Microsoft Press

Upgrading to
Microsoft®
Windows® 2000
Training
Kit
Beta Edition

PUBLISHED BY
Microsoft Press
A Division of Microsoft Corporation
One Microsoft Way
Redmond, Washington 98052-6399

Library of Congress Cataloging-in-Publication Data
Upgrading to Microsoft Windows 2000 Training Kit, Beta Edition / Microsoft
    Corporation.
        p. cm.
    ISBN 1-57231-894-5
        1. Microsoft Windows (Computer file)   2. Operating systems
(Computers)   I. Microsoft Corporation.
QA76.76.O63M52413226   1999
005.4'469--dc21   ,   99-33261
                                                                 CIP

Printed and bound in the United States of America.

2 3 4 5 6 7 8 9   WCWC   4 3 2 1 0 9

Distributed in Canada by Penguin Books Canada Limited.

A CIP catalogue record for this book is available from the British Library.

Microsoft Press books are available through booksellers and distributors worldwide. For further information about international editions, contact your local Microsoft Corporation office or contact Microsoft Press International directly at fax (425) 936-7329. Visit our Web site at mspress.microsoft.com.

Active Directory, ActiveX, BackOffice, Microsoft, Microsoft Press, Microsoft Press and Design, PowerPoint, Win32, Windows, and Windows NT are either registered trademarks or trademarks of Microsoft Corporation in the United States and/or other countries. Other product and company names mentioned herein may be the trademarks of their respective owners.

The example companies, organizations, products, people, and events depicted herein are fictitious. No association with any real company, organization, product, person, or event is intended or should be inferred.

Program Manager: Jeff Madden
Project Editor: Michael Bolinger

Author: Rick Wallace

Contents

About This Book

Welcome to *Upgrading to Microsoft Windows 2000 Training, Beta Edition*. This kit introduces you to the Windows 2000 family of products, prepares you to install the Windows 2000 software, and prepares you to upgrade your Microsoft Windows NT 4.0 network to a Windows 2000 network.

This kit concentrates on Windows 2000 Advanced Server and on Transmission Control Protocol/Internet Protocol (TCP/IP), the network protocol of choice for Windows 2000. It also emphasizes the Domain Name System (DNS), which is an Internet and TCP/IP standard name service and required for Windows 2000 domains and directory services based on Active Directory technology. Active Directory directory services integrate the Internet concept of a namespace with Windows 2000 directory services. Active Directory directory services use DNS as the domain naming and location service, so Windows 2000 domain names are also DNS names. In fact, the core unit of logical structure in Active Directory directory services is the domain. In this kit, you will learn how to install, navigate, and administer the Windows 2000 Active Directory directory services.

This course also supports the Microsoft Certified Systems Engineer program.

Note For more information on becoming a Microsoft Certified Systems Engineer, see the section titled "The Microsoft Certified Professional Program" later in this introduction.

The "Getting Started" section of this introduction provides important setup instructions that describe the hardware and software requirements to complete the procedures in this course. It also provides information about the networking configuration necessary to complete some of the hands-on procedures. Read through this section thoroughly before you start the lessons.

Intended Audience

Anyone who wants to learn more about Windows 2000 will find this book useful. However, this book was primarily designed for people currently administering and supporting Windows NT 4.0. This book was developed for information system (IS) professionals who need to plan upgrades, perform or manage the transition of Windows NT 4.0 networks to Windows 2000 networks, and support these networks before, during, and after the upgrade to Windows 2000

Prerequisites

- Experience administering or supporting a Windows NT 4.0 network
- A thorough knowledge of TCP/IP and Dynamic Host Configuration Protocol (DHCP)
- Experience creating and managing user accounts and controlling access to resources in a Windows NT 4.0 network

Features of This Book

Each chapter opens with a "Before You Begin" section, which prepares you for completing the chapter.

▶   Each chapter is divided into lessons. Many step-by-step practices are provided for you to perform the procedures on your test machine to help you learn the different facets of administering a Windows 2000 network. These practices are placed at the end of lessons and consist of one or more exercises or procedures. Each procedure is marked with a triangle as shown in the margin next to this paragraph.

Some additional procedures are placed outside the practices in the general text material to outline techniques in a more general way or to present procedures that can't be carried out with the minimum hardware configuration required for this Training Kit. You will find the minimum hardware requirements for this Training Kit listed later under "Hardware Requirements" in the "Getting Started" section of this chapter.

Important The additional procedures that are not included within the practice sections are intended as general information to advance your knowledge of Windows 2000. Because many of the practices build upon procedures you do in earlier practices, if you work through the additional procedures in the general text of the book you may alter the state of your test machine and may not be able to carry out subsequent practices exactly as they are presented.

Each lesson ends with a short summary of the lesson material. The "Review" section at the end of the chapter allows you to test what you have learned in the chapter. Appendix A, "Questions and Answers," contains all of the book's practice questions and review questions and the corresponding answers.

Notes

Notes appear throughout the lessons. There are several types, which are described as follows:

- Notes marked **Tip** contain explanations of possible results or alternative methods.
- Notes marked **Important** contain information that is essential to completing a task.
- Notes marked **Note** contain supplemental information.
- Notes marked **Caution** contain warnings about possible loss of data.

Conventions

This book uses the following conventions:

- Hands-on procedures that you may follow are presented in numbered lists of steps (1, 2, and so on). A triangular bullet (▶) indicates the beginning of a procedure.
- The word *select* is used for highlighting folders, filenames, text boxes, menu bars, and option buttons, and for selecting options in a dialog box.
- The word *click* is used for carrying out a command from a menu or dialog box.

Notational Conventions

This book uses the following notational conventions:

- Characters or commands that you type appear in **bold lowercase** type.
- *Italic* in syntax statements indicates placeholders for variable information. *Italic* is also used for book titles.
- Names of files and folders appear in title caps, except when you are to type them directly. Unless otherwise indicated, you can use all lowercase letters when you type a filename in a dialog box or at a command prompt.
- Filename extensions when used alone appear in all uppercase characters (for example, .DOC); filename extension in filenames appear in lowercase.
- Acronyms appear in all uppercase.
- Monospace type represents code samples, examples of screen text, or entries that you might type at a command prompt or in initialization files.
- Square brackets [ ] are used in syntax statements to enclose optional items. For example, [*filename*] in command syntax indicates that you can choose to type a filename with the command. Type only the information within the brackets, not the brackets themselves.

- Braces { } are used in syntax statements to enclose required items. Type only the information within the braces, not the braces themselves.
- Icons represent specific sections in the book as follows:

Icon	Represents
	A hands-on practice. You should perform the practice to give yourself an opportunity to use the skills being presented in the lesson.
	Chapter review questions. These questions at the end of each chapter allow you to test what you have learned in the lessons. You will find the answers to the review questions in Appendix A, "Questions and Answers" at the end of the book.

Keyboard Conventions

- A plus sign (+) between two key names means that you must press those keys at the same time. For example, "Press Alt+Tab" means that you hold down Alt while you press Tab.

- A comma (,) between two or more key names means that you must press each of the keys consecutively, not together. For example, "Press Alt, F, X" means that you press and release each key in sequence. "Press Alt+W, L" means that you first press Alt and W together, and then release them and press L.

- You can choose menu commands with the keyboard. Press the Alt key to activate the menu bar, and then sequentially press the keys that correspond to the highlighted or underlined letter of the menu name and the command name. For some commands, you can also press a key combination listed on the menu.

- You can select or clear check boxes or option buttons in dialog boxes with the keyboard. Press the Alt key, and then press the key that corresponds to the underlined letter of the option name. Or you can press Tab until the option is highlighted, and then press the Spacebar to select or clear the check box or option button.

Chapter and Appendix Overview

This self-paced training course combines discussions, notes, hands-on practices, and review questions to teach you how to install, configure, administer, and support Windows 2000. The course is designed to be completed from beginning to end. If you choose not to complete the book from beginning to end, see the "Before You Begin" section in each chapter. Hands-on practices that require preliminary work from preceding chapters refer to the appropriate chapters.

The book is divided into the following chapters:

- The "About This Book" section you are now reading contains a self-paced training overview and introduces the components of this training. Read this section thoroughly to get the greatest educational value from this self-paced training and to plan which lessons you will complete.

- Chapter 1, "The Microsoft Windows 2000 Platform," describes the Microsoft Windows 2000 family of products, which includes Window 2000 Professional, Windows 2000 Server, Windows 2000 Advanced Server, and Windows 2000 Datacenter Server. This chapter presents the features and benefits of using Windows 2000.

- Chapter 2, "Installing Windows 2000," reviews the Windows 2000 installation process and provides a hands-on practice in which you install Windows 2000 Advanced Server. It also presents information on automating installations, performing remote installations, and troubleshooting common problems that may occur during the installation process.

- Chapter 3, "Configuring the DNS Service," introduces DNS and name resolution. DNS is a distributed database that is used in TCP/IP networks to translate computer names to IP addresses. It also presents the skills and knowledge necessary to install and configure the DNS Service, to configure DNS clients, and to troubleshoot the DNS Service.

- Chapter 4, "Implementing Active Directory Directory Services," introduces Windows 2000 Active Directory directory services. Active Directory directory services use DNS as the domain naming and location service so Windows 2000 domain names are also DNS names. In fact, the core unit of logical structure in the Active Directory structure is the domain. This chapter presents the skills and knowledge necessary to plan, install, and configure your network's Active Directory structure.

- Chapter 5, "Administering Active Directory Directory Services," explains how to use the Active Directory Users and Computers administrative tool to create and manage user and computer accounts. User accounts still provide users with the ability to log on to a domain to gain access to network resources or to log on at a computer to gain access to resources on that computer, but the tool for creating them is new. This chapter also explains how groups have changed since Windows NT 4.0. There are two types of groups: security groups and distribution groups. These types of groups have a scope attribute that determines who can be a member of the group and where you can use that group in the network. This chapter explains how to create and manage groups and how to control access to Active Directory objects.

- Chapter 6, "Managing Desktop Environments with Group Policy," introduces you to group policies, which are another method for defining a user's desktop environment, and which are typically set for the entire domain or network to enforce corporate policies. This chapter teaches you what group policies are and how to apply and configure group policies.

- Chapter 7, "Managing Software by Using Group Policy," introduces Windows Installer and the Software Installation and Maintenance Technology. Both of these features help reduce the time required to deploy and manage software. This chapter provides the skills and knowledge necessary for you to publish software rather than install it. This chapter also explains how to deploy both mandatory and optional upgrades.

- Chapter 8, "Managing File Resources," explains how the methods of providing access to file and print resources in Windows 2000 have improved upon those available in Windows NT 4.0. It explains how to create and share file resources, how to create and use Dfs trees, and how to use the new disk defragmentation utility. This chapter also explains the changes in NTFS permission configuration, disk quotas, and file encryption.

- Chapter 9, "Configuring Remote Access," introduces the new protocols for use with remote access in Windows 2000, as well as the new wizards and interfaces for configuring all types of network connections. The Network Connection wizard, for example, provides a simple interface for creating and configuring basic inbound and outbound connections, while Routing and Remote Access is a more robust management tool for configuring connections on domain controllers. This chapter gives you an understanding of the new options and interfaces in Windows 2000 so that you can connect computers and configure protocols correctly to meet your organization's remote access requirements.

- Chapter 10, "Supporting DHCP and WINS," explains the enhanced implementations of DHCP and the Windows Internet Naming Service (WINS) included in the Windows 2000 Server family of products. These enhancements reduce the amount of time you spend configuring, administering, and troubleshooting your DHCP servers and clients, your DNS servers, and your WINS servers and clients.

- Chapter 11, "Managing Disks," introduces the two disk storage types Windows 2000 provides. Basic disks are not new to Windows 2000; they use the partitions found in earlier versions of Windows and MS-DOS. Dynamic disks are new to Windows 2000 and use volumes that provide more efficient use of space than partitions in computers with multiple hard disks. This chapter also introduces the Disk Management tool, which consolidates all disk management tasks for both local and remote administration. It provides shortcut menus to show you which tasks you can perform on the selected object, and includes wizards to guide you through creating partitions and volumes and upgrading disks.

- Chapter 12, "Implementing Disaster Protection," explains the features included in Windows 2000 that are designed to help you recover from computer disasters. These disaster protection features include support for fault-tolerant volumes, advanced startup options, the Recovery Console, and the Backup utility. This chapter helps prepare you to develop and implement effective disaster protection and recovery plans.

- Chapter 13, "Upgrading a Network to Windows 2000," explains some of the benefits of upgrading a Microsoft Windows NT 4.0 network to Microsoft Windows 2000, including improved security, easier management, and improved administration. It also explains how the process of upgrading a Windows NT 4.0 network to Windows 2000 varies depending on your existing Windows NT 4.0 network infrastructure and your organization's business requirements. This chapter examines the upgrade process, specifically as it relates to upgrading each of the Windows NT 4.0 domain models.

- Appendix A, "Questions and Answers," lists all of the practice questions and review questions from the book, shows the page number where the question appears, and provides the suggested answer.

- Appendix B, "Creating Setup Disks," explains how to create the four Windows 2000 Server Setup disks. Unless your computer supports booting from a CD-ROM drive, you must have the four Windows 2000 Server Setup disks to complete the installation of Windows 2000 Server.

Getting Started

This self-paced training course contains hands-on practices to help you learn about Windows 2000. Some practices and some exercises within practices are marked as optional. To complete these, you must have two networked computers or be connected to a larger network. Both computers must be capable of running Windows 2000. If you have only one machine, read through the steps and familiarize yourself with the procedure as best you can.

Caution Several exercises may require you to make changes to your server. This may have undesirable results if you are connected to a larger network. Check with your network administrator before attempting these exercises.

Hardware Requirements

Each computer must have the following minimum configuration. All hardware should be on the Windows 2000 Hardware Compatibility List (HCL). You'll find this list in the HCL.TXT file in the \Support directory of the Windows 2000 installation CD-ROM.

- Pentium 166 MHz or Compaq Alpha-based processor

- The computer must be connected to a network hub; it is not necessary for any additional computers to be connected to the hub.

- 64 MB of RAM

- 2 GB hard disk with 1 GB of free space to install Windows 2000 Advanced Server and create partitions
- 12× CD-ROM drive
- SVGA monitor capable of 800×600 resolution (1024×768 recommended)
- Microsoft Mouse or compatible pointing device

Software Requirements

The following software is required to complete the procedures in this course.

- Windows 2000 Advanced Server Beta 3 or later release version.

Note Because multiple interim beta versions of Windows 2000 are being released during the beta cycle, readers may find some discrepancies in such items as menu names and dialog boxes. The practices in this book were written based on Release Candidate 1 of the operating system.

Setup Instructions

Set up your computer according to the manufacturer's instructions.

For the exercises that require networked computers, you need to make sure the computers can communicate with each other. The first computer will be designated as a domain controller, and will be assigned the computer account name Server1 in the domain domain.com. The second computer will act as a stand-alone server for most of the optional practices in this course.

Caution If your computers are part of a larger network, you *must* verify with your network administrator that the computer names, domain name, and other information used in setting up Windows 2000 as described in Chapter 2 do not conflict with network operations. If they do conflict, ask your network administrator to provide alternative values and use those values in all of the exercises in this book.

The installation of Windows 2000 is part of this kit and is covered in Chapter 2. If you are installing two computers, follow the same instructions on both computers.

The Microsoft Certified Professional Program

The Microsoft Certified Professional (MCP) program provides the best method to prove your command of current Microsoft products and technologies. Microsoft, an industry leader in certification, is on the forefront of testing methodology. Our exams and corresponding certifications are developed to validate your mastery of critical competencies as you design and develop, or implement and support, solutions with Microsoft products and technologies. Computer professionals who become Microsoft certified are recognized as experts and are sought after industry-wide.

The Microsoft Certified Professional program offers six certifications, based on specific areas of technical expertise:

- **Microsoft Certified Professional (MCP).** Demonstrated in-depth knowledge of at least one Microsoft operating system. Candidates may pass additional Microsoft certification exams to further qualify their skills with Microsoft BackOffice products, development tools, or desktop programs.

- **Microsoft Certified Professional + Internet.** MCPs with a specialty in the Internet qualified to plan security, install and configure server products, manage server resources, extend servers to run CGI scripts or ISAPI scripts, monitor and analyze performance, and troubleshoot problems.

- **Microsoft Certified Systems Engineer (MCSE).** Qualified to effectively plan, implement, maintain, and support information systems in a wide range of computing environments with Microsoft Windows 95, Microsoft Windows 98, Microsoft Windows NT, and the Microsoft BackOffice integrated family of server software.

- **Microsoft Certified Systems Engineer + Internet (MCSE + Internet).** MCSEs with an advanced qualification to enhance, deploy, and manage sophisticated intranet and Internet solutions that include a browser, proxy server, host servers, database, and messaging and commerce components. In addition, an MCSE+Internet-certified professional is able to manage and analyze Web sites.

- **Microsoft Certified Solution Developer (MCSD).** Qualified to design and develop custom business solutions with Microsoft development tools, technologies, and platforms, including Microsoft Office and Microsoft BackOffice.

- **Microsoft Certified Trainer (MCT).** Instructionally and technically qualified to deliver Microsoft Official Curriculum through a Microsoft Authorized Technical Education Center (ATEC).

Microsoft Certification Benefits

Microsoft certification, one of the most comprehensive certification programs available for assessing and maintaining software-related skills, is a valuable measure of an individual's knowledge and expertise. Microsoft certification is awarded to individuals who have successfully demonstrated their ability to perform specific tasks and implement solutions with Microsoft products. Not only does this provide an objective measure for employers to consider, it also provides guidance for what an individual should know to be proficient. And as with any skills-assessment and benchmarking measure, certification brings a variety of benefits to the individual and to employers and organizations.

Microsoft Certification Benefits for Individuals

As a Microsoft Certified Professional, you receive many benefits:

- Industry recognition of your knowledge and proficiency with Microsoft products and technologies
- Access to technical and product information directly from Microsoft through a secured area of the MCP Web site
- Logos to enable you to identify your Microsoft Certified Professional status to colleagues or clients
- Invitations to Microsoft conferences, technical training sessions, and special events
- A Microsoft Certified Professional certificate
- Subscription to *Microsoft Certified Professional Magazine* (North America only), a career and professional development magazine

Additional benefits, depending on your certification and geography, include the following:

- A complimentary one-year subscription to the Microsoft TechNet Technical Information Network, providing valuable information on monthly CD-ROMs.
- A one-year subscription to the Microsoft Beta Evaluation program. This benefit provides you with up to 12 free monthly CD-ROMs containing beta software (English only) for many of Microsoft's newest software products.

Microsoft Certification Benefits for Employers and Organizations

Through certification, computer professionals can maximize the return on investment in Microsoft technology. Research shows that Microsoft certification provides organizations with the following:

- Excellent return on training and certification investments by providing a standard method of determining training needs and measuring results
- Increased customer satisfaction and decreased support costs through improved service, increased productivity, and greater technical self-sufficiency
- Reliable benchmark for hiring, promoting, and career planning
- Recognition and rewards for productive employees by validating their expertise
- Retraining options for existing employees so they can work effectively with new technologies
- Assurance of quality when outsourcing computer services

To learn more about how certification can help your company, see the following backgrounders, white papers, and case studies available on the Internet at

http://www.microsoft.com/mcp/mktg/bus_bene.htm:

- Financial Benefits to Supporters of Microsoft Professional Certification, IDC white paper (1998wpidc.doc 1,608 KB)
- Prudential Case Study (prudentl.exe 70 KB self-extracting file)
- The Microsoft Certified Professional Program Corporate Backgrounder (mcpback.exe 50 KB)
- A white paper (mcsdwp.doc 158 KB) that evaluates the Microsoft Certified Solution Developer certification
- A white paper, MCSE Criterion Validity Study White Paper, Oct. 1998 (SysEngrCert.doc 342 KB), that evaluates the Microsoft Certified Systems Engineer certification
- Jackson Hole High School Case Study (jhhs.doc 180 KB)
- Lyondel Case Study (lyondel.doc 21 KB)
- Stellcom Case Study (stellcom.doc 132 KB)

Requirements for Becoming a Microsoft Certified Professional

The certification requirements differ for each certification and are specific to the products and job functions addressed by the certification.

To become a Microsoft Certified Professional, you must pass rigorous certification exams that provide a valid and reliable measure of technical proficiency and expertise. These exams are designed to test your expertise and ability to perform a role or task with a product, and are developed with the input of professionals in the industry. Questions in the exams reflect how Microsoft products are used in actual organizations, giving them "real-world" relevance.

Microsoft Certified Product Specialists are required to pass one operating system exam. Candidates may pass additional Microsoft certification exams to further qualify their skills with Microsoft BackOffice products, development tools, or desktop applications.

Microsoft Certified Professional + Internet specialists are required to pass the prescribed Microsoft Windows NT Server 4.0, TCP/IP, and Microsoft Internet Information System exam series.

Microsoft Certified Systems Engineers are required to pass a series of core Microsoft Windows operating system and networking exams, and BackOffice technology elective exams.

Microsoft Certified Solution Developers are required to pass two core Microsoft Windows operating system technology exams and two BackOffice technology elective exams.

Microsoft Certified Trainers are required to meet instructional and technical re-quirements specific to each Microsoft Official Curriculum course they are certi-fied to deliver. In the United States and Canada, call Microsoft at (800) 636-7544 for more information on becoming a Microsoft Certified Trainer. Outside the United States and Canada, contact your local Microsoft subsidiary.

Technical Training for Computer Professionals

Technical training is available in a variety of ways, with instructor-led classes, online instruction, or self-paced training available at thousands of locations worldwide.

Self-Paced Training

For motivated learners who are ready for the challenge, self-paced instruction is the most flexible, cost-effective way to increase your knowledge and skills.

A full line of self-paced print and computer-based training materials is available direct from the source—Microsoft Press. Microsoft Official Curriculum course-ware kits from Microsoft Press are designed for advanced computer system professionals and are available from Microsoft Press and the Microsoft Devel-oper Division. Self-paced training kits from Microsoft Press feature print-based instructional materials, along with CD-ROM-based product software, multimedia presentations, lab exercises, and practice files. The Mastering Series provides in-depth, interactive training on CD-ROM for experienced developers. They're both great ways to prepare for Microsoft Certified Professional (MCP) exams.

Online Training

For a more flexible alternative to instructor-led classes, turn to online instruction. It's as near as the Internet and it's ready whenever you are. Learn at your own pace and on your own schedule in a virtual classroom, often with easy access to an online instructor. Without ever leaving your desk, you can gain the expertise you need. Online instruction covers a variety of Microsoft products and technolo-gies. It includes options ranging from Microsoft Official Curriculum to choices available nowhere else. It's training on demand, with access to learning resources 24 hours a day.

Online training is available through Microsoft Authorized Technical Education Centers.

Authorized Technical Education Centers

Authorized Technical Education Centers (ATECs) are the best source for instructor-led training that can help you prepare to become a Microsoft Certified Professional. The Microsoft ATEC program is a worldwide network of qualified technical training organizations that provide authorized delivery of Microsoft Official Curriculum courses by Microsoft Certified Trainers to computer professionals.

For a listing of ATEC locations in the United States and Canada, call the Microsoft fax service at (800) 727-3351. Outside the United States and Canada, call the fax service at (206) 635-2233.

Technical Support

Every effort has been made to ensure the accuracy of this book. If you have comments, questions, or ideas regarding this book, please send them to Microsoft Press using either of the following methods:

E-Mail:

tkinput@microsoft.com

Postal Mail:

Microsoft Press
Attn: Microsoft Windows 2000 Beta Training Kit Editor
One Microsoft Way
Redmond, WA 98052-6399

Microsoft Press provides corrections for books through the World Wide Web at the following address:

http://mspress.microsoft.com/support/

Please note that product support is not offered through the above mail addresses. For further information regarding Microsoft software support options, please connect to http://www.microsoft.com/support/ or call Microsoft Support Network Sales at (800) 936-3500.

For information about ordering the full version of any Microsoft software, please call Microsoft Sales at (800) 426-9400 or visit www.microsoft.com.

C H A P T E R   1

The Microsoft Windows 2000 Platform

About This Chapter

This chapter presents an overview of the Microsoft Windows 2000 operating system, and the four products that make up this family. The Windows 2000 family of products consists of Windows 2000 Professional, Windows 2000 Server, Windows 2000 Advanced Server, and Windows 2000 Datacenter Server. The information contained in this chapter is based on the beta version of Windows 2000.

Before You Begin

To complete this chapter

- You must have the working knowledge of using Microsoft Windows NT 4.0. See "Prerequisites" on page xvi for more details.

- You must have the working knowledge of installing and configuring Windows NT 4.0.

- You must have an understanding of Dynamic Host Configuration Protocol (DHCP), Windows Internet Naming Service (WINS), Internet Protocol (IP) subnetting, and routing.

Lesson 1: Overview of the Windows 2000 Platform

The Microsoft Windows 2000 family of operating systems builds upon Microsoft Windows NT technology by adding many features and enhancements. This lesson introduces you to the family of Windows 2000 products. It explains some of the key differences between these products and the environment for which each product is designed.

After this lesson, you will be able to

- Identify the four operating systems included in the Windows 2000 platform.

Estimated lesson time: 5 minutes

Introduction to the Windows 2000 Platform

Windows 2000 is more reliable, more scalable, and easier to deploy, manage, and use than previous versions of Windows. The Windows 2000 platform significantly reduces costs, enables a new generation of applications, and provides an organization with a solid infrastructure upon which to build their digital nervous system.

The Windows 2000 platform consists of four operating systems. Once you understand the capabilities of each of the Windows 2000 operating systems, you will be able to select the best product to meet the current and future needs of your organization. Table 1.1 describes the operating systems that are included in the Windows 2000 platform.

Table 1.1   The Windows 2000 Platform

Operating system	Description
Windows 2000 Professional	Replaces Microsoft Windows 95, Microsoft Windows 98, and Microsoft Windows NT Workstation 4.0 in a business environment. It is the desktop operating system for businesses of all sizes.
Windows 2000 Server	Contains all of the features in Windows 2000 Professional, and provides services that simplify network management. This version of Windows 2000 is ideal for file and print servers, Web servers, and workgroups, and provides improved network access for branch offices.

(continued)

Operating system	Description
Windows 2000 Advanced Server	Contains all of the features in Windows 2000 Server, and provides increased scalability and system availability. This version of Windows 2000 is designed for servers used in a large enterprise network and for database intensive work.
Windows 2000 Datacenter Server	Contains all of the features in Windows 2000 Advanced Server, and supports more memory and more CPUs per computer. This version of Windows 2000 is the most powerful and functional server operating system. It's designed for large data warehouses, online transaction processing (OLTP) and large-scale simulations, and server consolidation projects.

Lesson Summary

Windows 2000 consists of a family of four separate products: Windows 2000 Professional, Windows 2000 Server, Windows 2000 Advanced Server, and Windows 2000 Datacenter Server. You learned the purpose of each of these products and how and when to use each of them.

Lesson 2: Windows 2000 Professional

Windows 2000 Professional is easier to use and manage and provides greater compatibility, file management capabilities, and security than previous versions of Windows. This lesson discusses how Windows 2000 Professional improves the capabilities of previous versions of Windows in four areas: ease of use, simplified management, increased hardware support, and enhanced file management and security.

After this lesson, you will be able to

- Identify features and enhancements in Microsoft Windows 2000 Professional.

Estimated lesson time: 15 minutes

Ease of Use

Windows 2000 Professional includes changes to the look and functionality of the desktop, windows, and the Start menu, making it easier to use than previous versions of Windows. Besides these user interface enhancements, Windows 2000 Professional also contains features that improve support for mobile users and make printing easier and more flexible.

User Interface Enhancements

The enhancements and features that improve the Windows 2000 Professional user interface include the following:

- **Customized Start menu.** Personalized Menus can be activated to keep track of the programs you use and to update the Programs menu so that it presents only the programs that you use most often. Applications that you use less frequently are hidden from normal view, making the Start menu easier to use.

  Note To activate Personalized Menus, click Start, point to Settings, and then click Taskbar & Start Menu. Click the Start Menu Options tab and select Use Personalized Menus.

- **Logon and shutdown dialog boxes.** Logon and shutdown dialog boxes are easier to use with fewer, better organized choices.
- **Task Scheduler.** The enhanced Task Scheduler allows users to schedule scripts and programs to run at specific times.

Support for Mobile Users

Windows 2000 Professional supports the latest laptop technologies based on the Advanced Configuration and Power Interface (ACPI), which allows you to change or remove devices without turning off the computer. ACPI also lengthens battery life with power management and suspend or resume capabilities.

Features in Windows 2000 Professional that provide support for mobile users include the following:

- **Network Connections wizard.** Consolidates all of the processes for creating network connections. Users can now set up the following networking features from one wizard:
  - Dial-up connections
  - Virtual private networks (VPNs)
  - Incoming calls
  - Direct connections to another computer
- **Virtual private network (VPN) support.** Provides secure access to corporate networks from off-site locations by using a local Internet service provider (ISP) rather than using a long distance, dial-up connection.
- **Offline folders.** Allows you to copy documents that are stored on the network onto your local computer, making it easier to access data when you are not connected to the network.
- **Synchronization Manager.** Compares items on the network to items that you opened or updated while working offline. Synchronization occurs when you log on, and any changes made offline to files and folders, Web pages, and e-mail messages are saved to the network.

Printing Support

Printing in Windows 2000 Professional has been improved to assist you in providing a more flexible network of printers. Windows 2000 Professional includes the following printing features and enhancements:

- **Internet Printing Protocol (IPP).** Allows users to send documents to any printer in a Microsoft Windows 2000 network that is connected to the Internet. Internet printing enables users to do the following:
  - Print to a Uniform Resource Locator (URL) over an intranet or the Internet.
  - View printer and job-related information in Hypertext Markup Language (HTML) format from any browser.
  - Download and install printer drivers over the Internet.
- **Add Printer wizard.** Simplifies the process of connecting to local and network printers from within a program. You no longer need to open the Printers system folder or specify driver models, printer languages, or ports when you add printers.
- **Image Color Management 2.0.** Allows you to send high-quality color documents to a printer or another computer with greater speed and reliability than ever before. New color profiles ensure that the colors you see on your monitor match those on your scanner and printer.

Simplified Management

Windows 2000 Professional includes many features that help reduce the overall cost of managing the computing environment, from installation of the operating system and applications to day-to-day desktop management and support.

Setup Tools

Windows 2000 simplifies the process of setting up a computer with the following setup tools:

- **Disk duplication.** Allows you to use the Windows 2000 System Preparation Tool to create an image of a computer's hard disk. You can then use a third-party tool to duplicate the hard disk on similarly configured computers.

- **Setup Manager wizard.** Guides you through the process of creating answer files for unattended installation scripts without requiring you to learn the codes that were previously necessary for unattended installations.

Configuration Management Capabilities

The configuration management capabilities in Windows 2000 create a more consistent environment for the end user and help ensure that users have any data, applications, and operating system settings that they need.

Windows 2000 includes the following configuration management enhancements:

- **Add/Remove Programs wizard.** Simplifies the process of installing and removing programs. Users can install applications by pointing directly to a location on the corporate network or Internet. The user interface provides additional feedback and sort options to view installed or available applications by size, frequency of use, and time of last use.

- **Windows Installer service.** Manages application installation, modification, repairs, and removal. It provides a standard format for managing the components of a software package, and an application programming interface (API) for managing applications and tools.

Troubleshooting Tools

Windows 2000 Professional includes diagnostic and troubleshooting tools that make it easier to support the operating system. Troubleshooting tools in Windows 2000 Professional include the following:

- **Automated System Recovery (ASR).** Allows users to save a complete state of their system and provides a way to restore that state for disaster recovery purposes. This feature helps to reduce the amount of time spent trying to recover files or repairing a system, even when a key component, such as a hard disk, fails.

- **Compatibility tool.** Detects and warns the user if certain installed applications or components will cause an upgrade to fail or if the components will not work after an upgrade is complete.

- **Troubleshooters.** Included in Windows 2000 online Help as troubleshooting wizards that can be used to solve many common computer problems.

Increased Hardware Support

Microsoft Windows 2000 Professional now supports more than 6,500 hardware devices, such as infrared devices, scanners, digital cameras, and advanced multimedia devices that Windows NT Workstation 4.0 did not support. Some of the enhancements to hardware support in Windows 2000 Professional are shown in Figure 1.1.

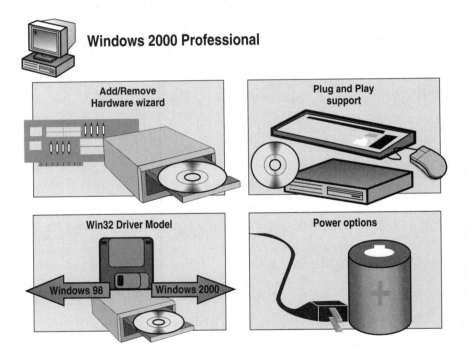

Figure 1.1   Enhancements to hardware support

- **Add/Remove Hardware wizard.** Allows you to add, remove, troubleshoot, and upgrade computer peripherals. When a device is not working properly, you can use the wizard to stop operation and safely remove the device.

- **Win32 Driver Model (WDM).** Provides a common model for device drivers across Windows 98 and Windows 2000. Drivers that are written to the WDM will work in both Windows 98 and Windows 2000.

- **Plug and Play support.** Enhances previous Plug and Play functionality and allows the following:

    - Automatic and dynamic reconfiguration of installed hardware
    - Loading of appropriate drivers
    - Registration for device notification events
    - Changeable and removable devices

- **Power options.** Prevent unnecessary power drains on your system by directing power to devices as they need it. The options available to you depend on your hardware. These options include the following:

    - Standby. While on standby, your monitor and hard disks turn off and your computer uses less power.
    - Hibernation. The hibernate feature turns off your monitor and hard disk, saves everything in memory on disk, and turns off your computer. When you restart your computer, your desktop is restored exactly as you left it.

Enhanced File Management

Windows 2000 Professional provides significant enhancements to file management capabilities. Features that enhance file management in Windows 2000 Professional include the following:

- **NTFS file system.** Supports file encryption and enables you to add disk space to an NTFS volume without having to restart the computer. It also supports distributed link tracking, and per-user disk quotas to monitor and limit disk space use.

- **FAT32 file system.** Supports FAT32 file system for compatibility with Windows 95 Operating System Release (OSR) 2 systems and later. FAT32 is an enhanced version of the FAT file system for use on disk volumes larger than 2 GB.

- **Disk Defragmenter utility.** Rearranges files, programs, and unused space on your computer's hard disk so that programs run faster and files open more quickly.

- **Backup utility.** Helps to protect data from accidental loss due to hardware or storage media failure. The backup utility in Windows 2000 allows you to schedule backups to occur automatically. You can back up data to a wide variety of storage media, such as the following:

    - Tape drives
    - External hard disks
    - Zip disks
    - Recordable CD-ROMs
    - Logical drives

- **Volume Mount Points.** Allows you to connect, or mount, a local drive at any empty folder on a local NTFS-formatted volume.

Security Features

Windows 2000 Professional is the most secure Windows desktop operating system for either a stand-alone computer or any type of public or private network. Security features and enhancements in Windows 2000 Professional include the following:

- **Kerberos 5.** Supports single logon, allowing faster authentication and faster network response. Kerberos 5 is the primary security protocol for domains in Windows 2000.
- **Encrypting File System (EFS).** Strengthens security by encrypting files on your hard disk so that no one can access them without using the correct password.
- **Internet Protocol Security (IPSec).** Encrypts Transmission Control Protocol/Internet Protocol (TCP/IP) traffic to secure communications within an intranet and provides the highest levels of security for virtual private network (VPN) traffic across the Internet.
- **Smart card support.** Enables portability of credentials and other private information between computers at work, home, or on the road. This eliminates the need to transmit sensitive information, such as authentication tickets and private keys, over networks.

Lesson Summary

Windows 2000 Professional improves the capabilities of previous versions of Windows in five main areas: ease of use, simplified management, increased hardware support, enhanced file management, and security.

Some of the ease of use improvements include enhancements to the user interface, such as a customized Start menu that presents only the programs that you use most often, and improved logon and shutdown dialog boxes. Windows 2000 Professional includes support for the latest laptop technologies based on ACPI and provides a Network Connections wizard and VPN support. It provides offline folders that allow you to copy documents stored on the network to your local computer for access when you are offline, and it provides a Synchronization Manager that compares items on the network to items that you opened or updated while working offline and synchronizes them.

Printing in Windows 2000 Professional has also been improved. Internet Printing Protocol (IPP) allows users to print to a URL over an intranet or the Internet, view printer and job-related information in HTML format from any browser, and download and install printer drivers over the Internet. The Windows 2000 Add Printer wizard simplifies the process of connecting to local and network printers from within a program, and Image Color Management 2.0 allows you to send high-quality color documents to a printer or another computer with greater speed and reliability than ever before.

Windows 2000 also simplifies the process of setting up a computer. The Windows 2000 System Preparation Tool allows you to create an image of a computer's hard disk so that you can use a third-party tool to duplicate the hard disk on similarly configured computers. The Setup Manager wizard guides you through the process of creating answer files for unattended installation scripts.

Microsoft Windows 2000 Professional now supports more than 6,500 hardware devices, such as infrared devices, scanners, digital cameras, and advanced multimedia devices. Other enhancements to hardware support include an Add/Remove Hardware wizard that allows you to add, remove, troubleshoot, and upgrade computer peripherals, a Win32 Driver Model that allows device drivers written to the WDM to work in both Windows 98 and Windows 2000, enhanced Plug and Play support, and power options that prevent unnecessary power drains on your system by directing power to devices as they need it.

Windows 2000 Professional enhancements to file management capabilities include a disk defragmenter utility and an NTFS file system that supports file encryption, distributed link tracking, and per-user disk quotas to monitor and limit disk space use. There is a backup utility that allows you to back up data to a wide variety of storage media: tape drives, external hard disks, zip disks, recordable CD-ROMs, and logical drives.

Windows 2000 Professional is the most secure Windows desktop operating system for either a stand-alone computer or any type of public or private network. Security features and enhancements in Windows 2000 Professional include support for Kerberos 5; EFS, which strengthens security by encrypting files on your hard disk; and IPSec, which encrypts TCP/IP traffic and provides the highest levels of security for VPN traffic across the Internet.

Lesson 3: Windows 2000 Server

Windows 2000 Server builds on the strengths of Windows NT Server 4.0 by providing a faster, more reliable platform that is easier to manage and lowers your total cost of ownership (TCO) by integrating easily with existing systems.

Windows 2000 Server supports new systems with up to two-way symmetric multiprocessing (SMP), dramatically increases system performance, and provides the following benefits: simplified management, enhanced file management and security, improved networking and communications, and improved printing support.

After this lesson, you will be able to

- Identify features and enhancements in Windows 2000 Server.

Estimated lesson time: 10 minutes

Simplified Management

Windows 2000 Server helps administrators manage their networks more easily from a central location, dramatically decreasing the TCO. It offers several features and enhancements that provide the foundation for simplifying management of your entire network.

Figure 1.2 lists the four main ways that Windows 2000 Server simplifies management of your network.

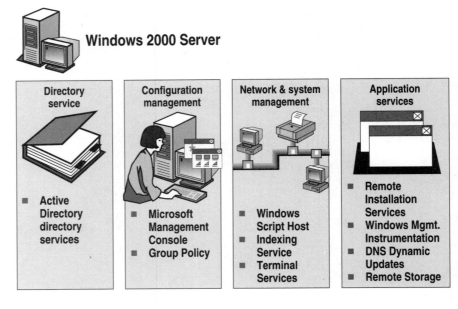

Figure 1.2   Four ways Windows 2000 Server simplifies management

Active Directory Directory Services

Directory services based on Active Directory technology are included in Windows 2000 Server. They extend the features of previous Windows-based directory services and are designed to work well in any size installation, from a single server with hundreds of objects to thousands of servers with millions of objects.

Active Directory directory services provide a single, consistent, open set of interfaces for performing common administrative tasks, such as adding new users or managing printers. Active Directory directory services also make it easier for users to locate and access resources anywhere on the network.

Management Capabilities

Windows 2000 Server contains all of the same configuration management capabilities as Windows 2000 Professional. Additional configuration management capabilities in Windows 2000 Server include the following:

- **Microsoft Management Console (MMC).** Provides a common console for monitoring network functions and accessing administrative tools. The MMC is customizable, allowing administrators to create consoles that include only the administrative tools that they need.

- **Group Policy.** Gives administrators more control over which users have access to specific workstations, data, and applications, allowing administrators to define and control the state of computers and users in an organization.

- **Windows Scripting Host.** Allows administrators and users to save time by automating many actions, such as connecting to or disconnecting from a network server, creating multiple user accounts, or creating a large number of groups. Scripts can be run directly on the desktop or from the command prompt.

Network and System Management Features

Windows 2000 Server contains several tools that help you easily and more cost effectively install, configure, and administer your Windows 2000 network. Network and system management features in Windows 2000 Server include the following:

- **Remote Installation Services (RIS).** Allows administrators to install Windows 2000 Professional on client computers throughout a network from a central location. RIS can dramatically decrease the cost of deploying new operating systems by reducing the amount of time an administrator spends moving from one client location to another.

- **Windows Management Instrumentation (WMI).** Improves administrative control by allowing administrators to correlate data and events from multiple sources and vendors on a local or enterprise basis.

- **Dynamic Updates in DNS or DNS UPDATE.** Reduces network administration costs by reducing the need for manual editing and replication of the Domain Name System (DNS) database each time that a change occurs in a DNS client's configuration.

Note For more information on dynamic updates in DNS or DNS UPDATE, see RFC 2136. An RFC (*Request for Comment*) is a document in which a standard, a protocol, or other information pertaining to the operation of the Internet is published. The RFC is actually issued *after* discussion and serves as the standard. You can find the text of each RFC that is cited in this book (as well as much associated discussion material) on the Internet. Use your Web browser and search, using any of the popular search engines on the Internet, to find the RFC of interest. In this case, search for "RFC 2136."

- **Remote Storage.** Monitors the amount of available space on a local hard disk. When the free space on the primary hard disk drops below the necessary level, Remote Storage automatically removes local data that has been copied to remote storage, providing the required free disk space.

Application Services

Windows 2000 Server is the first platform to provide an integrated set of services for building and deploying scalable, reliable applications. Application services in Windows 2000 Server include the following:

- **Indexing Service.** Automatically builds an index of your Web server that can be easily searched from any Web browser.
- **Terminal Services.** Allows clients to access Windows-based applications running entirely on the server and supports multiple client sessions on the server. The server manages all computing resources for each client that is connected to the server and provides all users who are logged on with their own environment.

Enhanced File Management and Security

Windows 2000 Server file management features improve resource availability and make it easier to manage your network storage requirements. Security features in Windows 2000 Server provide the highest levels of data protection and simplify administrative tasks.

File Management Enhancements

Windows 2000 Server provides significant enhancements to file management capabilities, enabling you to implement a more secure and manageable network. Enhancements to file management in Windows 2000 Server include the following:

- **Distributed file system (Dfs).** Simplifies the process of creating a single directory tree that includes multiple file servers and file shares in a group, division, or enterprise. This structure makes it easier for users to find and manage data on a network.

- **Disk quotas.** Provides more precise control of network-based storage. You can use disk quotas to monitor and limit disk space use, increasing bandwidth efficiency.

Security Features

Windows 2000 Server contains all of the same security features as Windows 2000 Professional, plus the following features:

- **Active Directory directory services security.** Allows administrators to create group accounts to more efficiently manage system security by allowing access to objects in Active Directory directory services based on group membership.

- **Security Templates.** Organizes all existing security attributes into one place, making it easier to administer security on a local computer.

- **Security Configuration and Analysis.** Allows you to import one or more saved configurations to a security database. Importing configurations builds a computer-specific security database that stores a composite configuration.

Improved Networking and Communications

Windows 2000 Server includes technologies that provide greater bandwidth control, secure network access from offsite locations, and support a new generation of communications solutions. Networking and communications features in Windows 2000 Server include the following:

- **Multiple-protocol routing.** Enables routing over multiple protocols, such as IP, Internetwork Packet Exchange (IPX), and AppleTalk on a local area network (LAN) or a wide area network (WAN). It also provides support for Open Shortest Path First (OSPF) and Routing Information Protocol version 2 (RIP 2).

- **Asynchronous Transfer Mode (ATM) support.** Allows a network to simultaneously transport a wide variety of network traffic, including voice, data, images, and video.

- **Remote Authentication Dial-in User Service (RADIUS).** Provides authentication and accounting services for distributed dial-up networking. Windows 2000 can act as a RADIUS client, a RADIUS server, or both.

Improved Printing Support

Windows 2000 Server makes printing easier and more flexible than ever before. Active Directory directory services integration with Windows 2000 Server, Advanced Server, and Datacenter Server make all shared printers in your domain available as objects in Active Directory directory services.

Publishing printers in Active Directory directory services allows users to quickly locate the most convenient printing resources through an improved user interface. Locating printers in a timely manner can dramatically improve productivity, particularly for users who travel or change offices frequently.

Windows 2000 Server contains all of the same printing support features as Windows 2000 Professional and also provides support for more than 2,500 different printers. This makes it easier for organizations to use the printing services in Windows 2000 Server with existing printers, new printers, and shared printer pools.

Lesson Summary

Windows 2000 Server builds on the strengths of Windows NT Server 4.0 but provides a faster, more reliable platform that is easier to manage and lowers your total cost of ownership. Active Directory directory services provide a single, consistent, open set of interfaces for performing common administrative tasks, and make it easier to locate and access resources anywhere on the network. The Active Directory directory services are designed to work well in any size installation, from a single server with hundreds of objects to thousands of servers with millions of objects.

Windows 2000 Server contains all of the same configuration management capabilities as Windows 2000 Professional and includes additional configuration management capabilities such as the MMC, which provides a common console for monitoring network functions and accessing administrative tools, and Group Policy, which allows administrators to control which users have access to specific workstations, data, and applications.

Windows 2000 Server has a number of features that help you easily and more cost effectively install, configure, and administer your Windows 2000 network. These features include RIS, which allows administrators to install Windows 2000 Professional on client computers throughout a network from a central location; DNS dynamic updates, which lower network administration costs by reducing the need for manual editing and replication of the DNS database; and Remote Storage, which monitors the available space on a local hard disk, and when the free space on the primary hard disk drops below the necessary level, automatically removes local data that has been copied to remote storage.

Windows 2000 Server is the first platform to provide an integrated set of services for building and deploying scalable, reliable applications. Application services in Windows 2000 Server include the Windows Script Host, which allows administrators and users to save time by automating many actions, such as connecting or disconnecting from a network server; Indexing Service, which automatically builds an index of your Web server that can be easily searched from any Web browser; and Terminal Services, which allows clients to access Windows-based applications running entirely on the server and supports multiple client sessions on the server.

Windows 2000 Server contains all of the file management capabilities and security features of Windows 2000 Professional. In addition, Windows 2000 Server enhancements to file management capabilities include Dfs, which makes it easier to create a single directory tree that includes multiple file servers and file shares and to find and manage data on a network, and disk quotas, which allows you to monitor and limit disk space use. Additional security features include Active Directory directory services security, which allows administrators to create group accounts and allow access to objects in Active Directory directory services based on group membership, and Security Templates, which organize all existing security attributes into one place.

Windows 2000 Server includes technologies that provide greater bandwidth control, secure network access from off-site locations, and support a new generation of communications solutions. Networking and communications features in Windows 2000 Server include multiple-protocol routing, support for OSPF, RIP 2, and ATM.

Windows 2000 Server contains all of the same printing support features as Windows 2000 Professional and provides support for more than 2,500 different printers. Active Directory directory services integration with Windows 2000 Server makes all shared printers in your domain available as objects in Active Directory directory services. Publishing printers in Active Directory directory services allows users to quickly locate the most convenient printing resources through an improved user interface. Locating printers in a timely manner can dramatically improve productivity, particularly for users who travel or change offices frequently.

Lesson 4: Windows 2000 Advanced Server and Windows 2000 Datacenter Server

Windows 2000 Advanced Server includes all of the same features as Windows 2000 Server and additional features that provide a highly scalable, interoperable, available, and manageable operating system. Windows 2000 Datacenter Server builds upon Windows 2000 Advanced Server.

After this lesson, you will be able to

- Identify features and enhancements in Windows 2000 Advanced Server.
- Identify key benefits of Windows 2000 Datacenter Server.

Estimated lesson time: 5 minutes

Windows 2000 Advanced Server

In addition to providing the features in Windows 2000 Server, Windows 2000 Advanced Server includes:

- **Enterprise Memory Architecture.** Allows applications that perform transaction processing or decision support on large data sets to keep more data in memory for greatly improved performance. Windows 2000 Advanced Server supports physical memories greater than 4 GB on Alpha-based and Intel Pentium II Xeon systems. Depending on the specific platform, physical memory sizes as large as 64 GB can be supported.

- **Increased SMP scalability.** Supports up to four processors.

- **Windows Clustering.** Allows you to connect multiple servers to form a cluster of servers that work together as a single system. Windows Clustering provides the following benefits:

- **High-availability.** Provides high availability for mission-critical applications, including the ability to automatically detect the failure of an application and quickly restart it on a different server. In addition, when one server in the cluster fails, another server in the cluster can be used to restore service to users.

- **Network load balancing.** Provides high availability and scalability for network-based services, such as TCP/IP and Web services.

- **Component load balancing clusters.** Allow you to create a cluster that does class load balancing across COM+ application server computers creating application clusters that allow organizations to scale applications by simply plugging in additional nodes.

Windows 2000 Datacenter Server

Windows 2000 Datacenter Server builds upon the features in Windows 2000 Advanced Server, making it the most powerful and functional server operating system ever offered by Microsoft.

Key benefits of Windows 2000 Datacenter Server include the following:

- Support for up to 16 processors or up to 32 processors through Original Equipment Manufacturers (OEMs)
- Support for up to 64 GB of memory on Intel-based systems and up to 32 GB on Alpha-based systems

Like Windows 2000 Advanced Server, Windows 2000 Datacenter Server provides both clustering and load balancing services as standard features. Windows 2000 Datacenter Server is optimized for the following:

- Large data warehouses
- Econometric analysis
- Large-scale simulations in science and engineering
- Online transaction processing
- Server consolidation projects
- Large-scale ISPs and Web-site hosting

Lesson Summary

Windows 2000 Advanced Server includes all of the same features as Windows 2000 Server and additional features that provide a highly scalable, interoperable, available, and manageable operating system. One of these additional features is Enterprise Memory Architecture, which allows applications that perform transaction processing or decision support on large data sets to keep more data in memory for greatly improved performance. Windows 2000 Advanced Server supports physical memories greater than 4 GB on Alpha-based and Intel Pentium II Xeon systems. Depending on the specific platform, physical memory sizes as large as 64 GB can be supported.

Windows 2000 Advanced Server also supports increased SMP scalability with support for up to four processors and Windows Clustering, which allows you to connect multiple servers to form a cluster of servers that work together as a single system. Two key benefits of Windows 2000 Datacenter Server are support for up to 16 processors, with support for up to 32 processors through OEMs, and support for up to 64 GB of memory. Like Windows 2000 Advanced Server, Windows 2000 Datacenter Server provides both clustering and load balancing services as standard features.

Review

Here are some questions to help you determine if you have learned enough to move on to the next chapter. If you have difficulty answering these questions, please go back and review the material in this chapter before beginning the next chapter. The answers to these questions are located in Appendix A, "Questions and Answers."

1. You have been asked to install a file and print server for your department of 50 people. Which operating system would you choose from the Windows 2000 platform?

2. Your department has now grown to support over 500 people, all of whom need access to your server's file services. They also require 24-hour access to these services. Which operating system from the Windows 2000 platform would you now choose?

3. Users in your organization are complaining that they cannot locate the printers that they need to print to. Identify the component in Windows 2000 that addresses this business problem, and explain how it addresses the problem.

4. Your organization provides users with access to a large number of programs for everyday use. The help desk is receiving many calls from people who are having difficulty finding the applications that they need because of a very large and confusing Start menu structure. How does Windows 2000 solve this problem?

5. Identify three of the features that make Windows 2000 Professional the best desktop operating system for a business environment.

6. List three of the features that help to simplify management of a Windows 2000 network.

C H A P T E R   2

Installing Windows 2000

About This Chapter

This chapter prepares you to install Microsoft Windows 2000. The information contained in this chapter is based on the beta version of Windows 2000.

Before You Begin

To complete this chapter

- You must have a computer that meets or exceeds the minimum hardware requirements listed in "Getting Started," on page xxi.
- You must have a beta version of Windows 2000 Advanced Server on CD-ROM.

Lesson 1: Preparing to Install

When you install Windows 2000, the Windows 2000 Setup program asks you to provide information about how you want to install and configure the operating system. Good preparation helps you avoid problems during and after the installation.

After this lesson, you will be able to

- Prepare to install the beta version of Microsoft Windows 2000 by completing preinstallation tasks such as identifying the hardware requirements and the required installation information.

Estimated lesson time: 30 minutes

Preinstallation Tasks

Before you start the installation, complete the following preinstallation tasks:

- Identify the hardware requirements to install Windows 2000, and make sure that your hardware meets these requirements.
- Determine whether your hardware is on the Hardware Compatibility List (HCL).
- Determine how you want to partition the hard disk on which you are going to install Windows 2000.
- Choose a file system for the installation partition.
- Choose a licensing mode for a server that will be running Windows 2000.
- Identify whether your computer will join a domain or a workgroup.
- Complete a checklist of preinstallation tasks to help ensure a successful installation.

Hardware Requirements

You must know the minimum hardware requirements for installing and operating Windows 2000 Professional, Windows 2000 Server, and Windows 2000 Advanced Server to determine if your hardware meets these requirements (see Figure 2.1 and Table 2.1). Make sure that your hardware meets or exceeds these requirements.

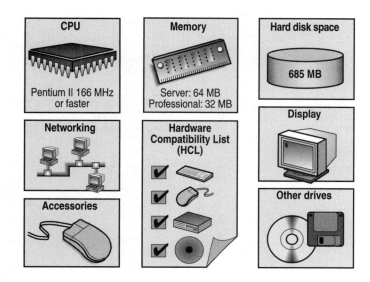

Figure 2.1   Hardware requirements

Table 2.1   Windows 2000 Hardware Requirements

Component	Windows 2000 Professional requirements	Windows 2000 Server or Advanced Server requirements
CPU	Pentium 166 megahertz (MHz) or higher or Compaq Alpha-based processor	Pentium 166 MHz (or higher) recommended or Compaq Alpha-based processor
Memory	32 megabytes (MB) (64 MB recommended)	64 MB for servers support-ing one to five clients (128 MB or higher recom-mended for most network environments)
	For Alpha-based computers: 48 MB (96 MB recommended)	For Alpha-based computers: 96 MB (128 MB recommended)
Hard disk space	One or more hard disks with a minimum of 685 MB (1 GB recommended) on the partition that will contain the system files	One or more hard disks with a minimum of 685 MB (1 GB recommended) on the partition that will con-tain the system files
	For Alpha-based computers: a minimum of 351 MB (1 GB recommended)	For Alpha-based computers: a minimum of 367 MB (1 GB recommended)

(continued)

Component	Windows 2000 Professional requirements	Windows 2000 Server or Advanced Server requirements
Networking	Network adapter card	One or more network adapter cards
Display	Video display adapter and monitor with video graphics adapter (VGA) resolution or higher	Video display adapter and monitor with video graphics adapter (VGA) resolution or higher
Other drives	CD-ROM drive, 12× or faster recommended (not required for installing Windows 2000 over a network)	CD-ROM drive, 12× or faster recommended (not required for installing Windows 2000 over a network)
	A high-density 3.5-inch disk drive as drive A, unless the computer supports starting the Setup program from a CD-ROM	A high-density 3.5-inch disk drive as drive A, unless the computer supports starting the Setup program from a CD-ROM
Accessories	Keyboard and mouse or other pointing device	Keyboard and mouse or other pointing device

Hardware Compatibility List

Before you install Windows 2000, verify that your hardware is on the Windows 2000 Hardware Compatibility List (HCL). Microsoft provides tested drivers for only those devices that are included on this list. Using hardware that is not listed on the HCL could cause problems during and after installation.

For a copy of the HCL, see the Hcl.txt file in the Support folder on the Windows 2000 CD-ROM.

You will also find the most recent versions of the HCL for released operating systems on the Internet at the Microsoft Web site (http://www.microsoft.com).

Note Microsoft supports only those devices that are listed on the HCL. If you have hardware that is not on this list, contact the hardware manufacturer to determine if there is a manufacturer-supported Windows 2000 driver for the component.

Disk Partitions

The Windows 2000 Setup program examines the hard disk to determine its existing configuration. Setup then allows you to install Windows 2000 on an existing partition or create a new partition on which to install Windows 2000.

New Partition or Existing Partition

Depending on the state of the hard disk, you can choose one of the following options during the installation:

- If the hard disk is unpartitioned, you must create and size the Windows 2000 partition.

- If the hard disk has partitions and has enough unpartitioned disk space, you can create the Windows 2000 partition by using the unpartitioned space.

- If the hard disk has an existing partition that is large enough, you can install Windows 2000 on that partition. Installing on an existing partition will overwrite any existing data.

- If the hard disk has an existing partition, you can delete it to create more unpartitioned disk space to use to create the Windows 2000 partition.

Remaining Free Hard Disk Space

Although you can use Setup to create other partitions, you should create and size only the partition on which you will install Windows 2000. After you install Windows 2000, use the Computer Management administrative tool to partition any remaining unpartitioned space on the hard disk.

Size of the Installation Partition

Microsoft recommends that you install Windows 2000 on a 1 GB or larger partition. Although Windows 2000 requires a minimum of about 685 MB of disk space for installation, using a larger installation partition provides flexibility in the future. Then, if required, you can install updates to Windows 2000, operating system tools, or other files that are required by Windows 2000.

File Systems

After you create the installation partition, Setup prompts you to select the file system with which to format the partition. As with Windows NT 4.0, Windows 2000 supports NT file system (NTFS) and file allocation table (FAT). New to Windows 2000 is support for FAT32. Figure 2.2 summarizes some of the features of these files systems.

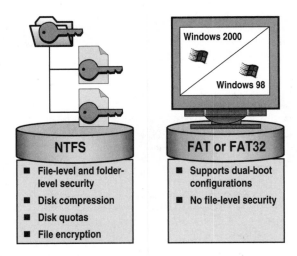

Figure 2.2   Summary of file systems features

NTFS

Use NTFS when the partition on which Windows 2000 will reside requires any of the following features:

- **File- and folder-level security.** NTFS allows you to control access to files and folders.
- **Disk compression.** NTFS compresses files to store more data on the partition.
- **Disk quotas.** NTFS allows you to control disk usage on a per-user basis. For additional information, see Chapter 8, "Managing File Resources."
- **Encryption.** NTFS allows you to encrypt file data on the physical hard disk.

The new version of NTFS in Windows 2000 supports remote storage, dynamic volumes, and the mounting of volumes to folders. Windows 2000 and Windows NT are the only operating systems that can access data on a local hard disk that is formatted with NTFS.

Important If you plan to promote a server to a domain controller, format the installation partition with NTFS.

Note If you do not format the installation partition as NTFS during installation, the Convert command allows you to convert the FAT or FAT32 partition to an NTFS partition with no loss of data. For example, if you want to convert the C: drive to NTFS, use the following command: **convert c: /fs:ntfs /v** at the command prompt. For more information on the Convert command, start a command prompt and type **convert /?** on the command line.

FAT and FAT32

FAT and FAT32 allow access by, and compatibility with, other operating systems. To dual boot Windows 2000 and another operating system, format the system partition with either FAT or FAT32.

Setup determines whether to format the hard disk with FAT or FAT32 based on the size of the installation partition.

Partition size	Format
Smaller than 2 GB	Setup formats the partition as FAT
Larger than 2 GB	Setup formats the partition as FAT32

FAT and FAT32 do not offer many of the features that are supported by NTFS (for example, file-level security). Therefore, in most situations, you should format the hard disk with NTFS. The only reason to use FAT or FAT32 is for dual booting. If you are setting up a computer for dual booting, you would only have to format the system partition as FAT or FAT32. For example, if drive C is the system partition, you could format drive C as FAT or FAT32 and format drive D as NTFS. However, Microsoft does not recommend dual booting a server.

Licensing

In addition to the license that is required to install and run Windows 2000 Advanced Server and the license that is required to install and run an operating system on each client computer, you also need to license each client connection to the server.

Client Access License

A Client Access License (CAL) gives client computers the right to connect to computers running Windows 2000 Advanced Server so that the client computers can connect to network services, shared folders, and print resources. When you install Windows 2000 Advanced Server, you will discover that the licensing modes in Windows 2000 are the same as in Windows NT 4.0: you can select the Per Seat or Per Server licensing mode.

The following services do not require Client Access Licenses:

- Anonymous or authenticated access to Windows 2000 Advanced Server with Microsoft Internet Information Services 4.0 (IIS) or a Web-server application that provides Hypertext Transfer Protocol (HTTP) sharing of Hypertext Markup Language (HTML) files.
- Telnet and File Transfer Protocol (FTP) connections.

Note If your company uses Microsoft BackOffice products, you must also have licenses for the BackOffice products. A Windows 2000 license does not cover BackOffice products.

Per Seat Licensing

The Per Seat licensing mode requires a separate CAL for each client computer that is used to access Windows 2000 Advanced Server for basic network services. After a client computer has a CAL, it can be used to access any computer running Windows 2000 Advanced Server on the enterprise network. Per Seat licensing is often more economical for large networks where client computers will be used to connect to more than one server.

Per Server Licensing

With Per Server licensing, CALs are assigned to a particular server. Each CAL allows one connection per client computer to the server for basic network services. You must have at least as many CALs that are dedicated to the server as the maximum number of client computers that will be used to concurrently connect to that server at any time.

Per Server licensing is preferred by small companies with only one computer running Windows 2000 Server or Windows 2000 Advanced Server. It is also useful for Internet or remote-access servers where client computers might not be licensed as Windows 2000 network client computers. In this situation, Per Server licensing allows you to specify a maximum number of concurrent server connections and reject any additional logon attempts.

Important If you are unsure which licensing mode to use, choose Per Server because you can change, only once, from Per Server to Per Seat licensing at no additional cost (by double-clicking the Licensing icon in Control Panel). It is not necessary to notify Microsoft to make this change. This is a one-way conversion; you cannot convert from Per Seat to Per Server.

Domain or Workgroup Membership

During installation, you must choose the type of network security group that you want the computer to join: a domain or a workgroup (see Figure 2.3).

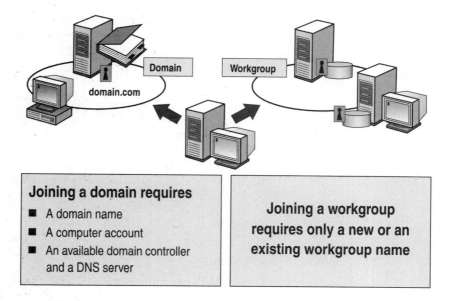

Figure 2.3   Domain or workgroup membership

Joining a Domain

During installation, you can add the computer on which you are installing Windows 2000 to an existing domain. Adding a computer to a domain is referred to as *joining a domain*. If you are installing Windows 2000 Server or Windows 2000 Advanced Server, the computer is added as a member server. A computer running Windows 2000 Server or Windows 2000 Advanced Server that is a member of a domain, and is not a domain controller, is called a *member server*.

Joining a domain during installation requires the following:

- **A domain name.** Ask the domain administrator for the Domain Name System (DNS) name for the domain that you want to join. An example of a DNS-compatible domain name is *microsoft.com,* where *microsoft* is the name of your organization's DNS-identity.

- **A computer account.** Before a computer can join a domain, you must create a computer account in the domain. You can ask a domain administrator to create the computer account before installation, or, if you have administrative privileges for the domain, you can create the computer account during installation. If you create the computer account during installation, Setup prompts you for a name and password of a user account with authority to add domain computer accounts.

- **An available domain controller and a server running the DNS Service (called the *DNS server*).** At least one domain controller in the domain that you are joining and one DNS server must be online when you install a computer in the domain.

Note You can join a domain during installation or after installation.

Important The exercises in this book will use the domain named *domain.com*. It is a special domain name reserved internationally for the use of authors and others in writing books like this one, so that no real company's domain name is used inadvertently. If you wish, you may also perform the practices in this book using *domain.com*. Otherwise, substitute your chosen domain name whenever you see *domain.com* in the text.

Joining a Workgroup

As with Windows NT 4.0, you will only join a workgroup if you are in a small network without a domain or in preparation for joining a domain later on.

During installation, you can add the computer on which you are installing Windows 2000 to an existing workgroup. Adding a computer to a workgroup is referred to as *joining a workgroup*. If you are installing Windows 2000 Server or Windows 2000 Advanced Server, the computer is added as a stand-alone server. A computer running Windows 2000 Server or Windows 2000 Advanced Server that is not a member of a domain is called a *stand-alone server*.

If you join a workgroup as a stand-alone server during installation, you must assign a workgroup name to your computer. The workgroup name that you assign can be the name of an existing workgroup or the name of a new workgroup that you create during installation.

Preinstallation Tasks Summary

The following is a preinstallation checklist that you can use to make sure you have all the necessary information available before you begin the installation process.

Task	Done
Verify that your components meet the minimum hardware requirements.	❏
Verify that all of your hardware is listed on the HCL.	❏
Verify that the hard disk on which you will install Windows 2000 has a minimum of 685 MB of free disk space, and preferably 1 GB.	❏
Select the file system for the Windows 2000 partition. Unless you need to dual boot operating systems or have clients running operating systems other than Windows NT or Windows 2000 that need access to information on this computer, format this partition with NTFS.	❏

Task	Done
Determine whether to use Per Server or Per Seat licensing. If you select Per Server licensing, note the number of Client Access Licenses that were purchased for the server.	❏
Determine the name of the domain or workgroup that you will join. If you join a domain, be sure that you write down the name for the domain; the name will be in the DNS format: *server.sub-domain.domain*. If you will be joining a workgroup, the name will be in the familiar 15-character NetBIOS naming convention: *Server_name*.	❏
Determine the name of the computer before installation	❏
Create a computer account in the domain that you are joining. You can create a computer account during the installation if you have administrative privileges in the domain.	❏
Create a password for the Administrator account.	❏

Lesson Summary

This lesson identified all the preinstallation tasks you must understand and complete before you install Windows 2000. The first task is to identify the hardware requirements for installing Windows 2000 and to ensure that your hardware meets these requirements. It is important that your hardware be on the Windows 2000 Hardware Compatibility List (HCL), so that it is compatible with Windows 2000. After you have determined that your hardware is on the HCL, you must determine how you want to partition the hard disk on which you are going to install Windows 2000. You must also determine whether you are going to format the partition as NTFS, so that you can have better security and a richer feature set, or as FAT or FAT32, so that other operating systems can access the data on the installation partition.

A Client Access License (CAL) gives client computers the right to connect to computers running Windows 2000 Server or Windows 2000 Advanced Server. With Per Seat licensing mode a separate CAL is required for each client computer that accesses a Windows 2000 computer. When a client computer has a CAL, it can be used to access any computer running Windows 2000 Server or Windows 2000 Advanced Server on the enterprise network. With Per Server licensing, CALs are assigned to a particular server. Each CAL allows one connection per client computer to the server, and you must have at least as many CALs that are dedicated to the server as the maximum number of client computers that will be used to concurrently connect to that server at any time.

During installation, your computer must join a domain or a workgroup. If your computer is the first one installed on the network, or if for some other reason there is no domain available for your computer to join, you can have the computer join a workgroup and then have the computer join a domain after the installation. This lesson also provided a checklist of preinstallation tasks that you can complete to help ensure a successful installation of Windows 2000.

Lesson 2: Installing Windows 2000 from a CD-ROM

This lesson looks at the four-stage process of installing Windows 2000 from a CD-ROM. These four stages are as follows: run the Setup program, run the Setup wizard, install Windows networking, and complete the Setup program. After you learn about these four stages, you will install Windows 2000 on your computer.

After this lesson, you will be able to

- Install Windows 2000 Advanced Server from a CD-ROM.

Estimated lesson time: 90 minutes

The Windows 2000 Setup Program

Installing Windows 2000 is a four-step process that combines the Setup program, wizards, and informational screens to complete the installation.

Installing Windows 2000 from a CD-ROM onto a clean hard disk consists of these four stages:

1. Run the Setup program.

   The Setup program prepares the hard disk for later stages of installation and copies the necessary files to run the Setup wizard.

2. Run the Setup wizard.

   The Setup wizard requests setup information about the computer, which includes names, passwords, licensing modes, and so on.

3. Install Windows 2000 networking.

   After gathering information about the computer, the Setup wizard prompts you for networking information and then installs the networking components so that the computer can communicate with other computers on the network.

4. Complete the Setup program.

   To complete the installation, Setup copies files to the hard disk and configures the computer. The system restarts after installation is complete.

Each of these four steps is covered in more detail in the following sections.

Running the Setup Program

To start Setup, use the Setup boot disks. Insert the disk labeled Setup Disk 1 into drive A, and then turn on, or restart, the computer. If your computer supports booting from a CD-ROM drive, you can also start the installation by using the Windows 2000 CD-ROM.

Note   For instructions on how to create the Windows 2000 Setup boot disks, see Appendix B, "Creating Setup Disks."

The following steps describe running the Setup program on a clean disk drive (see Figure 2.4):

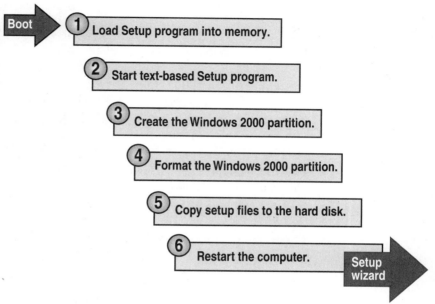

Figure 2.4   Steps in the Setup program

1. After the computer starts, a minimal version of Windows 2000 is copied into memory.

2. This version of Windows 2000 starts the text-mode portion of the Setup program and prompts you to read and accept a licensing agreement.

3. Setup prompts you to select the partition on which to install Windows 2000. You can select an existing partition or create a new partition by using unpartitioned space on the hard disk.

4. After you create the installation partition, Setup prompts you to select a file system for the new partition. Then, Setup formats the partition with the selected file system.

5. After formatting the Windows 2000 partition, Setup copies files to the hard disk and saves configuration information.

6. Setup restarts the computer and then starts the Windows 2000 Server Setup wizard, the graphical-user-interface-(GUI)-mode portion of Setup. As in Windows NT 4.0, by default the Windows 2000 operating system files are installed in the C:\Winnt folder.

Running the Setup Wizard

The GUI-based Windows 2000 Setup wizard leads you through the next stage of the installation process. It gathers information about you, your organization, and your computer.

After installing Windows 2000 security features and installing and configuring devices, the Windows 2000 Setup wizard asks you to provide the following information:

- **Regional settings.** Customize language, locale, and keyboard settings. You can configure Windows 2000 to use multiple languages and regional settings.
- **Name and organization.** Enter the name of the person and the organization to which this copy of Windows 2000 is licensed.
- **Licensing mode.** Select Per Server or Per Seat licensing. If you select Per Server, you must enter the number of Client Access Licenses that were purchased for this server. Each connection requires a Client Access License.
- **Computer name.** Enter a computer name of up to 15 characters. The computer name must be different from other computer, workgroup, or domain names on the network. The Windows 2000 Setup wizard displays a default name, using the organization name that you entered earlier in the setup process.
- **Password for Administrator account.** Specify a password for the Administrator user account, which the Windows 2000 Setup wizard creates during installation. The Administrator account provides administrative privileges that are required to manage the computer.
- **Windows 2000 optional components.** Add or remove additional components during the installation of Windows 2000.

Additional component	Description
Accessories and Utilities	Provides accessory programs—such as Calculator, Paint, WordPad, and others—and other utilities.
Certificate Services	Allows you to create and/or request X.509 digital certificates for authentication. Certificates provide a verifiable means of identifying users on nonsecure networks (such as the Internet), as well as providing the information necessary to conduct secure private communications.
Cluster Service	Enables two or more servers to work together to keep server-based applications highly available, regardless of individual component features. This service is available only in the Advanced Server and Datacenter versions of Windows 2000.
Indexing Service	Installs Index Server system files that enable comprehensive and dynamic full-text searches of data stored on the computer or network.

Additional component	Description
Internet Information Services (IIS)	Includes FTP and Web servers and the IIS administrative interface, common components, and documentation.
Management and Monitoring Tools	Includes tools for monitoring and improving network performance. These tools include the Connection Manager Administration Kit, the Directory Service Migration Tool (helps migrate Novell Directory Services to Windows 2000 Active Directory directory services), Network Monitor Tools (helps analyze and monitor packets of data transferred over the network), and Simple Network Management Protocol.
Message Queuing Services	Installs Microsoft Message Queuing (MSMQ) Routing Server or Client. MSMQ provides developers with a simplified asynchronous programming model and built-in transactional support so your message queues can participate in Microsoft Transaction Server (MTS) transactions.
	Queues act like caches, controlling the flow of data to destinations and ensuring that messages reach their destinations. Message queuing also allows applications to communicate across heterogeneous networks and to computers that might be temporarily offline.
Networking Services	Includes the Dynamic Host Configuration Protocol (DHCP) Service, the DNS Service, Transmission Control Protocol/Internet Protocol (TCP/IP) print server, file and print services, and other networking components.
Other Network File and Print Services	Enables sharing of files and printers on this computer with Macintosh and UNIX-based computers.
Remote Installation Services	Provides the ability to remotely install Windows 2000 Professional on remote boot–enabled client computers.
Remote Storage	Allows the user to use tape libraries as extensions of NTFS volumes, automatically moving data to and from tape media.
Script Debugger	Allows client and server side debugging of Active X Script Engines such as VBScript and JavaScript.
Terminal Services	Enables Windows 9x, Windows NT Workstation, and Windows-based Terminal super-thin clients to access a virtual Windows 2000 Professional desktop session and Windows-based applications.
Terminal Services Licensing	Allows user to configure the computer as a Terminal Services license server that provides client licenses.

Note IIS and Microsoft Script Debugger are selected by default.

- **Time and date.** Select the appropriate time zone, and adjust the date and time settings, if necessary.

After you complete this step in the installation, the Windows 2000 Setup wizard starts to install the Windows networking components.

Installing Windows 2000 Networking Components

After gathering information about your computer, the Windows 2000 Setup wizard guides you through installing the Windows 2000 networking components (see Figure 2.5).

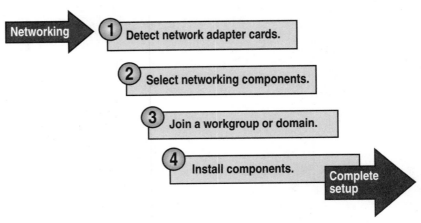

Figure 2.5   Installing Windows networking components

The following list describes the steps for installing Windows 2000 networking:

1. Detect network adapter cards. The Windows 2000 Setup wizard detects and configures any network adapter cards that are installed on the computer. After configuring network adapters, it locates a server running the DHCP Service (DHCP server) on the network.

2. Select networking components. Choose to install networking components with typical or customized settings. The typical installation includes the following options:

   - **Client for Microsoft Networks.** This component allows your computer to gain access to network resources.

   - **File and Printer Sharing for Microsoft Networks.** This component allows other computers to gain access to file and print resources on your computer.

- **TCP/IP.** This protocol is the default networking protocol that allows your computer to communicate over local area networks (LANs) and wide area networks (WANs).

You can install other clients, services, and network protocols (such as NetBIOS Enhanced User Interface [NetBEUI], AppleTalk, and NWLink IPX/SPX/NetBIOS-compatible transport) now or anytime after you install Windows 2000.

3. Join a workgroup or domain. If you create a computer account in the domain for your computer during the installation, the Windows 2000 Setup wizard prompts you for the name and password.

4. Install components. The Windows 2000 Setup wizard installs and configures the Windows networking components that you selected.

Completing the Installation

After installing the networking components, the Windows 2000 Setup wizard automatically starts the final steps in the installation process (see Figure 2.6).

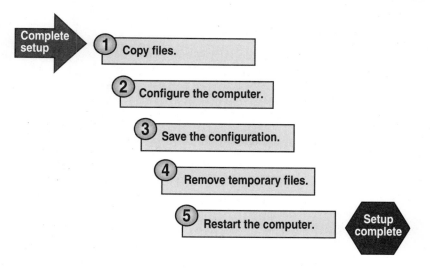

Figure 2.6   The final steps in completing the installation

The following list describes the tasks involved in completing the installation:

1. Copy files. Setup copies any remaining files, such as accessories and bitmaps.

2. Configure the computer. Setup applies the configuration settings that you specified in the Windows 2000 Setup wizard.

3. Save the configuration. Setup saves your configuration settings to the local hard disk. The next time that you start Windows 2000, the computer will use this configuration automatically.

4. Remove temporary files. To save hard disk space, Setup deletes any files that it installed for use only during installation.

5. Restart the computer. After completing the preceding steps, Setup restarts the computer. This finishes the installation of a stand-alone or member server from a CD-ROM.

6. Displays the Configure Server wizard. After you log on, Windows 2000 displays the Configure Server wizard, which allows further configuration of the computer. This step completes the installation of Windows 2000 from a CD-ROM as a stand-alone or member server. Creation of domain controllers will be discussed in Chapter 5, "Administering Active Directory Directory Services."

Practice: Installing Windows 2000 from a CD-ROM

In this practice, you install the beta version of Windows 2000 Advanced Server from a CD-ROM.

Note If your computer is configured with an El-Torito compatible CD-ROM drive, you can install Windows 2000 without using the Setup disks. You can run the Setup program by restarting the computer with the CD-ROM inserted in the CD-ROM drive and then skip to Step 4 in this practice.

▶ **To begin the text-mode installation phase of Windows 2000 Advanced Server Setup**

1. Insert the Windows 2000 Advanced Server beta CD-ROM into the CD-ROM drive.

   Note If your computer will boot from the CD-ROM drive, start the computer and go to step 4.

2. Insert the disk labeled Setup Boot Disk into drive A, and then turn on, or restart, the computer.

3. When prompted, insert Setup Disk 2 into drive A and proceed as directed with the other two Setup disks.

4. When Setup displays the Setup Notification message, read it, and then press Enter to continue.

   Setup displays the Welcome To Setup screen.

Notice that, in addition to the initial installation of Windows 2000, you can use Windows 2000 Setup to repair or recover a damaged Windows 2000 installation.

5. Read the Welcome To Setup screen and press Enter to continue.

   Setup displays the License Agreement screen.

6. Read the license agreement, and then press F8 to agree with the licensing terms.

Note If you are installing Windows 2000 Advanced Server on a computer that already has a Windows 2000 operating system installed on drive C, and you see a message about repairing a damaged installation, press Esc to bypass the message.

Setup displays the Windows 2000 Server Setup screen, prompting you to select an area of free space or an existing partition on which to install Windows 2000. This stage of Setup provides a way for you to create and delete partitions on your hard disk.

7. Press Enter to select the default C: partition.

Note If you are installing Windows 2000 on a computer that already has an operating system installed on drive C, you will be prompted to continue setup or to select a different partition. Press C to continue with the installation.

Setup displays a list of file system choices.

8. Ensure that the NTFS file system option is highlighted and press Enter.

Note If you are installing Windows 2000 on a computer that already has an operating system installed on drive C, you will be prompted to format the drive or to select a different partition. Press F to format the drive.

Setup examines the hard drive, formats the selected partition, and then copies files to the Windows 2000 installation folders.

9. When Setup prompts you to restart the computer, remove all the disks from the disk drives, and then press Enter.

Important If your computer supports booting from the CD-ROM drive and you do not remove the Windows 2000 Advanced Server CD-ROM before Setup restarts the computer, the computer might reboot from the Windows 2000 Advanced Server CD-ROM. This will cause Setup to start again from the beginning. If this happens, remove the CD-ROM and then restart the computer.

The computer restarts. A message box appears prompting you to insert the CD-ROM labeled Windows 2000 Advanced Server into your CD-ROM drive.

> **Note** If you are installing Windows 2000 in a dual-boot configuration on a computer that already has an operating system installed on drive C, you will not have to restart your computer. Proceed to step 2 in the next procedure.

▶ **To begin the graphics-mode installation phase of Windows 2000 Advanced Server Setup**

1. Insert the CD-ROM labeled Windows 2000 Advanced Server into your CD-ROM drive, and then click OK.

   The Windows 2000 Server Setup wizard appears.

2. Click Next to continue, unless Setup has already moved to the next page.

   Setup configures NTFS folder and file permissions for the operating system files, detects the hardware devices in the computer, and then installs and configures device drivers to support the detected hardware. This process will take several minutes.

   Setup prompts you to customize Windows 2000 for different regions and languages.

3. Select the appropriate system locale, user locale, and keyboard layout or ensure that they are correct for your language and location, and then click Next to continue.

   Setup displays the Personalize Your Software page, prompting you for your name and organization name. Setup uses your organization name to generate the default computer name. Many applications that you install later will use this information for product registration and document identification.

4. In the Name box, type your name; in the Organization box, type the name of your organization; and then click Next.

   Setup displays the Licensing Modes page.

5. Click Per Server. Number Of Concurrent Connections, enter 30 for the number of concurrent connections, and then click Next.

> **Important** Per Server and 30 concurrent connections are suggested values to be used in this practice. You should use a legal number of concurrent connections based on the actual licenses that you own.

   Setup displays the Computer Name And Administrator Password page.

6. Type **Server1** in the Computer Name box.

> **Note** Windows 2000 displays the computer name in all capital letters, no matter how you type it in.

If your computer is on a network, check with the network administrator before assigning a name to your computer. Throughout the rest of this self-paced training kit, the practice sections will refer to Server1. If you do not name your computer Server1, everywhere the materials reference Server1, you will have to substitute the name of your computer.

7. In the Administrator Password box and in the Confirm Password box, type **password**, and then click Next.

Important For the practice sections in this self-paced training kit, you will use *password* for the Administrator account. You should always use a complex password for the Administrator account (one that others cannot easily guess). Microsoft recommends mixing uppercase and lowercase letters, numbers, and symbols (for example Lp6*g9).

Setup displays the Windows 2000 Components page indicating components that will be installed by default. You can use the components page to add or remove components.

Important After the installation is complete, you use Add/Remove Components in Control Panel to add or remove components.

---

8. Click Next to continue.

   Setup displays the Modem Dialing Information page.

9. In the What Area Code (Or City Code) Are You In Now? box, type your appropriate area or city code.

10. In the If You Dial A Number To Get An Outside Line, What Is It? box, type the number you dial to get an outside line. If this option doesn't apply to your phone line, leave the box empty.

11. Select either the Tone Dialing option or the Pulse Dialing option, and then click Next.

   The Date And Time Settings page appears.

12. Set the appropriate date and time for your location.

13. Under Time Zone, select the time zone for your location.

14. Select the Automatically Adjust Clock For Daylight Saving Changes check box if you want Windows 2000 to automatically change the time on your computer for daylight saving time changes, and then click Next.

   Setup displays the Networking Settings page.

> **Note** If you have configured your computer for dual booting with another operating system that can also adjust your clock for daylight saving time changes, enable this feature for only one operating system. Enable this feature on the operating system you use most frequently so that the daylight saving adjustment will occur only once.

15. Ensure that Typical Settings is selected, and then click Next.

    Setup displays the Workgroup Or Computer Domain page.

    In this practice you are installing Windows 2000 Advanced Server as a stand-alone server in a workgroup. In a later practice, you will create and join a new Windows 2000 domain.

16. On the Workgroup Or Computer Domain page, make sure that No, This Computer Is Not On A Network, Or Is On A Network Without A Domain is selected, that the workgroup name is WORKGROUP, and then click Next.

    Setup displays the Installing Components page, displaying the status as Setup installs and configures the remaining operating system components according to the options that you have specified. This process will take several minutes.

    Setup then displays the Performing Final Tasks page and displays the status as Setup finishes copying files, making and saving configuration changes, and deleting temporary files.

    Setup displays the Completing The Windows 2000 Setup Wizard page.

17. Remove the CD-ROM from the CD-ROM drive, and then click Finish to continue setting up Windows 2000 Advanced Server.

> **Important** If your computer supports booting from the CD-ROM drive and you do not remove the Windows 2000 Advanced Server CD-ROM before Setup restarts the computer, the computer might reboot from the Windows 2000 Advanced Server CD-ROM. This will cause Setup to start again from the beginning. If this happens, remove the CD-ROM and then restart the computer.

    The computer restarts.

▶ **To log on as Administrator for the first time**

1. Log on by pressing Ctrl+Alt+Delete.

2. In the Log On To Windows dialog box, in the User Name box, type **Administrator**, if necessary, and in the Password box, type **password**

3. Click OK.

    The Windows 2000 Configure Your Server window appears.

Note Prior to or following the display of the Windows 2000 Configure Your Server window, if Setup detects any additional peripherals attached to your computer, such as a printer, the Found New Hardware wizard might open. Click the Next button to start the wizard and select appropriate options when you are prompted. Setup will copy the necessary driver files to the hard drive. Click the wizard's Finish button to continue.

---

4. Click Next to continue to the next wizard page.

5. Clear the Show This Screen At Startup check box, and then close the Windows 2000 Configure Your Server window.

Lesson Summary

Installing Windows 2000 Advanced Server is a four-stage process. The four stages are as follows: run the Setup program, run the Setup wizard, install Windows 2000 networking, and complete the Setup program.

To start Setup, insert Setup Disk 1 into drive A, or if your computer supports booting from a CD-ROM, insert the Windows 2000 Advanced Server CD-ROM into your CD-ROM drive and turn on, or restart, the computer. A minimal version of Windows 2000 is copied into memory and starts the Setup program. Setup then starts the text-mode portion of Setup, prompts you to read and accept a licensing agreement, to select the partition on which to install Windows 2000, and to select a file system for the new partition. Setup copies files to the hard disk, saves configuration information, restarts the computer, and then starts the Windows 2000 Setup wizard, the GUI-mode portion of Setup.

After installing Windows 2000 security features and installing and configuring devices, the Windows 2000 Setup wizard prompts you for information about you, your organization, and your computer. The information requested includes the following: language, locale, and keyboard settings, the name of the person and the organization to which this copy of Windows 2000 is licensed, the licensing mode, the computer name (up to 15 characters), the password for the Administrator user account, and any Windows 2000 optional components you want to install.

The third stage is the installation of Windows 2000 networking. The Setup wizard detects and configures any network adapter cards that are installed in the computer, and prompts you to choose to install networking components with typical or customized settings. By default, the client for Microsoft networks, the file and printer sharing for Microsoft networks, and TCP/IP are installed. You can choose to install other clients, services, and network protocols now or anytime after you install Windows 2000. The Setup wizard also prompts you to decide whether the computer will join a workgroup or domain, and then installs and configures the Windows networking components that you selected.

During the last stage, completing the installation, Setup copies any remaining files, such as accessories and bitmaps, applies the configuration settings that you specified, saves your configuration settings to the local hard disk, deletes any files that it installed for use only during installation, and restarts the computer. This finishes the installation of a stand-alone or member server from a CD-ROM.

After you log on, Windows 2000 displays the Configure Your Server window, which allows you to further configure your computer. This step completes the installation of Windows 2000 from a CD-ROM as a stand-alone or member server.

Lesson 3: Installing Windows 2000 over the Network

In addition to installing from a CD-ROM, you can install Windows 2000 over the network. This lesson demonstrates the similarities and differences between installing from a CD-ROM and installing over the network. The major difference is the location of the source files needed to install Windows 2000. This lesson also lists the requirements for an over-the-network installation.

After this lesson, you will be able to

- Identify the steps for completing a network installation of Windows 2000.

Estimated lesson time: 10 minutes

Preparing for a Network Installation

In a network installation, the Windows 2000 installation files are located in a shared location on a network file server, which is called a *distribution server*. From the computer on which you want to install Windows 2000 (the target computer), you connect to the distribution server and then run the Setup program.

The requirements for a network installation are shown in Figure 2.7 and are explained in more detail in the list that follows.

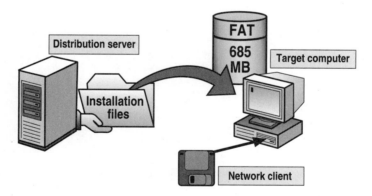

Figure 2.7   Requirements for a network installation

- **Locate a distribution server.** The distribution server contains the installation files from the I386 (or Alpha) folder on the Windows 2000 CD-ROM. These files reside in a common network location in a *shared folder.* This shared folder allows computers on the network to gain access to the installation files. Contact a network administrator to obtain the path to the installation files on the distribution server.

Note Once you have created or located a distribution server, you can use the over-the-network installation method to concurrently install Windows 2000 on multiple computers.

- **Create a FAT partition on the target computer.** The target computer requires a formatted partition on which to copy the installation files. Create a 685 MB (1 GB or larger recommended) partition and format it with the FAT file system.
- **Install a network client.** A network client is software that allows the target computer to connect to the distribution server. On a computer without an operating system, you must boot from a client disk that includes a network client, which enables the target computer to connect to the distribution server.

Installing over the Network

The Windows 2000 Setup program copies the installation files to the target computer and creates the Setup boot disks. After Setup copies the installation files, you start the installation on the target computer by booting from the Setup boot disks. From this point on, you install Windows 2000 in the same way as you do when installing from a CD-ROM.

The steps shown in Figure 2.8 describe the process for installing Windows 2000 over the network.

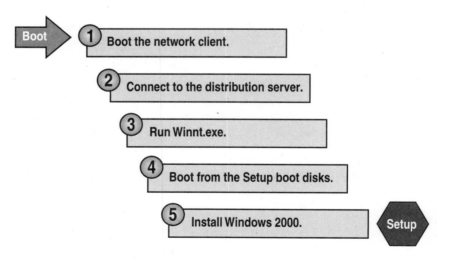

Figure 2.8   Installing Windows 2000 over the network

These steps describe the process for installing Windows 2000 over the network:

1. On the target computer, boot from the network client.

2. Connect to the distribution server. After you start the network client on the target computer, connect to the shared folder on the distribution server that contains the Windows 2000 installation files.

3. Run Winnt.exe or Winnt32.exe to start the Setup program. Winnt.exe and Winnt32.exe reside in the shared folder on the distribution server. When you run Winnt.exe from the shared folder, it creates the Win_nt.~bt temporary folder on the target computer and copies the Windows 2000 installation files from the shared folder on the distribution server to the Win_nt.~bt folder on the target computer.

Note Setup does not create the Setup floppy disks as it did in Windows NT 4.0.

4. Install Windows 2000. Setup restarts the local computer and begins installing Windows 2000.

Modifying the Setup Process Using Winnt.exe

You can modify a server-based installation by changing how Winnt.exe runs the setup process. Table 2.2 describes the switches that you can use with Winnt.exe to control Setup.

Table 2.2   Available Switches for Winnt.exe

Switch	Description
/a	Enables accessibility options.
/e:*command*	Specifies the command to be executed at the end of GUI setup.
/i:*inffile*	Specifies the file name (no path) of the setup information file. The default is Dosnet.inf.
/r:*folder*	Specifies the optional folder to be installed.
/rx:*folder*	Specifies the optional folder to be copied.
/s:*source_ path*	Specifies the source location of Windows 2000 files. Must be a full path of the form x:\[path] or \\server\share\[path]. The default is the current folder.
/t:*drive_letter*	Specifies a drive to contain temporary setup files. If not specified, Setup will attempt to locate a drive for you—the drive with the most available space.
/u:*script_file*	Performs an unattended installation by using an optional script file. Unattended installations also require use of the /s switch.
/udf:*id, UDF_file*	Indicates an identifier (id) that Setup uses to specify how a Uniqueness Database File (UDF) modifies an answer file. The /udf parameter overrides values in the answer file, and the identifier determines which values in the UDF are used.

Note Winnt.exe no longer includes switches for creating Setup disks. To create the Setup disks, run the Makeboot.exe program from the Bootdisk folder on the Windows 2000 CD-ROM. Use the command line **makeboot a:**.

Modifying the Setup Process Using Winnt32.exe

You can modify a server-based installation by changing how Winnt32.exe runs the setup process. Table 2.3 describes some of the switches that you can use with Winnt32.exe to control Setup.

Table 2.3   Available Switches for Winnt32.exe

Switch	Description
/copydir: *folder_name*	Creates an additional folder within the systemroot folder (the folder that contains the Windows 2000 system files). For example, if your source folder contains a folder called My_drivers, type **/copydir:My_drivers** to copy the My_drivers folder to your system folder. You can use the /copydir switch to create as many additional folders as you like.
/copysource: *folder_name*	Creates an additional folder within the systemroot folder. Setup deletes files created with /copysource after installation completes.
/cmd: *command_line*	Executes a command before the final phase of Setup.
/cmdcons	Copies additional files to the hard disk that are necessary to load a command-line interface for repair and recovery purposes.
/debug[*level*] [:file_name]	Creates a debug log at the specified level. By default, it creates C:\Winnt32.log at level 2 (the warning level).
/s:*source_ path*	Specifies the source location of Windows 2000 installation files. To simultaneously copy files from multiple paths, use a separate /s switch for each source path.
/syspart: *drive_letter*	Copies Setup startup files to a hard disk and marks the drive as active. You can then install the drive in another computer. When you start that computer, Setup starts at the next phase. Use of /syspart requires use of the /tempdrive switch.
/tempdrive: *drive_letter*	Places temporary files on the specified drive and installs Windows 2000 on that drive.
/unattend [number] :*answer_ file*	Performs an unattended installation. The answer file provides your custom specifications to Setup. If you do not specify an answer file, all user settings are taken from the previous installation. You can specify the number of seconds between the time that Setup finishes copying the files and when it restarts. You can specify the number of seconds only on a computer running Windows 2000 that is upgrading to a newer version of Windows 2000.

Switch	Description
/udf:id [,*UDF_file*]	Indicates an identifier (id) that Setup uses to specify how a Uniqueness Database File (UDF) modifies an answer file. The .UDF file overrides values in the answer file, and the identifier determines which values in the .UDF file are used. For example, /udf:RAS_user, Our_company.udf overrides settings that are specified for the RAS_user identifier in the Our_company.udf file. If you do not specify a .UDF file, Setup prompts the user to insert a disk that contains the $Unique$.udf file.

Lesson Summary

The main difference between an over-the-network installation and an installation from CD-ROM of Windows 2000 is the location of the source files. Once you connect to the shared folder containing the source files and start Winnt.exe or Winnt32.exe the installation proceeds like an installation from CD-ROM. There are several switches for Winnt.exe and Winnt32.exe to modify the installation process.

Lesson 4: Automating Installations

This lesson presents two methods that will help you to automate Windows 2000 installations. When you must install Windows 2000 on computers with varying configurations, scripting provides automation with increased flexibility. You will learn how the improved Setup Manager makes it easy to create the Unattend.txt files that are necessary for scripted installations. You will then learn how installing Windows 2000 on several identical computers, by using a disk duplication tool, can save you time and effort.

After this lesson, you will be able to

- Describe how to automate installations of Windows 2000 by using the Windows 2000 Setup Manager wizard.
- Describe how to automate installations of Windows 2000 by using disk duplication.

Estimated lesson time: 15 minutes

Automating Installations by Using the Windows 2000 Setup Manager Wizard

The computers in most networks are not identical but still have many similarities. It is possible to use installation scripts to specify the variations in the hardware configurations of the computers that are to receive installations. The new Windows 2000 Setup Manager wizard allows you to quickly create a script for a customized installation of Windows 2000 without cryptic text file syntax. Knowing how to use Setup Manager enables you to perform customized installations on workstations and servers that meet the specific hardware and network requirements of your organization (see Figure 2.9).

Although it is still possible to use Unattend.txt files created with a simple text editor, such as Notepad, use Setup Manager to reduce errors in syntax. To access Setup Manager, it is first necessary to install the Windows 2000 Resource Kit. Do this by running Setup.exe from the \Support\Reskit folder on the Windows 2000 CD-ROM.

Note Some interim beta releases do not include the Resource Kit. If the Resource Kit is not present on your current beta release, look for it on earlier betas you may have received or on later betas that you may receive. Even if you can't access the Resource Kit, read through this section to familiarize yourself with how Setup Manager works.

To run the Setup Manager wizard, click Start, point to Programs, point to Resource Kit, and select Tools Management Console. Then expand the Microsoft

Resource Kits, Windows 2000 Resource Kit, and Tools Categories folders in the console pane. Click the eployment Tools folder in the console pane, and then double-click the Setupmgr shortcut icon in the details pane. A sample answer file, named Unattend.txt, is also included on the Windows 2000 CD-ROM.

Setup Manager does the following:

- Provides a new, easy-to-use graphical interface with which you can create and modify answer files and Uniqueness Database Files (UDFs).
- Makes it easy to specify computer-specific or user-specific information.
- Simplifies the inclusion of application setup scripts in the answer file.
- Creates the distribution folder that you use for the installation files.

When you start Setup Manager, you will be presented with three options:

- Create a new answer file.
- Create an answer file based on the configuration of the computer on which the wizard is running.
- Modify an existing answer file.

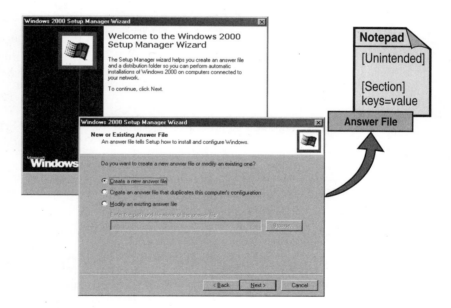

Figure 2.9 Windows 2000 Setup Manager wizard

Note Automating a domain controller installation requires the manual creation of an answer file.

If you select Create A New Answer File, you will then need to choose the type of answer file you want to create. Setup Manager can create the following types of answer files:

- Unattend.txt for setup of Windows 2000 Professional.
- Unattend.txt for setup of Windows 2000 Server.
- Remboot.sif for use with Remote Installation Services. (Remote Installation Services will be discussed later in this chapter.)
- Sysprep.inf for use with the System Preparation Tool. (The System Preparation Tool will also be discussed later in this chapter.)

The remainder of the Setup Manager wizard allows you to specify a level of user interaction with the Setup program and to enter all the information required to complete Setup.

Tip If you are installing Windows 2000 by booting from a CD-ROM drive, you can create an answer file designed for this purpose. In Setup Manager, specify the installation folder, and on the distribution folder page select No, This Answer File Will Be Used To Install From A CD. Save the file as a:\winnt.sif. Winnt.exe will search for this file when you boot from the CD-ROM.

If there are several domain controllers in your organization, you may find it efficient to automate these installations. When you automate a domain controller installation, you can automate installation of the server as you normally would and then automate the promotion of the server to a domain controller with a second answer file.

To start a domain controller promotion immediately after Setup completes, specify the following command to run after Setup completes: **dcpromo / answer:<*answer file*>**.

Note The Sysdiff.exe utility is often used in conjunction with Setup Manager to install Windows using difference files. The use of Sysdiff.exe has not changed from Windows NT 4.0.

Automating Installations by Using Disk Duplication

When you install Windows 2000 on several computers with identical hardware configurations, the most efficient installation method to use is disk duplication. By creating a disk image of a Windows 2000 installation and copying that image onto multiple destination computers, you save time in the rollout of Windows 2000. This method also creates a convenient baseline that you can easily copy again onto a computer that is experiencing significant problems.

Disk imaging and duplication technologies are improved in Windows 2000. One of the tools that you will use for disk duplication is the improved System Preparation Tool (Sysprep.exe) that now ships with Windows 2000. Knowing how to use the System Preparation Tool can help support professionals prepare master disk images for efficient mass installations.

Examining the Disk Duplication Process

To install Windows 2000 by using disk duplication, you first need to install and configure Windows 2000 on a test computer. After Windows 2000 is installed and configured, you need to install and configure any applications on the test computer. Run Sysprep.exe on the test computer to prepare the computer for duplication.

Optionally, you can run Setup Manager to create a Sysprep.inf file. Sysprep.inf provides answers to the Mini-Setup program on the destination computers. You can also use this file to specify customized drivers. Setup Manager creates a Sysprep folder at the root of the drive image and places Sysprep.inf in this folder. The Mini-Setup program checks for Sysprep.inf in the Sysprep folder at the root of the drive in which Windows 2000 is being installed.

Restart the test computer and run a third-party disk image copying tool to create a master disk image. Save the new disk image on a shared folder or CD-ROM. Copy this image to the multiple destination computers.

End users can then start the destination computers. The Mini-Setup wizard will prompt the user for computer-specific variables, such as the administrator password for the computer and the computer name. If a Sysprep.inf file was provided, the Mini-Setup wizard will be bypassed and the system will load Windows 2000 without user intervention.

Note When you use disk duplication, the mass storage controllers and hardware abstraction layers (HALs) for the test computer and all destination computers must be identical.

Using the System Preparation Tool

A familiarity with the features of Sysprep.exe, the program for preparing a disk for duplication, will help you use this utility effectively.

The System Preparation Tool (Sysprep.exe) in Windows 2000 prepares the master computer to be duplicated. After you run Sysprep.exe on the master computer, you can use a third-party tool to capture the image and copy it to the destination computers. When the user restarts the destination computer, the Setup wizard appears but requires very little input to complete. You can also automate the completion of the Setup wizard further by creating a Sysprep.inf file.

One of the primary functions of the System Preparation Tool is to delete security identifiers (SIDs) and all other user-specific or computer-specific information. New SIDs are generated when the destination computers are restarted after the disk image is loaded.

The System Preparation Tool prepares a hard disk for duplication. Table 2.4 describes the switches that you can use to customize Sysprep.exe.

Table 2.4   Available Switches for Sysprep.exe

Switch	Description
/quiet	Runs with no user interaction
/pnp	Forces Setup to detect Plug and Play devices on the destination computers
/reboot	Restarts the source computer
/nosidgen	Does not regenerate SIDs on the destination computers

Lesson Summary

There are two utilities in Windows 2000 that will help you automate installations: Setup Manager and the System Preparation Tool. Setup Manager makes it easy to create the Unattend.txt files that are necessary for scripted installations. Setup Manager provides an easy-to-use graphical interface with which you can create and modify answer files and UDFs.

You install Setup Manager by running Setup.exe from the \Support\Reskit folder on the Windows 2000 CD-ROM. Setup Manager makes it easy to specify computer-specific or user-specific information, and to include application setup scripts in the answer file. Setup Manager also creates the distribution folder that you use for the installation files.

The System Preparation Tool (Sysprep.exe) prepares the master computer to be duplicated. One of the primary functions of the System Preparation Tool is to delete security identifiers (SIDs) and all other user-specific or computer-specific information. There are four switches that you can use to customize Sysprep.exe.

After you run Sysprep.exe on the master computer, you can use a third-party tool to capture the image and copy it to the destination computers. When the user restarts the destination computer, the Setup wizard appears but requires very little input to complete. You can also automate the completion of the Setup wizard further by creating a Sysprep.inf file.

Lesson 5: Performing Remote Installations

The most efficient method of deploying Windows 2000 Professional is to use remote installation. You can perform remote installations of Windows 2000 Professional if you have a Windows 2000 Server or Windows 2000 Advanced Server infrastructure in place and the computers in your network support remote booting.

After this lesson, you will be able to

- Describe how to deploy Windows 2000 with remote installation.

Estimated lesson time: 10 minutes

Understanding Remote Installation

Remote installation is the process of connecting to a server running Remote Installation Services (RIS), called the RIS server, and then starting an automated installation of Windows 2000 Professional on a local computer. Remote installation enables administrators to install Windows 2000 Professional on client computers throughout a network from a central location. This saves time since administrators do not need to visit all the computers in a network, thereby reducing the cost of deploying Windows 2000 Professional.

RIS provides the following benefits:

- Enables remote installation of Windows 2000 Professional
- Simplifies server image management by eliminating hardware-specific images and by detecting Plug and Play hardware during Setup
- Supports recovery of the operating system and computer in the event of computer failure
- Retains security settings after restarting the destination computer
- Reduces TCO (total cost of ownership) by allowing either users or technical staff to install the operating system on individual computers

Installing and Configuring Remote Installation Services

Before beginning a rollout of Windows 2000 Professional using Remote Installation Services, you should become familiar with the prerequisites for the service and you must install the service using the Remote Installation Services Setup wizard.

Prerequisites

The RIS server can be a domain controller or a member server. Table 2.5 lists the network services required for RIS and their RIS function. These network services do not have to be installed on the same computer as RIS, but they must be available somewhere on the network.

Table 2.5   Network Services Required for RIS

Network service	RIS function
Domain Name System (DNS)	RIS relies on the DNS server for locating both the directory service and client computer accounts.
DHCP	Client computers that can perform a network boot receive an IP address from the DHCP server.
Active Directory directory services	RIS relies upon Active Directory directory services in Windows 2000 for locating existing client computers as well as existing RIS servers.

Remote installation requires that RIS (included on the Windows 2000 Server and Windows 2000 Advanced Server CD-ROMs) be installed on a volume that is shared over the network. This shared volume must meet the following criteria:

- The shared volume cannot be on the same drive that is running Windows 2000 Server or Windows 2000 Advanced Server.
- The shared volume must be large enough to hold the RIS software and the various Windows 2000 Professional images.
- The shared volume must be formatted with NTFS.

Remote Installation Services Setup Wizard

When your network meets the prerequisites for RIS, you can run the Remote Installation Services Setup wizard, which does the following:

- Installs the RIS software
- Copies the Windows 2000 Professional installation files to the server
- Adds .SIF files, which are a variation of an Unattend.txt file
- Configures the Client Installation wizard screens that will appear during a remote installation

When installation of RIS is complete, you can configure RIS using the server's computer object in the Active Directory Users and Computers snap-in, located in the Administrative Tools folder. You will learn more about the management of Active Directory objects in Chapter 5, "Administering Active Directory Directory Services."

Configuring Clients for Remote Installation

Client computers that support remote installation must have one of the following configurations:

- A configuration meeting the Net PC specification.
- A network adapter card with a Pre-Boot Execution Environment (PXE) boot read-only memory (ROM) version .99c or greater and basic input/output system (BIOS) support for starting from the PXE boot ROM. PXE defines

the way in which a PC should load its operating system from a remote boot server.

- A supported network adapter card and a remote installation boot disk.

Net PCs

The Net PC is a highly manageable platform with the ability to perform a network boot, manage upgrades, and prevent users from changing the hardware or operating system configuration. Additional requirements for the Net PC are as follows:

- The network adapter must be set as the primary boot device within the system BIOS.

- The user account that will be used to perform the installation must be assigned the user right Log On As A Batch Job. This is set using Group Policy, which is discussed in Chapter 6, "Managing Desktop Environments with Group Policy."

Note The Administrator group does not have the right to log on to a batch job by default and thus will need to be assigned this right prior to attempting a remote installation.

- Users must be assigned permission to create computer accounts in the domain that they are joining. The domain is specified in the Advanced Settings dialog box on the RIS server.

Computers Not Meeting the Net PC Specification

Computers that do not directly meet the Net PC specification can still interact with the RIS server. To enable remote installation on a computer that does not meet the Net PC specification, perform the following steps:

1. Install a network adapter card with a PXE boot ROM version .99c or greater.

2. Set the BIOS to start from the PXE boot ROM.

3. The user account that will be used to perform the installation must be assigned the user right Log On As A Batch Job.

4. Users must be assigned permission to create computer accounts in the domain that they are joining. The domain is specified in the Advanced Settings dialog box on the RIS server.

If the network adapter card is not equipped with a PXE boot ROM or the BIOS does not allow starting from the network adapter, create a remote installation boot disk by running the Windows 2000 Remote Boot Disk Generator, or Rbfg.exe. The Rbfg.exe utility is found in the \RemoteInstall\Admin\I386 folder on the RIS server. You will also need to set the user rights and permissions as listed above for a Net PC.

Lesson Summary

If you have a Windows 2000 Server or Windows 2000 Advanced Server infrastructure in place, and the computers in your network support remote boot, the most efficient method of deploying Windows 2000 Professional is to use remote installation. Remote installation is the process of connecting to an RIS server and then starting an automated installation of Windows 2000 Professional on a local computer. Remote installation enables administrators to install Windows 2000 Professional on client computers throughout a network from a central location. This saves time since administrators do not need to visit all the computers in a network, thereby reducing the cost of deploying Windows 2000 Professional.

Client computers that support remote installation must have one of the three following configurations: a configuration meeting the Net PC specification, and the network adapter must be set as the primary boot device within the system BIOS; a network adapter card with a Pre-Boot Execution Environment (PXE) boot ROM and BIOS support for starting from the PXE boot ROM; or a supported network adapter card and a remote installation boot disk.

Finally, the user account that will be used to perform the installation must be assigned the user right Log On As A Batch Job, and users must be assigned permission to create computer accounts in the domain that they are joining. The domain is specified in the Advanced Settings dialog box on the RIS server.

Lesson 6: Troubleshooting Windows 2000 Setup

Your installation of Windows 2000 should complete without any problems. However, this lesson covers some common issues that you might encounter during installation.

After this lesson, you will be able to

- Troubleshoot Windows 2000 installations.

Estimated lesson time: 5 minutes

Resolving Common Problems

Table 2.6 lists some common installation problems and offers solutions to resolve them.

Table 2.6   Troubleshooting Tips

Problem	Solution
Media errors	If you are installing from a CD-ROM, use a different CD-ROM. To request a replacement CD-ROM, contact Microsoft or your vendor.
	If one of your Setup disks is not working, try using a different set of Setup disks. You can make a new set of Setup disks by running Makeboot.bat.
Nonsupported CD-ROM drive	Replace the CD-ROM drive with one that is supported, or if that is not possible, try another method of installing, such as installing over the network, and then after you have completed the installation, you can add the adapter card driver for the CD-ROM drive if it is available.
Insufficient disk space	Use the Setup program to create a partition by using existing free space on the hard disk.
	Delete and create partitions as needed to create a partition that is large enough for installation.
	Reformat an existing partition to create more space.
Failure of dependency service to start	In the Windows 2000 Setup wizard, return to the Network Settings dialog box and verify that you installed the correct protocol and network adapter. Verify that the network adapter has the proper configuration settings, such as transceiver type, and that the local computer name is unique on the network.

(continued)

Problem	Solution
Inability to connect to the domain controller	Verify that the domain name is correct.
	Verify that the server running the DNS Service and the domain controller are both running and online. If you cannot locate a domain controller, install into a workgroup and then join the domain after installation.
	Verify that the network adapter card and protocol settings are set correctly.
	If you are reinstalling Windows 2000 and using the same computer name, delete and then recreate the computer account.
Failure of Windows 2000 to install or start	Verify that Windows 2000 is detecting all of the hardware and that all of the hardware is on the HCL.

Lesson Summary

You might encounter some common problems when installing Windows 2000. Installation problems could be caused by bad media, in which case you will have to get a new CD-ROM to be able to install. You might also encounter problems with your installation if your hardware is not on the HCL. If your CD-ROM drive is not on the HCL, you can swap it out for a supported drive or install over the network and add the driver to support the CD-ROM drive if it is available.

If you failed to complete your preinstallation tasks and there is not enough room on any of the partitions to install Windows 2000, you can create a new partition from unused space on the hard disk, if the space is available; you can delete some existing partitions so that you can create one that is large enough to install Windows 2000; or you can format an existing partition to provide enough space to install Windows 2000.

You also learned some tips to try in case you cannot connect to the domain controller. If you cannot connect to the domain controller, you can complete the installation by having a the computer join a workgroup. After you have completed the installation and determine what is preventing you from connecting to the domain controller, you can have the computer join the domain.

Review

Here are some questions to help you determine if you have learned enough to move on to the next chapter. If you have difficulty answering these questions, please go back and review the material in this chapter before beginning the next chapter. The answers to these questions are located in Appendix A, "Questions and Answers."

1. Your company has decided to install Windows 2000 Professional on all new computers that are purchased for desktop users. What should you do before you purchase new computers to ensure that Windows 2000 can be installed and run without difficulty?

2. You are attempting to install Windows 2000 Professional from a CD-ROM; however, you have discovered that your computer does not support booting from the CD-ROM drive. How can you install Windows 2000?

3. You are installing Windows 2000 Advanced Server on a computer that will be a member server in an existing Windows 2000 domain. You want to add the computer to the domain during installation. What information do you need, and what computers must be available on the network, before you run the Setup program?

4. You are using the CD-ROM to install Windows 2000 Advanced Server on a computer that was previously running another operating system. How should you configure the hard disk to simplify the installation process?

5. You are installing Windows 2000 over the network. Before you install to a client computer, what must you do?

C H A P T E R   3

Configuring the DNS Service

About This Chapter

Domain Name System (DNS) is a distributed database that is used in Transmission Control Protocol/Internet Protocol (TCP/IP) networks to translate computer names to Internet Protocol (IP) addresses. This chapter helps you understand DNS and name resolution. It also presents the skills and knowledge necessary to install and configure the DNS Service.

Before You Begin

To complete this chapter

- You must have installed the beta version of Windows 2000 Advanced Server on a computer that meets or exceeds the minimum hardware requirements listed in "Getting Started," on page xxi. The computer should be installed as a stand-alone computer in a workgroup and TCP/IP should be the only installed protocol.

Lesson 1: Understanding DNS

DNS is most commonly associated with the Internet. However, private networks use DNS extensively to resolve computer names and to locate computers within their local networks and the Internet. DNS provides the following benefits:

- DNS names are user-friendly, which means that they are easier to remember than IP addresses.
- DNS names remain more constant than IP addresses. An IP address for a server can change, but the server name remains the same.
- DNS allows users to connect to local servers by using the same naming convention as the Internet.

Note For more information on DNS, see RFC 1034 and RFC 1035. To read these RFCs (Requests for Comment), use your Web browser to search for "RFC 1034" and "RFC 1035" on the Internet.

After this lesson, you will be able to

- Explain the function of DNS and its components.

Estimated lesson time: 15 minutes

Domain Name Space

The domain name space is the naming scheme that provides the hierarchical structure for the DNS database. Each node represents a partition of the DNS database. These nodes are referred to as domains.

The DNS database is indexed by name; therefore, each domain must have a name. As you add domains to the hierarchy, the name of the parent domain is appended to its child domain (called a subdomain). Consequently, a domain's name identifies its position in the hierarchy. For example, in Figure 3.1, the sales.microsoft.com domain name identifies the sales domain as a subdomain of the microsoft.com domain and microsoft as a subdomain of the com domain.

The hierarchical structure of the domain name space consists of a root domain, top-level domains, second-level domains, any subdomains, and host names.

Note The term *domain,* in the context of DNS, is not related to *domain* as used in the Microsoft Windows 2000 directory services. A Windows 2000 domain is a grouping of computers and devices that are administered as a unit.

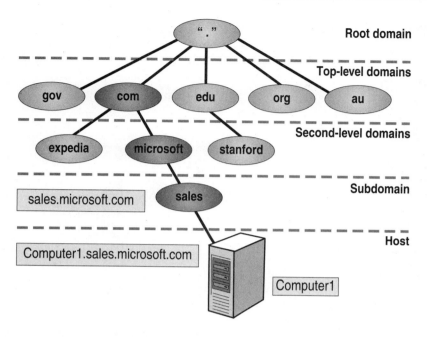

Figure 3.1   Hierarchical structure of a domain name space

Root Domain

The root domain is at the top of the hierarchy and is represented as a period (.). The Internet root domain is managed by several organizations, including Network Solutions, Inc.

Top-Level Domains

Top-level domains are two- or three-character name codes. Top-level domains are organized by organization type or geographic location. Table 3.1 provides some examples of top-level domain names.

Table 3.1   Top-Level Domains

Top-level domain	Description
gov	Government organizations
com	Commercial organizations
edu	Educational institutions
org	Noncommercial organizations
au	Country code of Australia

Top-level domains can contain second-level domains and host names.

Second-Level Domains

Organizations, such as Network Solutions, Inc., assign and register second-level domains to individuals and organizations for the Internet. A second-level name has two name parts: a top-level name and a unique second-level name. Table 3.2 provides some examples of second-level domains.

Table 3.2   Second-Level Domain Examples

Second-level domain	Description
ed.gov	United States Department of Education
microsoft.com	Microsoft Corporation
stanford.edu	Stanford University
w3.org	World Wide Web Consortium
pm.gov.au	Prime Minister of Australia

Subdomains

Organizations can create additional names that extend their DNS tree to represent departments, divisions, or other geographic locations. Subdomains have three name parts: a top-level name, a unique second-level name, and a unique name representing the department or location—for example, sales.microsoft.com.

Host Names

Host names refer to specific computers on the Internet or a private network. For example, in Figure 3.1, Computer1 is a host name. A host name is the leftmost portion of a *fully qualified domain name (FQDN),* which describes the exact position of a host within the domain hierarchy. Computer1.sales.microsoft.com. (including the end period, which represents the root domain) is an FQDN (see Figure 3.1).

DNS uses a host's FQDN to resolve a name to an IP address. The host name does not have to be the same as the computer name. By default, TCP/IP setup uses the computer name for the host name, replacing illegal characters, such as the underscore (_), with a hyphen (-).

Note For the accepted domain naming conventions, see RFC 1035.

Domain Naming Guidelines

When you create a domain name space, consider the following domain guidelines and standard naming conventions:

- **Limit the number of domain levels.** Typically, DNS host entries should be three or four levels down the DNS hierarchy and no more than five levels down the hierarchy. The numbers of levels increase the administrative tasks.

- **Use unique names.** Each subdomain must have a unique name within its parent domain to ensure that the name is unique throughout the DNS name space.

- **Use simple names.** Simple and precise domain names are easier for users to remember and enable users to search intuitively and locate Web sites or other computers on the Internet or an intranet.

- **Avoid lengthy domain names.** Domain names can be up to 63 characters, including the periods. The total length of an FQDN cannot exceed 255 characters. Case-sensitive naming is not supported.

- **Use standard DNS characters and Unicode characters.**

  - Windows 2000 supports the following standard DNS characters: A–Z, a–z, 0–9, and the hyphen (-), as defined in RFC 1035.

  - The DNS Service also supports the Unicode character set. The Unicode character set includes additional characters not found in the American Standard Code for Information Interchange (ASCII) character set, that are required for languages such as French, German, and Spanish.

Note Use Unicode characters only if all servers running the DNS Service in your environment support Unicode. For more information on the Unicode character set, see RFC 2044.

Zones

A zone represents a discrete portion of the domain name space. Zones provide a way to partition the domain name space into manageable sections.

- Multiple zones in a domain name space are used to distribute administrative tasks to different groups. For example, Figure 3.2 depicts the microsoft.com domain name space divided into two zones. The two zones allow one administrator to manage the microsoft and sales domains and another administrator to manage the development domain.

- A zone must encompass a contiguous domain name space. For example in Figure 3.2, you could not create a zone that consists of only the sales.microsoft.com and development.microsoft.com domains, because these two domains are not contiguous.

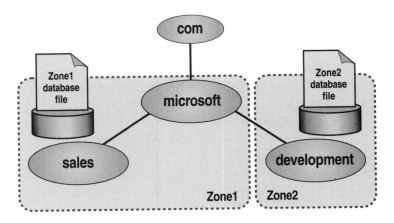

Figure 3.2 Domain name space divided into zones

The name-to-IP address mappings for a zone are stored in the zone database file. Each zone is anchored to a specific domain, referred to as the zone's root domain. The zone database file does not necessarily contain information for all subdomains of the zone's root domain, only those subdomains within the zone.

In Figure 3.2, the root domain for Zone1 is microsoft.com, and its zone file contains the name-to-IP-address mappings for the microsoft and sales domains. The root domain for Zone2 is development, and its zone file contains the name-to-IP-address mappings for the development domain only. The zone file for Zone1 does not contain the name-to-IP-address mappings for the development domain, although development is a subdomain of the microsoft domain.

Name Servers

A DNS name server stores the zone database file. Name servers can store data for one zone or multiple zones. A name server is said to have authority for the domain name space that the zone encompasses.

One name server contains the master zone database file, referred to as the *primary zone database file,* for the specified zone. As a result, there must be at least one name server for a zone. Changes to a zone, such as adding domains or hosts, are performed on the server that contains the primary zone database file.

Multiple name servers act as a backup to the name server containing the primary zone database file. Multiple name servers do the following:

- **Perform zone transfers.** The additional name servers obtain a copy of the zone database file from the name server that contains the primary database zone file. This is called a *zone transfer*. These name servers periodically query the name server containing the primary zone database file for updated zone data.

Note To configure the zone transfer interval rate, use the DNS snap-in.

- **Provide redundancy.** If the name server containing the primary zone database file fails, the additional name servers can provide service.

- **Improve access speed for remote locations.** If there are a number of clients in remote locations, use additional name servers to reduce query traffic across slow wide area network (WAN) links.

- **Reduce the load on the name server containing the primary zone database file.**

Zone Transfers

Zone transfer is the process of replicating a zone file to multiple name servers, and is achieved by copying the zone file information from the master server to the secondary server. The master server is the source of the zone information, and can be either a primary or secondary server. The zone transfer process is initiated when one of the following occurs:

- The master server sends a notification of a change in the zone to the secondary server or servers.

- The secondary server queries the primary server for changes to the zone file. This occurs when the DNS Server Service on the secondary server starts, or the secondary server's refresh interval has expired. The refresh interval in the SOA (Start of Authority) resource record is set to 15 minutes by default.

Replication Methods

There are two methods used for zone replication.

- Full zone transfer (AXFR), replicates the entire zone file. AXFR zone update is used and supported by most DNS implementations. When the refresh interval elapses on a secondary server, it queries its zone master server using an AXFR query. The secondary server detects whether its local copy of a zone is current to its zone master source by comparing serial numbers for the zone. If the secondary server detects that its copy of the zone database file is not current, it pulls the entire contents of the zone database file from the master server.

Note BIND 4.9.3 DNS servers and Windows NT 4.0 DNS support AXFR only.

- Incremental zone transfer (IXFR), replicates only changes to the zone file. IXFR zone update is new to the Windows 2000 DNS Server Service, and can reduce the amount of zone data that is transferred to fully update a zone. IXFR allows the transfer of only records that have been changed or added, rather than transferring the entire zone file. Changes and additions are kept in a cache at the primary server and are transferred to a requesting DNS secondary server if it is determined that the secondary server does not have the updated information. Synchronization is kept through the use of serial numbers for each zone file.

Note For more information on incremental zone transfer, see RFC 1995

Zone Transfer Properties

How often zone transfers should occur is a function of how often names and IP address mappings change within your domain. Unnecessary zone transfers could cause excessive network and server loads.

You configure primary and secondary zones with the information necessary to initiate and request zone transfers by using the State Of Authority (SOA) tab of the zone's Properties dialog box and the Notify dialog box (via the Zone Transfers tab). You can change the default zone transfer timers by using the State Of Authority (SOA) tab. You can also change the following values that affect zone transfer:

- **Serial Number.** Identifies changes in a zone. Normally, the serial number does not need to be modified and it is automatically incremented on a primary server each time a zone is changed. In some instances, however, setting a larger serial number for a primary zone can be useful to force all secondary zone servers to update zone data.

- **Refresh Interval.** Controls how often a secondary server will poll a primary server for new data. The default setting is 60 minutes. A smaller value can be used where high-speed network links are used between a primary zone server and secondary servers. This value can also be increased where network connection speeds are slower, or connections are only started on demand.

- **Retry Interval.** Controls how often retries occur. A retry interval is the length of time that a secondary server should wait before retrying a refresh if a primary server is offline. Normally, this value is set to some fraction of the refresh interval. The default is 10 minutes.

- **Expire Interval.** Controls the length of time that a secondary server will use its current zone data to answer queries if the server fails to contact the primary zone server. After the length of the expire time has been reached by a secondary with no further contact to the primary server, the secondary will cease to provide name service. Therefore, this value should be set to a length that is greater than the length of time used by a major server outage. The default is 24 hours, but larger values are commonly used for many installations.

- **Minimum (default) TTL.** Applies by default to all resource records in the zone and determines how long names returned by a zone's name servers will be cached on other name servers that receive this data. The minimum Time to

Live (TTL) value affects name caching performance throughout all servers in a zone. This value can be increased to a value of one to five days where zone changes are infrequent, and temporarily decreased during periods when major updates or revisions to a zone are being made. The default for this value is 60 minutes.

DNS Notify

DNS Notify is a revision to DNS that requests that the source server for a zone notify certain secondary servers in that zone of changes to the zone file. The secondary servers can then check to see whether they need to initiate a zone transfer. This process can help improve the consistency of zone data among secondary servers.

The following list describes the order in which the DNS Notify process works:

1. The local zone file on a primary server is updated. When the updated zone file is written to the hard disk, the serial number field in the SOA resource record is updated to indicate that the zone file has been updated.

2. The primary server then sends a notify message to other name servers that are part of a notify set.

3. All secondary name servers that receive the notify message respond by initiating an SOA type query back to the notifying server (usually the primary server) to determine if that server's zone file is a later version than the current copy of the zone file on the secondary server.

4. If a notified server determines that the serial number used in the SOA resource record of the notifying server's zone file is higher (more recent) than the serial number used in the SOA resource record for its current zone copy, a zone transfer is initiated. Otherwise, no update occurs and the notified server logs the attempted notify-update transaction as an error.

Note For more information on DNS Notify, see RFC 1996.

To determine which secondary servers in a zone to send the changes to, the source server for the primary zone contains a notify list, which is a list of the IP addresses for the secondary servers. The source server for the zone notifies only the listed servers when zone updates occur. To configure the notify list, open the zone Properties dialog box, click the Zone Transfers tab, and then click the Notify button. Select the Notify These Server Only option, type the IP address of each secondary server to notify when the zone is updated, and click the Add button. The notify list can also be used to restrict access to secondary servers that attempt to request zone updates.

Lesson Summary

DNS is most commonly associated with the Internet. However, many private networks also use DNS to resolve computer names and to locate computers within their local networks and the Internet. One benefit of DNS is that DNS names are user-friendly and are less likely to change than IP addresses. Another benefit is that it allows users to connect to local servers by using the same naming convention as the Internet.

The domain name space is the naming scheme that provides the hierarchical structure for the DNS database. The DNS database is indexed by name, so each domain (node) must have a name. The hierarchical structure of the domain name space consists of a root domain, top-level domains, second-level domains, any subdomains, and host names. Host names refer to specific computers on the Internet or a private network. A host name is the leftmost portion of a fully qualified domain name (FQDN), which describes the exact position of a host within the domain hierarchy.

Domain naming guidelines include limiting the number of domain levels, using unique names, and using simple names. Zones provide a way to partition the domain name space into smaller sections. A zone represents a discrete portion of the domain name space. A DNS name server stores the zone database file. There are two methods of replicating the zone database file. The first method is to do a full zone transfer (AXFR), which replicates the entire zone file. The second method is to do an incremental zone transfer (IXFR), which replicates only changes to the zone file. IXFR zone update is new to the Windows 2000 DNS Server Service, and it can reduce the amount of zone data that is transferred to fully update a zone.

Lesson 2: Resolving Names

The process of resolving names to IP addresses is called *name resolution*. Name resolution is similar to looking up a name in a telephone book; the name is associated with a telephone number. For example, when you connect to the Microsoft Web site, you use the name, www.microsoft.com. DNS resolves www.microsoft.com to its associated IP address. The mapping of names to IP addresses is stored in the DNS distributed database.

DNS name servers resolve forward and reverse lookup queries. A forward lookup query resolves a name to an IP address. A reverse lookup query resolves an IP address to a name. A name server can only resolve a query for a zone for which it has authority. If a name server cannot resolve the query, it passes the query to other name servers that can resolve the query. The name server caches the query results to reduce the DNS traffic on the network.

After this lesson, you will be able to

- Explain the name resolution process.

Estimated lesson time: 5 minutes

Forward Lookup Query

The DNS Service uses a client/server model for name resolution. To resolve a forward lookup query, a client passes a query to a local name server. The local name server either resolves the query or queries another name server for resolution.

In Figure 3.3 the client uses the following procedure to query the name server for an IP address of www.microsoft.com:

1. The client passes a forward lookup query for www.microsoft.com to its local name server.
2. The local name server checks its zone database file to determine whether it contains the name-to-IP-address mapping for the client query. The local name server does not have authority for the microsoft.com domain. So it passes the query to one of the DNS root servers, requesting resolution of the host name. The root name server sends back a referral to the com name server.
3. The local name server sends a request to a com name server, which responds with a referral to the microsoft name server.
4. The local name server sends a request to the microsoft name server. The microsoft name server receives the request. Because the microsoft name server has authority for that portion of the domain name space, it returns the IP address for www.microsoft.com to the local name server.
5. The name server sends the IP address for www.microsoft.com to the client.

6. The name resolution is complete, and the client can access www.microsoft.com.

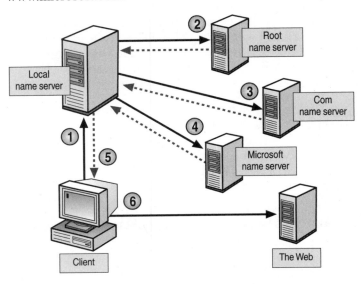

Figure 3.3 Resolving a forward lookup query

Name Server Caching

When a name server is processing a query, it might be required to send out several queries to find the answer. With each query, the name server discovers other name servers that have authority for a portion of the domain name space. The name server caches these query results to reduce network traffic.

When a name server receives a query result (see Figure 3.4), the following actions take place:

1. The name server caches the query result for a specified amount of time, referred to as Time to Live (TTL).

Note The zone that provided the query results specifies the TTL. TTL is configured by using the DNS snap-in. The default value is 60 minutes.

---

2. Once the name server caches the query result, TTL starts counting down from its original value.

3. When TTL expires, the name server deletes the query result from its cache.

Caching query results enables the name server to resolve other queries to the same portion of the domain name space quickly.

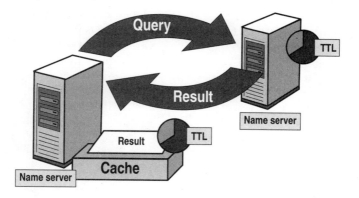

Figure 3.4 Caching query results

Note Use shorter TTL values to help ensure that data about the domain name space is more current across the network. Shorter TTL values *do* increase the load on name servers, however. A longer TTL value decreases the time required to resolve information. However, if a change does occur, the client will not receive the updated information until the TTL expires and a new query to that portion of the domain name space is resolved.

Reverse Lookup Query

A reverse lookup query maps an IP address to a name. Troubleshooting tools, such as Nslookup, use reverse lookup queries to report back host names. Additionally, certain applications implement security based on the ability to connect to names, not IP addresses.

Because the DNS distributed database is indexed by name and not by IP address, a reverse lookup query would require an exhaustive search of every domain name. To solve this problem, a special second-level domain called *in-addr.arpa* was created.

The in-addr.arpa domain follows the same hierarchical naming scheme as the rest of the domain name space; however, it is based on IP addresses instead of domain names as follows:

- Subdomains are named after the numbers in the dotted-decimal representation of IP addresses.
- The order of the IP address octets is reversed.
- Companies administer subdomains of the in-addr.arpa domain based on their assigned IP addresses and subnet mask.

For example, Figure 3.5 shows a dotted-decimal representation of the IP address 169.254.16.200. A company that has an assigned IP address range of 169.254.16.0 to 169.254.16.255 with a subnet mask of 255.255.255.0 will have authority over the 16.254.169.in-addr.arpa domain.

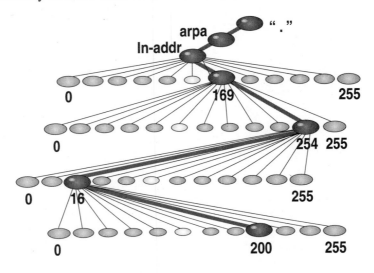

Figure 3.5   The in-addr.arpa domain

Lesson Summary

Name resolution is the process of resolving names to IP addresses. The mapping of names to IP addresses is stored in the DNS distributed database. DNS name servers resolve forward lookup queries. When a client passes a forward lookup query to its local name server, the local name server checks its zone database file to determine whether it contains the name-to-IP-address mapping for the client query. If the local name server does not have authority, it passes the query to one of the DNS root servers, requesting resolution of the host name. The root name server sends back a referral to the com name server, and the local name server sends a request to a com name server, which responds with a referral to a name server that can resolve the forward lookup query. The local name server sends a request to the name server to which it was referred, and since the name server has authority for that portion of the domain name space, it returns the requested IP address to the local name server. The name server sends the IP address to the client, and the name resolution is complete. Name servers cache these query results to reduce the DNS traffic on the network.

In addition to forward lookup queries, DNS name servers resolve reverse lookup queries. A reverse lookup query resolves an IP address to a name. Because the DNS distributed database is indexed by name and not by IP address, a special second-level domain called in-addr.arpa was created. The in-addr.arpa domain follows the same hierarchical naming scheme as the rest of the domain name space; however, it is based on IP addresses instead of domain names.

Lesson 3: Installing the DNS Service

Now that you have been introduced to DNS, the Windows 2000 DNS Service, and name resolution, you are ready to learn how to install the Microsoft DNS Server Service on a computer running Windows 2000 Server.

After this lesson, you will be able to

- Install the DNS Service.

Estimated lesson time: 25 minutes

Preinstallation Configuration

Computers running Windows 2000 are configured as Dynamic Host Configuration Protocol (DHCP) clients by default. Therefore, you must configure TCP/IP with a static IP address before installing the DNS Server Service. Configure the following options on the server on which you are going to install the DNS Service:

- Assign a static IP address in the Internet Protocol (TCP/IP) Properties dialog box.
- Configure the appropriate IP address of the DNS server and DNS domain name. Using My Network Places, click the Advanced button in the Internet Protocol (TCP/IP) Properties dialog box to configure the advanced TCP/IP settings. On the DNS tab, type the DNS address and domain name.

Installation Process

Install the DNS Service anytime after the Windows 2000 initial setup, or you can choose to install the DNS Service during setup. In addition to installing the DNS Service and enabling the service automatically (without restarting the computer), the DNS installation process does the following:

- Installs the DNS snap-in and adds the DNS shortcut to the Administrative Tools menu. The DNS snap-in is the Microsoft Management Console (MMC) snap-in that you use to manage local and remote DNS name servers.
- Adds the following key for the DNS Service to the registry:
  HKEY_LOCAL_MACHINE\SYSTEM\CurrentControlSet\Services\DNS
- Creates the C:\Winnt\System32\Dns folder, which contains the DNS database files that are described in Table 3.3.

Note Generally, you will not need to edit the DNS database files. However, you might use them to troubleshoot DNS. For additional information and sample files, see the C:\Winnt\System32\Dns\Samples directory.

Table 3.3   DNS Database

Filename	Description
Domain.dns	The zone database file that maps host names to IP addresses for a zone.
z.y.w.x.in-addr.arpa	The reverse lookup file that maps IP addresses to host names.
Cache.dns	The cache file that contains the required host information for resolving names outside of authoritative domains. The default file contains records for all of the root servers on the Internet.
Root	The root file that controls how the DNS Service starts. In Windows 2000, the root file is optional, because the root settings are also stored in the registry.

Note The root file is not defined in an RFC and is not needed for RFC compliance. The root file is a part of the Berkeley Internet Name Daemon (BIND)–specific implementation of DNS. If you are migrating from a BIND DNS server, copying the root file allows easy migration of your existing configuration.

Practice: Installing and Configuring the DNS Service

In this practice you will configure TCP/IP as part of the preinstallation configuration required to install the DNS Service, and then you will install the DNS Service.

Exercise 1: Configuring TCP/IP for DNS

In this exercise, you will configure TCP/IP for DNS. This is part of the configuration you do to prepare to install Microsoft DNS Server.

▶   **To configure TCP/IP for DNS**

1. Log on as Administrator.

2. Right-click My Network Places, and then click Properties.

   The Network And Dial-Up Connections window appears.

3. Right-click Local Area Connection, and then click Properties.

   The Local Area Connection Properties dialog box appears, displaying the network adapter in use and the network components used in this connection.

4. Click Internet Protocol (TCP/IP), and then verify that the check box to the left of the entry is selected.

5. Click Properties.

   The Internet Protocol (TCP/IP) Properties dialog box appears.

6. Select Use The Following IP Address.

7. Type **192.168.1.201** in the IP Address box. In the Subnet Mask box, ensure that 255.255.255.0 is the value and leave the Default Gateway box empty.

   If you are not using these suggested values, enter the IP address, Subnet Mask, and Default Gateway that you are using.

   Important Be careful when manually entering IP configuration settings, especially numeric addresses. The most frequent cause of TCP/IP connection problems is incorrectly entered IP address information.

   ---

8. Ensure that the Use The Following DNS Server Addresses option is selected.

9. Type **192.168.1.201** in the Preferred DNS Server box.

   Note In this exercise you only have one computer, so you are installing the DNS Service on your computer, making your computer the DNS server. That is why you type in the IP address of your computer for the Preferred DNS Server address. If you are on a network, you may use the address of an available DNS server instead of your computer's address. If you are using an existing DNS server, you do not have to install the DNS Service on your computer, so you can skip Exercise 2.

   ---

10. Click Advanced.

    The Advanced TCP/IP Settings dialog box appears.

11. Click the DNS tab.

12. In the DNS Suffix For This Connection box, type **domain.com** (if you are on a network, check with your network administrator to make sure it is OK to use this as your DNS domain name), and then click OK.

13. Click OK to close the Internet Protocol (TCP/IP) Properties dialog box.

14. Click OK to close the Local Area Connection Properties dialog box.

15. If you get a Local Network dialog box indicating that you must shut down and restart your computer before these changes take effect, click Yes to restart your computer, log back on as Administrator when your computer restarts, and skip to the next procedure.

16. If you did not get the Local Network dialog box mentioned in step 15, close the Network And Dial-Up Connections window.

▶ **To configure the DNS domain name of your computer**

1. Right-click My Computer, and then click Properties.

   The System Properties dialog box appears.

2. On the Network Identification tab, click Properties.

   The Identification Changes dialog box appears.

3. Click More.

The DNS Suffix And NetBIOS Computer Name dialog box appears.

4. In the Primary DNS Suffix Of This Computer box, type **domain.com**, and then click OK.

5. Click OK to close the Identification Changes dialog box.

A Network Identification warning box appears, stating that you must reboot this computer for the changes to take effect.

6. Click OK.

7. Click OK to close the System Properties dialog box.

A System Settings Change box appears, asking if you want to restart your computer.

8. Click Yes to restart your computer.

Exercise 2: Installing the DNS Service

In this exercise, you will install the Microsoft DNS Server Service.

▶ **To install the DNS Service**

1. Log on as Administrator.

2. Open Control Panel.

3. Double-click Add/Remove Programs.

The Add/Remove Programs window appears.

4. Click Add/Remove Windows Components.

The Windows Components wizard appears.

5. Click Next to continue.

6. Click Networking Services, but do not select the check box to the left of the component.

Note If the DHCP Service or any other optional networking component is installed on your computer, a check mark will appear in the box to the left of Networking Services.

---

7. Click Details.

8. In the Subcomponents Of Networking Services list box, select the check box to the left of Domain Name System (DNS).

9. Click OK.

You are returned to the Windows Components page.

10. Click Next.

The Configuring Components page appears, and a status indicator begins tracking the configuration process. After a few moments, the Insert Disk dialog box appears.

11. Insert the CD-ROM you used to install Windows 2000 on your computer, and then click OK.

Note If the Files Needed dialog box appears, ensure that the path to the source files is correct, and then click OK.

Setup copies the required files to the hard disk.

12. Click Finish to close the Windows Components wizard.

13. Close the Add/Remove Programs window.

14. Close Control Panel.

15. Remove the CD-ROM.

Lesson Summary

There are some configuration changes you need to make before you install the Microsoft DNS Server Service. As a part of this preinstallation configuration, you should assign the computer on which you are going to install the DNS Service a static IP address, and you should configure the appropriate IP address of the DNS server and DNS domain name.

You can install the DNS Service anytime after the Windows 2000 initial setup, or you can choose to install the DNS Service during setup. In the practice portion of this lesson, you did the preinstallation configuration and then you installed the DNS Service. In addition to installing the DNS Service, the DNS installation process installs DNS and adds a shortcut for it to the Administrative Tools menu on the Start menu's Programs menu.

Lesson 4: Configuring the DNS Service

Once the DNS Service is installed, you can configure it by using the DNS snap-in. When you start the DNS snap-in for the first time, a wizard appears and guides you through the process of configuring the following options:

- A root name server
- A forward lookup zone
- A reverse lookup zone

You can also use the DNS snap-in to add additional entries, called *resource records,* to the zone database file and to configure the DNS Service for *Dynamic DNS (DDNS),* which enables automatic updates to your zone files by other servers or services.

After this lesson, you will be able to

- Configure the DNS Service.
- Configure Dynamic DNS.
- Configure the DHCP Service for DNS.

Estimated lesson time: 45 minutes

Configuring a DNS Name Server

When you start the DNS snap-in for the first time, a wizard appears and provides you the option of configuring the server as a root name server. Root name servers store the location of name servers with authority for all the top-level domains in the domain name space (for example, the com domain). These top-level name servers can then provide a list of name servers with authority for the second-level domains (for example, the microsoft.com domain).

Configure a root name server for your intranet only when the following conditions apply:

- You are not connecting to the Internet. Therefore, the root level domain is for your intranet only.
- You are using a proxy service to gain access to the Internet. You are creating the root of your local DNS domain name space, and the proxy service will do the translation and connection necessary to access the Internet.

Creating Forward Lookup Zones

A forward lookup zone enables forward lookup queries. On name servers, you must configure at least one forward lookup zone for the DNS Service to work.

To create a new forward look up zone, right-click the Forward Lookup Zone folder, and a wizard guides you through the process. The wizard presents the following configuration options: Zone Type, Zone Name, and Zone Database File Name.

Zone Type

There are three types of zones that you can configure:

- **Standard Primary.** A standard primary zone is the master copy of a new zone and is stored in a standard text file. You administer and maintain a primary zone on the computer at which you create the zone.

- **Standard Secondary.** A standard secondary zone is a replica of an existing zone. Secondary zones are read-only and are stored in standard text files. A primary zone must be configured in order to create a secondary zone. When creating a secondary zone, you must specify the DNS server, called the master server, which will transfer zone information to the name server containing the standard secondary zone. You create a secondary zone to provide redundancy and to reduce the load on the name server containing the primary zone database file.

- **Active Directory Integrated.** An Active Directory Integrated zone is the master copy of a new zone. The zone uses directory services based on Active Directory technology to store and replicate zone files.

Note For more information on Active Directory directory services, see Chapter 4, "Implementing Active Directory Directory Services."

Zone Name

Typically, a zone is named after the highest domain in the hierarchy that the zone encompasses—that is, the root domain for the zone. For example, for a zone that encompasses both microsoft.com and sales.microsoft.com, the zone name would be microsoft.com.

Zone Database File Name

The zone database file name defaults to the zone name with a .DNS extension; for example, if your zone name is microsoft.com, the default zone database file name is microsoft.com.dns.

When migrating a zone from another server, you can import the existing zone file. You must place the existing file in the *systemroot*\System32\DNS folder on the target computer before creating the new zone.

Note Traditionally, zone database files are maintained on servers that are running the DNS Server Service. In Microsoft Windows 2000, the zone database can be stored in Active Directory directory services. In this case, the zone is called an *Active Directory–integrated zone*.

Creating Reverse Lookup Zones

A reverse lookup zone enables reverse lookup queries. Reverse lookup zones are not required. However, a reverse lookup zone is required to run troubleshooting tools, such as Nslookup, and to record a name instead of an IP address in Internet Information Services (IIS) log files.

To create a new reverse lookup zone, right-click the Reverse Lookup Zone folder in DNS Manager, and a wizard guides you through the process. The wizard presents the configuration options described in the following sections.

Zone Type

For the zone type, select Standard Primary, Standard Secondary, or Active Directory Integrated, as defined above.

Network ID and Subnet Mask

Enter your network ID and subnet mask; for example, an IP address of 169.254.16.200 and a subnet mask of 255.255.0.0 would result in a network ID of 169.254. All reverse lookup queries within the 169.254. network are resolved in this new zone.

Zone File Name

The network ID and subnet mask determine the default zone file name. DNS reverses the IP octets and adds the in-addr.arpa suffix. For example, the reverse lookup zone for the 169.254 network becomes 254.169.in-addr.arpa.dns.

When migrating a zone from another server, you can import the existing zone file. You must place the existing file in the *systemroot*\System32\DNS directory on the target computer before creating the new zone.

Adding Resource Records

Once you create your zones, you can use DNS Manager to add resource records. Resource records are entries in the zone database file. To add a resource record, right-click the zone to which you want to add the record, click New, and then select the type of record that you want to add.

There are many different types of resource records. When a zone is created, DNS automatically adds two resource records: the Start of Authority (SOA) and the Name Server (NS) resource records.

Table 3.4 describes these records, along with the most commonly used resource records.

Table 3. 4   Types of Resource Records

Resource record	DNS Manager name	Description
SOA	Start of Authority	Identifies which name server is the authoritative source of information for data within this domain. The first record in the zone database file must be the Start of Authority record.
NS	Name Server	Lists the name servers that are assigned to a particular domain.
A	Host	Lists the host name-to-IP-address mappings for a forward lookup zone.
PTR	Pointer	Points to another part of the domain name space. For example, in a reverse lookup zone, it lists the IP-address-to-name mapping.
SRV	Service	Identifies which servers are hosting a particular service in a single query operation. For example, if a client needs to find a server to validate logon requests, the client can send a query to the DNS server to obtain a list of domain controllers and their associated IP addresses.
CNAME	Alias	Creates an alias, or alternate name, for the specified host name. You can use a canonical name (CNAME) record to use more than one name to point to a single IP address. For example, you can host a File Transfer Protocol (FTP) server, such as ftp.microsoft.com, and a Web server, such as www.microsoft.com, on the same computer.
MX	Mail Exchanger	Identifies which mail exchanger to contact for a specified domain and in what order to use each mail host.
HINFO	Host Information	Identifies the central processing unit (CPU) and operating system used by the host. Use this record as a low-cost resource-tracking tool.

Note For more information on resource records, see RFC 1034, RFC 2052, and RFC 2065.

Configuring Dynamic DNS

The DNS Service includes a dynamic update capability called Dynamic DNS (DDNS). With DNS, when there are changes to the domain for which a name server has authority, you must manually update the zone database file on the preferred name server. With DDNS, name servers and clients within a network automatically update the zone database files.

Dynamic Updates

You can configure a list of authorized servers to initiate dynamic updates. This list can include secondary name servers, domain controllers, and other servers that perform network registration for clients, such as servers running the DHCP Service or the Microsoft Windows Internet Name Service (WINS).

DDNS and DHCP

DDNS interacts with the DHCP Service to maintain synchronized name-to-IP-address mappings for network hosts. By default, the DHCP Service allows clients to add their own A (Host) records to the zone, and the DHCP Service adds the PTR (Pointer) record to the zone (see Figure 3.6). The DHCP Service cleans up both the A (Host) and PTR records in the zone when the lease expires.

Note To send dynamic updates, use the DHCP snap-in to configure the DHCP server to point to the appropriate DNS servers.

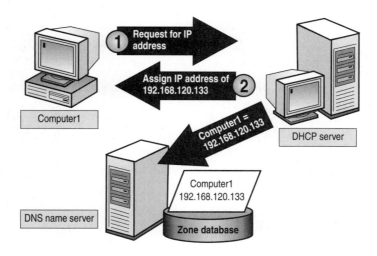

Figure 3.6 Dynamic DNS

DNS Management

Use the DNS snap-in to configure a zone for DDNS as follows:

1. From the DNS snap-in, right-click the forward or reverse lookup zone that you want to configure, and then click Properties.
2. On the General tab, under Dynamic Update, click one of the following options:
   - **None.** Do not allow dynamic updates for this zone.
   - **Allow Updates.** Allow all dynamic DNS update requests for this zone.
   - **Allow Secure Updates.** Allow only dynamic DNS updates that use secure DNS for this zone.

   The Allow Secure Updates option only appears if the zone type is Active Directory Integrated. If you click Allow Secure Updates, the requestor's permission to update the records in the zone database is tested by using mechanisms specified in a subsequent secure DNS update protocol.

Note For more information on Dynamic DNS, see RFC 2136 and RFC 2137.

Practice: Configuring the DNS Service

In this practice, you will create a forward lookup zone, create a reverse lookup zone, and configure the DNS Service to allow Dynamic DNS.

Exercise 1: Creating Zones

In this exercise, you will configure the DNS Service by creating a forward lookup zone and a reverse lookup zone.

▶ **To create a forward lookup zone and a reverse lookup zone**

1. Click Start, point to Programs, point to Administrative Tools, and then click DNS.
2. Click your server in the console tree.

   Information about configuring the DNS server appears in the details pane.
3. From the Action menu, select Configure The Server.

   The Configure DNS Server wizard appears.
4. In the Configure DNS Server wizard, click Next.
5. On the Root Server page, ensure that the This Is The First DNS Server On This Network option is selected, and then click Next.
6. On the Create Forward Lookup Zone page, verify that Yes, Create A Forward Lookup Zone is selected, and then click Next.

   The Zone Type page appears.

7. Verify that the Standard Primary option is selected, and then click Next.

The Zone Name page appears.

8. Type **domain.com** and then click Next.

Note If you are on a network, check with your network administrator to make sure it is OK to use this as your DNS domain name. This should be the same domain name that you used in step 12 of the "To configure TCP/IP for DNS" procedure in Exercise 1 in Lesson 3.

The Zone File page appears.

9. Ensure that the Create A New File With This File Name option is selected and that the name of the file to be created is domain.com.dns.

Note If you did not use domain.com as the domain name in step 8, this will be the domain name you typed in step 8 with a .DNS extension on the end.

---

10. Click Next.

11. On the Create Reverse Lookup Zone page, verify that Yes, Create A Reverse Lookup Zone is selected, and then click Next

12. On the Zone Type page, verify that the Standard Primary option is selected, and then click Next.

13. Ensure that the Network ID And Subnet Mask option is selected, and type **192.168.1** in the Network ID box.

If you are on a network and did not use 192.168.1.201 as your IP address, type in the first three octets of your static IP address. This should be the same IP address that you used in step 7 of the "To configure TCP/IP for DNS" procedure in Exercise 1 in Lesson 3.

Note In the Name box at the bottom of the screen, notice that the in-addr arpa name is filled in and is 1.168.192 in-addr. arpa. If you did not use 192.168.1.201, your name will match the IP address and subnet mask that you're using.

---

14. Click Next.

The Zone File page appears.

15. Ensure that the Create A New File With This File Name option is selected and that the name of the file to be created is 1.168.192 in-addr.arpa.dns.

Note If you did not use 192.168.1.201 as your IP address in step 7 of the procedure in Exercise 1 in Lesson 3, the filename will match the IP address and subnet mask that you used.

---

16. Click Next.

The Completing The Configure DNS Server Wizard page appears.

17. Review the information on the Completing The Configure DNS Server Wizard page, and then click Finish.

If you used the suggested name and IP address, your information should match the information shown in Figure 3.7.

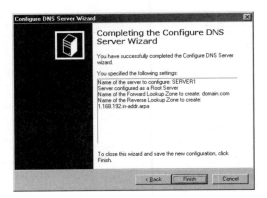

Figure 3.7   Lookup zone information upon completing the Configure DNS Server wizard

Exercise 2: Configuring Dynamic DNS Service

In this exercise, you will configure the DNS Service to allow dynamic updates.

▶   **To configure Dynamic DNS**

1. In the console tree, expand Server1.

   Note If you did not use Server1 as your server name, expand your server.

2. Expand Forward Lookup Zones, expand Domain.com, right-click Domain.com, and then click Properties.

   Note If you did not use Domain.com as your DNS domain name, right-click your DNS domain name.

   The Domain.com Properties dialog box appears.

3. In the Allow Dynamic Updates? drop-down list on the General tab, click Yes, and then click OK.

   This configures Dynamic DNS for the forward lookup zone.

4. Expand Reverse Lookup Zones, and expand 192.168.1.*x* Subnet.

Note There is nothing to expand, but the plus sign in front of 192.168.1.*x* Subnet will go away.

5. Right-click 192.168.1.*x* Subnet, and then click Properties.

   The 192.168.1.*x* Subnet Properties dialog box appears.

6. In the Allow Dynamic Updates? drop-down list on the General tab, click Yes, and then click OK.

   This configures the Dynamic DNS for the reverse lookup zone.

Exercise 3: Testing Your DNS Server

In this exercise, you will confirm that your DNS Service is working.

▶ **To test your DNS Service using the DNS snap-in**

1. In the console tree, right-click Server1, and then click Properties.

   Note If you did not use Server1 as your server name, right-click the appropriate server name.

   The SERVER1 Properties dialog box appears.

   Note If you did not use Server1 as your server name, the dialog box will reflect your server name.

2. Click the Monitoring tab.

3. Under Select A Test Type, select both the A Simple Query Against This DNS Server and the A Recursive Query To Other DNS Servers check box options.

4. Click Test Now.

   Note If the test results in the SERVER1 Properties dialog box are obscured by the DNS window, minimize the DNS window to see them.

   Under Test Results, you should see PASS in both the Simple Query and Recursive Query columns.

5. Click OK and restore the DNS window.

▶ **To create a pointer record for your DNS server**

1. In the console tree, click Reverse Lookup Zones.

2. Click 192.168.1.*x* Subnet.

> **Note** If you did not use 192.168.1.201 as the static IP address for your server name, click the appropriate subnet.

What types of records exist in the reverse lookup zone?

3. In the console tree, right-click 192.168.1.*x* Subnet. Point to New and then click Pointer.

> **Note** If you did not use 192.168.1.201 as the static IP address for your server name, click the appropriate subnet.

4. In the Host IP Number box, type in the selected octet, **201**, of your IP address.
5. In the Host Name box, type the fully qualified domain name of your computer, followed by a period. In our example, if your computer name is Server1, type **server1.domain.com.** *Remember to include the trailing period.*
6. Click OK.

   A Pointer record appears in the details pane.
7. Close the DNS tool.

▶   **To test your DNS server using Nslookup**

1. Open a command prompt.
2. At the command prompt, type **nslookup** and then press Enter.

   Record your results in the following table.

Parameter	Value
Default server	
Address	

3. Type **exit** and then press Enter.
4. Close the command prompt.

Lesson Summary

You can configure the DNS Service by using the DNS snap-in. When you start the DNS snap-in for the first time, a wizard appears and guides you through the process of configuring a root name server, a forward lookup zone, and a reverse lookup zone. Root name servers store the location of name servers with authority for all the top-level domains in the domain name space, and the top-level name servers can provide a list of name servers with authority for the second-level domains. In the practice portion of this lesson, you configured your DNS Service by creating a forward lookup zone and a reverse lookup zone.

You can also use the DNS snap-in to add additional entries, called resource records, to the zone database file and to configure the DNS Service for Dynamic DNS (DDNS), which enables automatic updates to your zone files by other servers or services.

Lesson 5: Configuring a DNS Client

Now that you know how to install and configure the DNS Service on computers running Windows 2000 Server or Windows 2000 Advanced Server, you need to know how to configure your DNS clients. In this lesson you will learn what needs to be done to configure your DNS clients.

After this lesson, you will be able to

- Configure a DNS client.

Estimated lesson time: 5 minutes

You must install TCP/IP on a client running Windows 2000 before configuring the client to use the DNS Service. To configure a client to use the DNS Service, you would do the following:

1. Right-click My Network Places, and then click Properties.
2. Right-click Local Area Connection, and then click Properties.
3. Select Internet Protocol (TCP/IP), and then click Properties.
4. In the Internet Protocol (TCP/IP) Properties dialog box, select Use The Following DNS Server Addresses.
5. Verify or type in the IP address of the Preferred DNS server, and if there is an Alternate DNS server, type in that name as well for this client, and then click Advanced.
6. In the Advanced TCP/IP Settings dialog box (see Figure 3.8), click the DNS tab.
7. In the DNS Server Addresses, In Order Of Use box, you can use the up arrow and down arrow buttons to set the client search order when sending queries to a name server.

   A client will attempt to send its query requests to the name server at the top of the search order list. If that name server is not responding, the client will send the query request to subsequent name servers on the search order list.

   Configure some of the clients to use the secondary server as the initial name server. This reduces the load on the primary server.
8. In the DNS Suffix For This Connection box, type the name of the DNS domain name.
9. In the Append These DNS Suffixes (In Order) box, click Add to add the names of the domains to search in order.

   When searching for a host name in the zone database file, a DNS server first searches for the name only and then for the name combined with each specified domain suffix.
10. Click OK.

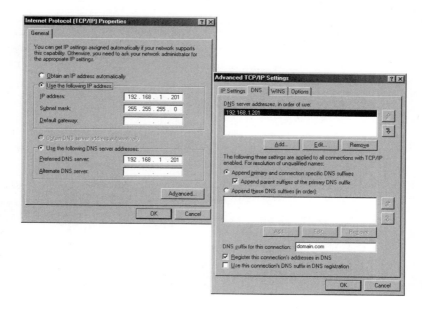

Figure 3.8   Advanced TCP/IP Settings dialog box

Lesson Summary

You must first install TCP/IP on a client running Windows 2000 Advanced
Server before you can configure the client to use the DNS Service. Once you
have TCP/IP installed, you can use the Advanced button to access the DNS tab
and configure the IP addresses of the DNS servers and the DNS domain names
your client will be using.

Lesson 6: Troubleshooting the DNS Service

This lesson discusses how to troubleshoot name servers by using the DNS monitoring and logging options and the Nslookup command-line utility.

After this lesson, you will be able to:
- Troubleshoot the DNS Service.

Estimated lesson time: 5 minutes

Monitoring the DNS Server

DNS has an option that allows you to monitor the DNS Service. In the DNS tool, right-click the name server to monitor, click Properties, and then click the Monitoring tab. Test the name server by performing two types of queries:

- **A Simple Query Against This DNS Server.** Select this option to perform a simple query test of the DNS server. This will be a local test using the DNS client on this computer to query the name server.

- **A Recursive Query To Other DNS Servers.** Select this option to perform a more complex, recursive query test of the name server. This query tests the name server by forwarding a recursive query to another name server.

Setting Logging Options

The DNS tool allows you to set additional logging options for debugging purposes. Right-click the name server, click Properties, and then click the Logging tab. You can select from 11 options: Query, Notify, Update, Questions, Answers, Send, Receive, UDP, TCP, Full Packets, and Write Through.

Using Nslookup

Nslookup is the primary diagnostic tool for the DNS Service, and it is installed along with TCP/IP. Use Nslookup to view any resource record and direct queries to any name server, including UNIX DNS implementations.

Nslookup has two modes: interactive and noninteractive.

- When you require more than one piece of data, use interactive mode. To run interactive mode, at the command prompt, type **Nslookup**. To exit interactive mode, type **exit**.

- When you require a single piece of data, use noninteractive mode. Type the Nslookup syntax at the command line, and the data is returned.

The syntax for Nslookup is as follows:

```
nslookup [-option ...] [computer-to-find | - [server]]
```

Table 3.5 describes the optional parameters for Nslookup.

Table 3.5   Nslookup Optional Parameters

Syntax	Description
-option...	Specifies one or more Nslookup commands. For a list of commands, type a question mark (**?**) in interactive mode to open Help.
computer-to-find	If the computer to find is an IP address, Nslookup returns the host name. If the computer to find is a name, Nslookup returns an IP address. If the computer to find is a name and does not have a trailing period, the default DNS domain name is appended to the name. To look up a computer outside the current DNS domain, append a period to the name.
-server	Use this server as the DNS name server. If the server is omitted, the currently-configured default name server is used.

Lesson Summary

You can troubleshoot name servers by using the DNS tool for monitoring and logging options and the Nslookup command-line utility. You can test the name server by performing a simple query or by performing a recursive query. A simple query performs a local test using the DNS client on this computer to query the name server. A recursive query performs a more complex, recursive query test of the name server. This query tests the name server by forwarding a recursive query to another name server.

You also learned that Nslookup is the primary diagnostic tool for the DNS Service. It is installed along with the TCP/IP protocol. You can use Nslookup to view any resource record and direct queries to any name server, including UNIX DNS implementations.

Review

Here are some questions to help you determine if you have learned enough to move on to the next chapter. If you have difficulty answering these questions, please go back and review the material in this chapter before beginning the next chapter. The answers to these questions are located in Appendix A, "Questions and Answers."

1. What is the function of each of the following DNS components?

   Domain name space

   Zones

   Name servers

2. Why would you want to have multiple name servers?

3. What is the difference between a forward lookup query and a reverse lookup query?

4. When would you configure a server as a root server?

5. Why do you create forward and reverse lookup zones?

6. What is the difference between Dynamic DNS and DNS?

C H A P T E R   4

Implementing Active Directory Directory Services

About This Chapter

You use a directory service to uniquely identify users and resources on a network. Microsoft Active Directory directory services in Microsoft Windows 2000 Advanced Server is a significant enhancement over the directory services provided in previous versions of Windows. Directory services based on Active Directory technology provide a single point of network management, allowing you to add, remove, and relocate users and resources easily.

This chapter introduces you to Active Directory directory services and to how to plan your Active Directory directory services implementation. It also presents the skills and knowledge necessary to install and explore Active Directory directory services. Finally, you will be introduced to configuring Active Directory replication by creating a site, configuring a site link, and configuring a global catalog server.

Before You Begin

To complete this chapter

- You must have a computer that meets or exceeds the minimum hardware requirements listed in "Getting Started," on page xxi.
- You must have installed the beta version of Windows 2000 Advanced Server. The computer should be installed as a stand-alone computer in a workgroup and TCP/IP should be the only installed protocol.
- Your computer should be using a static IP address.
- You must have installed DNS on your server, as outlined in Chapter 3, or you must have a DNS server available on your network.
- You must have a beta version of Windows 2000 Advanced Server on CD-ROM.

Note The Active Directory directory services features are also included with the Server and Datacenter Server editions of Windows 2000, but the practice exercises in this chapter are based on Windows 2000 Advanced Server.

Lesson 1: Introduction to Active Directory Directory Services

Before you implement Active Directory directory services, it is important to understand the overall purpose of a directory service and the role that Active Directory directory services play in a Windows 2000 network. In addition, you should know about the key features of Active Directory directory services, which have been designed to provide flexibility and ease of administration.

After this lesson, you will be able to

■ Explain the purpose and function of Active Directory directory services.

Estimated lesson time: 15 minutes

Directory Service

Active Directory directory services provide a set of directory services that are included in Windows 2000 Advanced Server. A *directory service* is a network service that identifies all resources on a network and makes them accessible to users and applications.

Active Directory directory services includes the *directory,* which stores information about network resources, as well as all the services that make the information available and useful. The resources stored in the directory, such as user data, printers, servers, databases, groups, computers, and security policies, are known as objects.

Simplified Administration

Active Directory directory services organize resources hierarchically in domains. A *domain* is a logical grouping of servers and other network resources under a single domain name. The domain is the basic unit of replication and security in a Windows 2000–based network. Each domain includes one or more domain controllers. A *domain controller* is a computer running Windows 2000 Advanced Server that stores a complete replica of the domain directory.

To simplify administration, all domain controllers in the domain are peers. You can make changes to any domain controllers, and the updates are replicated to all other domain controllers in the domain. Active Directory directory services further simplify administration by providing a single point of administration for all objects on the network. Since Active Directory directory services provide a single point of logon for all network resources, an administrator can log on to one computer and administer objects on any computer in the network.

Scalability

In Active Directory directory services, the directory stores information by organizing the directory into sections that permit storage for a very large number of objects. As a result, the directory can expand as an organization grows, allowing you to scale from a small installation with a few hundred objects to a very large installation with millions of objects.

Note You can distribute directory information across several computers in a network.

Open Standards Support

Active Directory directory services, like all directory services, are primarily a namespace. A *namespace* is any bounded area in which a name can be resolved. *Name resolution* is the process of translating a name into some object or information that the name represents.

Active Directory directory services integrate the Internet concept of a namespace with Windows 2000 directory services. This allows you to unify and manage the multiple namespaces that now exist in the heterogeneous software and hardware environments of corporate networks. Active Directory directory services use Domain Name System (DNS) for its name system and can exchange information with any application or directory that uses Lightweight Directory Access Protocol (LDAP) or Hypertext Transfer Protocol (HTTP).

Note Active Directory directory services also share information with other directory services that support LDAP version 2 and version 3, such as Novell Directory Services (NDS).

Domain Name System

The Active Directory namespace is based on the DNS naming scheme, which allows for interoperability with Internet technologies. Following DNS standards, the domain name of a child domain is the relative name of that child domain appended with the name of the parent domain. The name of the child object in an object hierarchy always contains the name of the parent domain.

Because Active Directory directory services use DNS as its domain naming and location service, Windows 2000 domain names are also DNS names. Windows 2000 Advanced Server uses Dynamic DNS (DDNS), which enables clients with dynamically assigned addresses to register directly with a server running the DNS Service and update the DNS table dynamically. DDNS eliminates the need for other Internet naming services, such as Windows Internet Name Service (WINS), in a homogeneous environment.

Note For Active Directory directory services and associated client software to function correctly, you must have installed and configured the DNS Service.

Support for LDAP and HTTP

Active Directory directory services further embrace Internet standards by directly supporting LDAP and HTTP. LDAP is an Internet standard for accessing directory services, which was developed as a simpler alternative to the Directory Access Protocol (DAP). For more information about LDAP, use your Web browser to search on the Internet for "RFC 1777" and retrieve the text of this Request for Comment. Active Directory directory services support both LDAP version 2 and version 3. HTTP is the standard protocol for displaying pages on the World Wide Web. You can display every object in Active Directory directory services as an HTML page in a Web browser. Thus, users receive the benefit of the familiar Web-browsing model when querying and viewing objects in Active Directory directory services.

Note Active Directory directory services use LDAP to exchange information between directories and applications.

Support for Standard Name Formats

Active Directory directory services support several common name formats. Consequently, users and applications can access Active Directory directory services by using the format with which they are most familiar. Table 4.1 describes some standard name formats supported by Active Directory directory services.

**Table 4.1   Standard Name Formats
Supported by Active Directory Directory Services**

Format	Description
RFC 822	RFC 822 names are in the form *somename@somedomain* and are familiar to most users as Internet e-mail addresses.
HTTP URL	HTTP Uniform Resource Locators (URLs) are familiar to users with Web browsers and take the form http://*somedomain*/*path-to-page*.
UNC	Active Directory directory services supports the Universal Naming Convention (UNC) used in Windows 2000 Advanced Server–based networks to refer to shared volumes, printers, and files. An example is \\myco.com\xl\budget.xls.
LDAP URL	An LDAP URL specifies the server on which the Active Directory directory services reside and the attributed name of the object. Active Directory directory services support a draft to RFC 1779 and use the attributes in the following example: LDAP://someserver.myco.com/CN=jimsmith,OU=sys, OU=product,OU=division,DC=devel CN represents CommonName OU represents OrganizationalUnitName DC represents DomainComponentName

Lesson Summary

The three server editions of Windows 2000 provide directory services based on Active Directory technology. Active Directory directory services provide a set of directory services that are included in Windows 2000 Advanced Server. A directory service is a network service that identifies all resources on a network and makes them accessible to users and applications. Active Directory directory services include the directory, which stores information about network resources, such as user data, printers, servers, databases, groups, computers, and security policies. The directory can scale from a small installation with a few hundred objects to a very large installation with millions of objects.

Active Directory directory services use DNS as the domain naming and location service. Therefore, Windows 2000 domain names are also DNS names. Windows 2000 Advanced Server uses Dynamic DNS (DDNS), so clients with dynamically assigned addresses can register directly with a server running the DNS Service and update the DNS table dynamically. Finally, in a homogeneous environment DDNS eliminates the need for other Internet naming services, such as WINS.

Lesson 2: Active Directory Structure and Site Replication

Active Directory directory services provide a method for designing a directory structure that meets the needs of your organization. As a result, before installing Active Directory directory services, you should examine your organization's business structure and operations.

Many companies have a centralized structure. Typically, these companies have strong information technology (IT) departments that define and implement the network structure down to the smallest detail. Other organizations, especially large enterprises, are very decentralized. These companies have multiple businesses, each of which is very focused. They need decentralized approaches to managing their business relationships and networks.

With the flexibility of Active Directory directory services, you can create the network structure that best fits your company's needs. Active Directory directory services completely separate the logical structure of the domain hierarchy from the physical structure.

After this lesson, you will be able to

- Explain Active Directory directory services' structure and replication.

Estimated lesson time: 15 minutes

Logical Structure

In Active Directory directory services, you organize resources in a logical structure. Grouping resources logically enables you to find a resource by its name rather than by its physical location. Since you group resources logically, Active Directory directory services make the network's physical structure transparent to users. The logical structure is composed of objects, organizational units, domains, trees, and forests.

Object

An *object* is a distinct, named set of attributes that represents a network resource. Object *attributes* are characteristics of objects in the directory. For example, the attributes of a user account might include the user's first and last names, department, and e-mail address (see Figure 4.1).

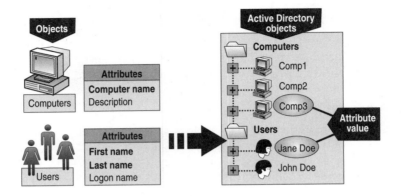

Figure 4.1   Active Directory directory services objects and attributes

In Active Directory directory services, you can organize objects in *classes*, which are logical groupings of objects. For example, an object class might be user accounts, groups, computers, domains, or organizational units.

Organizational Units

An *organizational unit (OU)* is a container that you use to organize objects within a domain into logical administrative groups. An OU can contain objects such as user accounts, groups, computers, printers, applications, file shares, and other OUs (see Figure 4.2).

- Use OUs to structure Active Directory directory services based on a company's
  - Organizational structure
  - Network administrative model
- Assign permissions to OUs to delegate administrative control

The OU hierarchy within a domain is independent of the OU hierarchy structure of other domains—each domain can implement its own OU hierarchy. There are no restrictions on the depth of the OU hierarchy. However, a shallow hierarchy performs better than a deep one, so you should not create an OU hierarchy any deeper than necessary.

Note You can delegate administrative tasks by assigning permissions to OUs.

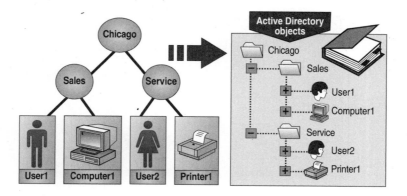

Figure 4.2   Resources organized in a logical hierarchical structure

Domain

The core unit of logical structure in Active Directory directory services is the domain (see Figure 4.3). Grouping objects into one or more domains allows your network to reflect your company's organization.

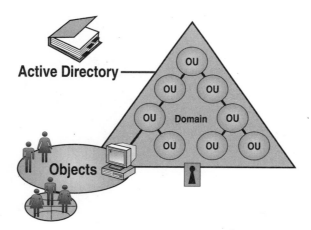

Figure 4.3   A domain is the core unit of logical structure.

All network objects exist within a domain, and each domain stores information about only the objects that it contains. Theoretically, a domain directory can contain up to 10 million objects, but 1 million objects per domain is more practical.

A domain is a security boundary. Access to domain objects is controlled by access control lists (ACLs). ACLs contain the permissions associated with objects that control which users can gain access to an object and what type of access users can gain to the objects. In Windows 2000, objects include files, folders, shares, printers, and Active Directory directory services objects. All security polices and settings—such as administrative rights, security policies, and ACLs—do not cross from one domain to another. The domain administrator has absolute rights to set policies only within that domain.

Tree and Forest

A *tree* is a grouping or hierarchical arrangement of one or more Windows 2000 domains. A *forest* is a grouping or hierarchical arrangement of one or more trees (See Figure 4.4).

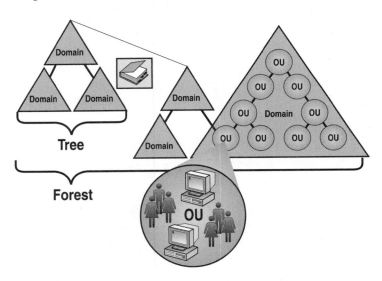

Figure 4.4   Structure of a tree and a forest

Both a tree and a forest are namespaces. Since a namespace is any bounded area in which a name can be resolved, using a common namespace allows you to unify and manage multiple hardware and software environments in your network. There are two types of namespaces:

- **Contiguous namespace.** The name of the child object in an object hierarchy always contains the name of the parent domain. A tree is a contiguous namespace because the name of any child object in a tree always contains the name of the parent tree.

- **Disjointed namespace.** The names of a parent object and of a child of the same parent object are not directly related to one another. A forest is a disjointed namespace because all trees in a forest do not share a common naming structure.

Since all trees in a forest do not share a common naming structure, you could use a forest to group the various divisions of a company that do not use the same naming scheme and that operate independently, but that need to communicate with an entire organization.

Sites and Replication Within a Site

A *site* is a combination of one or more Internet Protocol (IP) subnets, which should be connected by a high-speed link. Typically, a site has the same boundaries as a local area network (LAN). When you group subnets on your network, you should combine only those subnets that have fast, cheap, and reliable network connections with one another. "Fast" network connections are at least 512 kilobits per second (Kbps). An available bandwidth of 128 Kbps and higher is sufficient. Defining sites as a set of subnets allows you to configure the Active Directory directory services access and replication topology to take advantage of the physical network.

You create sites for two primary reasons:

- To optimize replication traffic
- To enable users to connect to a domain controller by using a reliable, high-speed connection

With Active Directory directory services, sites are not part of the namespace. When you browse the logical namespace, you see computers and users grouped into domains and OUs, not sites. Sites contain only computer objects and connection objects used to configure replication between sites.

Note A single domain can span multiple geographical sites, and a single site can include user accounts and computers belonging to multiple domains.

Active Directory directory services also include a replication feature. Replication ensures that changes to a domain controller are reflected in all domain controllers within a domain (see Figure 4.5).

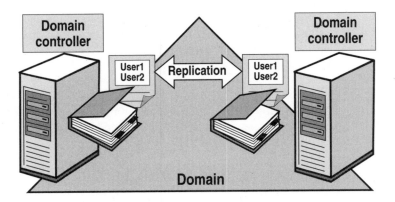

Figure 4.5   Replication within a site

To understand replication, you must understand domain controllers. A domain controller is a computer running Windows 2000 Server, Windows 2000 Advanced Server, or Windows 2000 Datacenter that stores a replica of the domain directory. A domain can contain one or more domain controllers. The following list describes the functions of domain controllers:

- Each domain controller stores a complete copy of all Active Directory directory services information for that domain, manages changes to that information, and replicates those changes to other domain controllers in the same domain.

- Domain controllers in a domain automatically replicate all objects in the domain to each other. When you perform an action that causes an update to Active Directory directory services, you are actually making the change at one of the domain controllers. The domain controller then replicates the change to all other domain controllers within the domain. You can control replication of traffic between domain controllers in the network by specifying how often replication occurs and the amount of data that Windows 2000 replicates at one time.

- Domain controllers immediately replicate certain important updates, such as a user account being disabled.

- Active Directory directory services use multimaster replication, in which no one domain controller is the master domain controller. Instead, all domain controllers within a domain are peers, and each domain controller contains a copy of the directory database that can be written to. Domain controllers might hold different information for short periods of time until all domain controllers have synchronized changes to Active Directory directory services.

- Having more than one domain controller in a domain provides fault tolerance. If one domain controller is offline, another domain controller can provide all required functions, such as recording changes to Active Directory directory services.

- Domain controllers manage all aspects of user domain interaction, such as locating Active Directory objects and validating user logon attempts.

Within a site, Active Directory directory services automatically generate a ring topology for replication among domain controllers in the same domain. The topology defines the path for directory updates to flow from one domain controller (DC) to another until all domain controllers receive the directory updates (see Figure 4.6).

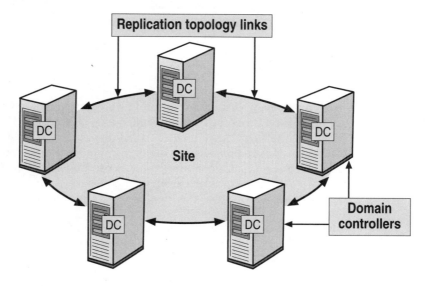

Figure 4.6   Replication topology

The ring structure ensures that there are at least two replication paths from one domain controller to another; if one domain controller is down temporarily, replication still continues to all other domain controllers.

Active Directory directory services periodically analyze the replication topology within a site to ensure that it is still efficient. If you add or remove a domain controller from the network or a site, Active Directory directory services reconfigure the topology to reflect the change.

Lesson Summary

Active Directory directory services provide a method to design a directory structure to meet the needs of your organization's business structure and operations. Active Directory directory services completely separate the logical structure of the domain hierarchy from the physical structure. In Active Directory directory services, grouping resources logically enables you to find a resource by its name rather than by its physical location. Since you group resources logically, Active Directory directory services make the network's physical structure transparent to users.

The core unit of logical structure in Active Directory directory services is the domain. All network objects exist within a domain, and each domain stores information only about the objects that it contains. An organizational unit (OU) is a container that you use to organize objects within a domain into logical administrative groups, and an OU can contain objects such as user accounts, groups, computers, printers, applications, file shares, and other OUs. A tree is a grouping or hierarchical arrangement of one or more Windows 2000 domains that share a contiguous namespace, and a forest is a grouping or hierarchical arrangement of one or more trees that form a disjointed namespace.

The physical structure of Active Directory directory services is based on sites. A site is a combination of one or more Internet Protocol (IP) subnets, connected by a high-speed link. Active Directory directory services also include replication to ensure that changes to a domain controller are reflected in all domain controllers within a domain. Within a site, Active Directory directory services automatically generate a ring topology for replication among domain controllers in the same domain. The ring structure ensures that there are at least two replication paths from one domain controller to another; if one domain controller is down temporarily, replication still continues to all other domain controllers. If you add or remove a domain controller from the network or a site, Active Directory directory services reconfigure the topology to reflect the change.

Lesson 3: Active Directory Concepts

Several new concepts are introduced with Active Directory directory services. It is important that you understand their meaning as applied to Active Directory directory services.

After this lesson, you will be able to

- Explain concepts associated with Active Directory directory services.

Estimated lesson time: 15 minutes

Schema

The schema contains a formal definition of the contents and structure of Active Directory directory services, including all attributes, classes, and class properties, as shown in Figure 4.7. For each object class, the schema defines what attributes an instance of the class must have, what additional attributes it can have, and what object class can be a parent of the current object class.

Note All domains within a single tree and all trees in a forest share a common schema.

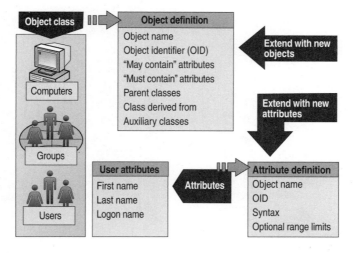

Figure 4.7 Schema is extensible.

Installing Active Directory directory services on the first domain controller in a network creates a default schema. The default schema contains definitions of commonly used objects and properties (such as user accounts, computers, printers, groups, and so on). The default schema also contains definitions of objects and properties that Active Directory directory services use internally to function.

The Active Directory schema is extensible, which means that you can define new directory object types and attributes and new attributes for existing objects (see Figure 4.7). You can extend the schema by using the Active Directory Schema Manager snap-in or the Active Directory Services Interface (ADSI). Both of these tools are available in the Windows 2000 Resource Kit.

The schema is implemented and stored in the global catalog, and it can be updated dynamically. As a result, an application can extend the schema with new attributes and classes and then can use the extensions immediately.

Note Write access to the schema is limited to members of the Administrators group, by default.

Global Catalog

The global catalog is the central repository of information about objects in a tree or forest, as shown in Figure 4.8. Active Directory directory services automatically generate the contents of the global catalog from the domains that make up the directory through the normal replication process.

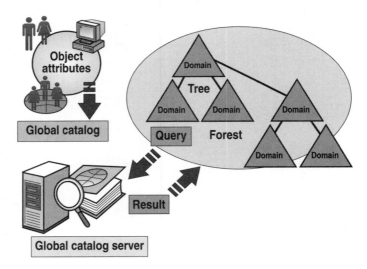

Figure 4.8   The global catalog contains information about objects.

Note All domains within a single tree and all domains in a forest share a common global catalog.

The global catalog is a service and a physical storage location that contains a replica of selected attributes for every object in Active Directory directory services. By default, the attributes stored in the global catalog are those most frequently used in search operations (such as a user's first and last names, logon name, and so forth), and those necessary to locate a full replica of the object. As a result, you can use the global catalog to locate objects anywhere in the network without replication of all domain information between domain controllers.

When you install Active Directory directory services on the first domain controller in a new forest, that domain controller is, by default, a global catalog server. A *global catalog server* is a domain controller that stores a copy of the global catalog and processes queries to the global catalog (see Figure 4.8). Global catalog servers improve the performance of forestwide searches in Active Directory directory services. For example, if you search for all of the printers in a forest, a global catalog server processes the query against the global catalog and then returns the results. Without a global catalog server, this query would require a search of every domain controller in every domain in the forest.

The configuration of the initial global catalog server should have the capacity to support several hundred thousand to one million objects, with the potential for growth beyond those numbers. You can designate additional domain controllers as global catalog servers by using the Active Directory Sites and Services snap-in. When considering which domain controllers to designate as global catalog servers, base your decision on the ability of your network structure to handle replication and query traffic. The more global catalog servers that you have, the greater the replication traffic. However, the availability of additional servers can provide quicker responses to user inquiries. It is recommended that every major site in your enterprise have a global catalog server.

Trust Relationships

A *trust relationship* is a link between two domains such that the trusting domain honors logon authentications of the trusted domain.

Note Authentication with Windows 2000 trust relationships supports the Kerberos 5 protocol, which is an industry standard for authentication across different operating systems.

Active Directory directory services support two forms of trust relationships: one-way, nontransitive trusts and two-way, transitive trusts.

One-Way, Nontransitive Trusts

In a one-way trust relationship, if DomainA trusts DomainB, DomainB does not automatically trust DomainA (see bottom portion of Figure 4.9).

In a nontransitive trust relationship, if DomainA trusts DomainB and DomainB trusts DomainC, then DomainA does not automatically trust DomainC.

Networks running Windows NT 4.0 and earlier versions of Windows NT use one-way, nontransitive trust relationships. You manually create one-way, nontransitive trust relationships between existing domains. As a result, a Windows NT 4.0 (or earlier Windows NT) network with several domains requires the creation of many trust relationships.

Active Directory directory services support this type of trust for connections to existing Windows NT 4.0 and earlier domains and to allow the configuration of trust relationships with domains in other trees.

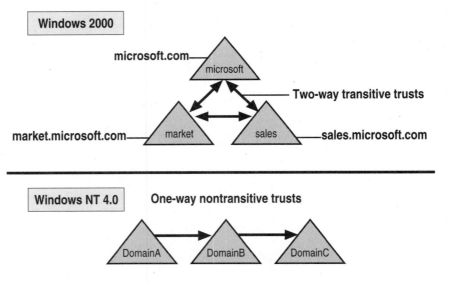

Figure 4.9   Trust relationships

Two-Way, Transitive Trusts

A two-way, transitive trust is the relationship between parent and child domains within a tree and between the top-level domains in a forest. This is the default; trust relationships among domains in a tree are established and maintained *automatically*. Transitive trust is a feature of the Kerberos authentication protocol, which provides the distributed authentication and authorization in Windows 2000 (see top portion of Figure 4.9).

In a two-way trust relationship, if DomainA trusts DomainB, then DomainB trusts DomainA. In a transitive trust relationship, if DomainA trusts DomainB and DomainB trusts DomainC, then DomainA trusts DomainC. Therefore in a two-way, transitive trust relationship, if DomainA trusts DomainB and DomainB trusts DomainC, then DomainA trusts DomainC and DomainC trusts DomainA.

If a two-way, transitive trust exists between two domains, you can assign permissions to resources in one domain to user and group accounts in the other domain, and vice versa.

Two-way, transitive trust relationships are the default in Windows 2000. When you create a new child domain, a trust relationship is established automatically with its parent domain, which imparts a trust relationship with every other domain in the tree. As a result, users in one domain can access resources to which they have been granted permission in all other domains in a tree.

Naming Conventions

Every object in Active Directory directory services is identified by a name. Active Directory directory services use a variety of naming conventions: distinguished names, relative distinguished names, globally unique identifiers, and user principal names.

Distinguished Name

Every object in Active Directory directory services has a *distinguished name (DN),* which uniquely identifies an object and contains sufficient information for a client to retrieve the object from the directory. The DN includes the name of the domain that holds the object, as well as the complete path through the container hierarchy to the object.

For example, the following DN identifies the James Smith user object in the microsoft.com domain:

/DC=COM/DC=Microsoft/OU=Dev/CN=Users/CN=James Smith

Table 4.2 describes the attributes in the example.

Table 4.2   Distinguished Name Attributes

Attribute	Description
DC	DomainComponentName
OU	OrganizationalUnitName
CN	CommonName

DNs must be unique. Active Directory directory services do not allow duplicate DNs.

Relative Distinguished Name

Active Directory directory services support querying by attributes, so you can locate an object even if the exact DN is unknown or has changed. The *relative distinguished name (RDN)* of an object is the part of the name that is an attribute of the object itself. In the preceding example, the RDN of the James Smith user object is James Smith. The RDN of the parent object is Users.

You can have duplicate RDNs for Active Directory objects, but you cannot have two objects with the same RDN in the same OU. For example, if a user account is named Amy Jones, you cannot have another user account called Amy Jones in the same OU. However, objects with duplicate RDN names can exist in separate OUs because they have different DNs (see Figure 4.10).

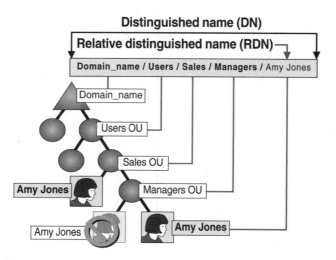

Figure 4.10   Distinguished names and relative distinguished names

Globally Unique Identifier

A *globally unique identifier* (GUID) is a 128-bit number that is guaranteed to be unique. GUIDs are assigned to objects when the objects are created. The GUID never changes, even if you move or rename the object. Applications can store the GUID of an object and use the GUID to retrieve that object regardless of its current DN.

User Principal Name

User accounts have a "friendly" name, the user principal name (UPN). The UPN is composed of a "shorthand" name for the user account and the DNS name of the tree where the user account object resides. For example, user James Smith in the microsoft.com tree might have a UPN of JamesS@microsoft.com.

Lesson Summary

The schema contains a formal definition of the contents and structure of Active Directory directory services, including all attributes, classes, and class properties. For each object class, the schema defines what attributes an instance of the class must have, what additional attributes it can have, and what object class can be a parent of the current object class. The schema is extensible, and installing Active Directory directory services on the first domain controller in a network creates a default schema.

The global catalog is a service and a physical storage location that contains a replica of selected attributes for every object in Active Directory directory services. Active Directory directory services automatically generate the contents of the global catalog from the domains that make up the directory through the normal replication process. By default, the attributes stored in the global catalog are those most frequently used in search operations (such as a user's first and last names, logon name, and so forth), and those necessary to locate a full replica of the object. As a result, you can use the global catalog to locate objects anywhere in the network without replication of all domain information between domain controllers.

There are two types of namespaces: contiguous namespaces and disjointed namespaces. In a contiguous namespace, the name of the child object in an object hierarchy always contains the name of the parent domain. A tree is an example of a contiguous namespace. In a disjointed namespace, the names of a parent object and of a child of the same parent object are not directly related to one another. A forest is an example of a disjointed namespace.

Lesson 4: Introduction to Planning

When you decide to establish a Windows 2000 network environment, you must consider how to implement a DNS namespace and Active Directory directory services. First, examine the business structure and operation of your organization.

In many organizations, the IS department defines and implements the network structure down to the smallest detail. Other organizations, especially large enterprises, take a decentralized approach to managing business relationships and networks. These organizations might have multiple business units, each with different requirements for managing their network resources.

When planning the implementation of a namespace and Active Directory directory services for your organization, consider the following issues: physical office locations, future growth and reorganization, and access to network resources. This lesson introduces some of the general considerations in planning for your Active Directory directory services implementation.

After this lesson, you will be able to

- Explain considerations for planning an Active Directory directory services implementation.

Estimated lesson time: 10 minutes

Planning a Namespace

If your network already has a presence on the Internet, you must decide whether to extend the external namespace for internal use or to create a new namespace.

Extending an Existing Namespace

You can extend an existing namespace to include it in Windows 2000 Advanced Server domains. You should consider using the same namespace for internal and external resources when you want to do the following:

- Have consistent tree names for internal and external resources
- Use the same logon and user names for internal and external resources
- Reserve no more than one DNS namespace

When you use the same namespace, you must create two separate DNS zones for your organization. One zone provides name resolution for internal resources, and the other provides name resolution for external resources, such as Web servers, File Transfer Protocol (FTP) servers, mail servers, and so on.

Creating a New Internal Namespace

You also can have different namespaces for internal and external resources. In this configuration, all internal corporate servers use one namespace, while external resources, such as Internet and FTP servers, use a different namespace. This configuration requires you to reserve two namespaces with an Internet DNS registration authority. Consider using different namespaces for internal and external resources when you want to have the following:

- A clear distinction between internal and external resources
- Separate internal and external resource management
- Simple client browser and proxy client configuration

Planning a Site

You maintain a domain structure and a site structure separately in Active Directory directory services. A single domain can include multiple sites, and a single site can include multiple domains, or parts of multiple domains.

As you plan sites, consider the availability of bandwidth for the replication traffic that occurs within a domain. For example, assume that you have offices in Phoenix, Arizona, and Flagstaff, Arizona, and assume that both offices are in the same site. In this case, the domain controllers in each office would be replicating frequently. However, by establishing each office as a separate site, you can specify a replication schedule to take advantage of hours when there is less demand on network resources, when more connections are available, or even when dial-up connections are less expensive.

Use the following guidelines as you plan how to combine subnets into sites:

- Combine only those subnets that share fast, inexpensive, and reliable network connections of at least 512 Kbps.
- Configure sites so that replication within the site occurs at times or intervals that do not interfere with network performance.

Planning Organizational Units

In a single domain, you can organize user accounts and resources by using a hierarchy of OUs to reflect the structure of your company. Just as your organization can have multiple levels of management, you can establish multiple levels of management within a domain based on OUs.

Consider creating an OU if you want to do the following:

- Reflect your company's structure and organization within a domain (see Figure 4.11). Without OUs, all user accounts are maintained and displayed in a single list, regardless of a user's department, location, or role.

- Delegate administrative control over network resources while maintaining the ability to manage them. You can grant administrative permissions to user accounts or groups at the OU level.

- Accommodate potential changes in your company's organizational structure. You can move user accounts between OUs easily, while moving user accounts between domains generally requires more time and effort.

- Group objects to allow administrators to locate similar network resources more easily to perform administrative tasks. For example, you could group all user accounts for temporary employees in an OU.

- Restrict visibility of network resources in Active Directory directory services. Users can view only the objects to which they have access.

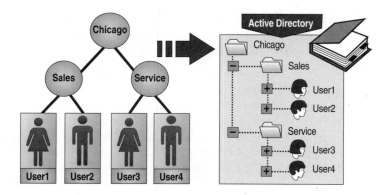

Figure 4.11   Organizational units

Lesson Summary

Planning for implementing Active Directory directory services can be extremely complex. For example, when you plan the implementation of a namespace and Active Directory directory services for your organization, you must consider the following issues: physical office locations, future growth and reorganization, and access to network resources. If your network already has a presence on the Internet, you must decide whether to extend the external namespace for internal use or to create a new namespace.

When you plan your sites, you must consider the availability of bandwidth for the replication traffic within a domain. You might also want to determine how to take advantage of hours when there is less demand on network resources, when more connections are available, or even when dial-up connections are less expensive.

You also have to plan your OU structure. Your OU structure could reflect your company's structure and organization within a domain, allow you to delegate administrative control over network resources while maintaining the ability to manage them, or restrict visibility of network resources in Active Directory directory services.

Lesson 5: Installing Active Directory Directory Services

This lesson presents information on installing Active Directory directory services, including using the Active Directory Installation wizard. In addition, the lesson addresses the database and shared system volume that Active Directory directory services create during installation. Finally, the lesson discusses domain modes.

After this lesson, you will be able to
- Install Active Directory directory services.

Estimated lesson time: 30 minutes

The Active Directory Installation Wizard

You use the Active Directory Installation wizard to perform the following tasks:

- Adding a domain controller to an existing domain
- Creating the first domain controller of a new domain
- Creating a new child domain
- Creating a new domain tree

To launch the Active Directory Installation wizard, you can use the Windows 2000 Configure Server wizard to start the Active Directory wizard or you can run Dcpromo.exe. When you run the Active Directory Installation wizard on a stand-alone server, it steps you through the process of installing Active Directory directory services on the computer and creating a new domain controller.

As you install Active Directory directory services, you can choose whether to add the new domain controller to an existing domain or create the first domain controller for a new domain.

Adding a Domain Controller to an Existing Domain

If you choose to add a domain controller to an existing domain, you create a peer domain controller. You create peer domain controllers for redundancy and to reduce the load on the existing domain controllers.

Creating the First Domain Controller for a New Domain

If you choose to create the first domain controller for a new domain, you create a new domain. You create domains on your network to partition your information, which enables you to scale Active Directory directory services to meet the needs of very large organizations. When you create a new domain, you can create a new child domain or a new tree. If you choose to create a new child domain, the new domain is created as a child domain in an existing domain. When you create a new domain tree, the new domain does not become part of an existing domain. You can create a new tree in an existing forest, or you can create a tree and start a new forest.

Note Running Dcpromo.exe on a domain controller allows you to remove Active Directory directory services from the domain controller and demotes the domain controller to a stand-alone server. If you remove Active Directory directory services from all domain controllers in a domain, you also delete the directory database for the domain, and the domain no longer exists.

The Database and Shared System Volume

Installing Active Directory directory services creates the database and database log files, as well as the shared system volume. Table 4.3 describes the purpose and location of these files.

Table 4.3   Types of Files Created by Installing Active Directory Directory Services

Type of file created	Description
Database and database log files	The database is the directory for the new domain, and the log file temporarily stores changes made to the Active Directory database.
	The default location for the database and database log files is *systemroot*\Ntds.
	For best performance, place the database and the log file on separate hard disks.
Shared system volume	The shared system volume is a folder structure that exists on all Windows 2000 domain controllers. It stores scripts and some of the Group Policy objects for both the current domain as well as the enterprise. The file replication services use the shared system volume to replicate files and Group Policy information among domain controllers. The default location for the shared system volume is *systemroot*\Sysvol.
	The shared system volume must be located on a partition or volume formatted with NTFS.

Replication of the shared system volume occurs on the same schedule as replication of Active Directory directory services. As a result, you might not notice file replication to or from the newly created system volume until two replication periods have elapsed (typically, 10 minutes). This is because the first file replication period updates the configuration of other system volumes so that they are aware of the newly created system volume.

Domain Modes

There are two domain modes: mixed mode and native mode.

Mixed Mode

When you first install a Windows 2000 Advanced Server domain controller or upgrade an existing domain controller running an ealier version of Windows NT to Windows 2000 Advanced Server, the domain controller runs in mixed mode. Mixed mode allows the domain controller to interact with any domain controllers in the domain that are running previous versions of Windows NT Server. Domain controllers running previous versions of Windows NT Server are called *down-level domain controllers*.

Native Mode

When all the domain controllers in the domain run Windows 2000 Advanced Server, and you do not plan to add any more down-level domain controllers to the domain, you can switch the domain from mixed mode to native mode.

Several things happen during the conversion from mixed mode to native mode:

- Support for down-level replication and down-level domain controllers ceases. Therefore all the domain controllers in your domain must be running Windows 2000.

- You can no longer add new down-level domain controllers to the domain.

- The server that served as the primary domain controller during migration is no longer the domain master; all domain controllers begin acting as peers.

Note The change from mixed mode to native mode is one way only; you cannot change from native mode to mixed mode.

Use the following procedure to switch the domain mode:

1. Start the Active Directory Domains and Trusts snap-in.
2. Right-click the domain name, and then click Properties.
3. On the General tab, click Change To Native Mode.
4. In the Warning dialog box, click Yes, and then click OK.

Practice: Installing Active Directory Directory Services and Viewing Your Domain

In this practice, you will promote your stand-alone server to a domain controller by installing Active Directory directory services on it. You will use My Network Places to confirm that your domain exists and then use the Active Directory Users and Computers snap-in to view your domain. The last thing you will do in this practice is change the mode of your domain from the default mixed mode to native mode.

Exercise 1: Promoting a Stand-Alone Server to a Domain Controller

In this exercise, you will run Dcpromo.exe to install Active Directory directory services on your stand-alone server, making it a domain controller in a new domain.

▶ **To install Active Directory directory services on a stand-alone server**

1. Click Start and then click Run.
2. Type **dcpromo** and then click OK.

   The Active Directory Installation wizard appears.
3. Click Next to continue.

   The Domain Controller Type page appears.
4. Ensure that the Domain Controller For A New Domain option is selected, and then click Next.

   The Create Tree Or Child Domain page appears.
5. Ensure that the Create A New Domain Tree option is selected, and then click Next.

   The Create Or Join Forest page appears.
6. Ensure that the Create A New Forest Of Domain Trees option is selected, and then click Next.

   The New Domain Name page appears.
7. Type **domain.com** in the Full DNS Name For New Domain box, and then click Next.

   Note If you are not using domain.com as your DNS domain name, type the name you are using.

   The NetBIOS Domain Name page appears.
8. Ensure that DOMAIN appears in the Domain NetBIOS Name box, and then click Next.

   The Database And Log Locations page appears.

9. Ensure that C:\Winnt\Ntds is the location of both the database and the log, and click Next.

Note If you did not install Windows 2000 on the C drive or in the Winnt directory, both locations should default to the Ntds folder on the drive and in the folder where you installed Windows 2000.

The Shared System Volume page appears.

10. Ensure that the Sysvol folder location is C:\Winnt\Sysvol.

Note If you did not install Windows 2000 on the C drive or in the Winnt directory, the Sysvol location should default to a Sysvol folder on the drive and in the folder where you installed Windows 2000.

What is the one Sysvol location requirement?

What is the function of Sysvol?

11. Click Next to accept C:\Winnt\Sysvol (or the default path on your system) as the path for Sysvol.

The Windows NT 4.0 RAS Servers page appears.

12. Click Next to accept the default option No, Do Not Change The Permissions.

The Directory Services Restore Mode Administrator Password page appears.

13. Type **password** in the Password and Confirm Password boxes, and then click Next.

Note For simplicity you are using *password* for the Administrator's password. You should always use a complex password for the Administrator account and, in this case, a password that is not the same as your Administrator password.

The Summary page appears with a list of the options you selected.

14. Review the contents of the Summary page, and then click Next.

The Configuring Active Directory progress indicator appears as Active Directory directory services are installed on the server. This process will take several minutes.

15. When the Completing The Active Directory Installation Wizard page appears, click Finish, and then click Restart Now.

Exercise 2: Viewing Your Domain

In this exercise, you will view your domain.

▶ **To explore My Network Places**

1. Log on as Administrator.
2. Double-click My Network Places.

   The My Network Places window appears.
3. Double-click Entire Network, and then click the Entire Contents link.

   The Microsoft Windows Network icon appears.
4. Double-click the Microsoft Windows Network icon.

   The Microsoft Windows Network window appears, and the Domain icon should be listed.
5. Close the Microsoft Windows Network window.

Exercise 3: Using the Active Directory Users and Computers Snap-In

In this exercise, you will use the Active Directory Users and Computers snap-in to view your domain.

▶ **To use Active Directory Users and Computers**

1. Click Start, point to Programs, point to Administrative Tools, and then click Active Directory Users And Computers.
2. In the console tree, expand domain.com.

   Note If you did not use domain for your domain name, double-click your domain name.

   What selections are listed under domain?

3. In the console tree, click Domain Controllers.

   Notice that SERVER1 appears in the details pane.

   Note If you did not use SERVER1 as your server name, the name of your server appears in the details pane.

   ---

4. Leave the Active Directory Users And Computers window open.

Exercise 4: Changing Your Domain from Mixed Mode to Native Mode

In this exercise, you will change your domain mode from mixed mode to native mode.

▶ **To change your domain from mixed mode to native mode**

1. In the console tree, click domain.com to select it.

Note If you did not use domain.com for your domain name, click your domain name.

---

2. Click Action and then click Properties on the Action menu.

   The Domain.com Properties dialog box appears.

3. On the General tab, click the Change Mode button.

   An Active Directory Service dialog box displays a warning that once the domain mode is changed to native mode, you cannot change back.

4. Click Yes, and then click OK to close the Properties dialog box for your domain.

   An Active Directory message box displays a message indicating that the operation completed successfully and that it may take 15 minutes or more for the information to replicate to all domain controllers.

5. Click OK, and close all open windows.

Lesson Summary

To install Active Directory directory services, you can use the Windows 2000 Configure Your Server wizard to start the Active Directory Installation wizard. You can also go to a command prompt and type **dcpromo** to launch the Active Directory Installation wizard. You use the Active Directory Installation wizard to add a domain controller to an existing domain, to create the first domain controller of a new domain, to create a new child domain, and to create a new domain tree.

When installing Active Directory directory services, a database and a log file are created. The database is the directory for the new domain, and the log file temporarily stores changes made to the Active Directory directory services database. The default location for the database and database log files is *systemroot*\Ntds. A shared system volume is also created when you install Active Directory directory services. The shared system volume is a folder structure that exists on all Windows 2000 domain controllers. It stores scripts and some of the Group Policy objects for both the current domain as well as the enterprise. The file replication services use the shared system volume to replicate files and Group Policy information among domain controllers. The default location for the shared system volume is *systemroot*\Sysvol.

When you first install or upgrade a domain controller to Windows 2000 Advanced Server, the domain controller runs in mixed mode. Mixed mode allows domain controllers to interact with any domain controllers in the domain that are running previous versions of Windows NT Server (down-level domain controllers). When all the domain controllers in the domain run Windows 2000, and you do not plan to add any more down-level domain controllers to the domain, you can switch the domain from mixed mode to native mode. Native mode does not support down-level replication. When you change from mixed mode to native mode, the server that was the primary domain controller during migration is no longer the domain master; all domain controllers in native mode act as peers.

In the practice section of this lesson, you used Dcpromo.exe to start the Active Directory Installation wizard so that you could install Active Directory directory services on your computer, promote your computer to a domain controller, and create a domain. You then viewed your domain using My Network Places and the Active Directory Users and Computers tool. Finally, you changed your domain controller from mixed mode to native mode.

Lesson 6: Configuring Active Directory Replication

Active Directory directory services automatically configure a default topology to enable replication within a domain. For a network that includes multiple locations, however, you must customize the replication topology to minimize the impact of replication traffic on the network.

To configure Active Directory replication, you need to map your physical network to Active Directory directory services by creating sites and site links. A *site* is a combination of one or more Internet Protocol (IP) subnets that are connected by a high-speed link. A *site link* is a connection between two or more sites.

When you create a site link, you specify values that reflect information about available connections, preferred connection times, and available bandwidth. Active Directory directory services use this information to determine the times and connections for replication that will afford the best performance for your network.

After this lesson, you will be able to

- Describe Active Directory replication.

Estimated lesson time: 30 minutes

Understanding Replication Between Sites

In a Windows NT 4.0 network, replication is single master. All changes to a domain are made on the primary domain controller. The changes are then replicated directly to the backup domain controllers in the domain. In a Windows NT 4.0 network, the only way to control the flow of replication traffic is by creating multiple domains in different physical locations.

In Windows 2000, however, all domain controllers are peers, and replication is multimaster. As a result, you can make changes to a domain on any domain controller, and those changes replicate to every other domain controller in the domain. In a Windows 2000 network, you can control the flow of replication traffic by configuring sites and site links that map your network's physical structure to Active Directory directory services.

Within a site, Windows 2000 automatically configures replication, though you can modify the configuration to optimize replication. Between sites, however, you must configure replication manually.

When you install Active Directory directory services, the Active Directory Installation wizard creates a default topology that accommodates replication for a single location with high-speed connectivity. However, if your network includes multiple locations, Active Directory replication will not be optimized for your network structure.

Figure 4.12 demonstrates how the default replication topology requires a change on a domain controller in Atlanta to replicate across the slow wide area network (WAN) link four times to update every domain controller in the domain.

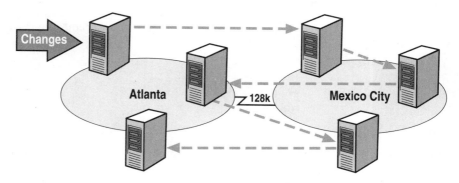

Figure 4.12   Default replication topology

To optimize replication traffic, you need to customize the default replication topology by mapping the physical structure of your network to Active Directory directory services.

Figure 4.13 demonstrates how the customized replication topology enables a change on a domain controller in Atlanta to replicate to all domain controllers in Atlanta and cross the slow WAN link only a single time before replicating to all domain controllers in Mexico City.

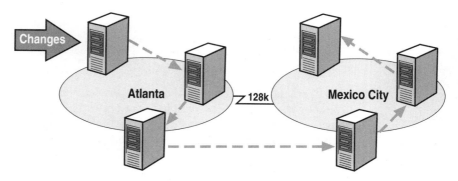

Figure 4.13   Customized replication topology

Examining Site Link Placement

In Windows 2000, you define a network model of sites and site links within Active Directory directory services to control the flow of replication traffic. Based on the model you define, Active Directory directory services create connections that enable replication. If any connection in the replication topology fails, Active Directory directory services modify the remaining connections to maintain replication within the network.

Figure 4.14 provides examples of site link placement in three basic network models.

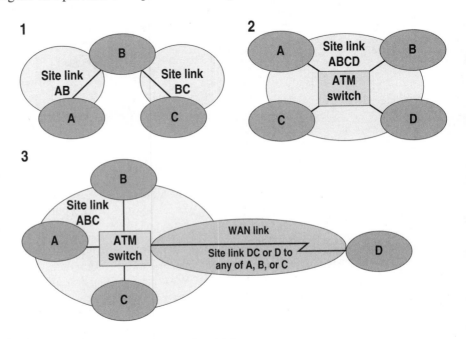

Figure 4.14   Three basic network models

Sites Connected by Routers

In example 1 in Figure 4.14, routers connect multiple sites, and the cost of traffic among the sites in the example is not uniform. For example, the cost associated with sending traffic from A to B is not the same as the cost associated with sending traffic from A to C. As a result, you must create a site link to define each WAN connection. The relative cost of each connection depends on the speed of that connection.

For example, if site link AB models a network connection of 128 Kbps and site link BC models a network connection of 256 Kbps, the cost of site link AB will be twice as much as the cost of site link BC.

Sites Connected by Network Equipment at Uniform Speeds

In example 2 in Figure 4.14, a switch connects multiple sites. Because the cost of traffic flowing from one site to any other site in the example is the same, you can create a site link that defines the connection between all four sites. While you must assign a cost to the site link, the value you assign is arbitrary unless you intend to create another site link in the network.

Sites Connected by Network Equipment at Different Speeds

In example 3 in Figure 4.14, a switch connects multiple sites, including a remote site. The connection speed to the remote site is different from the connection speed to the other sites in the model, and therefore has a different cost.

Example 3 includes two site links:

- One site link defines the connection between the sites that are using similar bandwidths.
- One site link defines the connection between the switch area and the remote site. The cost of connecting to the remote site (D) is the same for each of the sites in the switch area, so any of the sites (A, B, or C) can be part of the site link.

Creating and Configuring a Site

After you assess a cost for each WAN connection, you map your physical network to Active Directory directory services by configuring sites and then configuring site links to define the connections between those sites.

Configuring a site involves creating a site and configuring a subnet in Active Directory directory services. *Subnets* define the IP address ranges that exist within a site. When you configure a subnet, you must associate it with a site.

Important To create sites and configure subnets in Active Directory directory services, you must log on as a member of the Enterprise Admins group. The Enterprise Admins group exists in the root domain of the forest.

When you create a site, you must associate it with a site link. Before you configure the site links that map the connectivity in your network, you must specify the default site link, DEFAULTIPSITELINK.

Note The Active Directory Installation wizard creates the default site link during installation.

You create sites in Active Directory directory services to optimize replication traffic and to enable users to connect to a domain controller by using a reliable, high-speed connection. To create and configure a site, use the Active Directory Sites and Services snap-in. Right-click Sites, and then click New Site. You must provide a site name, and select a site link.

Configuring a Subnet in Active Directory Directory Services

A subnet in Active Directory directory services provides the link between IP addresses and sites. You can only associate a subnet with one site; however, you can associate a site with multiple subnets. When you configure a subnet in Active Directory directory services, you must specify the network/bit-masked identifier for the subnet. The network/bit-masked identifier includes the subnet ID for the subnet and the number of bits masked by the subnet mask.

For example, if your subnet ID is 10.14.208.0 and your subnet mask is 255.255.240.0, to determine that the network/bit-masked identifier would be 10.14.208.0/20, do the following steps.

Note that the subnet mask is represented by four decimal numbers separated by a period. Each number can be referred to as an octet, which means it can be represented by 8 binary digits (bits). To calculate the number of bits masked, you could do the following:

1. Start Calculator, and on the View menu of Calculator, select Scientific.

   Scientific mode of Calculator allows you to convert decimal numbers to binary, which will allow you to calculate the number of bits.

2. Make sure the Dec radio button is selected.

   This sets Calculator in decimal mode, which means any numbers entered will be understood as decimal.

3. Enter the first octet of your subnet mask into Calculator.

   If your subnet mask was 255.255.248.0, the first octet is 255. The first octet is always on the left.

4. Click the Bin radio button.

   The number you now see is the binary representation of the decimal number you entered first. Notice that there are eight 1 bits.

5. Click the Dec radio button to change Calculator back to decimal mode.

6. Continue entering the second, third, and fourth octet into Calculator and converting them to binary. Record the number of 1 bits in the table below. Add the numbers in the second column and record the total.

Octet	Number of 1 bits
1st	8
2nd	8
3rd	4
4th	0
Total	20

The total is the number of bits masked by your subnet mask.

7. Close Calculator.

To configure a subnet in Active Directory directory services, use Active Directory Sites and Services. Expand Sites to see Subnets. When you select New Subnet, you must provide the network/bit-masked identifier and a site with which to associate this subnet.

Configuring a Site Link

After you configure the sites for your network, you create site links in Active Directory directory services to map the connections between the sites. For each site link, you need to specify the following properties to define the connections in your network:

- **Cost.** By default, the cost of a site link is 100.

- **Replication interval.** The replication interval defines the frequency of replication. By default, replication occurs every three hours.

- **Schedule.** The schedule declares the time periods during which the link is available. For instance, you might make a site link representing a dial-up line unavailable during business hours when phone rates are high. By default, replication can occur at all times.

Note You specify site link properties on the General tab of the Properties dialog box for a site link.

To create a site link, open Active Directory Sites and Services, expand Sites, and then expand Inter-Site Transports. Right-click IP or SMTP, depending on which transport protocol you want the site link to use, and click New Site Link. In the Name box, type the name for the site link. Click two or more sites to include in this site link, and then click Add.

Note You must specify either Internet Protocol (IP) or Simple Mail Transport Protocol (SMTP) as the transport protocol for communication between sites. The preferred protocol is IP because SMTP has limited replication capabilities.

After you configure the sites and site links for your network, Active Directory directory services directs the flow of replication traffic accordingly.

Configuring a Global Catalog Server

After you configure Active Directory replication for your network, you configure a global catalog server for each site in your network to accomplish the following goals:

- Improving the performance of forestwide queries, by providing a partial list of attributes for every object in Active Directory directory services
- Reducing the time required for user logon, by ensuring that logon traffic remains within that site
- Enhancing the reliability of user logon, by ensuring that there are multiple global catalog servers to complete user logon

To configure a domain controller as a global catalog server, use Active Directory Sites and Services. In the console tree, right-click NTDS Settings, click Properties, and on the General tab, select the Global Catalog Server check box.

Note Active Directory directory services automatically configures the first domain controller in a forest as a global catalog server.

Review

Here are some questions to help you determine if you have learned enough to move on to the next chapter. If you have difficulty answering these questions, please go back and review the material in this chapter before beginning the next chapter. The answers to these questions are located in Appendix A, "Questions and Answers."

1. List three of the items that you should check on a server before running the Active Directory Installation wizard.

2. You have installed Active Directory directory services on your corporate network and have upgraded all domain controllers running Windows NT 4.0 to Windows 2000. You now want to create security-type universal groups. What should you do and what console should you use to make the change?

3. You are the administrator of a network in a remote location, and the network connection from the main office to that location has failed. You find you are still able to create user accounts even though the connection has failed, and users are noticing no difference in logon speed. What would you need at the remote location for this to be possible?

4. Your company has one remote office connected by a 64 Kbps WAN link. Technical support is receiving calls from users in the remote office who are complaining that it is sometimes taking over five minutes to log on. You have configured a domain controller and a global catalog server in the remote office. What is a potential source of the problem? Describe the steps you would take to improve logon times.

5. You have three locations (A, B, C) that are connected to a central site (D) by 128 Kbps WAN links, and another remote location (E) connected to the central site by a 256 Kbps WAN link. You create a site for each location. What site links should you create to enable replication to take place, and given only the bandwidth information about the links, what cost should be associated with each site link?

C H A P T E R   5

Administering Active Directory Directory Services

About This Chapter

The Active Directory directory services in Microsoft Windows 2000 are composed of objects that represent network resources, such as users, computers, and printers. You use a directory service to uniquely identify objects, organize these objects into organizational units (OUs), and manage the access to these resources.

After you create the structure of Active Directory directory services, you must populate it with network objects. Although user and computer accounts are basically the same in Windows 2000 as they were in Microsoft Windows NT 4.0, the procedures for creating these accounts and the interface that you use to create them are new in Windows 2000.

Before You Begin

To complete this chapter

- You must have a computer that meets or exceeds the minimum hardware requirements listed in "Getting Started," on page xxi.

- You must have installed the beta version of Windows 2000 Advanced Server on a computer meeting the specifications listed in the preceding bullet. The computer should be installed as a domain controller in a domain and TCP/IP should be the only installed protocol.

- Your computer should be using a static IP address.

Lesson 1: Creating Organizational Units

Organizational units (OUs) are objects (containers) that can contain other objects, such as user accounts, groups, computer accounts, and other OUs. OUs cannot contain objects from other domains. OUs can be employed to organize the objects in Active Directory directory services that represent your network resources. Employing OUs to contain and organize the objects in Active Directory directory services is similar to using folders to contain and organize other folders and files.

After this lesson, you will be able to

- Create organizational units.
- Move Active Directory objects.

Estimated lesson time: 15 minutes

Hierarchical Structure

OUs can contain other OUs, so you can create a logical hierarchy that represents your company's organizational structure or administrative needs. If you create a hierarchical structure to represent your company's organizational structure, you can base it on your company's departmental or geographical boundaries. For example, if your company has divisions in Brussels, Hong Kong, and New York, you could create a separate OU for each location.

Setting up an OU hierarchy allows you to delegate administrative control over a number of user accounts, groups, or other resources. You delegate administrative control by assigning specific permissions for OUs, and the objects that they contain, to other individuals and groups. By setting up an OU for each division in your company, you could then easily manage and delegate control of each division.

You can also base your OU hierarchy on your company's network administrative model. For example, at your company there might be one administrator who is responsible for all user accounts and a different administrator who is responsible for all printers. In this case, you would create an OU for users and a different OU for printers.

Permissions

You must have Read, List Contents, and Create Organizational Unit Objects permissions on the parent container (domain or OU) to create OUs within that container. List Contents is not specifically required to create an OU, but you cannot view the newly created OU without it. By default, members of the Administrators group have the permissions to create OUs anywhere. To create an OU, you would do the following:

1. Open Active Directory Users And Computers from the Administrative Tools menu.

   The Active Directory Users And Computers window displays several default containers directly beneath the domain. Users, Computers, and Builtin are containers that are not OUs. Because you cannot create OUs within these containers, or apply Group Policy to them, you should create different OUs to contain your users and computers.

   Note You may need to expand your domain, by clicking the plus sign to the left of the domain in the console pane, to see the default containers.

   ---

2. Right-click the container (domain or OU) in which you want to create a new OU.

3. Point to New, and click Organizational Unit.

4. Type in the name of the OU, and click OK.

Practice: Creating Organizational Units

In this practice, you will create four OUs: Sales, Administration, Production, and Servers. You will create four user accounts in the Sales OU, and then you will move two of these user accounts into the Administration OU.

Exercise 1: Creating an Organizational Unit

In this exercise, you will create four organizational units.

► **To create an organizational unit**

1. Log on as Administrator.

2. Click Start, point to Programs, point to Administrative Tools, and click Active Directory Users And Computers.

3. In the console tree, right-click domain.com, point to New on the shortcut menu, and then click Organizational Unit.

   The New Object – Organizational Unit dialog box appears.

   Note When you create an OU, the only required information is the name. The dialog box indicates the location where the object will be created.

   ---

4. In the Name box, type **Sales**, and then click OK.

5. Repeat steps 3 and 4 to create an Administration OU, a Production OU, and a Servers OU.

6. Leave the Active Directory Users And Computers window open.

Lesson Summary

Organizational units (OUs) can be used to organize the objects in Active Directory directory services that represent your network resources. OUs contain objects, including other OUs, so you can create a logical hierarchy of OUs to represent your company's organizational structure or administrative needs. Setting up an OU hierarchy allows you to delegate administrative control over user accounts, groups, or other resources, by assigning specific permissions for OUs, and the objects that they contain, to other individuals and groups.

You must have Read, List Contents, and Create Organizational Unit Objects permissions on the parent container (domain or OU) to create OUs within that container. List Contents is not specifically required to create an OU, but you cannot view the newly created OU without it. By default, members of the Administrators group have the permissions to create OUs anywhere.

Lesson 2: Creating User and Computer Accounts

You use objects, user accounts, and computer accounts to represent users and computers so that you can control network access and manage the use of network resources. To add a user or a computer account to an OU, you must have the permission to add new objects to the OU. By default, members of the Administrators group have permission to add objects anywhere in the domain.

After this lesson, you will be able to

- Create domain user accounts.
- Describe how to create computer accounts.

Estimated lesson time: 30 minutes

Creating User Accounts

User accounts are employed to authenticate the user, as well as to assign permissions to gain access to network resources. You can use the Active Directory Users and Computers administrative tool on any available domain controller to create a new user account. After you create the account, it is replicated to all other domain controllers in the domain.

When you create the user account, you must first select the container in which to create it. You can create user accounts at the domain level, but doing so limits your delegation options and increases the complexity of managing your network. To create a domain user account, you would do the following:

1. Open the Active Directory Users and Computers administrative tool.
2. Right-click the OU in which you want to create the user account, point to New, and then click User. Figure 5.1 shows the New Object – User dialog box. The fields in Figure 5.1 are explained in Table 5.1.

Table 5.1 describes the domain user account options that you can configure.

Table 5.1   Configurable Domain User Account Options

Option	Description
First Name	The user's first name. This field or the Last Name field is required.
Last Name	The user's last name. This field or the First Name field is required.
Full Name	The user's complete name. This name must be unique within the OU or container where you create the user account. Active Directory directory services display this name in the OU or container where the user account is located.

Option	Description
User Logon Name	The user's unique logon name based on your naming conventions. This is required and must be unique within the enterprise.
User Logon Name (Pre–Windows 2000	The user's unique logon name that is used to log on from computers running earlier versions of Windows, such as Windows NT 4.0 or 3.51. This is required and must be unique within the domain.

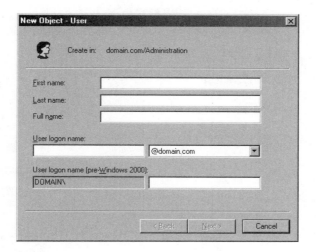

Figure 5.1   The New Object – User dialog box

Note The user logon name, combined with the domain name in the box that appears to the right of the User Logon Name box, is the User Principal Name (UPN). The UPN uniquely identifies the user throughout the entire enterprise. An example of a UPN would be user5@domain1.domain.com.

After you enter the information about the user, you can set the password requirements for the user account by clicking the Next button to display the password options shown in Figure 5.2.

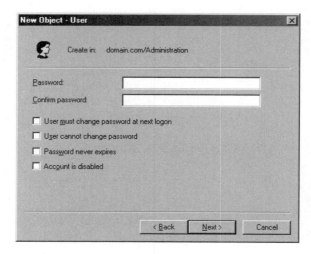

Figure 5.2   The New Object – User dialog box's password settings

Table 5.2 describes the password options that you can configure.

Table 5.2   Configurable Password Options

Option	Description
Password	Enter the password that is used to authenticate the user. For greater security, you should *always* assign a password.
Confirm Password	Confirm the password by typing it a second time to make sure that you typed it correctly.
User Must Change Password At Next Logon	Select this check box if you want the user to change his or her password the first time that he or she logs on. This ensures that the user is the only person who knows the password.
User Cannot Change Password	Select this check box if you have more than one person using the same domain user account (such as Guest), or to maintain control over user account passwords. This allows only administrators to control passwords.
Password Never Expires	Select this check box if you want the password to never change.
Account Disabled	Select this check box to prevent the use of this account—for example, on an account for a new employee who has not yet started.

Each user account that you create is associated with a set of default attributes. You can use the attributes that you define for a domain user account to search for users in Active Directory directory services. For this reason, you should provide detailed attribute definitions for each domain user account that you create.

After you create a domain user account, you can configure personal and account attributes, logon options, and dial-in settings.

The tabs in the Properties dialog box for a user contain information about each user account. When the Advanced Features for the Active Directory Users and Computers snap-in are active, the tabs are General, Address, Account, Profile, Telephones, Organization, Published Certificates, Member Of, Dial-In, Object, Security, and if you are using Terminal Services, Environment, Sessions, Remote Control, and Terminal Services Profile.

Right-click the user account, and then click Properties to open the Properties dialog box for a user account.

Note To create a local user account on a computer, open Computer Management and select the Local Users And Groups tool in the System Tools group.

Moving Objects

In Active Directory directory services, you can easily move objects between OUs within your domain structure. Active Directory directory services simplify your job as an administrator by allowing you to move objects whenever organizational or administrative functions change. For example, when an employee moves from one department to another, it is a lot easier to move the user account than to have to delete the user account, recreate a new user account, and make sure that all rights and permissions are correctly reestablished.

When you move objects between OUs

- Permissions that are assigned directly to objects remain the same.
- The objects inherit permissions from the new OU. Any permissions inherited from the previous OU will no longer affect the objects.
- You can move multiple objects at the same time.

Similar to moving users, you use the Active Directory Users and Computers tool to move an object. In the Active Directory Users And Computers window, right-click the object you want to move, and then click Move. In the Move dialog box, click on the container that you want the object moved to, and then click OK.

Locating Objects

In Active Directory directory services, you can also easily locate resources throughout the network, regardless of the physical location of the object. Use the Active Directory Users and Computers tool to locate groups in Active Directory directory services. Click Find on the Action menu in the Active Directory Users

And Computers window to open the Find dialog box. The Find dialog box, shown in Figure 5.3, allows you to search Active Directory directory services to locate different types of objects. The search criteria that are available vary (as does the dialog box's title bar) depending on the type of object you selected in the Find list.

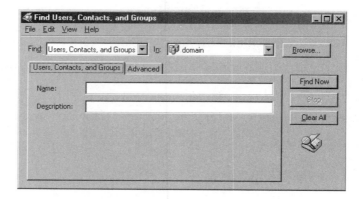

Figure 5.3   The Find dialog box

After a search successfully completes, the search results are displayed. You can then perform administrative functions on the objects that are listed. The functions that are available depend on the type of object you located. For example, if you searched for computer accounts, you can delete the computer account, disable or reset the computer account, move the computer account to another OU, or adjust the computer account's attributes.

Note Users can use Search, available on the Start menu, to find objects in Active Directory directory services. The Search commands in Windows Explorer and My Network Places can also be used to locate objects in Active Directory directory services.

Practice: Creating and Managing Domain User Accounts

In this practice, you will create user accounts based on information given in Exercise 1. After creating the user accounts you will modify the user account properties, specifically the logon hours properties, for one of the user accounts. You will test the user account you modified to verify that the logon restrictions you set up are working, and finally, you will move two of the user accounts from the OU in which they were created to another OU.

Exercise 1: Creating User Accounts

In this exercise, you will create four user accounts.

▶ **To create a domain user account**

1. In the console tree, right-click Production, point to New, and then click User.

   Notice that the New Object – User dialog box shows that the new user account is being created in the location domain.com/Production.

2. Create the user account by typing **User** in the First Name box, **One** in the Last Name box, and **User1** in the User Logon Name box.

3. If you are on a network where there are multiple domains, in the box to the right of the User Logon Name box, select @domain.com.

Note If you did not follow the naming convention suggested in this kit, select the appropriate domain name.

---

4. Click Next to continue.

5. In the Password and Confirm Password boxes, use the information in the following table to determine the password to type or whether you should leave these boxes blank (you are not assigning a password). Use the information in the table to determine how to set the password options as well.

First name	Last name	User logon name	Password	Change password
User	One	User1	Blank	Must
User	Two	User2	Blank	Must
User	Three	User3	User3	Must
User	Four	User4	User4	Cannot

6. After you have assigned the appropriate password options, click Next.

7. Verify that the user account options are correct, and then click Finish.

   Notice that the user account that you just created now appears in the details pane of the Active Directory Users And Computers window.

8. Repeat steps 1–7 to create User Two, User Three, and User Four. Add these users to the Print Operators group.

Note As you continue with the exercises in this chapter, you will be asked to log on to the domain controller as a user other than Administrator. To be able to log on to a domain controller, you will need to make the user account a member of a group that has a right to log on to domain controllers (for example, the Print Operators group). To add a user to the Print Operators group, click the Builtin node in the console pane, right-click Print Operators in the details pane, and click Properties. In the user's Properties dialog box, click the Members tab, click Add, select the user you want to add to the group, click Add, and then click OK twice.

Exercise 2: Modifying User Account Properties

In this exercise, you will configure the Logon Hours properties for one of the user accounts that you created in Exercise 1.

▶ **To modify user account properties**

1. In the Production OU, right-click User2, and then click Properties.
2. Click the Account tab, and then click Logon Hours.

> **Note** A blue block indicates that the user is allowed to log on during that hour. A white block indicates that the user cannot log on.

By default, when can a user log on?

3. Restrict User2's logon hours, so that User2 can only log on from 6:00 PM until 6:00 AM.

> **Note** To restrict the user's logon hours, click the start time of the first period during which you want to prevent the user from logging on, and then drag the pointer to the end time for the period. A frame will outline the blocks for all of the selected hours. Click Logon Denied. The outlined area is now a white block, indicating that the user will not be permitted to log on during those hours.

4. Click OK to close the Logon Hours For User Two dialog box.
5. Click OK to close the User Two Properties dialog box, and then close the Active Directory Users And Computers window.

Exercise 3: Testing the User Account

In this exercise, you will log on using User1 for which you modified the logon hours in Exercise 2 to test the effects of the account settings.

▶ **To test restrictions on logon hours**

1. Attempt to log on as User1 with no password.

   Windows 2000 displays a Logon Message message box, indicating that you must change your password.

> **Note** If Windows 2000 displays a message that the local policy of your system does not permit you to interactively log on User1 to your server, log on as Administrator, add your User1 account to the Print Operators group, log off as Administrator, and then log on as User1 again.

2. Click OK.

The Change Password dialog box appears.

3. In the Change Password dialog box, in the New Password and Confirm New Password boxes, type **User1** and then click OK.

Windows 2000 displays the Change Password message box indicating that your password was changed.

4. Click OK to close the Change Password message box.

Were you able to successfully log on as User1? Why or why not?

5. Repeat steps 1 – 3 for User Two; use User2 as the new password.

Note If Windows 2000 displays a message that the local policy of your system does not permit you to interactively log on User2 to your server, log on as Administrator, add your User2 account to the Print Operators group, log off as Administrator, and then log on as User2 again.

Were you able to successfully log on as User Two? Why or why not?

Note If you are doing the lab between the hours of 6:00 AM and 6:00 PM, you can use the Date/Time icon in Control Panel to change your system clock to verify that the logon settings are working. If you do change your system time, remember to set the correct time after you complete your test.

Exercise 4: Moving a User Account from One OU to Another OU

User One and User Three have been transferred from Production to Administration. In this exercise, you will move the user objects for User One and User Three to reflect the transfer.

▶ **To move a user account**

1. Log on as Administrator, and open Active Directory Users And Computers from the Start menu.

2. In the Production OU, select both User One and User Three, right-click, and then click Move.

3. In the Move dialog box, expand your domain, click Administration, and then click OK.

Notice that the user accounts that you moved no longer appear in the Production OU.

4. To verify that the user accounts were moved to the correct location, in the console tree, click Administration.

Notice that the user objects for User One and User Three are now located in the Administration OU.

5. Close the Active Directory Users And Computers window.

6. Log off.

Creating Computer Accounts

Computer accounts are similar to user accounts in that they can be used to authenticate and audit the computer, as well as being used to assign permissions to gain access to network resources.

Since all domain controllers in a Windows 2000 domain are peers, you can use the Active Directory Users and Computers tool on any available domain controller to create a new computer account. After you create the account, Active Directory directory services replicate it to all other domain controllers in the domain.

When you create the computer account, select the container in which to create it. You can create computer accounts at the domain level, but doing so limits your delegation options and increases the complexity of managing your network. To create a computer account, you also use the Active Directory Users and Computers tool. Right-click on the container in which you want to create the computer account, point to New, and then click Computer. Type in the name of the computer.

Note The computer name must be unique within the enterprise.

For added security, you might want to change the selection in the User Or Group box. You can enter any user or group to join a computer to a domain. During the process of joining the computer to the domain, a dialog box appears that prompts you for an account that has the right to join the computer to the domain. The person who joins the computer to the domain must enter a user name and password that matches the value you designate in this box. As with user accounts, each computer account that you create is associated with a set of default attributes. You can use the attributes that you define for a computer account to search for a computer in the Active Directory directory services. For this reason, you should provide detailed attribute definitions for each computer account that you create.

Lesson Summary

You use objects, user accounts, and computer accounts to represent users and computers so that you can control network access and manage the use of network resources. To add a user or a computer account to an OU, you must have the permission to add new objects to the OU. By default, members of the Administrators group have permission to add objects anywhere in the domain. User accounts are employed to authenticate the user, as well as to assign permissions to gain access to network resources. You can use the Active Directory Users and Computers tool on any available domain controller to create a new user account. After you create the account, it is replicated to all other domain controllers in the domain.

Lesson 3: Managing Groups

Active Directory directory services provide support for different types of groups, as well as offering options for the scope of a group—that is, whether or not the group spans multiple domains or is limited to a single domain.

After this lesson, you will be able to

- Create and modify groups.
- Delete groups.
- Explain how to move and locate objects in Active Directory directory services.

Estimated lesson time: 50 minutes

Understanding Group Types

Active Directory directory services allow for flexibility by providing two distinct types of groups: security groups and distribution groups.

Security Groups

Windows 2000 uses only security groups, which you use to assign or deny rights and permissions to groups of users and computers so that they can gain access to resources. Programs that are designed to search Active Directory directory services can also use security groups for nonsecurity-related purposes, such as sending e-mail messages to a number of users at the same time. A security group also has all the capabilities of a distribution group. Since Windows 2000 uses only security groups, this chapter will focus on security groups.

Distribution Groups

Applications, such as Microsoft Exchange, use distribution groups as lists for nonsecurity-related functions. Distribution groups cannot be used for security purposes; you cannot use distribution groups to assign permissions. Use distribution groups when the only function of the group is nonsecurity related, such as sending e-mail messages to a group of users at the same time.

If you have no plans to use a particular group for security purposes, you should create a distribution group rather than a security group. During the logon process, Windows 2000 creates an access token that contains the list of security groups to which the user belongs. Using distribution groups rather than security groups improves logon performance by reducing the size of the access token.

Understanding Group Scope

Security and distribution groups have a scope attribute. The scope of a group determines who can be a member of the group and where you can use that group in the network. There are three group scopes that are available: universal, global, and domain local.

Universal Groups

Universal groups can contain user accounts, global groups, and other universal groups from any Windows 2000 domain in the forest. The domain must be operating in native mode to create security groups with universal scope.

You can grant permissions to universal groups for all domains in the forest, regardless of the location of the universal group.

Global Groups

Global groups, in a native mode domain, can contain user accounts and global groups from the domain in which the group exists. In a mixed mode domain, they can contain only user accounts from the domain in which the group exists.

You can grant permissions to global groups for all domains in the forest, regardless of the location of the global group. The membership of a global group is limited to its domain, but the group can be assigned permissions throughout the forest.

Domain Local Groups

Domain local groups, in a native mode domain, can contain user accounts, global groups, and universal groups from any domain in the forest, as well as domain local groups from the same domain. In a mixed mode domain, they can contain user accounts and global groups from any domain.

You can grant permissions to domain local groups only for objects within the domain in which the domain local group exists. The membership of a domain local group can be forestwide, but the group can only be assigned permissions within its own domain.

Group Scope and Performance

A list of universal group memberships is maintained in the global catalog. Global and domain local groups are listed in the global catalog, but their membership is not. Each change to the membership of a universal group is replicated to all global catalog servers. By minimizing the use of universal groups, you will help reduce the size of the global catalog and thereby reduce the amount of traffic on your network caused by replication of the global catalog.

Consider limiting membership in universal groups to other groups, as opposed to user accounts. This allows you to adjust the user accounts that are members of the universal group by adjusting the membership of the groups that are members of the universal group. Since this does not directly affect the membership of the universal group, no replication traffic is generated.

Limiting the use of universal groups can also help you to reduce the size of access tokens when resources are in different domains. If you use global and domain local groups, the access tokens contain the global and domain local groups that are applicable to the domain in which the resource exists. If you use universal groups, the access token contains a list of all of the universal groups the user belongs to, even if those universal groups are not used in that domain.

Limit the use of universal groups to groups that are widely used in your enterprise and are relatively static as far as membership changes.

Creating Groups

Creating groups eases administrative overhead by combining accounts that require similar access to network resources into a single object to which you can assign rights and permissions.

Planning Groups

The recommended strategy for using both global and domain local groups is to put user accounts (A) into global groups (G) and then to put global groups into domain local groups (DL) and assign resource permissions (P) to the domain local groups. This strategy (AGDLP) provides for the most flexibility and reduces the complexity of assigning access permissions to network resources.

For example, suppose your network has several global groups that all require the same access permissions to network resources in a particular domain. If you put all of these global groups into a single domain local group, you can then assign the appropriate permissions for each resource to that single domain local group, and the user accounts in the global groups would have the appropriate permissions. If the permission requirements for the resources ever change, you can simply adjust the domain local group's membership. If, on the other hand, you assigned permissions directly to the global groups, you would need to manually adjust the individual permissions on all of the network resources.

Creating a Group in Active Directory Directory Services

To create a group, open the Active Directory Users and Computers tool, right-click the appropriate container or OU, point to New, and then click Group. Figure 5.4 shows the New Object – Group dialog box, and Table 5.3 describes the options that you must provide in the New Object – Group dialog box.

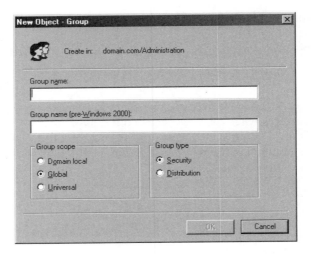

Figure 5.4 The New Object – Group dialog box

Table 5.3 New Object – Group Dialog Box Options

Option	Description
Group Name	The name of the new group. The name must be unique within the container in which you create the group.
Group Name (Pre–Windows 2000)	The name the group is referred to from client computers running versions of Windows earlier than Windows 2000. This name must be unique within the domain.
Group Scope	The group scope. Choose Domain Local, Global, or Universal.
Group Type	The type of group. Choose Security or Distribution.

After you create a group, you add members. Members of groups can include user accounts, other groups, and computers.

Note Add a computer to a group to give access to a shared resource on that computer (for example, the remote backup utility).

Adding Members to a Group

To add members to a group, use the Active Directory Users and Computers tool. In the Active Directory Users And Computers window, right-click the group to which you want to add a member, click Properties, and then click the Members tab. On the Members tab, click Add.

In the Look In list, select a domain from which to display user accounts and groups, or select Entire Directory to view user accounts and groups from anywhere in Active Directory directory services. From this list, select the user account or group that you want to add, and then click Add. If you are adding more than one user account or group, you can continue to select the account or group and click Add. Once you have finished adding user accounts or groups to selected groups, click OK.

Note You can also add a user account or group to a group by using the Member Of tab in the Properties dialog box for that user account or group. Use this method to quickly add the same user or group to multiple groups.

Modifying Groups

In addition to changing the membership of a group and the permissions granted to that group, you can modify a group by changing the type and scope. You can also delete groups when they are no longer needed.

Changing Group Type

You can change a group's type from security to distribution or from distribution to security at any time when the domain is in native mode. You cannot change a group's type when the domain is in mixed mode. You change the type of the group on the General tab of the Properties dialog box for the group.

Changing Group Scope

As your network changes, you might need to change a group's scope. For example, you might want to change an existing domain local group to a universal group when you need to assign permissions to allow users to gain access to resources in other domains. You change the scope of a group on the General tab of the Properties dialog box for the group.

Here are some important points to remember about changing group scope:

- You can only change the scope of a group when the domain is in native mode; you cannot change group scope in mixed mode.
- You can change a global group to a universal group, but only if the global group that you are converting is not a member of another global group.
- You can change a domain local group to a universal group, but only if the domain local group that you are converting does not contain another domain local group.
- You cannot change a universal group to any other group scope because all other groups have more restrictive membership and scope than universal groups.

Deleting a Group

When you delete a group, you delete only the group and remove the permissions and rights that are associated with it. Deleting a group does not delete the user accounts that are members of the group.

Each group that you create has a unique, nonreusable identifier, called the security identifier (SID). Windows 2000 uses the SID to identify the group and the permissions that are assigned to it. When you delete a group, Windows 2000 does not use the SID for that group again, even if you create a new group with the same name. Therefore, you cannot restore access to resources by recreating the group.

To delete a group, open the Active Directory Users and Computers tool, right-click the group, and then click Delete.

Practice: Creating Groups

In this practice, you will create and add members to a global group, a domain local group, and a universal group.

Exercise 1: Creating a Global Group and Adding Members

In this exercise, you will create a global group and add members.

▶ **To create a global group in a domain**

1. Log on as Administrator.
2. Open the Active Directory Users and Computers tool.
3. In the console tree, expand domain.com.
4. In the console tree, click Administration.
5. Right-click Administration, point to New, and then click Group.

   The New Object – Group dialog box appears.
6. Type **Managers** in the Group Name box.
7. Verify that the Group Scope option is set to Global, and that the Group Type option is set to Security, and then click OK.

   Windows 2000 creates the group and displays it in the details pane.

▶ **To add members to a global group**

1. Double-click Managers.

   The Managers Properties dialog box displays the properties of the group.
2. To view the members of the group, click the Members tab.

   This list is currently empty.
3. To add a member to the group, click Add.
4. In the Select Users, Contacts, Computers, Or Groups dialog box, in the Look In box, verify that your domain is selected.
5. In the list, click User One, and then click Add.
6. In the list, click User Two, and then click Add.

7. Click OK.

User One and User Two are now members of the Managers global group.

8. Click OK to close the Managers Properties dialog box.

Leave the Active Directory Users And Computers window open.

Exercise 2: Creating a Domain Local Group and Adding Members

In this exercise, you will create a domain local group and add members. You will use the group to assign permissions to gain access to an inventory database. Because you use the group to assign permissions, you will make it a domain local group. You will then add members to the group.

▶ **To create a domain local group in a domain**

1. Right-click Administration, point to New, and then click Group.

The New Object – Group dialog box appears.

2. Type **Inventory** in the Group Name box.

3. For the Group Scope option, click Domain Local, and for the Group Type option, confirm that Security is selected.

4. Click OK.

Windows 2000 creates the domain local group and displays it in the details pane.

Leave the Active Directory Users And Computers window open.

▶ **To add members to a domain local group**

1. Right-click Inventory, and click Properties.

The Inventory Properties dialog box displays the properties of the group.

2. To add a member to the group, click the Members tab, and then click Add.

3. In the Select Users, Contacts, Computers, Or Groups dialog box, in the Look In box, select Entire Directory.

The Select Users, Contacts, Computers, Or Groups dialog box displays user accounts and groups from all domains and shows the location of each user account or group as *domain / Users*. In your case there is only one domain.

4. Click the Name column heading.

The Select Users, Contacts, Computers, or Groups dialog box displays all entries in the list alphabetically by name.

5. Click Managers.

6. Click Add, and then click OK.

The Managers group is now a member of the Inventory domain local group.

7. Click OK to close the Inventory Properties dialog box.

Leave the Active Directory Users And Computers window open.

Exercise 3: Creating a Universal Group and Adding Members

In this exercise, you will create a universal group. You will then test what members you can add to this group.

▶   **To create a universal group**

1. Right-click Administration, point to New, and then click Group.

   The New Object – Group dialog box appears.

2. Type **Universal1** in the Group Name box.

3. For the Group Scope option, click Universal, and for the Group Type option, ensure that Security is selected.

4. Click OK.

   Windows 2000 creates the universal group and displays it in the details pane.

5. Repeat steps 1–4 to create a universal group named Universal2.

▶   **To add members to a universal group**

1. Right-click Universal1, and then click Properties.

   The Universal1 Properties dialog box appears.

2. Click the Members tab, and then click Add.

3. In the Select Users, Contacts, Computers, Or Groups dialog box, in the Look In box, select your domain.

4. In the list, click Managers, and then click Add.

5. Click OK.

6. Click OK to close the Universal1 Properties dialog box.

   Were you able to successfully add the Managers global group to the universal group? Why or why not?

7. Attempt to repeat steps 1 through 5 to add the Inventory domain local group to the universal group.

   Was the Inventory domain local group available for you to add to the universal group? Why or why not?

8. In the Universal1 Properties dialog box, click OK.

Exercise 4: Deleting a Group

In this exercise, you will delete a universal group.

▶ **To delete a universal group**

1. Right-click Universal2, and then click Delete.
2. When prompted, click Yes to delete the group named Universal2.
3. Close the Active Directory Users And Computers window.

Lesson Summary

Active Directory directory services provide two types of groups: security groups and distribution groups. You use security groups to assign or deny rights and permissions to groups of users and computers so that they can gain access to resources. A security group has all the capabilities of a distribution group. Applications, such as Microsoft Exchange, use distribution groups as lists for nonsecurity-related functions. You use distribution groups when the only function of the group is nonsecurity related, such as sending e-mail messages to a group of users at the same time.

Security and distribution groups have a scope attribute. The scope of a group determines who can be a member of the group and where you can use that group in the network. There are three group scopes that are available: universal, global, and domain local.

After you plan your groups, you use the Active Directory Users And Computers tool to create a group, add members to a group, change the type or scope of a group, or delete a group. In Active Directory directory services, you can also easily move objects within your domain structure and locate resources throughout the network, regardless of the physical location of the object.

Lesson 4: Controlling Access to Active Directory Objects

Every object in Active Directory directory services has a security descriptor that defines who has the permissions to gain access to the object and what type of access is allowed. Windows 2000 uses these security descriptors to control access to objects. To reduce administrative overhead, you can group objects with identical security requirements into one OU. You can then assign access permissions to the entire OU and all of the objects within it.

After this lesson, you will be able to

- Explain how to control access to objects in Active Directory directory services with permissions.
- View permissions on Active Directory objects.
- Delegate control of an organizational unit.

Estimated lesson time: 55 minutes

Introducing Active Directory Permissions

Active Directory permissions provide security for resources by allowing you to control who can gain access to individual objects or object attributes, and the type of access that you will allow. You can use permissions to assign administrative privileges—for an OU, a hierarchy of OUs, or a single object—to a specific user or group.

An administrator or the object owner must assign permissions to the object before users can gain access to the object. Windows 2000 stores a list of user access permissions called the discretionary access control list (DACL), for every object in Active Directory directory services. The DACL for an object lists who can access the object and the specific actions that each user can perform on the object.

The object type determines which permissions you can select. Permissions vary for different object types. For example, you can assign the Reset Password permission for a user object, but not for a printer object.

Effective Permissions

A user can be a member of multiple groups, each with different permissions that provide different levels of access to objects. When you assign a permission to a user for access to an object, and that user is a member of a group to which you assigned a different permission, the user's effective permissions are the combination of the user and the group permissions. For example, if a user has the Read permission and is a member of a group with the Write permission, the user's effective permissions are Read and Write.

Allow and Deny Permissions

You can allow or deny permissions. Denied permissions take precedence over any permissions that you otherwise allow for user accounts and groups. If you deny permission for a user to gain access to an object, the user will not have that permission, even if you allow the permission for a group of which the user is a member. You should deny permissions only when it is necessary to do so for a specific user who is a member of a group with allowed permissions.

Note Always ensure that all objects have at least one user with the Full Control permission. Failure to do so can result in some objects being inaccessible, even to an administrator when he or she uses the Active Directory Users and Computers administrative tool.

Standard and Special Permissions

You can set standard and special permissions on objects. Standard permissions are the most frequently assigned permissions and are composed of special permissions. Special permissions provide you with a finer degree of control for assigning access to objects.

For example, the standard Write permission is composed of the special permissions Write All Properties, Add/Remove Self As Member, and Read Permissions.

Table 5.4 lists standard object permissions that are available for most objects (some object types have additional permissions that are available) and the type of access that each permission allows.

Table 5.4   Standard Object Permissions

Object permission	Allows the user to
Full Control	Change permissions and take ownership, plus perform the tasks that are allowed by all other standard permissions.
Read	View objects and object attributes, the object owner, and the Active Directory permissions.
Write	Change object attributes.
Create All Child Objects	Add any type of child object to an OU.
Delete All Child Objects	Remove any type of object from an OU.

Using Permission Inheritance

Permission inheritance in Active Directory directory services minimizes the number of times that you need to assign permissions for objects.

Applying Permissions to Child Objects

When you assign permissions, you can select to apply the permissions to subobjects (child objects), which propagates the permissions to all of the subobjects for a given object. To indicate that permissions are inherited, the check boxes for inherited permissions are unavailable in the user interface.

For example, you can assign the Full Control permission to a group for an OU that contains printers, and then apply this permission for all subobjects. The result is that all group members can administer all printers in the OU.

Preventing Permission Inheritance

You can prevent permission inheritance so that a child object does not inherit permissions from its parent object. When you prevent inheritance, only the permissions that you explicitly assign to the object will apply.

Use the Security tab in the Properties dialog box to prevent permission inheritance.

When you prevent permission inheritance, Windows 2000 allows you to do the following:

- **Copy previously inherited permissions to the object.** The new explicit permissions for the object are a copy of the permissions that it previously inherited from its parent object. Then, according to your needs, you can make any necessary changes to the permissions.

- **Remove previously inherited permissions from the object.** By removing these permissions, you will eliminate all permissions for the object. Then, according to your needs, you can assign any new permission for the object that you want.

Assigning Active Directory Permissions

Windows 2000 determines a user's authorization to use an object by checking the DACL for permissions granted to the user on that object. To add or change permissions for an object, you would do the following:

1. In the Active Directory Users And Computers window, on the View menu, click Advanced Features.
2. Right-click the object, click Properties, and then in the Properties dialog box, click the Security tab.
3. Perform either or both of the following steps:
   - To add a new permission, click Add, click the user account or group to which you want to assign permissions, click Add, and then click OK.
   - To change an existing permission, click the user account or group.
4. In the Permissions box, select the Allow check box or the Deny check box for each permission that you want to add or remove.

Standard permissions are sufficient for most administrative tasks. However, you might need to view the special permissions that constitute a standard permission. To view special permissions, you would do the following:

1. On the Security tab in the Properties dialog box for the object, click the Advanced button.
2. In the Access Control Settings dialog box, on the Permissions tab, click the entry that you want to view, and then click View/Edit.
3. To view the permissions for specific attributes, click the Properties tab.

Note Avoid assigning permissions for specific attributes of objects because this can complicate system administration—errors can result, such as objects in Active Directory directory services not being visible, which could prevent users from completing tasks.

To modify inheritance of the permission, you would do the following:

1. On the Security tab in the Properties dialog box for the object, click the Advanced button.
2. In the Access Control Settings dialog box, on the Permissions tab, click the entry that you want to view, and then click View/Edit.
3. In the Apply Onto box, select the desired option from the menu.

Changing Object Ownership

Every object has an owner. The person who creates the object automatically becomes the owner. The owner controls the permissions assigned for an object and to whom permissions are assigned.

As an administrator, you can take ownership of any object and then change the permissions for the object. If a member of the Administrators group creates an object or takes ownership, the Administrators group is the owner, rather than the individual member of the group.

Ownership for an object changes when either of the following occurs:

- The current owner, or any user with the Full Control permission, grants the Modify Owner permission to another user who takes ownership of the object.

  For example, if an employee who owns an object leaves the company, you can let another user take ownership of that object, thereby reassigning responsibility for the object.

- A member of the Administrators group takes ownership of any object.

Note Although members of the Administrators group can take ownership of any object, members of the Administrators group cannot transfer ownership. This restriction assures accountability.

To take ownership of an object, you would do the following:

1. In the Properties dialog box for an object, on the Security tab, click the Advanced button.
2. Click the Owner tab, and then click your user account. (If you are a member of the Administrators group, you can also click Administrators. This will make the Administrators group the owner.)
3. Click OK, and then click OK again to take ownership.

Delegating Administrative Control of Active Directory Objects

The structure of Active Directory directory services lends itself to more efficient management through the delegation of administrative control over objects. You can use the Delegation Of Control wizard and customized Microsoft Management Consoles to give specific users the rights to perform various administrative and management tasks, thus decreasing your workload and reflecting your business's hierarchy by placing the responsibility for network resources on the appropriate individuals.

You delegate administrative control of objects by assigning tasks at the OU level, thus allowing users or groups of users to administer the following types of control:

- Assigning to a user the permissions to create or modify objects in a specific OU.
- Assigning to a user the permissions to modify specific permissions for the attributes of an object, such as assigning the permission to reset passwords on a user account.

Because tracking tasks (or permission to perform specific tasks) at the OU level is easier than tracking tasks on objects or object attributes, the most common method of delegating administrative control is to assign tasks (or permission to perform specific tasks) at the OU level. Assigning tasks at the OU level allows you to delegate administrative control for the objects that are contained within the OU.

For example, you can delegate administrative control for an OU to the appropriate manager. By delegating control of the OU to the manager, you can decentralize administrative operations and issues. This reduces your administration time and costs by distributing administrative control closer to its point of service.

You can use the Delegation Of Control wizard to assign permissions at the OU level. For more specialized permissions, you must manually assign permissions at the object level.

Using the Active Directory Users and Computers tool, right-click the OU for which you want to delegate control, and then click Delegate Control to start the wizard.

Table 5.5 describes the Delegation Of Control wizard options.

Table 5.5   Delegation Of Control Wizard Options

Option	Allows the user to set
Users Or Groups	The user accounts or groups to which you want to delegate control
Tasks To Delegate	The tasks to assign to the object or objects.

Creating Customized Administrative Tools

One of the new features in Windows 2000 is the ability to create custom administrative tools using the Microsoft Management Console (MMC). Once you have delegated administrative control of a portion of Active Directory directory services, you can create your own unique set of administrative tools and distribute them to the delegated administrators. Saved as .MSC files, these custom administrative tools can be sent by e-mail, stored in a shared folder, or posted on the Web. They can also be assigned to users, groups, or computers with Group Policy settings.

Creating Customized Consoles

You can create custom MMC consoles to meet your administrative requirements by combining snap-ins that you use to perform common administrative tasks into a single console. To open MMC with an empty console, click the Start button, click Run, type **mmc** in the Open box, and then click OK. Click New on the MMC Console menu, add the desired snap-ins and extensions, name the console, and then save it.

Table 5.6 describes when to use the different commands on the MMC Console menu.

Table 5.6   MMC Console Menu Commands

Use this command	When
New	You want to create a new custom MMC console.
Open	You want to use a saved MMC console.
Save or Save As	You want to use the MMC console later.
Add/Remove Snap-In	You want to add or remove one or more snap-ins and their associated extensions to or from an MMC console.
Options	You want to configure the console mode and create a custom MMC console.

Saving a Console in Author Mode

When you create an MMC console, you can set the mode in which it will open. To set the mode, on the Console menu, select Options. You can select Author Mode or User Mode.

When you save an MMC console in Author mode, you enable full access to all MMC functionality, which includes modifying the MMC console. By default, all new MMC consoles are saved in Author mode. You can use Author mode to do the following:

- Add or remove snap-ins
- Create new windows
- View all portions of the console tree
- Save MMC consoles

Saving a Console in User Mode

If you plan to distribute an MMC console to other administrators and you do not want them to be able to modify the MMC console, save the MMC console in User mode. When you set an MMC console to User mode, users cannot add snap-ins to, remove snap-ins from, or save the MMC console. There are three types of User modes, which allow different levels of access and functionality.

Table 5.7 describes the three types of User modes.

Table 5.7   User Mode Types

Use this	When
Full Access	You want to allow users to navigate between snap-ins, open new windows, and gain access to all portions of the console tree.
Limited Access, Multiple Window	You do not want to allow users to open new windows or gain access to a portion of the console tree. You do want to allow users to view multiple windows in the console.
Limited Access, Single Window	You do not want to allow users to open new windows or gain access to a portion of the console tree. You want to allow users to view only one window in the console.

Practice: Delegating Control

In this practice, you will review the default security settings on Active Directory components. Then you will delegate to a user control over objects in an OU.

Exercise 1: Reviewing Active Directory Permissions

In this exercise, you will review the default security settings on Active Directory components.

Note Do not change any security settings in Active Directory directory services unless you are specifically instructed to do so in this exercise. Making changes could result in losing access to portions of Active Directory directory services.

▶ **To create objects in Active Directory directory services**

1. Log on as Administrator.
2. Open the Active Directory Users and Computers tool.
3. Expand domain.com
4. Right-click domain.com, point to New, and then click Organizational Unit.
5. In the Name box, type Security, and then click OK.
6. In the Security OU, create a user account with the first name Assistant and user logon name Assistant@domain.com. Assign a password of *password* and accept the defaults for all other options.
7. In the same OU, create another user account with the first name Secretary and user logon name Secretary@domain.com. Assign a password of *password* and accept the defaults for all other options.

▶ **To view default Active Directory permissions for an OU**

1. On the View menu, ensure that the Advanced Features option is selected.
2. In the console tree, right-click Security, and then click Properties.
3. Click the Security tab.
4. In the following table, list the groups that have permissions for the Security OU. If an account has special permissions, just record Special Permissions in the table. You will need to refer to these permissions in the next exercise.

User account or group	Assigned permissions
Authenticated Users	
System	
Domain Admins	
Enterprise Admins	
Account Operators	
Print Operators	

Why are all permission check boxes for some groups blank?

Are any of the default permissions inherited from the domain, which is the parent object? How can you tell?

▶ **To view special permissions for an OU**

1. In the Security Properties dialog box, on the Security tab, click the Advanced button.

   The Access Control Settings For Security dialog box appears.

2. To view the permissions for Account Operators, in the Permission Entries box, click each entry for Account Operators, and then click View/Edit.

   The Permission Entry For Security dialog box appears.

   What object permissions are assigned to Account Operators? What can Account Operators do in this OU?

   Do any objects within this OU inherit the permissions assigned to the Account Operators group? Why or why not?

3. Close all open dialog boxes, and then log off.

Exercise 2: Delegating Control

In this exercise, you will delegate to a user control over objects in an OU. Refer to the table you completed in the previous exercise to answer the questions below.

▶ **To test current permissions**

1. Log on to your domain as Assistant using a password of *password.*

   Note If Windows 2000 displays a message that the local policy of your system does not permit you to interactively log on Assistant to your server, log on as Administrator, add your Assistant account to the Print Operators group, log off as Administrator, and then log on as Assistant again.

   ---

2. Open the Active Directory Users and Computers tool.

3. In the console tree, expand your domain, and then click Security.

   What user objects are visible in the Security OU?

Which permissions allow you to see these objects? (Hint: refer to your answers in the preceding exercise.)

Attempt to change the logon hours for Secretary. Were you successful? Why or why not?

Attempt to change the logon hours for Assistant. Were you successful? Why or why not?

4. Close the Active Directory Users and Computers tool and log off.

▶ **To use the Delegation Of Control wizard to assign Active Directory permissions**

1. Log on to your domain as Administrator with a password of *password*.

2. Open the Active Directory Users and Computers tool.

3. In the console tree, expand your domain.

4. Right-click Security, and then click Delegate Control.

5. In the Delegation Of Control wizard, click Next.

   The Delegation Of Control wizard displays the Users Or Groups page.

6. Click Add.

7. In the Select Users, Computers, Or Groups dialog box, click Assistant, click Add, and then click OK.

8. Click Next.

   The Delegation Of Control wizard displays the Tasks To Delegate page. If you only want to delegate control for certain types of tasks, such as managing printers, you can select one or more predefined tasks.

9. Click the Create, Delete, And Manage User Accounts option, and then click Next.

10. Click Finish.

11. Close the Active Directory Users And Computers window and log off.

▶   **To test delegated permissions**

1. Log on to your domain as Assistant, using a password of *password*.

2. Open the Active Directory Users And Computers tool.

3. In the console tree, expand your domain, and then click Security.

4. Attempt to change the logon hours for both user accounts in the Security OU. Were you successful? Why or why not?

5. Attempt to change the logon hours for a user account in the Users container. Were you successful? Why or why not?

6. Close the Active Directory Users And Computers window and log off.

Lesson Summary

Active Directory permissions provide security for resources by allowing you to control who can gain access to individual objects or object attributes, and the type of access that you will allow. Windows 2000 stores a list of user access permissions, called the discretionary access control list (DACL), for every object in Active Directory directory services. The DACL for an object lists who can access the object and the specific actions that each user can perform on the object.

You can allow or deny permissions. Denied permissions take precedence over any permissions that you otherwise allow for user accounts and groups. If you deny permission for a user to gain access to an object, the user will not have that permission, even if you allow the permission for a group of which the user is a member. You should deny permissions only when it is necessary to do so for a specific user who is a member of a group with allowed permissions.

When you assign permissions, you can select to apply the permissions to subobjects (child objects), which propagates the permissions to all of the subobjects for a given object. To indicate that permissions are inherited, the check boxes for inherited permissions are dimmed in the user interface. You can prevent permission inheritance so that a child object does not inherit permissions from its parent object. When you prevent inheritance, only the permissions that you explicitly assign to the object will apply.

Review

Here are some questions to help you determine if you have learned enough to move on to the next chapter. If you have difficulty answering these questions, please go back and review the material in this chapter before beginning the next chapter. The answers to these questions are located in Appendix A, "Questions and Answers."

1. What strategy should you apply when you use domain local and global groups?

2. What determines whether users can locate an object using the global catalog?

3. What happens to the permissions of an object when you move it from one OU to another OU?

4. You want to delegate administrative control of all computer accounts in an OU to a specific user. What is the simplest method for assigning the needed permissions?

5. You have the Read permission for the Sales OU. Can you create other OUs within Sales?

6. What is the difference between the naming requirements for user accounts and for computer accounts?

C H A P T E R 6

Managing Desktop Environments with Group Policy

About This Chapter

Group Policy is the Windows 2000 tool that allows an administrator to manage desktop environments throughout the network by applying configuration settings to computers and users within a site, domain, or organizational unit. Group policy settings are contained in Group Policy Objects. This chapter introduces the Group Policy tool and how to use group policy settings to manage the desktop environments on your Windows 2000 networks.

Before You Begin

To complete this chapter

- You must have a computer that meets or exceeds the minimum hardware requirements listed in "Getting Started," on page xxi.

- You must have installed the beta version of Windows 2000 Advanced Server on a computer meeting the specifications listed in the preceding bullet. The computer should be installed as a domain controller in a domain and TCP/IP should be the only installed protocol.

- Your computer should be using a static IP address.

Lesson 1: Understanding Group Policy

You can lower your network's total cost of ownership (TCO) by using Group Policy in Microsoft Windows 2000 to create a managed desktop environment that is tailored to the user's job responsibilities and experience level. TCO is the cost that is involved in administering distributed personal computer networks. Recent studies on TCO cite lost user productivity as one of the major costs to corporations. Lost productivity is often due to user error, such as modifying system configuration files and thereby rendering the computer unusable. Group Policy provides the network administrator with greater control over computer configurations, thus reducing the potential for lost user productivity.

After this lesson, you will be able to

- Explain the capabilities and structure of Group Policy, including Group Policy Objects (GPOs), Group Policy Containers (GPCs), and Group Policy Templates (GPTs).

Estimated lesson time: 15 minutes

Group Policy Settings

Group Policy in Windows 2000 allows an administrator to establish a requirement for a user or a computer once and have that requirement continually enforced. For example, the administrator can implement group policy settings that will run a startup script on all computers in an organizational unit (OU) or audit all failed logon attempts in a domain.

You use the Group Policy tool and its extensions in Microsoft Management Console (MMC) to define group policy settings for desktop configurations for computers and users. You can specify group policy settings with the following Group Policy extensions:

- **Administrative Templates.** The Administrative Templates extension adds a node that allows you to control the registry-based group policy settings that configure the application settings and customize desktop appearances and behavior of system services.

- **Security Configuration Editor.** The Security Configuration Editor extension adds a node to Group Policy that includes options for local computer, domain, and network security settings. These settings allow you to configure security levels for a Group Policy Object, the local computer, IP Security, and public keys policy. For example, policies applied to user accounts include password policy, account lockout policy and Kerberos policy.

- **Software Installation (Computers) and Software Installation (Users).** The Software Installation extensions allow you to control the central management of software including installation, updates, and removal.

- **Scripts (Logon/Logoff) and Scripts (Startup/Shutdown).** The Scripts extensions allow you to configure scripts for when a computer starts and shuts down and when a user logs on and logs off.
- **Folder Redirection.** The Folder Redirection extension allows you to redirect folders like My Documents to network locations, so that users' folders are stored on the network rather than on the user's local computer.
- **Remote Installation Services.** The Remote Installation Services extension allows you to predefine configuration options such as operating system selection and client computer naming conventions to provide better disaster recovery and easier operating system and application management.

Group Policy Objects

In Windows 2000, you create a Group Policy Object (GPO) and then configure the settings for that specific GPO. The GPO is a virtual storage location for the group policy settings. The contents of the GPO are stored in two different locations, the Group Policy Container and the Group Policy Template.

Group Policy Container

The Group Policy Container (GPC) is an Active Directory object that contains GPO attributes and includes subcontainers for group policy information about computers and users. The GPC includes the following information:

- **Version information.** Ensures that the information in the GPC synchronizes with the Group Policy Template information.
- **Status information.** Indicates whether the GPO is enabled or disabled.
- **List of components (extensions).** Lists any of the Group Policy extensions that are used in the GPO.

Group Policy Template

The Group Policy Template (GPT) is a folder hierarchy in the Sysvol folder on domain controllers. The GPT is the container for all group policy information on administrative templates, security, software installation, scripts, and folder redirection.

When you create a GPO, Windows 2000 creates the corresponding GPT folder hierarchy. The name of the GPT folder is the globally unique identifier (GUID) of the GPO that you created.

For example, if you associate a GPO with the domain domain.com, and the GPO is assigned a GUID of {A3A2C853-F033-11D1-9BE4-00C0DFE00C63}, the resulting GPT folder name would be *systemroot*\Sysvol\Sysvol\domain.com\ Policies\{A3A2C853-F033-11D1-9BE4-00C0DFE00C63}

Group Policy Inheritance

When you create a GPO, you associate it with a selected Active Directory container, such as a site, domain, or organizational unit. Within the hierarchical structure of the Active Directory directory services, child containers inherit GPOs from parent containers. You must understand the processing order of GPOs to plan your group policy implementation. You can filter the scope of the GPO and delegate control of a GPO with permissions. The attributes of a GPO offer you other options for managing how you apply group policy settings.

Group policy settings are inherited, cumulative, and affect all computers and user accounts in the Active Directory container with which the GPO is associated. You can associate multiple Active Directory containers with the same GPO and multiple GPOs with a single Active Directory container.

Understanding Order of Inheritance

Windows 2000 evaluates GPOs starting with the Active Directory container furthest away (highest up the hierarchical structure) from the computer or user. The order of group policy inheritance is site, domain, and then organizational unit. With this order, the GPOs of the OU that the computer or user is a member of are the final group policy settings that Windows 2000 applies to the computer or user.

This default behavior allows a group policy setting in the Active Directory container closest to the computer or user to override a conflicting group policy setting in a container that is higher up in the Active Directory hierarchy.

When a group policy setting is configured for a parent OU, and the same group policy setting is not configured for a child OU, the objects in the child OU inherit the group policy setting from the parent OU. However, a group policy setting can be configured in the GPO for both the parent and child OU. In that case, the compatibility of the group policy settings determines the result.

When the parent OU and child OU both have a configured group policy setting and the settings are compatible, the settings from both OUs apply. If a group policy setting that is configured for a parent OU is incompatible with the same group policy setting that is configured for a child OU, the child OU does not inherit the group policy setting from the parent, but retains its own group policy setting.

Note A GPO that is linked to a site affects all computers in that site, regardless of the domain to which the computers belong. The GPO, however, is only stored in one domain. Because a single site can include multiple domains, a GPO that is associated with a site can be inherited by computers in multiple domains. All computers in the site must contact a domain controller in the domain that contains the GPO. You should consider the network traffic implications when you create a site GPO.

Order of Processing GPO Settings

The group policy settings in a GPO are processed in a specific order. Some group policy settings for users can affect computers also. For example, the permission to use the Run command on the Start menu can affect computers and users both. By understanding the order in which Windows 2000 processes group policy settings, you can avoid overwriting settings.

The group policy settings are processed in the following sequence:

1. When the computer starts, group policy settings for computers process. This is done synchronously by default.

2. Startup scripts run synchronously by default. This means that each script must complete or time out before the next one will start.

3. When a user logs on, group policy settings for users process. This is also done synchronously by default.

4. Logon scripts run. Logon scripts in GPOs run asynchronously by default. If you have scripts that are associated with a user object, they run last.

Note You can modify the synchronous and asynchronous processing of both group policies and scripts with a group policy setting.

Windows 2000 periodically refreshes group policy settings throughout the network. This is done by default on client computers every 90 minutes with a randomized offset of plus or minus 30 minutes. For domain controllers, the default period is every 5 minutes. You can change the default values by modifying the settings in Administrative Templates. You cannot schedule the application of a GPO to the client computers.

Note The processing of software installation and folder redirection settings in a GPO occurs *only* when a computer starts or when the user logs on, rather than on a periodic basis.

Lesson Summary

The Windows 2000 Group Policy tool allows an administrator to manage desktop environments throughout the network by applying configuration settings to computers and users within a site, domain, or organizational unit. Group policy settings are contained in Group Policy Objects. A GPO is a virtual storage location for the group policy settings whose contents are stored in two different locations, the Group Policy Container and the Group Policy Template.

You use the Group Policy tool and its extensions in MMC to define group policy settings for desktop configurations for computers and users. The extensions available for Group Policy include Administrative Templates, Security Settings, Software Installation, Scripts, Folder Redirection, and Remote Installation Service. These extensions allow you to specify additional group policy settings. The settings contained in the GPOs are applied in a specific order. When the computer is started, the group policy settings for the computers process. Next any startup scripts run. When a user logs on, the group policy settings for users process, and finally, if there are any logon scripts, they run.

Lesson 2: Applying Group Policy

The first step in applying group policy is creating GPOs. Once you create or link a GPO, you should verify that the appropriate permissions are set. To successfully apply group policy you also must understand how GPOs are applied as well as the order of inheritance for GPOs, and be able to modify how they are applied and inherited.

After this lesson, you will be able to

- Apply group policy by creating a GPO, managing the access permissions of GPOs, and managing the inheritance of GPOs through the structure of Active Directory directory services.

Estimated lesson time: 20 minutes

Creating a GPO

The steps for creating a GPO or linking an existing GPO to an Active Directory container are shown in Figure 6.1; these steps are explained below.

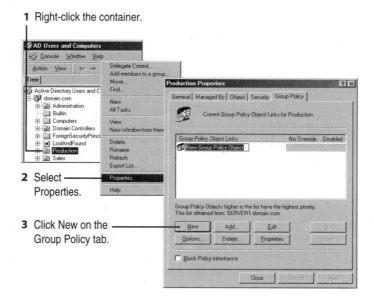

Figure 6.1 Creating a GPO

1. Open the Active Directory Users and Computers tool.
2. Right-click the Active Directory container (domain or OU) for which you want to create a GPO, and then click Properties.

3. On the Group Policy tab, choose New to create a new GPO, or choose Add to link an existing GPO.

The GPO that you create or link is displayed in the list of GPOs that are linked to the Active Directory container.

Note To create a GPO that is linked to a site, open the Active Directory Sites And Services snap-in and follow the previous procedure. By default, the site GPO is stored in the domain to which the creator of the GPO belongs. You can set another domain for the storage location when you create the site GPO. To change the storage location, click the Add button on the Group Policy tab, click the All tab in the Add A Group Policy Object Link dialog box, change the domain in the Look In box, and then create the GPO. You must be a member of the Enterprise Admins group to create a site GPO.

Managing GPO Permissions

After you create or link a GPO, you should verify that the appropriate permissions are set. The group policy settings in a GPO affect only users or computers that have the Apply Group Policy and Read permissions for that GPO. The default permissions are shown in Table 6.1.

Table 6.1   Default Permissions for a GPO

Group or account	Default permissions
Authenticated Users	Read Apply Group Policy
System Account Domain Admins Enterprise Admins	Read Write Create All Child Objects Delete All Child Objects

Modifying Permissions

To modify permissions for a GPO, you would do the following:

1. Open the Properties dialog box for the Active Directory container that is associated with the GPO.

2. On the Group Policy tab, select a GPO link and click Properties.

3. On the Security tab of the GPO's Properties dialog box, add or remove the Apply Group Policy permission for the desired objects by selecting or clearing the Allow check box (see Figure 6.2).

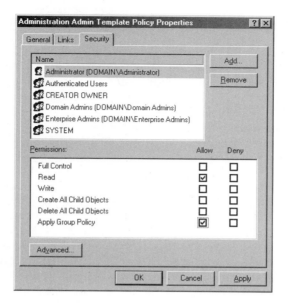

Figure 6.2 Modifying permissions for a GPO

Note When you set permissions on a GPO, select or clear the check boxes in the Allow column, rather than using the Deny column. Denying a permission always takes precedence over allowing a permission, and you might have inconsistent results if you use the Deny column.

Filtering the Scope of a GPO

You can filter the scope of a GPO by creating security groups and then assigning the Apply Group Policy and Read permissions to selected groups or removing the permissions from selected groups.

Delegating Control with Permissions

Members of the Domain Admins group can use permissions to identify which groups of administrators can modify policies in GPOs. To do this, the network administrator creates groups of administrators (for example, the Marketing Administrators group) and then assigns Read and Write permissions to selected GPOs for these groups. This allows the member of the Domain Admins group to delegate control of the GPO. Administrators with Read and Write permissions to a GPO can control all aspects of the GPO.

Managing Group Policy Inheritance

In addition to controlling the Read and Apply Group Policy permissions of a GPO, you can manage group policy by modifying inheritance options, disabling all or part of a GPO, and deleting a GPO.

Modifying Inheritance Options

You can modify the inheritance of a GPO by setting No Override, by changing the processing order of multiple GPOs, and by blocking Policy Inheritance.

- **No Override.** Use this option to prevent child containers from overriding a GPO that is set in a higher level GPO. This option is useful for enforcing group policy that represents companywide rules. The No Override option is set on a per-GPO basis. You may set this option on one or more GPOs as required. When more than one GPO is set as No Override, the GPO that is highest in the Active Directory hierarchy with a No Override option always takes precedence over the Block Policy Inheritance option. To set this option, on the Group Policy tab, click Options, and then select the No Override check box.

- **Changing the processing order of multiple GPOs.** The Group Policy tab lists the GPOs that are linked to the site, domain, or OU, and these GPOs are processed in order from bottom to top as listed on this tab. If incompatible group policy settings exist in different GPOs in the same site, domain, or OU, the group policy setting that is contained in the GPO that is higher in the list overrides the group policy settings that are contained in any other GPO. To change the order, select a GPO in the list and then use the Up button or the Down button to move the GPO within the list.

- **Block Policy Inheritance.** Use this option to allow a child container to block policy inheritance from parent containers. This option is useful when an OU requires unique group policy settings. The Block Policy Inheritance option applies to all GPOs from parent containers. In the case of a conflict, the No Override option always takes precedence over the Block Policy Inheritance option. To set this option, on the Group Policy tab, click Options, and then select the Block Policy Inheritance check box.

Disabling GPOs

You can disable the user settings of a GPO, the computer settings of a GPO, or the entire GPO.

When you create a GPO that only contains group policy settings for users, you should disable the computer settings to speed up the processing of the GPO. Conversely, when you create a GPO that only contains group policy settings for computers, you should disable the user settings. To disable the user or computer settings of a GPO, on the Group Policy tab, click Properties; click the General tab; and then click the Disable User Configuration Settings check box or the Disable Computer Configuration Settings check box (see Figure 6.3).

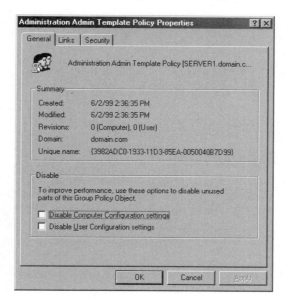

Figure 6.3   Disabling user or computer configuration settings

You can disable an entire GPO, which prevents it from being applied to the selected container. Disabling the GPO only affects its application to that container and any containers that inherit it. The GPO can still be linked to other containers and continues to apply to any containers to which it is linked, unless it is disabled in those containers as well. To disable the GPO, on the Group Policy tab, click Options and then click Disabled (see Figure 6.4).

Deleting GPOs

You can use Delete on the Group Policy tab to delete a GPO from a container. If the GPO is also associated with another Active Directory container, Delete removes the link from the selected container. If the GPO is only associated with the selected container, Delete permanently deletes the GPO.

Note Before you delete a GPO, you can verify which containers a GPO is linked to on the Links tab of the Properties dialog box for that GPO.

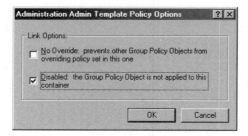

Figure 6.4   Disabling a GPO

Lesson Summary

The first step in applying group policy is creating GPOs. Use Active Directory Users And Computers to create a GPO, or to create a GPO that is linked to a site, use Active Directory Sites And Services. After you create or link a GPO, you should verify that the appropriate permissions are set. The group policy settings in a GPO affect only users or computers that have the Apply Group Policy and Read permissions for that GPO. In addition to controlling the Read and Apply Group Policy permissions of a GPO, you can manage group policy by modifying inheritance options, disabling all or part of a GPO, and deleting a GPO.

Lesson 3: Configuring Group Policy

You configure the group policy settings within a GPO by using the Group Policy tool and its extensions in MMC. The extensions in Group Policy display the configurable settings for administrative templates, scripts, security, and folder redirection, in addition to software installation and Remote Installation Services (RIS).

Note For information on the use of group policies for software installation, see Chapter 7, "Managing Software by Using Group Policy." For information on RIS, see Chapter 2, "Installing Windows 2000."

After this lesson, you will be able to

- Apply group policy by creating a GPO, managing the access permissions of GPOs, and managing the inheritance of GPOs through the structure of Active Directory directory services.
- Configure administrative templates, scripts, security, and folder redirection policies.

Estimated lesson time: 30 minutes

Group Policy Console

You use Group Policy in MMC to specify group policy settings for a GPO. The group policy settings are separated under Computer Configuration and User Configuration.

You can open Group Policy in two ways:

- On the Group Policy tab in the Properties dialog box for a site, domain, or OU, select the GPO that you want to view in Group Policy, and then click Edit.
- Add the Group Policy tool and any desired extensions to an MMC console and select the GPO you want to configure.

When you open Group Policy by clicking the Edit button, the Group Policy console opens. Figure 6.5 shows a Group Policy window with the Group Policy extensions expanded. When you manually add the Group Policy tool to an MMC console, you can select which extensions to include in the console that you create.

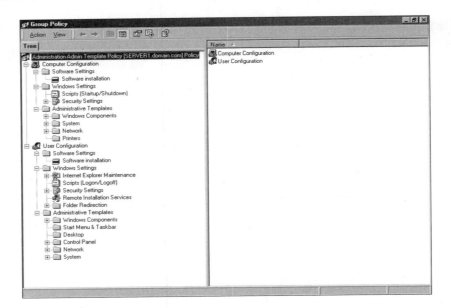

Figure 6.5   Group Policy nodes and extensions

Computer Configuration

Group policy settings that customize the desktop environment or enforce security policies on computers on the network are contained under the Computer Configuration node in the Group Policy window. Computer configuration policies apply when the operating system initializes.

Computer configuration settings include all computer-related policies that specify operating system behavior, desktop settings, application settings, security settings, assigned applications options, and computer startup and shutdown scripts.

User Configuration

Group policy settings that customize the user's desktop environment or enforce lockdown policies on users on the network are contained under the User Configuration node in the Group Policy window.

User configuration settings include all user-related policies that specify operating system behavior, desktop settings, application settings, security settings, assigned and published applications options, user logon and logoff scripts, and folder redirection options. User-related policies apply when users log on to the computer.

Settings Folders

The group policy settings in Computer Configuration and User Configuration are categorized into the following folders:

- Software Settings
- Windows Settings
- Administrative Templates

The subfolders and individual policies within each folder differ according to the item that you select. For example, Folder Redirection settings are displayed in the Windows Settings folder under User Configuration but not under Computer Configuration because folder redirection applies only to users.

Administrative Template Settings

The Administrative Templates extension includes all registry-based group policy information. Group policy settings that are specific to a user are written to the registry under HKEY_CURRENT_USER, and computer-specific settings are written under HKEY_LOCAL_MACHINE.

In previous versions of Windows, group policy settings remained in the registry until they were removed, either through an additional group policy setting or by directly editing the registry. Windows 2000, however, automatically removes group policy settings from the registry when the GPO that implemented the group policy no longer applies. To modify group policy settings in the Administrative Templates folder, you would do the following:

1. Open the GPO in Group Policy, expand Computer Configuration or User Configuration, and then expand the Administrative Templates folder.

2. Expand the item that represents the particular policy that you want to modify.

   For example, if you wanted to modify the desktop settings for a user, you would expand User Configuration\Administrative Templates\Desktop.

3. Once you have expanded the policy you want to modify, in the details pane, double-click the policy or right-click the policy, and then click Properties.

   You configure the group policy settings in the Administrative Templates folder by selecting the appropriate option:

   - If the Enabled option button on the Policy tab is selected, the setting is implemented. If this option was selected the last time that the user logged on, no changes are made (see Figure 6.6).

- ▪ If the Disabled option button on the Policy tab is selected, the setting is not implemented. If the group policy settings were previously implemented, they are removed from the registry (see Figure 6.6).

- ▪ If the Not Configured option button on the Policy tab is selected, Windows 2000 ignores the group policy setting and makes no changes to the computer (see Figure 6.6).

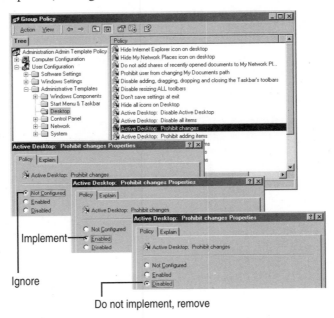

Figure 6.6   Modifying Administrative Template settings

You can move the Properties dialog box to one side so that you can see the group policy settings that are available and then use the Next Policy button and the Previous Policy button to move through the available group policies. In addition, the Properties dialog box has an Explain tab that provides detailed information regarding the purpose and use of individual group policy settings.

Script Settings

In previous versions of Windows NT, scripts were limited to logon scripts. In Windows 2000, the Group Policy tool allows you to assign scripts to both users and computers. For users, you can assign scripts that execute during the logon process, in addition to scripts that execute during the logoff process. For computers, you can assign scripts that execute during the startup process, in addition to scripts that execute during the shutdown process.

Windows 2000 Script Execution

Windows 2000 executes scripts according to the following rules:

- When you assign multiple logon/logoff or startup/shutdown scripts to a user or computer, the scripts are executed from top to bottom as listed in the corresponding Properties dialog box.

- When a computer shuts down, Windows 2000 first processes logoff scripts and then processes shutdown scripts.

- By default, the timeout value for processing scripts is two minutes. If a script requires more than two minutes to process, you must adjust the timeout value by modifying the wait time in the following location: Computer Configuration\Administrative Templates\System\Logon\.

Group Policy Settings for Scripts

The Scripts extension allows you to configure startup and shutdown scripts for a computer and logon and logoff scripts for a user. To set group policy settings for scripts, you would do the following:

1. Open the appropriate GPO in Group Policy.
2. Under either Computer Configuration (for startup and shutdown scripts) or User Configuration (for logon and logoff scripts), expand the Windows Settings folder.
3. Click the Scripts folder.
4. Right-click the appropriate script type (startup, shutdown, logon, or logoff) in the details pane, and then click Properties.
5. In the Properties dialog box, click Add, click Browse, select the script that you copied in the previous step, and then click Open.
6. Add any necessary script parameters, and then click OK. Then close the Properties dialog box.

Note Windows 2000 still enables you to assign scripts to users in the Properties dialog box for user objects; however, using the Group Policy tool is the preferred method of assigning scripts.

Practice: Implementing Administrative Templates and Script Policies

In this practice you will implement administrative templates.

Exercise 1: Creating a GPO

In this exercise, you will create a GPO at the domain level.

▶ **To create a GPO**

1. Log on as Administrator.
2. Open the Active Directory Users and Computers tool.
3. Expand domain.com.
4. Right-click Administration, and then click Properties.
5. On the Group Policy tab, click New.
6. Type **Administration Admin Template Policy** and then press Enter.

   Administration Admin Template Policy appears in the list of Group Policy Object Links.
7. Close the Administration Properties dialog box.

   Leave the Active Directory Users And Computers window open.

▶ **To create and allow the ADAdmin user to modify the GPOs in the Administration OU**

1. Create a user account named ADAdmin with a password of *password* in the Administration OU. Make ADAdmin a member of the Print Operators group.

   Note By making ADAdmin a member of the Print Operators group, ADAdmin can log on to the domain controller.
   ---

2. On the View menu, click Advanced Features (or ensure that it is active).
3. Right-click Administration, and then click Properties.
4. On the Security tab, add the ADAdmin user and grant both Read and Write permissions.
5. Click Advanced, click ADAmin, and then click View/Edit.
6. In the Apply Onto box, click This Object And All Child Objects, click OK, and then click OK to return to the Administration Properties dialog box.
7. Click OK to close the Administration Properties dialog box.
8. Leave Active Directory Users And Computers open.

▶ **To modify OU policy inheritance**

1. Right-click Production, and then click Properties.
2. On the Group Policy tab, click the Block Policy Inheritance check box, and then click OK.

    This setting will block all policy from parent containers.

3. Right-click Administration, and then click Properties.
4. On the Group Policy tab, right-click Administration Admin Template Policy, and then click No Override.
5. Click OK.

▶ **To create a custom administrative tool for the ADAdmin user**

1. Start the mmc.exe command from the Run dialog box.
2. On the Console menu, click Add/Remove Snap-In.
3. In the Add/Remove Snap-In dialog box, click Add, click Active Directory Users And Computers, click Add, and then click Close.
4. Click OK.

    Active Directory Users And Computers appears in the console pane below the console root.

5. Expand Active Directory Users And Computers, and then expand domain.com.
6. Right-click Administration, and then click New Window From Here.

    A new window appears with Administration as the root node.

7. Close the original Console Root window.
8. On the Console menu, click Options.
9. On the Console tab, change the name of the window to ADAdmin, and then in the Console Mode list, select User Mode – Limited Access, Single Window.
10. Click Do Not Save Changes To This Console, and then click OK.
11. On the Console menu, click Save As, and then in the Save In list click the drive C icon. Browse to C:\Documents and Settings\All Users\Start Menu\Programs\Administrative Tools in the list.
12. Type **ADAdmin** in the File Name box, and then click Save.
13. Close the ADAdmin console.

Exercise 2: Implementing Group Policy

In this exercise, you will implement Group Policy.

▶ **To set the required restrictions in Administrative Templates**

1. Open the Administration Properties dialog box.

2. On the Group Policy tab, click Administration Admin Template Policy, and then click Edit.

3. Expand User Configuration, and then expand the Administrative Templates folder.

4. Click Start Menu & Taskbar, and then double-click Remove Run Menu From Start Menu.

   The Remove Run Menu From Start Menu Properties dialog box appears.

5. On the Policy tab, click the Enabled option button.

6. Click OK.

   Notice that the value in the Setting column for this policy has changed to Enabled.

7. Using the following table, enable the remainder of the required restrictions:

Node	Policy
Start Menu & Taskbar	Disable Changes To Control Panel Settings
Desktop	Hide My Network Places Icon On Desktop
Windows Components\ Windows Explorer	Remove The "Map Network Drive" And "Disconnect Network Drive" Options

8. Close the Group Policy window, and then click OK to close the Administration Properties dialog box.

9. Close the Active Directory Users and Computers tool and log off.

Exercise 3: Testing Group Policy

In this exercise, you will log on as the ADAdmin user to test the group policy settings implemented in Exercise 2.

▶ **To test Group Policy**

1. Log on as ADAdmin with a password of *password*.

   Were the following restrictions enforced? Why or why not?

   No Run command on the Start menu.

   No access to Control Panel from the Start menu.

   No My Network Places icon on the desktop.

No Map Network Drive or Disconnect Network Drive on the Tools menu in Windows Explorer.

2. Log off.

Exercise 4: Removing Group Policy

In this exercise, you will remove the GPOs you created in the previous exercises.

▶ **To remove the GPOs**

1. Log on as Administrator.
2. Open the Active Directory Users and Computers tool.
3. Open the Administration Properties dialog box for the Administration OU.
4. On the Group Policy tab, click Administration Admin Template Policy, and then click Delete.

   The Delete dialog box appears.
5. Click Remove The Link And Delete The Group Policy Object Permanently, and then click OK.
6. When prompted to confirm the deletion, click Yes.
7. Click Close.
8. Close Active Directory Users And Computers and restart your computer.

Lesson Summary

You configure the group policy settings within a GPO by using the Group Policy snap-in and its extensions in MMC. The extensions in Group Policy display the configurable settings for administrative templates, scripts, security, and folder redirection, in addition to software installation and Remote Installation Services (RIS).

Group policy settings that customize the desktop environment or enforce security policies on computers on the network are contained under Computer Configuration in Group Policy. Computer configuration policies apply when the operating system initializes. Computer configuration settings include all computer-related policies that specify operating system behavior, desktop settings, application settings, security settings, assigned applications options, and computer startup and shutdown scripts.

Group policy settings that customize the user's desktop environment or enforce lockdown policies on users on the network are contained under User Configuration in Group Policy. User configuration settings include all user-related policies that specify operating system behavior, desktop settings, application settings, security settings, assigned and published applications options, user logon and logoff scripts, and folder redirection options. User-related policies apply when users log on to the computer.

The way that you implement group policy depends on the structure of your organization and network. However there are some general guidelines you should follow. Limit the use of the Block Policy Inheritance and No Override options. Also limit the use of GPOs linked across domains, and limit the number of GPOs that affect any given user or computer. Computer startup and user logon time are affected by the number of GPOs that must be processed. Make use of security groups to filter the effect of group policies because this will reduce the number of GPOs to be processed. Also disable the unused portion of a GPO. This will speed up the processing of GPOs.

Review

Here are some questions to help you determine if you have learned enough to move on to the next chapter. If you have difficulty answering these questions, please go back and review the material in this chapter before beginning the next chapter. The answers to these questions are located in Appendix A, "Questions and Answers."

1. Where do GPOs store group policy information?

2. In what order are GPOs implemented through the structure of Active Directory directory services?

3. Your company has decided to implement some restrictions on what users can and cannot do on their desktops. These restrictions need to be applied to all users in your single domain, with the exception of members of the Software Development group. If the Software Development group had their own organizational unit, how would you accomplish this? How would you accomplish this if all user accounts in the domain, including members of the Software Development group, were in the Users container?

CHAPTER 7

Managing Software by Using Group Policy

About This Chapter

Microsoft Windows 2000 includes a new technology called Software Installation and Maintenance that you use to deploy and manage software. It uses Group Policy and the new Windows Installer to allow you to reduce the amount of time spent deploying and managing software. This chapter covers how to use the Software Installation and Maintenance technology to deploy and manage software.

Before You Begin

To complete this chapter

- You must have a computer that meets or exceeds the minimum hardware requirements listed in "Getting Started," on page xxi.

- You must have installed the beta version of Windows 2000 Advanced Server on a computer meeting the specifications listed in the preceding bullet. The computer should be installed as a domain controller in a domain and TCP/IP should be the only installed protocol.

- Your computer should be using a static IP address.

Lesson 1: Introducing the Software Installation and Maintenance Technology

Windows 2000 ships with Microsoft Windows Installer and the Software Installation and Maintenance technology. Both are designed to help you deploy and manage software throughout an organization. This lesson helps you to understand the differences between them.

After this lesson, you will be able to

- Explain how the Microsoft Windows 2000 Software Installation and Maintenance technology uses Group Policy and its Software Installer node to manage software.
- Explain the four phases of the software life cycle: preparation, deployment, maintenance, and removal.

Estimated lesson time: 10 minutes

Windows Installer

Windows Installer introduces a file format, the Windows Installer package or .MSI file, which replaces the Setup.exe file. It also introduces a higher level of sophistication to software installation and maintenance. The benefits of Windows Installer include the following:

- **Custom installations that can be performed only when they are required.** For example, optional features in an application, such as clip art or a thesaurus, can be visible in a program without being installed. Although the menu commands will be accessible, the feature itself will not be installed until the user accesses the menu command. This method of installation helps reduce both the complexity of the application and the amount of hard disk space used by the application.
- **Resilient applications.** If a critical file is deleted or becomes corrupt, the application will automatically return to the installation source and acquire a new copy of the file, without the need for user intervention.
- **Clean removal.** Applications are uninstalled without leaving orphaned files and without inadvertently breaking another application (for example, by deleting a shared file required by another program).

These benefits are not limited to Windows 2000. Versions of Windows Installer will also be available for Windows NT 4.0, Windows 95, and Windows 98. However, using Windows 2000 does give administrators one major advantage: by combining the Windows Installer package files with the Software Installation and Maintenance technology, administrators can easily deploy and manage software throughout their entire organization.

The Software Installation and Maintenance technology uses Group Policy to deploy and manage software that has been packaged in the Windows Installer package file format.

Software Installation and Maintenance Technology

The Windows 2000 Software Installation and Maintenance technology allows you to deploy and manage software with Group Policy and Active Directory directory services. After an organization has obtained a Windows Installer package file, an administrator can create Group Policy Objects (GPOs) that are associated with the package file. These GPOs can do the following:

- Install applications on user computers. This can be done automatically, when a user logs on or a computer is turned on, or these applications can be made available for users to install when they need them.
- Upgrade a previous version of the application, or automatically apply software patches or service packs.
- Remove applications.

Most important, you can manage and deploy software without visiting the computer of every user in the organization. By working with Windows Installer package files, administrators can handle most software deployment and management tasks through the use of Group Policy.

Note The Software Installation and Maintenance technology operates using Group Policy. Therefore, these deployment and management features are only available for Windows 2000 clients. If you have client computers running other operating systems, you will need to replace or supplement the Software Installation and Maintenance technology with another deployment solution.

Software Life Cycle

The Software Installation and Maintenance technology allows the distribution of software in a manner that more closely aligns with the typical software life cycle. Instead of managing software manually, Group Policy can be used to install, modify, repair, and remove software more efficiently. To better understand how these new software deployment and management technologies function, it is useful to examine the four phases of the software life cycle: preparation, deployment, maintenance, and removal.

Preparation Phase

The preparation phase occurs before software is actually deployed to users or computers. For Windows 2000, this involves two key processes: package acquisition and package modification.

Package Acquisition

The Software Installation and Maintenance technology can only deploy and manage Windows Installer package files. This means you must have a package file for an application before that application can be deployed using Group Policy. Administrators have the following three options for acquiring package files:

- Obtain a package file from a software vendor.
- Repackage an application (create a package file using repackaging software).
- Create a text file with the .ZAP extension. These text files enable you to publish an application using Group Policy and are discussed later in this chapter.

Package Modifications

Modifications are similar to Windows Installer package files but have an .MST file extension. Modifications allow you to take one product (for example, Microsoft Excel), and create any number of custom installations. For example, you might create a version of Excel that leaves out the statistical analysis components for a human resource department and a second version that includes the statistical analysis components for an accounting department. You can then create GPOs, assign these different versions to different users, and install the software without requiring a technician to sit at each computer and specify the installation options.

Deployment Phase

In the deployment phase, software is actually installed on computers. Windows 2000 provides the following options for software deployment:

- **Assigning applications.** When an application is assigned to a user, that application is advertised on the computer desktop. Advertised applications aren't actually installed, but they *appear* as though they have been installed. A Start menu shortcut, desktop icons, and registry entries (for example, file associations) are created.

  The user can install the software by clicking the Start menu shortcut, double-clicking the desktop icon, or double-clicking a document type associated with that application (document invocation). Unless the user activates the installation, the application is not installed, which saves valuable hard disk space and administration time.

- **Publishing applications.** When an application is published, it is not advertised on the user desktop. However, users can install the application either through Add/Remove Programs or through document invocation.

Maintenance Phase

Windows 2000 makes it easy to upgrade or redeploy software. For example, suppose a service pack has been issued for your organization's word processing program. As an administrator, you place the service pack on the network, and modify a GPO to redeploy the application. The next time a user activates the program, the service pack will automatically be applied. There is no need to individually visit each workstation and install the service pack.

Removal Phase

Windows 2000 offers two methods for automatically removing applications:

- **Forced removal.** With a forced removal, software is automatically deleted from a computer, either the next time the computer is turned on (in the case of a computer policy), or the next time a user logs on (in the case of a user policy).

- **Optional removal.** With an optional removal, software is not automatically uninstalled from computers. For example, if a user already has Microsoft Word 97 installed, the user will be able to continue running that application. However, no new users will be able to install Word 97.

Lesson Summary

Microsoft Windows 2000 includes a new technology called Software Installation and Maintenance. It uses Group Policy and the new Windows Installer to reduce the amount of time you spend deploying and managing software. The Windows Installer package replaces the Setup.exe file and provides custom installations that can be performed only when they are required. It also makes applications resilient; if a critical file is deleted or becomes corrupt, the application will automatically return to the installation source and acquire a new copy of the file, without the need for user intervention. Applications are uninstalled without leaving orphaned files and without inadvertently breaking another application (for example, by deleting a shared file required by another program).

After you obtain a Windows Installer package file, you can create Group Policy objects (GPOs) that are associated with the package file. The Windows 2000 Software Installation and Maintenance technology allows you to deploy and manage software with Group Policy and Active Directory directory services. You can automatically install applications on user computers, upgrade previous versions of the application or apply software patches or service packs, and remove applications. Most important, you can manage and deploy software without visiting the computer of every user in the organization.

To help you understand how these new software deployment and management technologies function, this lesson examined the four phases of the software life cycle: preparation, deployment, maintenance, and removal. All of these four phases are handled by the Windows 2000 Software Installation and Maintenance technology.

Lesson 2: Deploying Software

In the past, deploying software required considerable time and effort. A technician had to visit each computer and perform the installation. Whenever the organization changed its software policy or the job responsibilities for a user, a technician had to provide the user with a revised set of applications. If a user did something to render a program inoperable, a technician had to visit the computer to make repairs.

The Software Installation and Maintenance technology helps to solve these problems by enabling software to be deployed and managed remotely. This is achieved by using the Software Installation node, which is an extension to Group Policy.

After this lesson, you will be able to

- Explain how to deploy software using Software Installation group policies.

Estimated lesson time: 30 minutes

Deploying New Applications

Deploying a new application involves a number of steps. These steps include acquiring the Windows Installer package file and placing the package and any related installation files in a shared folder on your network. The package file will be the .MSI file used by the Windows Installer. The related installation files are the application files that will be installed on the local hard disk. Once you have set up a shared folder on your network that contains the package and the required installation files, use the Active Directory Users and Computers tool to specify deployment options in one or more GPOs. To deploy a new application, you would do the following:

1. In Active Directory Users And Computers, right-click the OU and then click Properties.
2. In the OU's Properties dialog box, click the Group Policy tab, select a policy, and then click Edit.
3. In the new Group Policy window, double-click either Computer Configuration (if you want to deploy the application to a computer) or User Configuration (if you want to deploy the application to a user).
4. Double-click Software Settings.
5. Right-click Software Installation (see Figure 7.1), point to New, and then click Package.

   The Open dialog box appears.
6. Locate the package file, and then click Open.

   The Deploy Software dialog box appears.
7. Select a deployment method and then click OK.

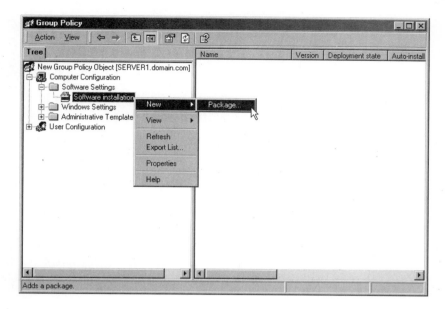

Figure 7.1 Displaying and selecting the Software Installation node in Group Policy

---

Note You can assign, publish, or disable an application using Software Installation defaults. Or you can select Configure Package Properties to bring up the package file's Properties dialog box, which allows you to set additional options for deployment.

Using Gradual Deployment

As with any new software installation, it is a good idea to start off slowly and do some testing before you deploy the software to the entire organization. To reduce the risk of deploying package files that do not work or do not meet your organization's needs, it is a good idea to deploy them gradually. It is best to ensure that a package file will install properly before releasing an application to the entire organization. Because application deployments are GPOs, you can use Group Policy to limit your deployment to particular groups.

When you create an application deployment GPO there are several things you should do:

1. Remove the Apply Group Policy permission for the Authenticated User group; be sure to remove the permission, but do not deny permission. If you do not remove this permission, the GPO will automatically be applied to all authenticated users in the Active Directory container.

2. Create a security group, for example Pilot Test1, and give this group the Read and Apply Group Policy permissions.

3. Apply the group policy, and make sure the Pilot Test1 group can install the software without any problem.

4. If they can, you can then reinstate the Apply Group Policy permission for the Authenticated User group. This will enable installation for all members of the Active Directory container.

Assigning Software Packages

Software is usually assigned when an application is required for a user to do his or her job. For example, you might assign Excel to the accounting group because accountants need this program to do their work. By assigning a software package to a user or group of users, you ensure that

- The application will always be available to the user, even if he or she logs on from a different computer. If the user logs on to a computer that does not have Excel, Excel will be installed when the user activates the program.

- The application will be resilient. If the software is deleted for any reason, it will be reinstalled the next time the user logs on and activates the program.

Assigning Software to Users

When you assign an application to a user, the program is advertised when the user logs on, but installation does not take place until the first time the user starts the application, by selecting it from the Start menu or by double-clicking an icon or a file type associated with the application (document invocation). If the user does not activate the program using one of these methods, the application will not be installed, which saves hard disk space and administrative load.

By initially only advertising applications, you can minimize the impact on the local hard disk while keeping applications available to the user at all times. For example, if a user logs on to another computer to briefly check her e-mail, you probably don't want all of the applications associated with her account to be installed on the computer that she is using just to check her e-mail. To assign an application to users, you would do the following:

1. Log on as Administrator and start the Active Directory Users and Computers tool.

2. Expand the domain containing the users to whom you want to assign an application.

3. If no GPO exists, right-click the OU containing the users; click Properties; and on the Group Policy tab, click the New button, type the name for the GPO, and then press Enter.

   The new GPO will appear in the list of Group Policy Object Links.

4. Select the appropriate GPO, and then click the Edit button.

5. Expand User Configuration, expand the Software Settings node, and then click the Software Installation node.

6. Right-click the Software Installation node, point to New, and then click Package.

7. In the File Name box, type the appropriate path to the package, and then click Open.

8. In the Deploy Software dialog box, click Assigned, and then click OK.

   The deployed application will appear in the list of deployed applications.

Assigning Software to Computers

By assigning a software package to a computer, you ensure that certain applications will be available on that computer regardless of who is using it. For example, a classroom used for Microsoft Office 2000 training would require Office 2000 installations on all of the computers. In cases like this, you would create the GPO under Computer Configuration rather than User Configuration.

When you assign an application to a computer, no advertising takes place. Instead, when the computer is turned on, the software is installed automatically.

Note When in doubt as to whether to assign an application to users or to computers, assign it to users. For example, sometimes you are hesitant about installing an application because you don't know if the user will actually use the program. In this case, it would be best to assign the application to the user. The application is advertised, but no files are copied and hard disk space is not wasted. If the user never starts the program, the adaptive menus in Windows 2000 will eventually hide the Start menu shortcuts, helping to reduce Start menu clutter and complexity.

The steps for assigning an application to computers is almost identical to the steps for assigning an application to users. To assign an application to computers, perform the steps for assigning an application to users and in step 5 expand Computer Configuration instead of expanding User Configuration.

Publishing Software Packages

When an application is published, it is not installed or advertised. However, the software is readily available, and a user can install an application in one of two ways: by using Add/Remove Programs or by using document invocation.

Using Add/Remove Programs

As in previous versions of Windows, when you start Control Panel and double-click the Add/Remove Programs icon, the set of programs available to you is displayed. You can then select the desired program and install the software. Many organizations set up shared folders, place the Setup files there, and allow users to connect to the network to install software themselves.

The new version of Add/Remove Programs includes the following improvements:

- **Provides friendly names for installation.** Users see names like *Microsoft Office 97* rather than names like \\ *Server1\ Msofc97 \ Setup.exe*.

- **Centralizes distribution.** Users can install all of their software using Add/Remove Programs without having to know the network locations for each Setup file.

- **Uses Windows Installer package files.** Windows Installer allows setup to be done with minimal user intervention.

- **Respects the access permissions placed on a package file.** If a user has permission to install Word and Excel, but not Microsoft PowerPoint, then only Word and Excel will appear in Add/Remove Programs.

Using Document Invocation

In Windows 2000, if a user double-clicks an unknown file type, the following steps take place:

1. The computer sends a query to Active Directory directory services to see if there are any applications associated with the file extension.

2. If Active Directory directory services contain such an application, the computer then checks to see if this application has either been published or assigned to the user.

3. If the application has been published or assigned to the user, the computer then checks to see if the application is set for Auto-Install This Application By File Extension Activation (which allows it to be installed automatically through document invocation).

4. If the administrator has set the application to Auto-Install, the application is installed.

Publishing Applications vs. Assigning Applications

In order to use Software Installation properly, it is important to understand the differences between publishing and assigning an application. The differences between published and assigned applications are as follows:

- **Published applications are not advertised.** There is no obvious way of knowing that a published application is available without starting Add/Remove Programs or double-clicking an unknown file type.

- **Published applications are not resilient.** If a published application is deleted, it will not automatically reinstall itself the next time a user logs on.

- **Applications can only be published to users, not computers.**

Using .ZAP Files

Software Installation normally works only with Windows Installer package files. However, you can get around this requirement by creating a text file, known as a .ZAP file for ZAW (Zero Administration Initiative for Windows) down-level application packages, that provides instructions for deploying the application. You should only use .ZAP files to publish applications when it is not feasible to use repackaging software to repackage an application and when a Windows Installer package file from a software vendor is unavailable.

A .ZAP file is a text file that can be parsed and executed by Software Installation. These files allow you to publish non–Windows Installer applications with the following limitations:

- The applications cannot be assigned to either users or computers. They can only be published.

- The applications do not automatically repair themselves when key files have been deleted or become corrupted. Instead, the application will invoke and rerun its setup program any time it is unable to start.

- The applications are rarely able to install without user intervention. These applications run the software's original setup program, and few of these programs support an unattended installation.

- The applications do not have the ability to install with elevated privileges. If you intend to deploy .ZAP files, users must have permission to install software on their local computers. Native package files install using the privileges assigned to the Windows Installer. This allows package files to be installed on computers regardless of the user's privileges. In other words, security is based on the GPO that deployed the application rather than on the individual user's security rights.

A .ZAP file can be created with Notepad or any other text editor. The file itself has two primary sections: the Application section [Application] and the File Extensions section [Ext].

Application Section

The Application section includes information on how to install the program in addition to information that will be displayed to users in Software Installation and in Add/Remove Programs. Your .ZAP file must include the FriendlyName and SetupCommand tags. All other tags within this section are optional. Optional tags add information about the program to Software Installation and Add/Remove Programs. The tags in the following example are explained in Table 7.1.

```
[Application]
FriendlyName = Microsoft Office 97
SetupCommand = setup.exe /unattend
DisplayVersion = 8.0
Publisher = Microsoft
URL = http://www.microsoft.com/office
```

Table 7.1   Application Section Tags

Tag	Comment
FriendlyName	The name that will be used in Software Installation and in Add/Remove Programs. Friendly names should be in the format of *Microsoft Office 97,* not executable file names like *Setup.exe.*
SetupCommand	The command used to install the application. The path should be relative to the .ZAP file. If the setup command is in the same folder as the .ZAP file, you only need to list the setup executable file name (for example, Setup.exe).
DisplayVersion	The version number of the program, as shown in Software Installation and in Add/Remove Programs.
Publisher	The publisher of the application, as shown in Software Installation and in Add/Remove Programs.
URL	The URL shown in Software Installation and in Add/Remove Programs. This should be a Web page that contains additional information about the application.

File Extension Section

The File Extensions section is optional. Include this section to associate the application with the file extensions saved in Active Directory directory services. To add this section, type the **[Ext]** heading, followed by a list of file extensions associated with the application (you do not have to type the period before the extension):

```
[Ext]
DOC=
DOT=
```

When an application is deployed with the .ZAP file, the contents of the .ZAP file will be parsed, and the application and its associated file extensions will be added to Active Directory directory services.

Performing Software Modifications

The various departments in your organization will use applications in different ways, and they might need customizations or options available when the application is deployed. For example, an international organization would like to deploy Word 2000 but there are large segments of the organization that require localized dictionaries. Rather than requiring local administrators to manually configure their users' computers with the local dictionary, you can use software modifications, or .MST files, to simultaneously deploy several different configurations of one application.

You create a separate GPO for each OU needing a different modification of the application. For example, you would create a Software Installation GPO in the Paris OU and apply a modification to it that installs the French dictionary. You would also create a GPO in the Bonn OU and apply the .MST file that installs the German dictionary.

Note You can add and remove modifications only during deployment of a package, not after the deployment has occurred.

To add modifications to an application package, you would do the following:

1. While you are adding a new package to a GPO or before the package has been deployed, click the Modifications tab in the application package's Properties dialog box.
2. On the Modifications tab, click Add and in the Open dialog box, select the path and filename of the modification file (.MST).
3. To complete the process, click Open, and then click OK.

You can add multiple modifications. The modifications are applied according to the order you specify in the Modifications list. You can arrange the order of the modifications in the list by selecting a modification from the list and using the Move Up button or the Move Down button.

Lesson Summary

The Software Installation and Maintenance technology helps reduce your total cost of ownership (TCO) by enabling software to be deployed and managed remotely. This is achieved by using Software Installation, which is an extension to Group Policy. To deploy a new application you must acquire the Windows Installer package file, and place the package and any related installation files in a shared folder on your network. The package file will be the .MSI file used by the Windows Installer. After you set up a shared folder containing the package and the required installation files, you use the Active Directory Users and Computers tool to specify deployment options in one or more GPOs.

When you deploy an application, you can assign it or publish it. Software is usually assigned when an application is required for a user to do his or her job. By assigning a software package to a user or group of users, you ensure that the application will always be available to the user, even if he or she logs on from a different computer. The application will also be resilient, so that if the software is deleted for any reason, it will be reinstalled the next time the user logs on and activates the program.

When you assign an application to a user, the program is advertised when the user logs on, but installation does not take place until the first time the user starts the application, by selecting it from the Start menu or by double-clicking an icon or a file type associated with the application (document invocation). If the user does not activate the program using one of these methods, the application will not be installed, which saves hard disk space and administrative load. By assigning a software package to a computer, you ensure that certain applications will be available on that computer regardless of who is using it. When you assign an application to a computer, no advertising takes place. Instead, when the computer is turned on, the software is installed automatically.

Software Installation normally works only with Windows Installer package files. However, you can create a text file (known as a .ZAP file for ZAW down-level application packages) that provides instructions for deploying the application. You should only use .ZAP files to publish applications when it is not feasible to use repackaging software to repackage an application and when a Windows Installer package file from a software vendor is unavailable. A .ZAP file cannot be assigned to either users or computers. A .ZAP file can only be published.

Lesson 3: Upgrading Software

You must be able to upgrade users' software to ensure that users' computers have the most current version of an organization's software. There are two types of upgrades: mandatory and optional. Knowing how to deploy both mandatory and optional upgrades helps you to keep existing software installations current. You should also understand the requirements and implications of upgrading software and know when to make an upgrade mandatory or optional.

After this lesson, you will be able to:
- Explain how to upgrade software using Software Installation group policies.
- Explain how to remove software using Software Installation group policies.

Estimated lesson time: 30 minutes

Deploying Mandatory Upgrades

Mandatory upgrades automatically replace an older version of a program with the upgraded version. For example, if users are currently using version 3.0 of a program, this version will be removed, and version 4.0 of the program will be installed.

To deploy a mandatory upgrade, in Software Installation, right-click the new version and click Properties. In the package file's Properties dialog box, select the Upgrades tab. In the Packages That This Package Will Upgrade section, click Add, and then select the older version of the program that you want to upgrade. If both versions of the program are native Windows Installer packages, this step will be done automatically because native Windows Installer packages detect the native package files that they update. If the older version has been installed, it will be replaced with the newer version the next time that the user activates the program. You can use this same strategy to change from one vendor's product to another.

Deploying Optional Upgrades

Optional upgrades allow users to use either the old or the new version of a program. After an optional upgrade, users can also install and use both versions of the application simultaneously. To deploy an optional upgrade, right-click the new version in Software Installation and click Properties. Then select the Upgrades tab in the package file's Properties dialog box.

In the Packages That This Package Will Upgrade section, click Add, and then select the older version of the program. If both versions of the program are native Windows Installer packages, this step will be done automatically. Clear the Required Upgrade For Existing Packages check box, and then click OK.

If the older version has been installed, existing shortcuts will still launch the older version. The next time the user logs on, the user can install either version from Add/ Remove Programs. Document invocation will only install the newer version if the GPO deploying the newer version has the highest order of precedence.

If the older version has not yet been installed, the next time that the user logs on, advertised shortcuts will start an installation of the newer version. The user can install either version from Add/Remove Programs, and document invocation will only install the later version if the GPO deploying the later version has the highest order of precedence.

If you want new users to install the newer version of the program but don't want to uninstall the application for people who are currently using the older version of the program, deploy the newer version as an optional upgrade, and then disable the older version. Disabling software is discussed later in this chapter.

Redeploying Software

Windows 2000 makes deploying service packs and software patches remarkably easy. When you mark a package file for redeployment, the application is readvertised to everyone who has been granted access to the program, either through assigning or publishing. Then, depending on how the original package was deployed, one of three things happen:

- If the application was published and installed, the Start menu, desktop shortcuts, and registry settings relevant to that application will be updated the next time that the user logs on. The first time that the user starts the application, the service pack or software patch will be automatically applied.

- If the application was assigned to a user, the Start menu, desktop shortcuts, and registry settings relevant to that application will be updated the next time that the user logs on. The first time that the user starts the application, the service pack or software patch will be automatically applied.

- If the application has been assigned to a computer, the service pack or software patch will be automatically applied the next time that the computer is turned on. The application does not need to be activated for this to occur.

To redeploy a software package, obtain the service pack or software patch from the application vendor and place the files in the appropriate installation folders. The service pack must include a new Windows Installer package file (.MSI file). If it does not, you will be unable to redeploy the software because the original package file will contain instructions for deploying the new files added by the service pack or software patch. Open the GPO that originally deployed the application. In Software Installation, right-click the package filename, point to All Tasks, and click Redeploy Application. In the Redeployment dialog box, click Yes.

Removing or Disabling Software

Windows 2000 provides two options for dealing with software you no longer want to deploy in your organization: you can either remove the applications, or you can disable them.

Removing Software

To remove software, right-click the package file name in Software Installation, point to All Tasks, and then click Remove. In the Remove Software dialog box, select one of the options explained in Table 7.2, and then click OK.

Table 7.2   Remove Software Options

Option	Description
Immediately Uninstall The Software From Users And Computers (Forced Removal)	Software is automatically deleted from a computer, either the next time the computer is turned on (in the case of a computer group policy setting), or the next time a user logs on (in the case of a user group policy setting). Removal will take place before the desktop appears.
Allow Users To Continue To Use The Software, But Prevent New Installations (Optional Removal)	Future installations of the software are not installed, but users can continue using existing installations.

Removing Non–Windows Installer Software

Only software that has been installed from a Windows Installer package file can be removed using Group Policy. When software is installed from a package file, an information cache is created on the local hard disk. This cache contains information regarding the applications that were installed, in addition to instructions on how to uninstall them. When you issue a Group Policy command to remove software, that command is directed to the local cache. If the steps for removing the software can be found in the information cache, the program will be removed. If those steps cannot be found, the order to remove the software will be ignored. Any software that was installed without using Windows Installer will have to be removed manually.

Lesson Summary

There are two types of upgrades: mandatory and optional. Mandatory upgrades automatically replace an older version of a program with the upgraded version. You can use this same strategy to change from one vendor's product to another.

Optional upgrades allow users to use either the old or the new version of a program. After an optional upgrade, users can install and use both versions of the application simultaneously. The next time the user logs on, the user can install either version from Add/Remove Programs. If the older version has been installed, existing shortcuts will still launch the older version, but document invocation will only install the newer version, if the GPO deploying the newer version has the highest order of precedence.

Windows 2000 also makes deploying service packs and software patches easy. When you mark a package file for redeployment, the application is readvertised to everyone who has been granted access to the program, either through assigning or publishing. In addition, Windows 2000 provides two options for dealing with software you no longer want to deploy in your organization: you can either immediately remove the applications, or you can allow users to continue to use them but prevent new installations.

Lesson 4: Managing Software

Without the management controls built into Software Installation, the value of having users automatically install software would have to be weighed against potential software installation hazards. Those hazards could include the following:

- Users encountering new file extensions (such as .GIF) that could install a number of different applications (such as Adobe Photoshop or Microsoft Internet Explorer)

- Users installing every program listed in Add/Remove Programs, whether they actually needed the programs or not

- Users being reassigned to positions that precluded the use of software that was installed for use only in their previous positions

To address these problems, Software Installation includes a number of options for managing software after it has been deployed. In particular, administrators have the ability to do the following:

- Associate file extensions with applications

- Prevent software from being installed through document invocation

- Control the programs listed in Add/Remove Programs in Control Panel

- Categorize programs listed in Add/Remove Programs in Control Panel

- Automatically uninstall software whenever a GPO no longer applies to an individual user

After this lesson, you will be able to

- Explain how to manage software using Software Installation group policies by configuring deployment options, managing file extension associations, and assigning software categories.

Estimated lesson time: 30 minutes

Associating File Extensions with Applications

Active Directory directory services include a list of file extensions and the applications associated with those extensions. This is the list used by the Windows Installer whenever a user double-clicks an unknown file type. System administrators cannot dictate the contents of this list, but they can determine the priority for installing applications upon document invocation.

For example, your organization could deploy Word 97, Word 2000, and Lotus Word Pro. Each word processor might be preferred in a different department, but all three of these programs use the .DOC file extension. You need to adjust the file extension priorities for each department so that users always receive the correct word processor.

To modify file extension priorities, open the GPO used to deploy the application. Expand User Configuration, right-click Software Installation, and then click Properties. In the Software Installation Properties dialog box, select the File Extensions tab and use the Up button and the Down button to set the priority order. The first application listed will be the first application installed. Application associations are managed on a per-GPO basis. Changing the priority order in a GPO affects only those users who have that GPO applied to them.

Note You can only associate document types with applications that have been deployed using Group Policy. For example, you cannot associate the .DOC file extension with WordPad unless you create a package file for deploying WordPad.

Creating Software Categories

Administrators can categorize the software deployed in their organizations. This allows users to choose from categories in Add/Remove Programs such as "Graphics" or "Microsoft Office" (see Figure 7.2) rather than from a long and arbitrary list of applications (see Figure 7.3).

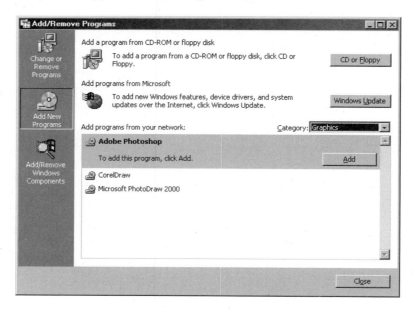

Figure 7.2   Add/Remove Programs listing a category of applications

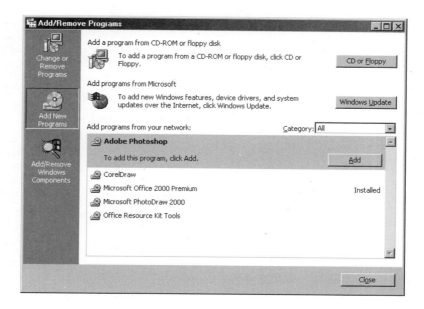

Figure 7.3   Add/Remove Programs listing all published applications

Software categories function on an Active Directory–wide basis. You can gain access to the Categories tab from within any OU. However, any changes you make will be reflected throughout Active Directory directory services.

You create a category by editing the GPO for any OU. Expand Software Settings, for either Computer Configuration or User Configuration. Right-click Software Installation, and select Properties. In the Software Installation Properties dialog box, click the Categories tab. Click the Add button, the Modify button, or the Remove button to create, edit, or remove a category.

You can assign a software package to a category at the time you deploy the application, or you can assign it anytime thereafter. Packages can also be listed under more than one category. You assign a package to a category from the Categories tab in the package's Properties dialog box.

Modifying Deployment Options

To change the deployment options for an application, right-click the package filename in Software Installation, and then click Properties. When the Properties dialog box appears, click the Deployment tab and set any combination of the options listed in Table 7.3.

Table 7.3   Deployment Tab Options

Option	Description
Deployment Type	You can change the deployment type for an application, changing an application from assigned to published, or vice-versa. This will affect new installations of the application, but will not affect users who have already installed the program.
Auto-Install This Application By File Extension Activation	Normally, applications are installed upon document invocation. There might be times, however, when you don't want applications to automatically install. If so, you can turn off Auto-Install, but only for published applications.
Uninstall This Application When It Falls Out Of The Scope Of Management	Administrators can choose to have applications uninstall when the deployment's GPO no longer applies to a particular user or group of users. For example, suppose Mary is a member of the Accounting OU, and accounting has been assigned Excel. If Mary is moved to the Human Resources OU, the Excel GPO will no longer apply to her. Administrators can decide whether to leave Excel on her computer or have it automatically uninstalled after she changes OUs.
Do Not Display This Package In The Add/Remove Programs Control Panel	One way to restrict the ability of users to install software is to prevent the application from being displayed in Add/Remove Programs in Control Panel. Users can still install software by document invocation or by accessing an advertised shortcut. However, they won't be able to install the software unless they actually need to use it.
Installation User Interface Options	Native Windows Installer packages often come with two different setup interfaces. The basic interface installs the software using default values. The maximum interface prompts the user to enter values. Administrators can choose which interface to expose to users during setup. Repackaged applications generally offer only a basic interface.

Resolving Common Problems

You might encounter problems when deploying software with Group Policy. Here are some suggested strategies for resolving some of the more common problems you might encounter.

- **Verify that the application appears in Add/Remove Programs.** If applications do not appear as expected, this is likely because of a problem in how those applications were deployed. To determine whether an application has been assigned or published to a user, log on as that user and start Add/Remove Programs. If the application appears in Add/Remove Programs but there is no Start menu shortcut, it means the application has been published rather than assigned. If the application does not appear in Add/Remove Programs, the application was never deployed, it was deployed in the wrong OU, or the user is a member of a security group that is being filtered out from the effects of this GPO.

- **Verify that the user has access to the network distribution point.** Sometimes an application cannot be installed because a user cannot gain access to the network distribution point (for example, the server hosting that network might be unavailable). You can verify access to the network distribution point by clicking Start, clicking Run, and then typing in the Universal Naming Convention (UNC) name of the shared folder and clicking OK. For example, to verify access to a folder called Software located on a server named Server1, type the following: **\\Server1\Software**.

- **Check for group policy conflicts.** It's possible to assign a user an application at one level of the Active Directory directory services (for example, the domain) and then deny them access to that application at a lower level (for example, an OU). If applications are not showing up as expected, it might be due to a group policy conflict. In addition, applications can also be assigned to computers, and computer policy always overrides user policy. If a user has been assigned Word, but Word has been marked for mandatory removal from a computer, that user will not get Word if he or she logs on from that computer.

Lesson Summary

Active Directory directory services include a list of file extensions and the applications associated with those extensions. This is the list used by the Windows Installer whenever a user double-clicks an unknown file type. System administrators cannot dictate the contents of this list, but you can determine the priority for installing applications upon document invocation. In the Software Installation Properties dialog box, select the File Extensions tab and use the Up button and the Down button to set the priority order. The first application listed will be the first application installed. Application associations are managed on a per-GPO basis. Changing the priority order in a GPO affects only those users who have that GPO applied to them.

You can categorize the software deployed in your organization. This allows users to choose from categories in Add/Remove Programs such as "Graphics" or "Microsoft Office" rather than from a long and arbitrary list of applications. You can also change the deployment options for an application. The options you can change include changing the deployment type for an application from assigned to published, or vice-versa. You can also restrict the ability of users to install software by preventing the application from being displayed in Add/Remove Programs in Control Panel. Users can still install software by document invocation or by accessing an advertised shortcut. However, they won't be able to install the software unless they actually need to use it.

Review

Here are some questions to help you determine if you have learned enough to move on to the next chapter. If you have difficulty answering these questions, please go back and review the material in this chapter before beginning the next chapter. The answers to these questions are located in Appendix A, "Questions and Answers."

1. What two new technologies in Windows 2000 provide the ability to manage software?

2. You need to deploy two new applications to users in your organization, Microsoft Excel 2000 and Microsoft Word 2000. All users in your company use Word 2000 on a daily basis. All users in the accounting department also use Excel 2000 on a daily basis. Some users outside of the accounting department need occasional access to Excel 2000. If you have a single domain and each department has their own organizational unit, how would you deploy these two applications?

3. Under what circumstances would you choose to assign an application to computers instead of users?

4. You have deployed an application to all users in your organization and now need to upgrade the application to the latest version. For compatibility reasons, you need to allow some users to continue to use the old version. How would you accomplish this?

C H A P T E R   8

Managing File Resources

About This Chapter

The methods of providing access to file and print resources in Windows 2000 have improved upon those available in Windows NT 4.0. This chapter explains how to create and share file resources and how to use Dfs trees. It also explains the changes in NTFS permission configuration, disk quotas, file encryption, and the new disk defragmentation utility. At the end of this chapter, you will be able to manage file resources in Windows 2000.

Before You Begin

To complete this chapter

- You must have a computer that meets or exceeds the minimum hardware requirements listed in "Getting Started," on page xxi.

- You must have installed the beta version of Windows 2000 Advanced Server on a computer meeting the specifications listed in the preceding bullet. The computer should be installed as a domain controller in a domain and TCP/IP should be the only installed protocol.

- Your computer should be using a static IP address.

- To complete the optional practices in this chapter, you need to have a network with two computers, one configured as a domain server and the other configured as a member server in the domain.

Lesson 1: Sharing and Publishing File Resources

Microsoft Windows 2000 allows file resources to be shared from the computer or published to directory services based on Active Directory technology. Publishing to Active Directory directory services makes resources easier to find because all the published shares can be centrally accessed. This lesson introduces the Computer Management administrative tool and Active Directory tools necessary to publish file resources in Windows 2000.

After this lesson, you will be able to

- Publish shared folders in Active Directory directory services.
- Differentiate between published folders and shared folders.

Estimated lesson time: 40 minutes

Computer Management

The Computer Management tool is an administrator's primary computer configuration tool. It uses two panes—the console tree (left pane) for navigating and tool selection and the details pane (right pane) for displaying the selection's data or attributes. All of the Computer Management features can be used from a remote computer, so an administrator can troubleshoot and configure a computer from any other computer on the same network. Computer Management provides access to the primary Windows 2000 administrative tools for viewing events, creating shares, and managing devices (see Figure 8.1).

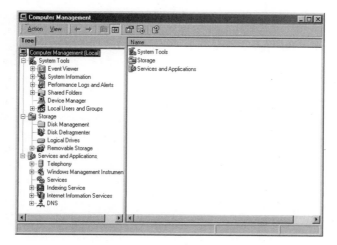

Figure 8.1   The Computer Management tool

There are three nodes in the console tree. In tree structures, a *node* is a location on the tree that has links to one or more items below it. Each of the three nodes in the console tree provides access to a set of management tools.

- **System Tools.** This node contains administrative tools including Event Viewer, Shared Folders, and Device Manager.
- **Storage.** This node contains the tools that relate to disks, including Disk Management and Logical Drives.
- **Services And Applications.** This node is dynamically populated depending on the computer that the tools are focused on. Examples of tools in the Services And Applications node include Services, Internet Information Services, and Indexing Service.

Shared Folders

On computers running Windows NT 4.0 and Windows 2000, you share folders to provide network users with access to file resources. When a folder is shared, users can connect to the folder over the network and gain access to the files that it contains, provided that they have the appropriate permissions.

You can use Windows Explorer or Computer Management to share a folder. Sharing a folder using Windows Explorer is the same in Windows 2000 as in Windows NT 4.0. To use Computer Management to share a folder, right-click the My Computer icon on the desktop, and then click Manage. In the Computer Management console tree, expand System Tools and click Shared Folders. Under Shared Folders, click Shares and all of the folders that are shared from the local computer appear in the details pane. You add a new shared folder by right-clicking the details pane and clicking New File Share. You can share an existing folder, or you can create and share a new folder. To complete the process of sharing a folder, follow the instructions in the wizard that appears. The new shared folder will then appear in the details pane of Computer Management.

Published Folders

Network administrators face many challenges in managing large, complex networks. One challenge is providing information about network resources to authorized users on a network, while at the same time keeping this information secure from unauthorized access. Another challenge is making it easy to find information on the network.

Active Directory directory services is designed to meet these challenges by storing information about network objects, offering rapid information retrieval, and providing security mechanisms that control access. Resources that you can make available (publish) in Active Directory directory services include objects, such as users, computers, printers, files, folders, and network services. Publishing information about shared resources, such as folders, files, and printers, makes it easy for users to find these resources on the network.

In Windows 2000, you can publish information about printers and shared folders in Active Directory directory services by using the Active Directory Users and Computers tool. To make a file resource accessible, you first share the resource and then publish the resource in the Active Directory database.

For example, to publish a folder, from the Administrative Tools menu, start the Active Directory Users and Computers tool. In the console tree, right-click the domain in which you want to publish the shared folders, point to New, and then click Shared Folder. You will be prompted for the Shared Folder Name and Network Path (see Figure 8.2). Enter the requested information and click OK. The shared folder name appears in the domain.

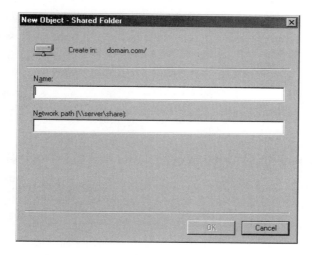

Figure 8.2   The New Object – Shared Folder dialog box

Practice: Sharing and Publishing Folders

In this practice, you will share a folder using Windows Explorer. Then you will share and publish a folder using Computer Management. Finally, you will observe the difference between a published folder and a shared folder.

Exercise 1: Sharing Folders

In this exercise, you will use first Windows Explorer and then the Computer Management tool to share a folder on a Windows NT file system (NTFS) partition.

▶   **To share a folder using Windows Explorer**

1. Log on as Administrator with a password of *password*.
2. Start Windows Explorer.

3. Create a folder named C:\Engineering Documents.

4. Right-click Engineering Documents, and then click Sharing.

   The Engineering Documents Properties dialog box appears.

5. On the Sharing tab, click the Share This Folder option and then click the Permissions button.

   The Permissions For Engineering Documents dialog box appears.

6. Clear the Full Control check box and the Change check box in the Allow column, and then click the Add button.

   The Select Users, Computers, Or Groups dialog box appears.

7. In the list of names, select Administrator, click Add, and then click OK.

8. Verify that Administrator is selected in the Name box, select the Full Control check box in the Allow column, and then click OK.

9. In the Engineering Documents Properties dialog box, click OK.

   Notice that the Engineering Documents folder changes to a shared folder icon.

10. Close Windows Explorer.

▶ **To share a folder using the Computer Management tool**

1. Open Computer Management from the Administrative Tools folder, expand System Tools, expand Shared Folders, and then click Shares.

   A list of shares on your computer appears.

2. Right-click Shares, and then click New File Share.

   The Create Shared Folder wizard appears, prompting you for the location of the folder you want to share.

3. In the Folder To Share box, type **C:\Research Documents** and type **RescDocs** in the Share Name box. Then click Next.

   The Set Permissions page appears and displays the available permissions for this shared folder.

4. Click Administrators Have Full Control, Other Users Have Read-Only Access and then click Finish.

   The Create Shared Folder dialog box displays a message that the folder has been shared out successfully and asks if you want to create another shared folder.

5. Click No.

   Notice that Research Documents is now listed in the Shares folder.

6. Close the Computer Management window.

Exercise 2: Publishing Shared Folders

In this exercise, you will publish a shared folder on the domain controller in Active Directory directory services.

▶ **To publish a shared folder in Active Directory directory services**

1. From the Administrative Tools menu, start the Active Directory Users and Computers tool.

2. Expand domain.com, and then click Computers. This is the OU in which you'll publish a folder named Research Documents.

3. Right-click Computers, point to New, and then click Shared Folder.

   The New Object – Shared Folder dialog box appears.

   Note Published folders need to have unique names because the name of a published folder's scope is global (that is, the entire network) versus local (that is, the server).

4. Type **Research Documents** in the Name box.

   Note A published folder is easy to search for because it is displayed in Active Directory directory services. A shared folder is available on a server and is more difficult to find unless you know the name of the server.

5. In the Network Path box, type **\\Server1\rescdocs** and then click OK.

   Notice that Research Documents appears as a shared folder.

   Note Engineering Documents does not appear as a shared folder in the Active Directory Users And Computers window because Engineering Documents is not a published folder. Active Directory directory services only displays published folders.

Lesson Summary

Microsoft Windows 2000 allows file resources to be shared from the computer or published to Active Directory directory services. When a folder is shared, users can connect to the folder over the network and gain access to the files that it contains, provided that they have the appropriate permissions. You can use Windows Explorer or Computer Management to share a folder.

Publishing to Active Directory directory services makes resources easier to find because all the published shares can be centrally accessed. Active Directory directory services also provides security mechanisms that control access to resources. The resources that you can make available (publish) in Active Directory directory services include objects, such as users, computers, printers, files, folders, and network services.

You publish information about printers and shared folders in Active Directory directory services by using the Active Directory Users and Computers tool. To make a file resource accessible, you first share the resource and then publish the resource in Active Directory directory services. Published folders need to have unique names because the name of a published folder's scope is global (that is, the entire network) versus local (that is, the server).

Lesson 2: Administering Shared Folders by Using Dfs

The distributed file system (Dfs) allows for the creation of a single logical directory tree from a variety of physical systems. Although this technology was available in Microsoft Windows NT 4.0, the administrative tool for configuring the Dfs tree has been enhanced in Windows 2000. An understanding of how to use the Distributed File System console can help ensure an effective Dfs structure.

After this lesson, you will be able to

- Create, configure, and test a Microsoft distributed file system for Windows 2000 Advanced Server.

Estimated lesson time: 35 minutes

Understanding Dfs

Dfs is a single hierarchical file system whose contents are distributed across the enterprise network. Dfs provides a logical tree structure for file system resources that can be anywhere on the network. Because the Dfs tree is a single point of reference, users can easily gain access to network resources regardless of the actual location of the resources. Dfs also facilitates administering multiple shared folders from a single location.

A Dfs share uses a tree structure that contains a root node and child nodes. To create a Dfs share, you must first create a Dfs root. Each Dfs root can have multiple child nodes beneath it, each of which points to a shared folder. The child nodes of the Dfs root represent shared folders that can be physically located on different file servers.

You can configure two types of distributed file systems:

- **Stand-alone Dfs.** Stores the Dfs topology on a single computer. This type of Dfs provides no fault tolerance if the computer that stores the Dfs topology or any of the shared folders that Dfs uses fail.

- **Fault-tolerant Dfs.** Stores the Dfs topology in Active Directory directory services. This type of Dfs allows child nodes to point to multiple identical shared folders for fault tolerance. In addition, it supports Domain Name System (DNS), multiple levels of child volumes, and file replication.

Navigating a Dfs-managed shared folder is easy because the user does not need to know the name of the server on which the folder is shared. This simplifies network access because users no longer need to locate the server where a specific resource is located on the network. After connecting to a Dfs root, users can browse and gain access to all resources below the root, regardless of the location of the server on which the resource is located.

Dfs also simplifies network administration. If a server fails, you can move a child node from one server to another without users being aware of the change. All that is required to move a child node is to modify the Dfs folder to refer to the new server location of the shared folders. Users continue to use the same Dfs path for the child node. Users can gain access to a shared folder through Dfs as long as they have the required permission to gain access to the shared folder.

Note Only client computers with Dfs client software can gain access to Dfs resources. Windows NT 4.0, Windows 98, and Windows 2000 all include a Dfs client. You must download and install a Dfs client for Windows 95.

Setting Up a Dfs Root

A stand-alone Dfs root is physically located on the server to which users initially connect. The first step in setting up a stand-alone Dfs is to create the Dfs root.

Stand-Alone Dfs Root

To create a stand-alone Dfs root, use the Distributed File System console to start the Create New Dfs Root wizard. Table 8.1 describes the wizard options that you configure to create a stand-alone Dfs root.

Table 8.1   Creating a Stand-Alone Dfs Root

Option	Description
Select The Dfs Root Type	The type of Dfs root. Select Create A Standalone Dfs Root to store the Dfs topology on a single computer. A stand-alone Dfs root does not use Active Directory directory services and does not provide fault tolerance.
Specify The Host Server For The Dfs Root	The initial connection point for all resources in the Dfs tree, or the host server. You can create a Dfs root on any computer running Windows 2000 Server.
Specify The Dfs Root Share	A shared folder to host the Dfs root. You can choose an existing shared folder or create a new share.
Name The Dfs Root	A descriptive name for the Dfs root.

Fault-Tolerant Dfs Root

A fault-tolerant Dfs root can be created only on a domain controller. Active Directory directory services store each Dfs tree topology and replicate the topology to every participating Dfs root server. Because changes to a Dfs tree are automatically synchronized with Active Directory directory services, you can always restore a Dfs tree topology if the Dfs root is offline for any reason. You can implement fault tolerance at the file and content level by assigning replicas to a Dfs child node. Any branch node on the Dfs tree can be serviced by a set of replicated resources. If a client connection to one replica fails for any reason, the Dfs client attempts a connection to another. The Dfs client cycles through the replicas until an available one is found.

To create a fault-tolerant Dfs root, use the Create New Dfs Root wizard. Table 8.2 describes the wizard options you configure to create a fault-tolerant Dfs root.

Table 8.2   Creating a Fault-Tolerant Dfs Root

Option	Description
Select The Dfs Root Type	The type of Dfs root. Click Create A Domain Dfs Root. A domain Dfs root uses Active Directory directory services to store the Dfs tree topology and supports DNS naming, file replication, and fault tolerance.
Select The Host Domain For The Dfs Root	The initial connection point for all resources in the Dfs tree, or the host domain. A domain can host multiple Dfs roots.
Specify The Host Server For The Dfs Root	The initial connection point for all resources in the Dfs tree, or the host server. You can create a Dfs root on any computer running Windows 2000 Server.
Specify The Dfs Root Share	A shared folder to host the Dfs root. You can choose an existing shared folder or create a new share.
Name The Dfs Root	Provide a descriptive name for the Dfs root.

To create a second root, right-click the domain, and then click New Root Replica Member. The only options for creating a second root are Specify Server To Host Dfs and Select Share For Dfs Root Volume.

Setting Up Dfs Child Nodes

In a network environment, it can be difficult for users to keep track of the physical locations of shared resources. When you use Dfs, the network and file system structures become transparent to users. This enables you to centralize and optimize access to resources based on a single tree structure.

After you create a Dfs root, you can create Dfs child nodes. To create a Dfs child node, in the Distributed File System console, click the Dfs root to which you will attach a child node. On the Action menu, click New Dfs Child Node. In the Add To Dfs dialog box, configure the options described in Table 8.3.

Table 8.3   Creating a New Dfs Child Node

Option	Description
Child Node	The name that users will see when they connect to Dfs.
Send The User To This Network Path	The Universal Naming Convention (UNC) name for the actual location of the shared folder to which the child node refers.
Comment	Additional information (optional) to help keep track of the shared folder (for example, the actual name of the shared folder).
Clients Cache This Dfs Referral For X Seconds	Length of time for which clients cache a referral to a Dfs child node. After the referral time expires, a client queries the Dfs server about the location of the child node, even if the client has previously established a connection with the child node.

The child node will appear below the Dfs root volume in the Distributed File System console.

Optional Practice: Creating a Dfs Tree

In this optional practice, you will share some existing folders, create and share some folders, create a new Dfs root, and then create some Dfs child nodes.

Note To complete all the procedures in this practice, you must have two computers running Windows 2000. This practice also assumes that one of the two computers is configured as a domain controller and the other computer is configured as a member server in the domain.

Exercise 1: Creating and Sharing Folders

In this exercise, you will create and share some folders.

Note If you have two computers, a domain controller and a member server in the domain, complete this exercise on both computers.

▶ **To create and share folders**

1. Log on as Administrator.
2. Start Windows Explorer and create and share the folders listed in the following table using all default permissions.

Folder	Share name
C:\Apps\Database	DB
C:\Apps\Wordprocessing	Word
C:\MoreApps\Maintenance	Maint
C:\MoreApps\CustomerService	Custom

3. Close Windows Explorer.

Exercise 2: Creating a Dfs

In this exercise, you create and configure a distributed file system (Dfs) on your computer.

Note If you have two computers, a domain controller and a member server in the domain, complete this exercise on both computers.

▶ **To create a new Dfs root**

1. Click the Start button, point to Programs, point to Administrative Tools, and then click Distributed File System.

   The Distributed File System window appears.

2. On the Action menu, click New Dfs Root.

   The New Dfs Root wizard appears.

3. Click Next.

   The wizard displays the Select The Dfs Root Type page.

   Notice that there are two types of Dfs roots you can create:

   ■ A fault-tolerant Dfs root that uses Active Directory directory services to store the Dfs tree topology and supports DNS, multiple levels of child volumes, and file replication.

   ■ A stand-alone Dfs root that does not use Active Directory directory services and that permits a single level of child volume.

Note In this exercise, you will create a stand-alone Dfs root.

---

4. Click Create A Standalone Dfs Root, and then click Next.

   The wizard displays the Specify The Host Server For The Dfs Root page. You will create a Dfs root on your own server.

5. In the Server Name box, confirm that the name of your server is displayed, and then click Next.

   The wizard displays the Specify Dfs Root Share page. Notice that you can use an existing share for the Dfs root or the wizard can create a new shared folder for you.

Note In this exercise, you will let the wizard create a new shared folder for you. You have to provide both the location of the folder on your computer and a share name.

---

6. Select the Create A New Share option.

7. Type **C:\Apps** in the Path To Share box, and then type **Shared Apps** in the Share Name box.

   A Distributed File System box appears that displays a prompt asking if you want to create the folder.

8. Click Yes.

   The wizard displays the Name The Dfs Root page. The wizard fills in the Dfs name for you.

9. Click Next.

   The wizard displays the Completing The New Dfs Root Wizard page, which contains a summary of the choices that you made. An example is shown in Figure 8.3.

Figure 8.3   A summary of choices for the new Dfs root

10. Confirm that the options that the wizard displays are correct, and then click Finish.

11. Close the Distributed File System window.

▶   **To add Dfs child nodes on the local computer**

Note If you have two computers, a domain controller and a member server in the domain, complete this procedure on both computers.

---

1. Open Distributed File System from the Administrative Tools menu.

2. In the Distributed File System window's console tree, click \\ *Server1*\ SharedApps (where *Server1* is the UNC name of your domain controller).

3. On the Action menu, click New Dfs Link.

   The Create A New Dfs Link dialog box appears.

4. Type **Word Processing** in the Link Name box.

5. In the Send The User To This Shared Folder box, type \\ *Server1***Word** (where *Server1* is the UNC name of your domain controller).

6. Click OK.

7. Repeat steps 1–5 to add a child node called Customer Service, which points to the shared folder *Server1*\Custom (where *Server1* is the UNC name of your domain controller).

The following table summarizes the nodes being created in this procedure and the next procedure.

Child node	Shared folder	Folder name
Word Processing	\\ *Server1*\Word	C:\Apps\Wordprocessing
Customer Service	\\ *Server1*\Custom	C:\MoreApps\CustomerService
Maintenance	\\ *second_computer*\Maint	C:\MoreApps\Maintenance
Database	\\ *second_computer*\DB	C:\Apps\Database

▶ **To add a Dfs child node on a remote computer**

Note This is an optional procedure. To complete this procedure, you must have two computers running Windows 2000. This procedure assumes that one of the two computers is configured as a domain controller and the other computer is configured as a member server in the domain.

1. In the console tree, click *Server*1\SharedApps (where *Server1* is the UNC of your domain controller).

2. On the Action menu, click New Dfs Link.

   The Create A New Dfs Link dialog box appears.

3. Type **Maintenance** in the Link Name box.

4. In the Send The User To This Shared Folder box, type *second_computer***Maint** (where *second_computer* is the UNC name of your non–domain controller computer), and then click OK.

5. Repeat steps 1–4 to add a child node called Database, which points to the shared folder *second_computer*\DB (where *second_computer* is the UNC name of your non–domain controller computer).

6. Close the Distributed File System window.

▶   **To test the Dfs**

Note To complete this procedure, you must have two computers running Windows 2000. This procedure assumes that one of the two computers is configured as a domain controller and the other computer is configured as a member server in the domain.

---

1. On the domain controller's desktop, double-click My Network Places, double-click the Computers Near Me icon, and then double-click *second_computer*.

   The *second_computer* window appears, displaying the shared resources on your second computer.

2. Double-click Shared Apps.

   The Shared Apps on *second_computer* window appears, displaying the child nodes of the Shared Apps Dfs.

3. Create a text file in the Word Processing child node, and name the text file WP1.

4. Create a text file in the Maintenance child node, and name the text file Maint1.

5. Close all open windows.

6. Open *second_computer*\Word.

   Notice that the file you created on your second computer's Dfs appears in a shared folder on your second computer's shared folder.

7. Close all open windows and log off.

Lesson Summary

The Microsoft distributed file system (Dfs) for Windows 2000 Advanced Server provides users with convenient access to shared folders that are distributed throughout a network. A Dfs share uses a tree structure containing a root and child nodes. The child nodes of the Dfs root represent shared folders that can be physically located on different file servers.

In a network environment, it might be difficult for users to keep track of the physical locations of shared resources. When you use Dfs, the network and file system structures become transparent to users. A user who navigates a Dfs-managed shared folder does not need to know the name of the server on which the folder is shared.

After connecting to a Dfs root, users can browse and gain access to all resources below the root, regardless of the location of the server on which the resource is located. If a server fails, you can move a child node from one server to another without users being aware of the change. All that is required to move a child node is to modify the Dfs folder to refer to the new server location of the shared folders. Users continue to use the same Dfs path for the child node.

Lesson 3: Using NTFS Special Access Permissions

The standard NTFS permissions generally provide all of the access control that you need to secure your resources. However, there are instances where the standard NTFS permissions do not provide the specific level of access that you want to assign to users. To create the specific level of access, you can assign NTFS special access permissions. When you assign special access permissions to folders, you can choose where to apply the permissions down the tree to subfolders and files.

After this lesson, you will be able to

- Explain how to use NTFS special permissions.
- Assign the Take Ownership permission and take ownership of a folder or file.

Estimated lesson time: 25 minutes

Understanding NTFS Special Access Permissions

Special access permissions provide you with a finer degree of control for assigning access to resources. The special access permissions, when combined, constitute the standard NTFS permissions. For example, the standard Read permission includes the Read Data, Read Attributes, Read Permissions, and Read Extended Attributes special access permissions.

Two of the special access permissions are especially useful for managing access to files and folders: Change Permissions and Take Ownership.

Change Permission

You can give other administrators and users the ability to change permissions for a file or folder without giving them the Full Control permission over the file or folder. In this way, the other administrator or user cannot delete or write to the file or folder but can assign permissions to the file or folder.

To give administrators the ability to change permissions, assign Change Permissions to the Administrators group for the file or folder.

Take Ownership

You can transfer ownership of files and folders from one user account or group to another user account or group. You can give someone the ability to take ownership and, as an administrator, you can take ownership of a file or folder.

The current owner or any user with the Full Control permission can assign the Full Control standard permission or the Take Ownership special access permission to another user account or group, allowing the user or a member of the group to take ownership.

Members of the Administrators group have the Take Ownership special access permission. This gives administrators the ability to take ownership of a file or folder, regardless of the other permissions that are assigned to the file or folder. If an administrator takes ownership, the Administrators group becomes the owner and any member of the Administrators group can change the permissions for the file or folder and assign the Take Ownership permission to another user account or group.

You cannot *assign* anyone ownership of a file or folder. The owner of a file, an administrator, or anyone with the Full Control permission, can assign Take Ownership permission to a user account or group, allowing the user or group member to take ownership. However, to become the owner of a file or folder, a user or group member with the Take Ownership permission must explicitly take ownership of the file or folder.

To take ownership of a file or folder, open the Properties dialog box for the file or folder in Windows Explorer, and select the Security tab. On the Security tab, click the Advanced button. The Access Control Settings dialog box appears. In the Access Control Settings dialog box, on the Owner tab, in the Change Owner To list, select your name. Select the Replace Owner On Subcontainers And Objects check box to take ownership of all subfolders and files that are contained within the folder.

Setting Special NTFS Permissions

If an employee leaves the company, an administrator can take ownership of the employee's files and assign the Take Ownership permission to another employee, and then that employee can take ownership of the previous employee's files. To set the Change Permissions or Take Ownership permissions, in the Properties dialog box for a file or folder, on the Security tab, click the Advanced button. In the Access Control Settings dialog box for a file or folder, on the Permissions tab, select the user account or group for which you want to apply NTFS special access permissions (see Figure 8.4).

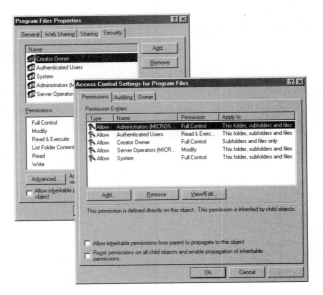

Figure 8.4 The Access Control Settings dialog box

After you have selected the user account or group, click the View/Edit button and the Permission Entry dialog box appears (see Figure 8.5).

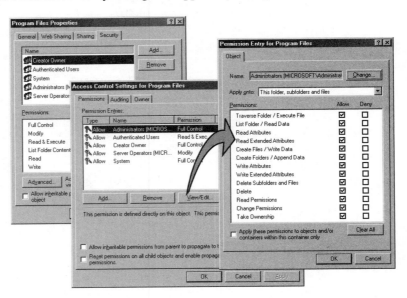

Figure 8.5 Setting special NTFS permissions for a file or folder

In the Permission Entry dialog box, you configure the options described in Table 8.4.

Table 8.4   Special NTFS Permissions

Option	Description
Name	Specify the user account or group name. To select a different user account or group, click the Change button.
Apply Onto	Specify the level of the folder hierarchy at which the special NTFS permissions are inherited. The default is This Folder, Subfolders And Files.
Permissions	Allow the special access permissions. To allow the Change Permissions or Take Ownership permissions, select the appropriate check box in the Allow column.
Apply These Permissions To Objects And/Or Containers Within This Container Only	Specify whether subfolders and files within a folder inherit the special access permissions from the folder. Select this check box to propagate the special access permissions to files and subfolders. Clear this check box to prevent permissions inheritance.
Clear All	Click this button to clear all selected permissions.

Understanding NTFS Permissions Inheritance

By default, permissions that you assign to the parent folder are inherited by and propagated to the subfolders and files that are contained in the parent folder. However, you can prevent permissions inheritance.

Allowing Permissions Inheritance

Files and subfolders inherit permissions from their parent folder. Whatever permissions you assign to the parent folder also apply to subfolders and files that are contained in the parent folder. When you assign NTFS permissions to give access to a folder, you assign permissions for the folder and for any existing files and subfolders, as well as for any new files and subfolders that are created in the folder.

Preventing Permissions Inheritance

You can prevent permissions that are assigned to a parent folder from being inherited by subfolders and files that are contained in the folder. The folder at which you prevent permissions inheritance becomes the new parent folder, and permissions that are assigned to this folder will be inherited by the subfolders and files that are contained in it.

Practice: Taking Ownership of a File

In this practice, you will observe the effects of taking ownership of a file. To do this, you will determine permissions for a file, assign the Take Ownership permission to a user account, and then take ownership as that user.

▶   **To determine the permissions for a file**

1. Log on to your domain as Administrator, and then start Windows Explorer.
2. In the C:\Apps folder, create a text document named Owner.txt.
3. Right-click Owner.txt, and then click Properties.

    Microsoft Windows 2000 displays the Owner Properties dialog box with the General tab active.
4. Click the Security tab to display the permissions for the Owner.txt file.
5. Click the Advanced button.

    Windows 2000 displays the Access Control Settings For Owner dialog box with the Permissions tab active.
6. Click the Owner tab.

    Who is the current owner of the Owner.txt file?

▶   **To assign permission to a user to take ownership**

1. In the Access Control Settings For Owner dialog box, click the Permissions tab.
2. Click Add.

    Windows 2000 displays the Select User, Computer, Or Group dialog box.
3. In the Look In box at the top of the dialog box, ensure that your domain is selected.
4. Under Name, click User Four, and then click OK.

    Windows 2000 displays the Permission Entry For Owner dialog box. Notice that all of the permission entries for User Four are blank.
5. In the Permissions list, select the Allow check box next to Take Ownership.
6. Click OK.

    Windows 2000 displays the Access Control Settings For Owner dialog box with the Permissions tab active.
7. Click OK to return to the Owner Properties dialog box.
8. Click OK to apply your changes and close the Owner Properties dialog box.
9. Close all applications, and then log off Administrator.

▶ **To take ownership of a file**

1. Log on to your domain as User4 with a password of *user4*, and then start Windows Explorer.

2. Expand the C:\Apps folder, and then click the C:\Apps folder in the console pane.

3. Right-click Owner.txt in the details pane, and then click Properties.

   Windows 2000 displays the Owner Properties dialog box with the General tab active.

4. Click the Security tab to display the permissions for Owner.txt.

5. Click Advanced to display the Access Control Settings For Owner dialog box, and then click the Owner tab.

   Who is the current owner of Owner.txt?

6. Under Name, select User Four, and then click Apply.

   Who is the current owner of Owner.txt?

7. Click OK to close the Access Control Settings For Owner dialog box.

   Windows 2000 displays the Owner Properties dialog box with the Security tab active.

8. Click OK to close the Owners Properties dialog box.

▶ **To test permissions for a file as the owner**

1. While you are logged on as User Four, assign User Four the Full Control permission for the Owner.txt file, and click Apply.

2. Clear the Allow Inheritable Permissions From Parent To Propagate To This Object check box.

   A Security dialog box appears to indicate that you are preventing any inheritable permissions from propagating to this object.

3. In the Security dialog box, click the Remove button.

4. Log off.

Lesson Summary

NTFS special access permissions provide you with a finer degree of control for assigning access to resources. Two of the special access permissions are especially useful for managing access to files and folders: Change Permissions and Take Ownership.

By assigning the Change Permissions permission to a user or group, you can give other administrators and users the ability to change permissions for a file or folder without giving them the Full Control permission over the file or folder. In this way, the other administrator or user cannot delete or write to the file or folder but can assign permissions to the file or folder. To give administrators the ability to change permissions, assign the Change Permissions permission to the Administrators group for the file or folder.

The current owner or any user with the Full Control permission can assign the Take Ownership special access permission to another user account or group, allowing the user or a member of the group to take ownership. An administrator can take ownership of a folder or file, regardless of assigned permissions. When an administrator takes ownership of a file or folder, the Administrators group becomes the owner and any member of the Administrators group can change the permissions for the file or folder and assign the Take Ownership permission to another user account or group.

By default, permissions that you assign to the parent folder are inherited by and propagated to the subfolders and files that are contained in the parent folder. However, you can prevent permission inheritance.

Lesson 4: Managing Disk Quotas on NTFS Volumes

You use disk quotas to manage storage growth in distributed environments. Disk quotas allow you to allocate disk space to users based on the files and folders that they own. You can set disk quotas, quota thresholds, and quota limits for all users and for individual users. You can also monitor the amount of hard disk space that users have filled and the amount that they have left against their quota.

After this lesson, you will be able to

- Manage disk quotas on NTFS volumes.

Estimated lesson time: 30 minutes

Using Disk Quotas

Windows 2000 disk quotas track and control disk usage on a per-user, per-volume basis. Windows 2000 tracks disk quotas for each volume, even if the volumes are on the same hard disk. Because quotas are tracked on a per-user basis, every user's disk space is tracked regardless of the folder in which the user stores files. Table 8.5 describes the characteristics of Windows 2000 disk quotas.

Table 8.5   Disk Quota Characteristics and Descriptions

Characteristic	Description
Disk usage is based on file and folder ownership.	Windows 2000 calculates disk space usage for users based on the files and folders that they own. When a user copies or saves a new file to an NTFS volume or takes ownership of a file on an NTFS volume, Windows 2000 charges the disk space for the file against the user's quota limit.
Disk quotas do not use compression.	Windows 2000 ignores compression when it calculates hard disk space usage. Users are charged for each uncompressed byte, regardless of how much hard disk space is actually used. File compression produces different degrees of compression for different types of files. Different uncompressed file types that are the same size might end up to be very different sizes when they are compressed.
Free space for applications is based on quota limit.	When you enable disk quotas, the free space that Windows 2000 reports to applications for the volume is the amount of space remaining within the user's disk quota limit.

Note You can apply disk quotas only to volumes formatted with the version of NTFS that is used in Windows 2000.

To monitor and control hard disk space usage, system administrators can do the following:

- Set a disk quota limit to specify the amount of disk space for each user.
- Set a disk quota warning to specify when Windows 2000 should log an event, indicating that the user is nearing his or her limit.
- Enforce disk quota limits and deny users access if they exceed their limit.
- Log an event when a user exceeds a specified disk space threshold. The threshold could be when users exceed their quota limit or when they exceed their warning level.

After you enable disk quotas for a volume, Windows 2000 collects disk usage data for all users who own files and folders on the volume. This allows you to monitor volume usage on a per-user basis. By default, only members of the Administrators group can view and change quota settings. However, you can allow users to view quota settings.

Setting Disk Quotas

You can enable disk quotas and enforce disk quota warnings and limits for all users and for individual users.

If you want to enable disk quotas, in the Properties dialog box for a disk, on the Quota tab, configure the options that are described in Table 8.6.

Table 8.6   Quota Tab Options

Option	Description
Enable Quota Management	Select this check box to enable disk quota management.
Deny Disk Space To Users Exceeding Quota Limit	Select this check box so that when users exceed their hard disk space allocation, they receive an "out of disk space" message and cannot write to the volume.
Do Not Limit Disk Usage	Click this option when you do not want to limit the amount of hard disk space for users.
Limit Disk Space To	Configure the amount of disk space that users can fill.
Set Warning Level To	Configure the amount of disk space that users can fill before Windows 2000 logs an event, indicating that a user is nearing his or her limit.
Quota Entries	Click this button to open the Quota Entries window, where you can add a new entry, delete an entry, and view the properties for a quota entry.

If you want to enforce quota limits for all users, you would do the following:

1. In the Limit Disk Space To box and the Set Warning Level To box, enter the values for the limit and warning level that you want to set.

2. Select the Deny Disk Space To Users Exceeding Quota Limit check box.

Windows 2000 will monitor usage and will not allow users to create files or folders on the volume when they exceed the limit.

If you want to enforce quota limits for a specific user, you would do the following:

1. In the Properties dialog box for a disk, on the Quota tab, click the Quota Entries button.

2. In the Quota Entries window (see Figure 8.6), double-click the user account for which you want to set a disk quota limit or create an entry by clicking New Quota Entry on the Quota menu.

3. Configure the disk space limit and the warning level for the individual user.

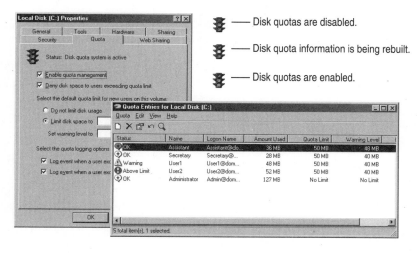

Figure 8.6 Configuring disk quotas

You can determine the status of disk quotas in the Properties dialog box for a disk. A traffic light icon designates the status (see Figure 8.6):

- A red (top) light indicates that disk quotas are disabled.

- A yellow (middle) light indicates that Windows 2000 is rebuilding disk quota information.

- A green (bottom) light indicates that the disk quota system is active.

You use the Quota Entries window to monitor usage for all users who have copied, saved, or taken ownership of files and folders on the volume. Windows 2000 will scan the volume and monitor the amount of disk space in use by each user. Use the Quota Entries window to view the following:

- The amount of hard disk space that each user fills.
- Users who are over their quota-warning threshold, which is signified by a yellow triangle (see Figure 8.6).
- Users who are over their quota limit, which is signified by a red circle (see Figure 8.6).
- The warning threshold and the disk quota limit for each user.

Practice: Configuring Disk Quotas

In this practice, you will configure the quota management settings for drive C to limit the data that users can store on the volume. You will then configure custom quota settings for a user account. Finally, you will remove the quota management limits.

Exercise 1: Assigning Disk Quotas

▶ **To configure default quota management settings**

1. Log on to your domain as Administrator and start Windows Explorer.
2. In Windows Explorer, right-click the drive C icon, and then click Properties.

   Windows 2000 displays the Local Disk (C:) Properties dialog box with the General tab active.
3. Click the Quota tab.

   Notice that disk quotas are disabled by default.
4. On the Quota tab, click the Enable Quota Management check box.

   Notice that the default disk space limit for new users is set to 1 KB.
5. Type **10** in the Limit Disk Space To box, and select MB in the drop-down list box to the right.
6. Type **6** in the Set Warning Level To box and select MB in the drop-down list box to the right.
7. Click Apply.

   Windows 2000 displays the Disk Quota message box, warning you that the disk volume will be rescanned to update disk usage statistics if you enable quotas.
8. Click OK to enable disk quotas.

▶ **To configure quota management settings for a user**

1. In the Local Disk (C:) Properties dialog box, click the Quota Entries button.

   Windows 2000 displays the Quota Entries For Local Disk (C:) window.

   Note Any user accounts that have stored files on drive C are listed along with the amount of disk space they are currently using, their quota limit, the warning level indicating the amount of disk space that can be used before a warning is generated, and the percentage of their quota limit in use.

2. On the Quota menu, click New Quota Entry.

   Windows 2000 displays the Select Users dialog box.

3. In the Look In box, ensure your domain is selected.

4. Near the top of the dialog box, in the Name column, select User Three, the user for which you want to set up a quota, and then click Add.

   User Three appears in the list at the bottom of the dialog box.

5. Click OK.

   Windows 2000 displays the Add New Quota Entry dialog box.

   What are the default settings for the user you just set a quota limit for?

6. Click OK to accept the default settings and return to the Quota Entries For Local Disk (C:) window.

7. Close the Quota Entries window and the Local Disk (C:) Properties dialog box.

Exercise 2: Disabling Quota Management

In this exercise, you will disable quota management settings for drive C.

▶ **To disable quota management settings for drive C**

1. Ensure you are logged on to your domain as Administrator and that Windows Explorer is open.

2. Right-click the drive C icon, and then click Properties.

   Windows 2000 displays the Local Disk (C:) Properties dialog box with the General tab active.

3. Click the Quota tab.

4. On the Quota tab, clear the Enable Quota Management check box.

   Notice that all quota settings for drive C are no longer available.

5. Click Apply.

   Windows 2000 displays the Disk Quota message box, warning you that if you disable quotas, the volume will be rescanned if you enable them later.

6. Click OK to close the Disk Quota message box.

7. Click OK to close the Local Disk (C:) Properties dialog box.

8. Close all applications.

Lesson Summary

Disk quotas are used to allocate disk space usage to users. You can set disk quotas, quota thresholds, and quota limits for all users and for individual users. You can also monitor the amount of hard disk space that users have filled and the amount that they have left against their quotas. Windows 2000 ignores compression when it calculates hard disk space usage. You can apply disk quotas only to NTFS volumes created by Windows 2000.

Windows 2000 disk quotas track and control disk usage on a per-user, per-volume basis. Windows 2000 tracks disk quotas for each volume, even if the volumes are on the same hard disk. Because quotas are tracked on a per-user basis, every user's disk space is tracked regardless of the folder in which the user stores files.

Lesson 5: Increasing Security with EFS

The Microsoft Encrypting File System (EFS) provides encryption for data in NTFS files stored on disk. EFS encryption is public key–based and runs as an integrated-system service, making it easy to manage, difficult to attack, and transparent to the file owner. If a user who attempts to access an encrypted NTFS file has the private key to that file, the file can be decrypted so that the user can open the file and work with it transparently as a normal document. A user without the private key is denied access.

Windows 2000 also includes the Cipher command-line utility, which provides the ability to encrypt and decrypt files and folders from a command prompt. Windows 2000 also provides a recovery agent. In the event that the owner loses the private key, the recovery agent can still recover the encrypted file.

After this lesson, you will be able to

- Encrypt folders and files.
- Decrypt folders and files.

Estimated lesson time: 40 minutes

Understanding EFS

EFS allows users to encrypt NTFS files by using a strong public key–based cryptographic scheme that encrypts all files in a folder. Users with roaming profiles can use the same key with trusted remote systems. No administrative effort is needed to begin, and most operations are transparent. Backups and copies of encrypted files are also encrypted if they are in NTFS volumes. Files remain encrypted if you move or rename them, and encryption is not defeated by temporary files created during editing and left unencrypted in the paging file or in a temporary file.

Enterprises can set policies to recover EFS-encrypted data when necessary. The recovery policy is integrated with overall Windows 2000 security policy. Control of this policy can be delegated to individuals with recovery authority, and different recovery policies can be configured for different parts of the enterprise. Data recovery discloses only the recovered data, not the key that was used to encrypt the file. Several protections are in place to ensure that data recovery is possible and that no data is lost in the case of total system failure.

EFS is implemented either from Windows Explorer or from the command line. It can be enabled or disabled for a computer, domain, or organizational unit (OU) by resetting recovery policy in the Group Policy console in MMC.

You can use EFS to encrypt and decrypt files on remote file servers but not to encrypt data that is transferred over the network. Windows 2000 provides network protocols, such as Secure Sockets Layer authentication, to encrypt data over the network.

Table 8.7 lists the key features provided by Windows 2000 EFS.

Table 8.7   EFS Features

Feature	Description
Transparent encryption	In EFS, file encryption does not require the file owner to decrypt and re-encrypt the file on each use. Decryption and encryption happen transparently on file reads and writes to disk.
Strong protection of encryption keys	Public-key encryption resists all but the most sophisticated methods of attack. Therefore, in EFS, the file-encryption keys that are used to encrypt the file are encrypted by using a public key from the user's certificate. (Note Windows 2000 uses X.509 v3 certificates.) The list of encrypted file-encryption keys is stored with the encrypted file and is unique to it. To decrypt the file-encryption keys, the file owner supplies a private key, which only the file owner has.
Integral data-recovery system	If the owner's private key is unavailable, the recovery agent can open the file using his or her own private key There can be more than one recovery agent, each with a different public key, but at least one public recovery key must be present on the system to encrypt a file.
Secure temporary and paging files	Many applications create temporary files while you edit a document, and these temporary files can be left unencrypted on the disk. On computers running Windows 2000, EFS is implemented at the folder level, so any temporary copies of an encrypted file are also encrypted, provided that all files are on NTFS volumes. EFS resides in the Windows operating system kernel and uses the nonpaged pool to store file encryption keys, ensuring that they are never copied to the paging file.

Encryption

The recommended method to encrypt files is to create an NTFS folder and then "encrypt" the folder. To "encrypt" a folder, in the Properties dialog box for the folder, select the General tab. On the General tab, click the Advanced button, and then click the Encrypt Contents To Secure Data check box. All files placed in the folder are encrypted. The folder is now marked for encryption. Folders that are marked for encryption are not actually encrypted; only the files within the folder are encrypted.

Note Compressed files cannot be encrypted, and encrypted files cannot be compressed.

After you encrypt the folder, when you save a file in that folder, the file is encrypted by using file encryption keys, which are fast symmetric keys designed for bulk encryption. The file is encrypted in blocks, with a different file encryption key for each block. All of the file encryption keys are stored, encrypted, in the Data Decryption Field (DDF) and the Data Recovery Field (DRF) in the file header.

Note By default, encryption provided by EFS is standard 56-bit encryption. For additional security, North American users can obtain 128-bit encryption by ordering the Enhanced CryptoPAK from Microsoft. Files encrypted by the CryptoPAK cannot be decrypted, accessed, or recovered on a system that supports the 56-bit encryption only.

You use a file that you encrypted just like you would use any other file. Encryption is transparent. You do not need to decrypt a file you encrypted before you can use it. When you open an encrypted file, your private key is applied to the DDF to unlock the list of file-encryption keys, allowing the file contents to appear in plain text. EFS automatically detects an encrypted file and locates a user certificate and associated private key. You open the file, make changes to it, and save it, like you would any other file. However, if someone else tries to open your encrypted file, he or she is unable to access the file and receives an access denied message.

Note Encrypted files cannot be shared.

Decryption

Decrypting a folder or file refers to unchecking the Encrypt Contents To Secure Data check box in a folder's or file's Advanced Attributes dialog box, which you access from the folder's or file's Properties dialog box. Once decrypted, the file remains decrypted until you check the Encrypt Contents To Secure Data check box. The only reason you might want to decrypt a file would be if other people needed access to the folder or file; for example, if you want to share the folder or make the file available across the network.

The Cipher Command

Windows 2000 also includes command-line utilities for the richer functionality that is required for some administrative operations. The Cipher command-line utility provides the ability to encrypt and decrypt files and folders from a command prompt.

The following example shows the available options for the Cipher command. Table 8.8 describes these options.

cipher [/e | /d] [/s:*folder_name*] [/i] [/f] [/q] [*file_name* [...]]

Table 8.8   Cipher Command Options and Descriptions

Option	Description
/e	Encrypts the specified folders. Folders are marked so that files that are added later will be encrypted.
/d	Decrypts the specified folders. Folders are marked so that files that are added later will not be encrypted.
/s	Performs the specified operation on files in the given folder and all subfolders.
/i	Continues performing the specified operation even after errors have occurred. By default, Cipher stops when an error is encountered.
/f	Forces the encryption operation on all specified files, even those that are already encrypted. Files that are already encrypted are skipped by default.
/q	Reports only the most essential information.
file_name	Specifies a pattern, file, or folder.

If you run the Cipher command without parameters, it displays the encryption state of the current folder and any files that it contains. You can specify multiple filenames and use wildcards. You must put spaces between multiple parameters.

Recovery Agent

If the owner's private key is unavailable, a person designated as the recovery agent can open the file using his or her own private key, which is applied to the DRF to unlock the list of file-encryption keys. If the recovery agent is on another computer in the network, send the file to the recovery agent. The recovery agent can bring his or her private key to the owner's computer, but it is never a good security practice to copy a private key onto another computer.

Note The default recovery agent is the administrator of the local computer unless the computer is part of a domain. In a domain, the domain administrator is the default recovery agent.

It is a good security practice to rotate recovery agents. However, if the agent designation changes, access to the file is denied. For this reason, it is recommended that recovery certificates and private keys be kept until all files that are encrypted with them have been updated.

The person designated as the recovery agent has a special certificate and associated private key that allow data recovery. To recover an encrypted file, the recovery agent would do the following:

1. Use Backup or another backup tool to restore a user's backup version of the encrypted file or folder to the computer where his or her file recovery certificate is located.

2. In Windows Explorer open the Properties dialog box for the file or folder, and on the General tab, click the Advanced button.

3. Clear the Encrypt Contents To Secure Data check box.

4. Make a backup version of the decrypted file or folder and return the backup version to the user.

Practice: Encrypting Files

In this practice, you will encrypt a folder and its files.

Exercise 1: Encryption

▶ **To encrypt a file**

1. In Windows Explorer, create C:\Secret\File1.txt and then click Properties.

   Windows 2000 displays the Properties dialog box with the General tab active.

2. Click Advanced.

   The Advance Attributes dialog box appears.

3. Click the Encrypt Contents To Secure Data check box and then click OK.

4. Click OK to close the Owner Properties dialog box.

   An Encryption Warning dialog box informs you that you are about to encrypt a file that is not in an encrypted folder. The default is to encrypt the folder and file, but you may also choose to encrypt only the file.

5. Click Cancel, and then click Cancel again to close the Owner Properties dialog box.

6. In Windows Explorer, right-click C:\Secret and then click Properties.

7. Click Advanced.

   The Advance Attributes dialog box appears.

8. Click the Encrypt Contents To Secure Data check box and then click OK.

9. Click OK to close the Apps Properties dialog box.

   The Confirm Attribute Changes dialog box informs you that you are about to encrypt a folder. You have two choices: You can encrypt only this folder, or you can encrypt the folder and all subfolders and files in the folder.

10. Select the Apply Changes To This Folder, Subfolders And Files option, and then click OK.

> **Note** If you see an Error Applying Attribute dialog box informing you that there is no recovery policy configured for your system, choose its Ignore button. For the purposes of this exercise you can ignore this warning. However, you should always have a recovery policy in place on a production computer.

11. In the Secret folder, right-click File1.txt and then click Properties.

    The File1 Properties dialog box appears.

12. Click Advanced.

    The Advanced Attributes dialog box appears. Notice the Encrypt Contents To Secure Data check box is selected.

13. Close the Advanced Attributes dialog box.

14. Close the Properties dialog box.

15. Close all windows and log off.

Exercise 2: Testing the Encrypted Files

In this exercise, you will log on using the User Three account and then attempt to open an encrypted file. You will then try to disable encryption on the encrypted files.

> **Note** This is the first time you are logging on as User3. Recall that the password is User3, but you will have to change it. Change the password to *user.*

▶ **To test encrypt files**

1. Log on as User3 with a password of User3.

2. When prompted, change User3's password to **user**.

3. Start Windows Explorer and open C:\Secret\File1.txt.

    What happens?

4. Close Notepad.

▶ **To attempt to disable the encryption**

1. Right-click C:\Secret\File1.txt and then click Properties.

2. Click Advanced.

3. Clear the Encrypt Contents To Secure Data check box and then click OK.

4. Click OK to close the File1 Properties dialog box.

    The Error Applying Attributes dialog box appears and informs you that access to the file is denied.

5. Click Cancel.

6. Close all open windows and dialog boxes.

7. Log off as User3 and log on as Administrator.

Exercise 3: Decrypting Folders and Files

In this exercise, you will decrypt the folder and file that you previously encrypted.

▶   **To decrypt files**

1. Start Windows Explorer.

2. Right-click C:\Secret\File1.txt, and then click Properties.

3. Click Advanced.

4. Clear the Encrypt Contents To Secure Data check box and then click OK.

5. Click OK to close the File1 Properties dialog box.

6. Close Windows Explorer and log off.

Lesson Summary

EFS provides the core file-encryption technology for storage of NTFS files on disk. EFS allows users to encrypt NTFS files by using a strong public key-based cryptographic scheme that encrypts all files in a folder. Users with roaming profiles can use the same key with trusted remote systems. Backups and copies of encrypted files are also encrypted if they are in NTFS volumes. Files remain encrypted if you move or rename them, and encryption is not defeated by leakage to paging files. Windows 2000 also provides a recovery agent. In the event an owner loses the private key, the recovery agent can still recover the encrypted file.

EFS is implemented either from Windows Explorer or from the command line, using commands such as Cipher. EFS can be enabled or disabled for a computer, domain, or organizational unit (OU) by resetting recovery policy in the Group Policy console in MMC.

You can use EFS to encrypt and decrypt files on remote file servers, but not to encrypt data that is transferred over the network. Windows 2000 provides network protocols, such as Secure Sockets Layer, to encrypt data over the network.

Lesson 6: Using Disk Defragmenter

Windows 2000 saves files and folders in the first available space on a hard disk and not necessarily in an area of contiguous space. This leads to file and folder fragmentation. When your hard disk contains a lot of fragmented files and folders, your computer takes longer to gain access to them because it requires several additional reads to collect the various pieces. Creating new files and folders also takes longer because the available free space on the hard disk is scattered. Your computer must save a new file or folder in various locations on the hard disk. This lesson introduces the Windows 2000 system tool, Disk Defragmenter, which helps organize your hard disks.

After this lesson, you will be able to

- Describe defragmentation.
- Use Disk Defragmenter to organize your hard disks.

Estimated lesson time: 15 minutes

Defragmenting Disks

The process of finding and consolidating fragmented files and folders is called *defragmenting*. Disk Defragmenter locates fragmented files and folders and defragments them. Disk Defragmenter moves the pieces of each file or folder to one location so that each file or folder occupies a single, contiguous space on the hard disk. Consequently, your system can gain access to and save files and folders more efficiently. By consolidating files and folders, Disk Defragmenter also consolidates free space, making it less likely that new files will be fragmented. Disk Defragmenter can defragment FAT, FAT32, and NTFS volumes.

The Disk Defragmenter window is split into three areas, as shown in Figure 8.7.

The upper portion lists the volumes that you can analyze and defragment. The middle portion provides a graphic representation of how fragmented the selected volume is. The lower portion provides a graphic representation of the volume during and after defragmentation. The display colors indicate the condition of the volume as follows:

- Red indicates fragmented files.
- Dark blue indicates contiguous (nonfragmented) files.
- Green indicates system files, which Disk Defragmenter cannot move.
- White indicates free space on the volume.

By comparing the Analysis Display band to the Defragmentation Display band, you can quickly see the improvement in the volume after defragmentation.

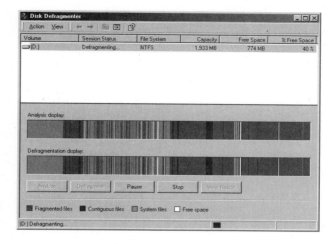

Figure 8.7 The Disk Defragmenter window

If you want to analyze and defragment a volume, in Disk Defragmenter, select one of the options that are described in Table 8.9.

Table 8.9   Disk Defragmenter Options

Option	Description
Analyze	Click this button to analyze the disk for fragmentation. After the analysis, the Analysis Display band provides a graphic representation of how fragmented the volume is.
Defragment	Click this button to defragment the disk. After defragmentation, the Defragmentation Display band provides a graphic representation of the defragmented volume.

Using Disk Defragmenter Effectively

The following list provides best practices for using Disk Defragmenter:

- Run Disk Defragmenter when the computer will receive the least usage. During defragmentation, data is moved around on the hard disk and the defragmentation process is microprocessor intensive. The defragmentation process will adversely affect access time to other disk-based resources.

- Educate users to defragment their local hard disks at least once a month to prevent accumulation of fragmented files.

- Analyze the target volume before you install large applications, and then defragment the volume if necessary. Installations complete more quickly when the target media has adequate contiguous free space. Additionally, gaining access to the application, after it is installed, is faster.

- NTFS compression can cause performance degradation when you copy and move files. When a compressed file is copied, it is uncompressed, copied, and then compressed again as a new file. Compress static data rather than data that changes frequently or is copied or moved frequently.

- Before you can delete a quota entry for a user account, all files that the user owns must be removed from the volume or another user must take ownership of the files.

- When you delete a large number of files or folders, your hard disk can become excessively fragmented, so be sure that you analyze it afterward. Generally, you should defragment hard disks on busy file servers more often than those on single-user client computers.

Lesson Summary

Windows 2000 saves files and folders in the first available space on a hard disk and not necessarily in an area of contiguous space. This leads to file and folder fragmentation. When your hard disk contains a lot of fragmented files and folders, your computer takes longer to gain access to these files and folders and to create new files and folders.

The Windows 2000 system tool, Disk Defragmenter, locates fragmented files and folders and defragments them. Consequently, your system can gain access to and save files and folders more efficiently. By consolidating files and folders, Disk Defragmenter also consolidates free space, making it less likely that new files will be fragmented. Disk Defragmenter can defragment FAT, FAT32, and NTFS volumes.

Review

Here are some questions to help you determine if you have learned enough to move on to the next chapter. If you have difficulty answering these questions, please go back and review the material in this chapter before beginning the next chapter. The answers to these questions are located in Appendix A, "Questions and Answers."

1. You are the administrator for your organization's network. Management would like to segregate documents so that marketing documents are available to everybody on the network while research and development documents are hidden in a shared folder. How can this be accomplished?

2. Users are distraught because information they need is scattered throughout the network on various servers. This forces them to remember the names of all of the servers and shared folders on the entire network, which is difficult at best. As the administrator, what can you do to alleviate this problem?

3. Your company utilizes a data center for centralized storage and control of corporate documents. Each user is allocated a certain amount of storage at the data center and the user's department is charged a monthly fee for usage. In the past, the data center's strategy has been to partition the drives on the servers to configure each user's allocation. This creates problems when the allocations must be changed. The data center is going to be upgrading all of its servers to Windows 2000. Which feature of Windows 2000 will make setting the allocations easier?

4. Users complain that access times to the data center's servers has increased over the past few months. What maintenance must be done and when should this be done?

C H A P T E R   9

Configuring Remote Access

About This Chapter

Microsoft Windows 2000 incorporates several new protocols for use with remote
access, in addition to new wizards and interfaces for configuring all types of
network connections. The Network Connection wizard, for example, provides a
simple interface for creating and configuring basic inbound and outbound connections, while Routing and Remote Access is a more robust management tool
for configuring connections on domain controllers. This chapter gives you an
understanding of the new options and interfaces in Windows 2000 so that you
can connect computers and configure protocols correctly to meet your
organization's remote access requirements.

Before You Begin

To complete this chapter

- You must have a computer that meets or exceeds the minimum hardware requirements listed in "Getting Started," on page xxi.

- You must have installed the beta version of Windows 2000 Advanced Server on a computer meeting the specifications listed in the preceding bullet. The computer should be installed as a domain controller in a domain and TCP/IP should be the only installed protocol.

- Your computer should be using a static IP address.

Lesson 1: Understanding the New Authentication Protocols in Windows 2000

Microsoft Windows NT 4.0 included support for several authentication protocols used to verify the credentials of users connecting to the network. These protocols included the following:

- Password Authentication Protocol (PAP)
- Challenge Handshake Authentication Protocol (CHAP)
- Microsoft Challenge Handshake Authentication Protocol (MS-CHAP)
- Shiva Password Authentication Protocol (SPAP)
- Point-to-Point Tunneling Protocol (PPTP)

Windows 2000 includes support for these and several additional protocols that significantly increase your authentication, encryption, and multilinking options. The new protocols supported by Windows 2000 include Extensible Authentication Protocol (EAP), Remote Authentication Dial-In User Service (RADIUS), Internet Protocol Security (IPSec), Layer-Two Tunneling Protocol (L2TP), and Bandwidth Allocation Protocol (BAP).

After this lesson, you will be able to

- Describe the new protocols supported by Windows 2000.

Estimated lesson time: 15 minutes

Extensible Authentication Protocol (EAP)

EAP allows for an arbitrary authentication mechanism to validate a dial-in connection. The exact authentication method to be used is negotiated by the dial-in client and the remote access server. EAP supports authentication by using the following:

- **Generic token cards.** These are physical cards used to provide passwords. Token cards can use several authentication methods, such as using codes that change with each use.
- **Message Digest 5 Challenge Handshake Authentication Protocol (MD5-CHAP).** This protocol encrypts user names and passwords with an MD5 algorithm.
- **Transport Level Security (TLS).** TLS is used for smart card support or other certificates. Smart cards require a card and reader. The smart card electronically stores the user's certificate and private key.

Through the use of the EAP application programming interfaces (APIs), independent software vendors can supply new client and server authentication modules for technologies such as token cards, smart cards, biometric hardware such as retina scanners, or one-time password systems. EAP allows for the support of authentication technologies that are not yet developed. EAP authentication methods are added on the Security tab of the remote access server's Properties dialog box.

Note For more information on EAP, see RFC 2284.

Remote Authentication Dial-In User Service (RADIUS)

The diversity of hardware and operating systems in today's enterprise networks requires remote user authentication to be vendor-independent and scalable. RADIUS support in Windows 2000 facilitates this kind of user authentication, while providing highly scalable authentication designs for performance and fault-tolerant designs for reliability.

RADIUS provides authentication and accounting services for distributed dial-up networking. Windows 2000 can act as a RADIUS client, a RADIUS server, or both. A RADIUS client, typically an Internet service provider (ISP) dial-up server, is a remote access server receiving authentication requests and forwarding requests to a RADIUS server. As a RADIUS client, Windows 2000 can also forward accounting information to a RADIUS accounting server. RADIUS clients are configured on the Security tab in the remote access server's Properties dialog box.

A RADIUS server validates the RADIUS client request. Windows 2000 Internet Authentication Services (IAS) performs authentication. As a RADIUS server, IAS stores RADIUS accounting information from RADIUS clients in log files. IAS is one of the optional components that can be installed during Windows 2000 installation or at a later time through Add/Remove Programs in Control Panel. IAS can then be found in Administrative Tools on the Programs menu (via the Start menu).

Note For additional information on RADIUS, see RFC 2138/2139.

Internet Protocol Security (IPSec)

IPSec is a framework of open standards for ensuring secure private communications over Internet Protocol (IP) networks by using cryptographic security services. IPSec provides aggressive protection against private network and Internet attacks, while retaining ease of use. Clients negotiate a security association (SA) that acts as a private key to encrypt the data flow.

Your network security administrator can use IPSec policies, rather than applications or operations systems, to configure IPSec security services. The policies provide variable levels of protection for most traffic types, in most existing networks. Your network security administrator can configure IPSec policies to meet the security requirements of a user, group, application, domain, site, or global enterprise.

Windows 2000 provides an administrative interface, IP Security Management, to create and manage IPSec policies (centrally at the group policy level for domain members, or locally on a nondomain computer). IP Security Management is a tool that you can add to any Microsoft Management Console (MMC). Configuring IPSec policies is beyond the scope of this course.

Note For additional information on security mechanisms for IP, see RFC 1825.

Layer-Two Tunneling Protocol (L2TP)

L2TP is very similar to PPTP in that its primary purpose is to create an encrypted tunnel through an untrusted network. L2TP differs from PPTP in that it provides tunneling, but not encryption. L2TP provides a secure tunnel by cooperating with other encryption technologies such as IPSec. IPSec does not require L2TP, but its encryption functions complement L2TP to create a secure virtual private network (VPN) solution.

Both PPTP and L2TP use PPP to provide an initial envelope for the data and then append additional headers for transport through the transit internetwork. Some of the key differences between PPTP and L2TP are as follows:

- PPTP requires an IP-based transit internetwork. L2TP requires only that the tunnel media provide packet-oriented, point-to-point connectivity. L2TP can use User Datagram Protocol (UDP), frame relay permanent virtual circuits (PVCs), X.25 virtual circuits (VCs), or Asynchronous Transfer Mode (ATM) VCs to operate over an IP network.

- L2TP supports header compression; PPTP does not. When header compression is enabled, L2TP operates with four bytes of overhead, compared to six bytes for PPTP.

- L2TP supports tunnel authentication, while PPTP does not. However, when either PPTP or L2TP is used in conjunction with IPSec, IPSec provides tunnel authentication so that layer-two tunnel authentication is not necessary.

- PPTP uses PPP encryption. L2TP requires IPSec for encryption.

The creation of L2TP ports for VPNs is discussed later in this chapter.

Note As of the release of this training kit, L2TP has not reached RFC status. The latest draft is available at http://ds.internic.net/internet-drafts/.

Bandwidth Allocation Protocol (BAP)

In Windows NT 4.0, Remote Access Service (RAS) supports basic multilink capabilities. It allows the combining of multiple physical links into one logical link. Typically, two or more Integrated Services Digital Network (ISDN) lines or modem links are bundled together for greater bandwidth.

In Windows 2000, BAP and Bandwidth Allocation Control Protocol (BACP) enhance multilink by dynamically adding or dropping links on demand. BAP is especially valuable to operations that have carrier charges based on bandwidth utilization. BAP and BACP are sometimes used interchangeably to refer to bandwidth-on-demand functionality. Both protocols are PPP control protocols and work together to provide bandwidth on demand. BAP provides a very efficient mechanism for controlling connection costs while dynamically providing optimum bandwidth.

You can enable multilink and BAP protocols on a serverwide basis from the PPP tab of each remote access server's Properties dialog box. You configure BAP settings through remote access policies. Using these policies, you can specify that an extra line is dropped if link utilization drops below 75 percent for one group and below 25 percent for another group. Remote access policies are described later in this chapter.

Note For more information on PPP multilink, see RFC 1990. For more information on BAP/BACP, see RFC 2125.

Lesson Summary

Windows NT 4.0 included support for several authentication protocols used to verify the credentials of users connecting to the network. These protocols included the following: Password Authentication Protocol (PAP), Challenge Handshake Authentication Protocol (CHAP), Microsoft Challenge Handshake Authentication Protocol (MS-CHAP), Shiva Password Authentication Protocol (SPAP), and Point-to-Point Tunneling Protocol (PPTP).

Windows 2000 includes support for these and several additional protocols that significantly increase your authentication, encryption, and multilinking options including the following:

- **Extensible Authentication Protocol (EAP).** EAP is an extension to the Point-to-Point Protocol (PPP) that works with dial-up, PPTP, and L2TP clients. EAP allows for an arbitrary authentication mechanism to validate a dial-in connection. The exact authentication method to be used is negotiated by the dial-in client and the remote access server.

- **Remote Authentication Dial-In User Service (RADIUS).** Windows 2000 RADIUS support allows user authentication to be vendor-independent and provides highly scalable authentication designs for performance and fault-tolerant designs for reliability.

- **Internet Protocol Security (IPSec).** IPSec is a framework of open standards for ensuring secure private communications over IP networks by using cryptographic security services. IPSec provides aggressive protection against private network and Internet attacks, while retaining ease of use. Clients negotiate a security association (SA) that acts as a private key to encrypt the data flow.

- **Layer-Two Tunneling Protocol (L2TP).** L2TP is very similar to PPTP in that its primary purpose is to create an encrypted tunnel through an untrusted network. L2TP differs from PPTP in that it provides tunneling but not encryption. L2TP provides a secure tunnel by cooperating with other encryption technologies such as IPSec. IPSec does not require L2TP, but its encryption functions complement L2TP to create a secure virtual private network (VPN) solution.

- **Bandwidth Allocation Protocol (BAP).** BAP and Bandwidth Allocation Control Protocol (BACP) enhance multilink by dynamically adding or dropping links on demand. BAP is especially valuable to operations that have carrier charges based on bandwidth utilization. BAP and BACP are sometimes used interchangeably to refer to bandwidth-on-demand functionality. BAP provides a very efficient mechanism for controlling connection costs while dynamically providing optimum bandwidth.

Lesson 2: Configuring Inbound Connections

Configuring inbound connections on a computer running Windows 2000 allows the computer to act as a dial-in server. You can configure inbound connections in Windows 2000 with the same Network Connection wizard used for outbound connections if the computer is not a member of a domain. (Outbound connections and the Network Connection wizard are discussed in the next lesson in this chapter.) However, you must use the Routing and Remote Access Service (RRAS) to configure inbound connections when the computer is a member of a domain or a domain controller. Experience with this administrative tool can help you set up VPNs and modem pools on a remote access server.

Note RRAS in Windows 2000 is also a full-featured software router and an open platform for routing and internetworking. The Windows 2000 RRAS extends the routing capabilities of the Windows NT 4.0 RRAS by adding IP multicast, network address translation (NAT), and additional VPN services. The routing functions of RRAS are outside the scope of this training kit.

After this lesson, you will be able to

- Install RRAS.
- Configure inbound connections in Windows 2000.
- Configure remote access to allow incoming VPN connections.

Estimated lesson time: 25 minutes

Configuring Inbound Dial-Up Connections

To configure and administer inbound connections on a computer that is a member of a domain, you must use RRAS. You must do several things to prepare to start and configure RRAS. First you must purchase the appropriate hardware, verify the compatibility of all of the hardware to be installed, install the hardware, and then verify that the hardware has been installed successfully. After the hardware is installed, you can install and configure Transmission Control Protocol/Internet Protocol (TCP/IP), Internet Packet Exchange (IPX), NetBIOS Enhanced User Interface (NetBEUI), and AppleTalk.

After installing the hardware and any appropriate protocols, you are ready to install RRAS. On the Start menu, point to Programs, point to Administrative Tools, and click Routing And Remote Access. Right-click the server name, and select Configure And Enable Routing And Remote Access (see Figure 9.1).

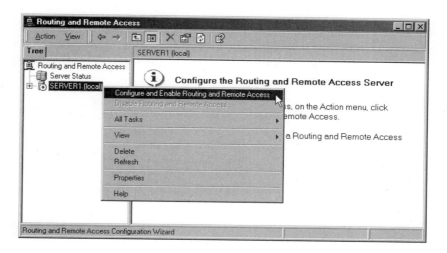

Figure 9.1   Initiating the RRAS configuration and enable process

The Routing And Remote Access Configuration wizard appears. Click Next to continue and on the first page of the wizard, select the Enable Remote Access check box. On the Dial-In Or Demand Dial Interfaces page, select one of the following four options to indicate how you want to configure the interfaces for dial-in access:

- Enable All Devices For Routing
- Enable All Devices For Remote Access
- Enable All Devices For Both Routing And Remote Access
- Configure Each Device Individually

On the Authentication And Encryption page, you can select the authentication methods you want to use by selecting the All Methods Including Clear Text Password option or the Only Methods Which Secure The User's Password option. You can also select the Encrypt All L2TP Connections check box to require all L2TP VPN connections to use IPSec encryption.

On the Remote Access page, you can review the protocols that have been installed on your server and select whether dial-in users have access to just this computer or all computers on the network. On the TCP/IP Server Settings (Remote Access) page, select Use DHCP or Use A Static Pool for assigning IP addresses to the dial-in clients. Click Finish to exit the wizard.

Finally, you need to verify that the service starts correctly and that the dial-up clients are allocated appropriate IP addresses, Domain Name System (DNS) server addresses, IPX network addresses, NetBIOS names, and so on when they are connected. You can configure remote access policies, authentication, and encryption settings.

Configuring Virtual Private Network Ports

When RRAS is started for the first time, Windows 2000 automatically creates five PPTP and five L2TP ports. You can configure these ports under the Ports node on the console tree (see Figure 9.2).

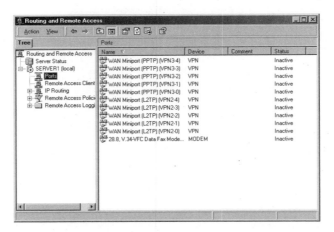

Figure 9.2   Port configuration

To configure VPN ports, in the console tree of the Routing And Remote Access window, right-click Ports, and then click Properties. In the Ports Properties dialog box, select a device. For VPN ports, these will read WAN Miniport (PPTP) and WAN Miniport (L2TP). Click the Configure button. In the Configure Ports dialog box, select the Remote Access (Inbound) check box to enable inbound VPN connections (see Figure 9.3). Optionally, you can increase or decrease the number of virtual ports available on the server. Click OK in the Configure Ports dialog box and in the Ports Properties dialog box.

Configuring Modem and Cable Ports

When RRAS is started for the first time, Windows 2000 automatically detects any modems that are installed and creates modem ports for them. Windows 2000 also creates ports for each parallel or serial cable connection it detects. You can also configure these ports manually under the Ports node on the console tree.

To configure modem or cable ports, in the console tree of the Routing And Remote Access window, right-click Ports, and then click Properties. In the Ports Properties dialog box, select a device, and then click the Configure button.

Note   Modem, parallel, and serial ports are listed individually, but are grouped together and can be configured either individually or together. To configure several ports simultaneously, hold down the Ctrl key or the Shift key to select multiple ports, and then click the Configure button.

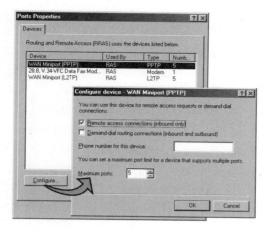

Figure 9.3   Enabling inbound connections

In the Configure Device dialog box, select the Remote Access Connections (Inbound Only) check box to enable inbound connections (see Figure 9.3). If you are configuring a modem port, enter a phone number.

When you are through configuring the ports, click OK in the Configure Device and Ports Properties dialog boxes.

Practice: Installing and Configuring RRAS

In this practice, you will use the Routing And Remote Access Configuration wizard to install and configure RRAS.

▶ **To install RRAS**

1. Log on as Administrator.

2. On the Start menu, point to Programs, point to Administrative Tools, and click Routing And Remote Access.

    The Routing And Remote Access window appears.

3. Right-click the Server1 icon, and select Configure And Enable Routing And Remote Access.

    The Routing And Remote Access Configuration wizard appears.

4. Click Next.

5. On the Routing And Remote Access page, select the Enable Remote Access check box, clear the Enable Server As A Router check box, and then click Next.

    The Dial-In Or Demand Dial Interfaces page appears.

6. Ensure that the Enable All Devices For Remote Access option is selected, and then click Next.

   The Authentication And Encryption page appears.

7. Select the Only Methods Which Secure The User's Password option, and then click Next.

   The Routing And Remote Access page appears.

8. Select the Access This Server Only option, and then click Next.

   The TCP/IP Settings page appears.

9. Select the Use A Static Pool option. Type **192.168.0.0** in the Address box. Type **255.255.255.0** in the Mask box. Click Next, and then click Finish.

   A Routing And Remote Access Administration message box appears, stating that RRAS is installed and asking if you want to start the service.

10. Click Yes to start the service.

   The service starts and the console tree is populated with additional nodes beneath Server1. Leave the Routing And Remote Access window open.

Lesson Summary

You configure inbound connections in Windows 2000 with the Network Connection wizard if the computer is not a member of a domain. However, RRAS is used to configure inbound connections when the computer is a member of a domain or a domain controller. When RRAS is started for the first time, Windows 2000 automatically creates five PPTP and five L2TP ports. You can configure these ports under the Ports node on the console tree.

When RRAS is started for the first time, Windows 2000 automatically detects any modems that are installed and creates modem ports for them. Windows 2000 also creates ports for each parallel or serial cable connection it detects. You can also configure these ports manually under the Ports node on the console tree.

Lesson 3: Configuring Outbound Connections

You can configure all outbound connections in Windows 2000 with the Network Connection wizard. Much of the work of configuring protocols and services is automated when you use this process. Understanding the options found in the wizard will help you to configure connections efficiently.

There are three basic types of outbound connections:

- Dial-up connections
- Connections to a VPN
- Direct connections to another computer through a cable

After this lesson, you will be able to

- Configure outbound connections in Windows 2000.

Estimated lesson time: 25 minutes

Creating Dial-Up Connections

Dial-up connections include outbound dial-up connection to either a private network or to an ISP. To create and configure an outbound dial-up connection, use the Network Connection wizard. To access the Network Connection wizard, right-click My Network Places, click Properties, and then double-click the Make New Connection icon. The Welcome To The Network Connection Wizard page will appear. Click Next to continue and the Network Connection Type page appears, as shown in Figure 9.4.

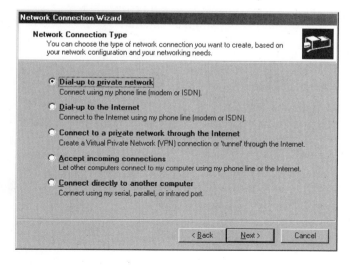

Figure 9.4   Select a type of connection on the Network Connection Type page.

On the Network Connection Type page, select Dial-Up To Private Network to create a connection to a private network or Dial-Up To The Internet to create a connection to an ISP.

Dial-Up to Private Network

If you select the Dial-Up To Private Network option and click Next, you will be prompted to enter the phone number of the computer or network to which you want to connect; this might be an ISP for an Internet connection or the modems for your private network. Enter the phone number, click Next, and you will be prompted to specify who can use this connection. If you want this connection to be made available to all users of this computer, select the For All Users option, and then click Next. If you want to reserve the connection for yourself, select the Only For Myself option. When you click Next, you will be prompted for one of the following:

- If you selected For All Users, and you want to let other computers gain access to resources through this dial-up connection, select the Enable Shared Access For This Connection check box, and then click Next. Type a name for the connection, and then click Finish.

- If you selected Only For Myself, you will be prompted to type a name for the connection, and then click Finish.

Dial-Up to the Internet

If you select Dial-Up To The Internet and click Next, you will be prompted to select one of the following two options in the Internet Connection wizard:

- **Connect Using My Phone Line.** If you already have an account with an ISP and have obtained all the necessary connection information, you can connect to your account using your phone line. If you choose this option and click Next, you will be prompted to enter the telephone number you dial to connect to your ISP or the modem for your private network. To complete the wizard, you will be prompted for the user name and password that you use to log on to your ISP, and you will be prompted to type in a name for the dial-up connection.

- **Connect Using My Local Area Network (LAN).** If you are connected to a local area network (LAN) that is connected to the Internet, you can access the Internet over the LAN. You will be prompted for a proxy server and other settings.

Note ISDN and X.25 connections are considered VPNs for the purposes of the Network Connection wizard.

Creating Connections to a Virtual Private Network

A VPN is a network that is created by using tunneling protocols such as PPTP or L2TP to create secure connections across an untrusted network. To create a new VPN connection you also use the Network Connection wizard. To access the Network Connection wizard, right-click My Network Places, click Properties, and then double-click the Make New Connection icon. The Welcome To The Network Connection Wizard page will appear. Click Next to continue and the Network Connection Type page appears.

On the Network Connection Type page, click Connect To A Private Network Through The Internet, click Next, and then do one of the following:

- If you need to establish a connection with your ISP or some other network before connecting to the VPN, click the Automatically Dial This Initial Connection option, select a connection from the list, and then click Next.

- If you do not want to automatically establish an initial connection, click the Do Not Dial The Initial Connection option, and then click Next.

When prompted, type the host name or IP address of the computer or network to which you are connecting, and then click Next. If you want this connection to be made available to all users of this computer, select the For All Users option, and then click Next. If you want to reserve the connection for yourself, select the Only For Myself option. When you click Next, you will be prompted for one of the following:

- If you selected For All Users and you want to let other computers gain access to resources through this dial-up connection, select the Enable Shared Access For This Connection check box, and then click Next. Type a name for the connection, and then click Finish.

- If you selected Only For Myself, type a name for the connection when prompted, and then click Finish.

Creating Direct Connections to Another Computer Through a Cable

The Network Connection wizard can also be used to create a direct (cable) connection to another computer. However, if you are a member of a domain and want to host a direct connection, you must use RRAS.

To create a direct cable connection to another computer, on the Network Connection Type page, click Connect Directly To Another Computer, click Next, and then do one of the following:

- If your computer will be the host for the connection, click Host and then click Next.

- If your computer will be the guest for the connection, click Guest (see Figure 9.5) and then click Next.

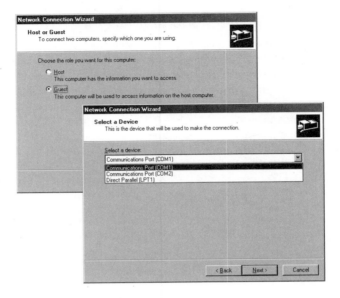

Figure 9.5   Connecting two computers using the Network Connection wizard

After specifying Host or Guest, you select the port that is connected to the other computer and then click Next. If you want this connection to be made available to all users of this computer, click the For All Users option. If you want to reserve the connection for yourself, click the Only For Myself option. When you click Next, you will be prompted for one of the following:

- If you selected For All Users, and you want to let other computers gain access to resources through this dial-up connection, select the Enable Shared Access For This Connection check box, and then click Next. Type a name for the connection, and then click Finish.

- If you selected Only For Myself, type a name for the connection when prompted, and then click Finish.

Practice: Configuring an Outbound Connection

In this practice, you will configure an outbound connection.

Note Before you complete this practice on a stand-alone computer configured as a domain controller, check that your Administrator account is set up to allow remote access. To do this, start the Active Directory Users and Computers tool and be sure to select Advanced Features on the View menu, open the Properties dialog box for the Administrator user, and click the Dial-In tab. In the Remote Access Permission (Dial-In Or VPN) group, ensure that the Allow Access option is selected.

▶ **To configure an outbound connection**

1. Ensure that you are logged on as Administrator.
2. Right click My Network Places, and click Properties.

   The Network And Dial-Up Connections window appears.
3. Double-click the Make New Connection icon.

   The Network Connection wizard appears.
4. Click Next.
5. On the Network Connection Type page, select Connect To A Private Network Through The Internet, and then click Next.
6. On the Destination Address page, type **192.168.1.201** and then click Next.

Note If your server is on a network and there is a valid address that you can use to test your outbound connection, use that address instead of 192.168.1.201.

---

7. On the Connection Availability page, select the Only For Myself option, and click Next.
8. Click Finish.

   The Connect Virtual Private Connection dialog box appears.
9. In the Connect Virtual Private Connection dialog box, ensure that the User name is set to Administrator, and type **password** for the password.

Note If your server is on a network and you entered a valid address in step 6, enter a valid user name and password in step 9.

---

10. Click Connect, read the Connection Complete dialog box, and then click OK.

Important You would not normally set up a virtual connection to your own computer. If your server is the only computer on the network, this was your only choice. If your server is on a network and you entered a valid address in step 6 and a valid user name and password in step 9, a message will also appear stating that Virtual Private Connection is now connected.

---

11. Double-click the connection icon in the system tray, click the Disconnect button, and then click Yes.
12. Close all windows and log off.

Lesson Summary

You can configure all outbound connections in Windows 2000 with the Network Connection wizard. Using the Network Connection wizard automates much of the work of configuring protocols and services. Understanding the options found in the wizard will help you to configure the three basic types of outbound connections efficiently. The three types of outbound connections are dial-up connections, connections to a VPN, and direct connections to another computer through a cable.

Lesson 4: Examining Remote Access Policies

Remote access policies allow the assignment of a connection type to a user according to a set of conditions such as group membership. Understanding how policies are applied helps you to provide customized access to the various users and groups in your organization. It is likely that the default policy settings are adequate for your remote access needs. However, it is important that you become familiar with remote access policies because using them effectively provides you with a great deal of flexibility in granting remote access permissions and usage.

After this lesson, you will be able to

- Explain remote access policy and profile concepts.
- Evaluate remote access policies and profiles.

Estimated lesson time: 10 minutes

Remote Access Policies

Windows 2000 RRAS and IAS both use remote access policies to accept connection attempts. Remote access policies are stored on the remote access server, not in the Active Directory database, so that policies can vary according to remote access server capabilities.

A remote access policy consists of three components that cooperate with Active Directory directory services to provide secure access to remote access servers. The three components of a remote access policy are its conditions, permissions, and profile.

Conditions

This is a list of parameters such as the time of day, user groups, Caller IDs, or IP addresses that is matched to the parameters of the client connecting to the server. The first policy that matches the parameters of the incoming connection request is processed for access permission and configuration.

Permissions

In Windows NT 3.5 and later, remote access was granted based on the Grant Dial-In Permission To User option in the User Manager tool or the Remote Access Administration tool. In Windows 2000, remote access connections are granted based on the dial-in properties of a user account and remote access policies.

The permission setting to allow or deny access on the remote access policy works together with the user's dial-in permissions in Active Directory directory services to create both positive and negative rules. For example, a policy could grant access to all users in Group A from 8 AM–5 PM, but the permissions for User X in Group A could be set to deny access in Active Directory directory services. On the other hand, another policy could deny access to Group A from 5 PM–8 AM, but the permissions for User Y in Group A could be set to allow access. As a result, Group A can gain access only from 8 AM–5 PM, but User X is denied access completely, and User Y is granted 24-hour access.

Profile

Each policy includes a profile of settings that are applied to the connection. If the settings of the connection do not match the user's dial-in settings or the profile properties, Windows 2000 denies access to the connection.

Remote Access Policy Evaluation

Windows 2000 evaluates a connection attempt based on logic that incorporates user and remote access permissions, policy conditions, and profile settings. Using this logic, both mixed- and native-mode networks can use Windows 2000 remote access servers.

Policy Logic

If all of the conditions of a remote access policy are met, the user's dial-in permission is checked by Active Directory directory services and can override the policy's permission. However, when dial-in permission on a user account is set to the Control Access Through Remote Access Policy option, it is the policy's permission that determines whether the user is granted access.

Granting access through the user's permissions or the policy's permissions is only the first step in accepting a connection. The connection attempt is then matched to the settings of the user account and the policy profile. If the connection attempt does not match the settings of the user account or the profile, the connection attempt is rejected.

Default Remote Access Policy

The default policy that is created when RRAS installs is named Allow Access If Dial-In Permission Is Enabled, meaning that the user's dial-in permission will control access. Table 9.1 describes the settings of the default policy.

Table 9.1   Default Policy Settings

Setting	Value
Conditions	Current date/time = any day, any time
Permissions	Deny Access
Profile	None

This default policy is designed to be sufficient for many organizations. However, you should be aware of the implications of the default policy on native- and mixed-mode domains.

Native Mode

If you set the dial-in permission on every user account to Control Access Through Remote Access Policy, and if you do not change the default remote access policy, all connection attempts will be rejected. However, if one user's dial-in permission is set to Allow Access, that user's connection attempts will be accepted. If you change the permission setting on the default policy to Grant Remote Access Permission, all connection attempts are accepted.

Mixed Mode

The default policy is always overridden in a mixed-mode domain, because the user's dial-in permission, Control Access Through Remote Access Policy, is not available on mixed-mode domain controllers. However, remote access policies are applied to users in a mixed-mode domain. If the user's dial-in permission is set to Allow Access, the user still must meet the conditions of a policy to gain access.

Note When converting from mixed mode to native mode, all users with a dial-in setting of Deny Access will be changed to Control Access Through Remote Access Policy. Users with a dial-in permission set to Allow Access will remain set to Allow Access.

Multiple Policies

It is often necessary to administer remote access using multiple remote access policies. You should create these policies carefully. If a connection attempt does not match any of the remote access policies, the connection attempt is rejected, even when a user's dial-in permission is set to Allow Access. The requirement that at least one policy's conditions are matched also means that if the default policy is deleted and no other remote access policies exist, users will not be able to gain access to the network, regardless of their individual dial-in permission settings.

Lesson Summary

Remote access policies allow the assignment of a connection type to a user according to a set of conditions such as group membership. Both Windows 2000 RRAS and IAS use remote access policies to accept connection attempts. If a connection attempt does not match any of the remote access policies, the connection attempt is rejected, even when a user's dial-in permission is set to Allow

Access. The requirement that at least one policy's conditions are matched also means that if the default policy is deleted and no other remote access policies exist, users will not be able to gain access to the network, regardless of their individual dial-in permission settings.

Remote access policies are stored on the remote access server, not in Active Directory directory services, so policies can vary according to remote access server capabilities. A remote access policy consists of three components that cooperate with Active Directory directory services to provide secure access to remote access servers. The three components of a remote access policy are its conditions, permissions, and profile.

Lesson 5: Creating a Remote Access Policy

A number of options and settings are available to you for configuring remote access. Creating a remote access policy involves the following three major steps:

- Configuring dial-in settings for users by using the Active Directory Users and Computers tool
- Creating a policy and its conditions by using the Routing and Remote Access tool
- Editing the policy's profile

These do not have to be completed in any order or at the same time. However, it is important to plan these policies thoroughly and address all three components of creating remote access policies in order to provide secure access to your users.

After this lesson, you will be able to

- Create a remote access policy.
- Create a remote access profile.

Estimated lesson time: 30 minutes

Configuring User Dial-In Settings

On a stand-alone server, the dial-in settings are found on the Dial-In tab of the Properties dialog box for a user account in the Users folder. For a server using Active Directory directory services, the dial-in settings are found on the Dial-In tab of the Properties dialog box for a user account in the Active Directory Users And Computers window. Figure 9.6 shows a user's Properties dialog box.

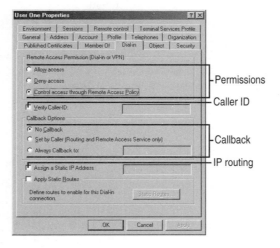

Figure 9.6 A user's Properties dialog box

Remote Access Permission

The Remote Access Permission (Dial-In Or VPN) property determines whether remote access is explicitly allowed, explicitly denied, or determined through remote access policies. If access is explicitly allowed, remote access policy conditions, user account properties, or profile properties can still deny the connection attempt. The Control Access Through Remote Access Policy option is only available on user accounts for stand-alone Windows 2000 remote access servers or members of a native Windows 2000 domain.

Verify Caller-ID

If the Verify Caller-ID check box is selected, the server verifies the caller's phone number. If the caller's phone number does not match the configured phone number, the connection attempt is denied.

All parts of the connection must support caller ID. Caller ID support on the remote access server consists of caller ID answering equipment and the driver that passes caller ID information to RRAS. If you configure a caller ID phone number for a user and you do not have support for the passing of caller ID information from the caller to RRAS, the connection attempt is denied.

Callback Options

If the Callback Options property is enabled, the server calls back a specific phone number (set by the caller or by the network administrator) during the connection process. To disable callback, select No Callback, and the user cannot use callback. To enable callback, select either of the two following options: Set By Caller (Routing And Remote Access Service Only) or Always Callback To. If you want the user to determine whether or not to use callback, select Set By Caller (Routing And Remote Access Service Only). If you want the user to always use callback, select Always Callback To.

Note If the Windows 2000 remote access server is a stand-alone server or a member of a native-mode domain, the callback number can be of unlimited size. If a Windows 2000 remote access server is a member of a mixed-mode domain, the callback number can only be 128 characters.

Assign a Static IP Address

If the Assign A Static IP Address check box option is enabled, the network administrator assigns a specific IP address to the user when a connection is made.

Apply Static Routes

If the Apply Static Routes check box option is selected, the network administrator defines a series of static IP routes that are added to the routing table of the remote access server when a connection is made. This setting is designed for use with demand-dial routing.

Note If a Windows 2000 remote access server is a member of a Windows NT 4.0 domain or a Windows 2000 mixed-mode domain, only the Remote Access Permission (Allow Access and Deny Access options) and Callback Options dial-in settings are available. You can also use the User Manager for Domains tool on Windows NT servers to grant or deny dial-in access and set callback options. When a Windows NT 4.0 remote access server uses a native-mode domain to obtain the dial-in properties of a user account, the Control Access Through Remote Access Policy option is interpreted as Deny Access. Callback settings are interpreted correctly.

Creating a Policy and Its Conditions in Routing and Remote Access

Remote access policy conditions are assigned attributes that are compared to the settings of a connection attempt. If there are multiple conditions in a policy, all of the conditions must correspond to the settings of the connection attempt to result in a match. The condition attributes you can set are described in the following list:

- **Called Station ID.** A character string identifying the phone number of the network access server (NAS). The phone line, hardware, and hardware driver must support reception of caller ID data. You can use a wildcard (asterisk) in this attribute, but the attribute is not used by Windows 2000 IAS.

- **Calling Station ID.** A character string identifying the phone number used by the caller. You can use a wildcard (asterisk) in this attribute, but the attribute is not used by Windows 2000 IAS.

- **Client Friendly Name.** A character string identifying the name of the RADIUS client computer requesting authentication. You can use a wildcard (asterisk) in this attribute, and the attribute is used by Windows 2000 IAS.

- **Client IP Address.** A character string identifying the IP address of the RADIUS client. You can use a wildcard (asterisk) in this attribute, and the attribute is used by Windows 2000 IAS.

- **Day And Time Restrictions.** The day of the week and the time of day for the server's connection attempt. You cannot use a wildcard (asterisk) in this attribute, and the attribute is not used by Windows 2000 IAS.

- **Framed Protocol.** The type of framing for incoming packets. Examples are PPP, AppleTalk, Serial Line Internet Protocol (SLIP), Frame Relay, and X.25. You cannot use a wildcard (asterisk) in this attribute, but the attribute is used by Windows 2000 IAS.

- **NAS IP Address.** A character string identifying the IP address of the NAS. You can use a wildcard (asterisk) in this attribute, and the attribute is used by Windows 2000 IAS.

- **NAS Identifier.** A character string identifying the NAS from which the request originated. You can use a wildcard (asterisk) in this attribute, but the attribute is not used by Windows 2000 IAS.

- **NAS Manufacturer.** The vendor of the NAS requesting authentication. You cannot use a wildcard (asterisk) in this attribute, but the attribute is used by Windows 2000 IAS.

- **NAS Port Type.** The type of media used by the caller. Examples are analog phone lines (Async), ISDN, and VPNs. You cannot use a wildcard (asterisk) in this attribute, and the attribute is not used by Windows 2000 IAS.

- **Service Type.** The type of service being requested. Examples include framed (such as PPP connections) and login (such as Telnet connections). For more information on RADIUS service types, see RFC 2138. You cannot use a wildcard (asterisk) in this attribute, but the attribute is used by Windows 2000 IAS.

- **Windows Groups.** The names of the Windows 2000 groups to which the user attempting the connection belongs. For a native domain-based remote access or IAS server, use universal groups. There is no condition attribute for a specific user name. You cannot use a wildcard (asterisk) in this attribute, and the attribute is not used by Windows 2000 IAS.

You can create a remote access policy and an associated profile under the Remote Access Policies node of the Routing And Remote Access console tree. Right-click the Remote Access Policies node, and then click New Remote Access Policy. In the Add Remote Access Policy dialog box, type the name of the profile in the Policy Friendly Name text box.

To configure a new condition, click the Add button, in the Select Attribute dialog box, click the attribute that you want to add, and then click OK. In the attribute dialog box, enter the information required by the attribute, and then click OK.

In the Permissions section, if you want to grant access to these users, click the Grant Remote Access Permission option, and if you want to deny access to these users, click the Deny Remote Access Permission option.

Configuring Profile Settings

The profile specifies what kind of access the user will be given if the conditions match. This access will only be granted if the connection attempt does not conflict with the settings of the user account or the profile. There are six different tabs that can be used to configure a profile:

- **Dial-In Constraints.** These options include settings for idle-time disconnect, maximum session time, day and time, phone number, and media type (ISDN, VPN, etc.).

- **IP.** These settings configure client IP address assignment and TCP/IP packet filtering. Separate filters can be defined for inbound or outbound packets.

- **Multilink.** These settings configure multilink and BAP. A line can be dropped if bandwidth drops below a certain level for a given length of time. Multilink can also be set to require the use of BAP.

- **Authentication.** These settings define the authentication protocols that are allowed for connections using this policy. The protocol selected must also be enabled in the server's properties.

- **Encryption.** These settings specify that IPSec or Microsoft Point to Point Encryption (MPPE) is prohibited, allowed, or required.

- **Advanced.** This tab allows for the configuration of additional network parameters that could be sent from non–Microsoft RADIUS servers.

You can create a remote access profile from the Add Remote Access Policy dialog box. To edit the policy's profile, click the Edit Profile button. In the Edit Dial-In Profile dialog box, configure the settings on any of the six tabs, and then click OK. Click OK to close the Add Remote Access Policy dialog box.

Optional Practice: Creating a Remote Access Policy and Profile

In this practice, you will create a user with dial-in capabilities. You will then create a global group and add the user to the group.

Note To complete all the procedures in this practice, you must have two computers.

▶ **To create a user with dial-in capabilities**

1. Log on to your domain as Administrator, and open Active Directory Users and Computers.

2. In the console tree, right-click Users, point to New, and then click User.

3. In the New Object – User dialog box, create a user named Rasuser with no password and accept all default settings. Click Next twice, and then click Finish.

4. In the details pane, double-click Rasuser.

5. In the Rasuser Properties dialog box, click the Dial-In tab. Select Allow Access, and then click OK.

► **To create a global group**

1. In the console tree, right-click Users, point to New, and then click Group.
2. In the New Object – Group dialog box, enter the name Rasgroup.
   Ensure that Global is selected in the Group Scope section, then click OK.
3. In the details pane, right-click Rasuser, and then click Add Members To A Group.
4. In the Select Group dialog box, select Rasgroup, and then click OK.
5. Click OK to close the message box that informs you the operation was successful.

► **To test the dial-in configuration**

Note This is one of the procedures that requires two computers.

1. Right-click the My Network Places icon and click Properties. Double-click the Virtual Private Network icon.
2. Connect as Rasuser, with no password.
3. Close the connection.

► **To configure a user's dial-in permissions to control access through remote access policy**

1. In the Active Directory Users And Computers window, double-click Rasuser.
2. In the Rasuser Properties dialog box, click the Dial-In tab.
3. Select the Control Access Through Remote Access Policy option, and then click OK.

► **To test the dial-in configuration**

Note This is one of the procedures that requires two computers.

1. Double-click the Virtual Private Network icon in the Network And Dial-Up Connections window.
2. Connect using Rasuser and no password.

   The Connect Virtual Private Connection dialog box appears informing you that the connection fails.

   Note The default remote access policy denies access to all attempts. To fix this, either control access through user settings or create another policy that grants access to this user.

3. Click Cancel.

▶ **To add a new policy that grants access to users in the Rasgroup**

1. In the Routing And Remote Access window's console tree, right-click Remote Access Policies, and select New Remote Access Policy.
2. On the Policy Name page, type **Allow Rasgroup access** in the Policy Friendly Name box. Click Next.
3. On the Conditions page, click Add.
4. In the Select Attribute dialog box, click Windows-Groups, and then click Add.
5. In the Groups dialog box, click Add. In the Select Groups dialog box, select Rasgroup and click Add.
6. Click OK twice.
7. On the Conditions page, click Next.
8. On the Permissions page, select the Grant Remote Access Permission option, and then click Next.
9. On the User Profile page, click Finish.
10. In the details pane, right-click the new policy and select Move Up.

▶ **To test the dial-in configuration**

Note This is one of the procedures that requires two computers.

---

1. Double-click the Virtual Private Connection icon in the Network And Dial-Up Connections window.
2. Connect using Rasuser and no password.

   The connection succeeds.

   Note Dial-in permissions of the user override the remote access policy permissions.

   ---

3. Close all open windows and log off.

Lesson Summary

When you create a remote access policy, you must configure the dial-in settings for users, create a policy and its conditions, and edit the policy's profile. You do not have to complete these in any order or at the same time. To configure a user's dial-in settings on a stand-alone server, use the dial-in settings found on the Dial-In tab of the Properties dialog box for a user account in the Users folder. To configure a user's dial-in settings on a server using Active Directory technology, the dial-in settings are found on the Dial-In tab of the Properties dialog box for a user account in the Active Directory Users And Computers window.

You can create a remote access policy and an associated profile under the Remote Access Policies node of the Routing And Remote Access console tree. In the If A User Matches The Specified Conditions section, if you want to grant access to these users, click the Grant Remote Access Permission option, and if you want to deny access to these users, click the Deny Remote Access Permission option. Finally, you edit the user's policy's profile. The profile specifies what kind of access the user will be given if the conditions match. This access will only be granted if the connection attempt does not conflict with the settings of the user account or the profile.

Review

Here are some questions to help you determine if you have learned enough to move on to the next chapter. If you have difficulty answering these questions, please go back and review the material in this chapter before beginning the next chapter. The answers to these questions are located in Appendix A, "Questions and Answers."

1. What are the advantages of using L2TP over using PPTP?

2. Describe the two new settings that must be configured using the Network Connection wizard in regard to sharing the connection.

3. Why are remote access policies stored on the remote access server and not in Active Directory directory services? Describe a scenario in which this is beneficial.

4. Which part of a remote access policy is overridden in a mixed-mode domain? Why? Which parts are still effective?

5. A user in the Sales Group has their dial-in permission set to Allow Access. The user attempts to connect during business hours using an ISDN connection, an IP address of 123.45.1.2, and CHAP authentication. Assuming the following policy is in effect on the remote access server, will the user's connection attempt be accepted?

Policy setting	Value
Client IP Address	123.45.*.*
Day And Time Restrictions	8AM–5PM, Mon–Fri
NAS Port Type	Asynch, ISDN, VPN
Windows Groups	Sales, Accounting
Permissions	Deny Access

C H A P T E R   1 0

Supporting DHCP and WINS

About This Chapter

The Microsoft Windows 2000 Server family of products includes enhanced implementations of the Dynamic Host Configuration Protocol (DHCP) and the Windows Internet Naming Service (WINS). These enhancements are designed to lower your total cost of ownership (TCO) by reducing the amount of time you spend configuring, administering, and troubleshooting your DHCP servers and clients, your Domain Name System (DNS) servers, and your WINS servers and clients.

Before You Begin

To complete this chapter

- You must have a computer that meets or exceeds the minimum hardware requirements listed in "Getting Started," on page xxi.

- You must have installed the beta version of Windows 2000 Advanced Server on a computer meeting the specifications listed in the preceding bullet. The computer should be installed as a domain controller in a domain and TCP/IP should be the only installed protocol.

- Your computer should be using a static IP address.

- You must have a beta version of Windows 2000 on CD-ROM.

Lesson 1: New DHCP Functionality

DHCP centralizes and simplifies Internet Protocol (IP) address management on Transmission Control Protocol/Internet Protocol (TCP/IP)-based networks. Windows 2000 includes an enhanced implementation of DHCP that provides additional tools that are designed to reduce the complexity of configuring and administering TCP/IP network clients. Enhancements to DHCP in Windows 2000 include the following:

- **Unauthorized DHCP server detection.** DHCP prevents unauthorized DHCP servers from creating address assignment conflicts.

- **Integration of DHCP with DNS.** When DHCP assigns an IP address to a client, the service can also register the IP address with DNS name servers that support the DNS dynamic update protocol. This can help to reduce the administrative effort required to manage DNS name servers.

- **Expanded scope support.** DHCP adds support for superscopes and multicast scopes, which you can use to streamline your ongoing administration of IP configurations.

- **Support for option classes.** DHCP supports the option classes, which you use to separate and distribute appropriate options for clients with similar or special configuration needs.

- **Automatic assignment of IP addresses.** DHCP clients running Windows 2000 can automatically assign a temporary IP configuration if a DHCP server is unavailable to provide one. Addresses are self-assigned from a network address range that is reserved for private TCP/IP usage and is not used on the Internet.

- **Enhanced monitoring and statistical reporting.** Windows 2000 includes the DHCP console, which provides a graphical display of statistical data to help you monitor system status, such as the number of available addresses versus the number of depleted addresses or the number of leases being processed per second.

After this lesson, you will be able to

- Describe the new DHCP functionality.
- Install the DHCP Server service.
- Authorize a DHCP server.
- Configure scopes, superscopes, and multicast scopes.

Estimated lesson time: 60 minutes

Authorizing a DHCP Server

In previous versions of Windows NT, the implementations of DHCP allowed any user to create DHCP servers on the network. These unauthorized DHCP servers often caused conflicts in IP address assignments. In Windows 2000, before a DHCP server can issue leases to DHCP clients, it must be authorized in the directory services based on Active Directory technology, and only members of the Enterprise Admins group, which exists in the root domain of the forest, can authorize a DHCP server in Active Directory directory services. Since unauthorized DHCP servers cannot issue leases to DHCP clients, the new implementation of DHCP that ships with Windows 2000 reduces IP address conflicts and the amount of time you spend on DHCP administration.

Authorization Status in a Domain

When a DHCP server that is a member of a domain starts, it contacts a domain controller to determine if it is authorized to operate on the network. If the DHCP server is authorized, the service starts properly. If the DHCP server is not authorized, the service logs an error in the system log.

Note If the DHCP server cannot contact a domain controller, it assumes that it is not authorized within the domain, logs an error in the system log, and does not respond to client requests.

Authorization Status in a Workgroup

When a DHCP server that is a member of a workgroup starts, it sends a broadcast message. If the DHCP server receives a response from a DHCP server in a domain, it assumes that it is unauthorized on the network. If the DHCP server receives a response only from workgroup DHCP servers, it determines that it can operate normally. As a result, a network can include multiple operational DHCP servers if all of them are in a workgroup.

Note In both a domain and workgroup environment, a DHCP server broadcasts periodically to determine if there is a change in its authorization status.

To authorize a DHCP server, you would do the following:

1. Log on to the domain with an account that is a member of the Enterprise Admins group.
2. On the Start menu, point to Programs, point to Administrative Tools, and then click DHCP.

3. In the console tree, right-click DHCP, and then click Manage Authorized Servers.

4. In the Manage Authorized Servers dialog box, click a server name and click Authorize.

5. In the Authorize DHCP Server dialog box, enter the name or IP address of the DHCP server to authorize, and then click OK.

6. In the DHCP dialog box, click Yes to confirm the authorization.

Updating DNS Name Servers Dynamically

In Windows 2000, you can configure the DHCP servers and the DNS servers to allow dynamic update of the DNS name servers. This is commonly referred to as Dynamic DNS (DDNS). With DDNS enabled, when DHCP assigns an IP address to a client, the service can also register the IP address with DNS name servers that support the DNS dynamic update protocol. In addition, when the IP address of the client changes, DHCP can automatically update the DNS name server.

Configuring DHCP to Allow Dynamic Updates

You must configure the DHCP server to perform dynamic updates. Otherwise, the ability to perform DNS dynamic updates is disabled. You configure DHCP to enable dynamic update of DNS name servers on the DNS tab of the Properties dialog box for a DHCP server (see Figure 10.1). On the DNS tab, select Automatically Update DHCP Client Information In DNS.

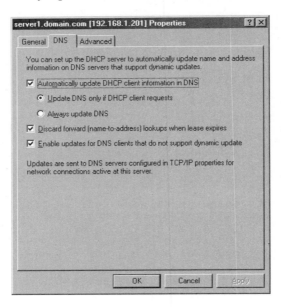

Figure 10.1   Configuring DHCP to automatically update client information in DNS name servers

When you configure DHCP to enable dynamic update of DNS name servers, you also must specify one of the following options:

- **Update DNS Only If DHCP Client Requests.** Specifies to update forward and reverse DNS lookup zones based on the type of request that the client makes during the lease process. This is selected by default. If this option is selected, the DHCP client updates the A (host address) resource record and the DHCP server updates the PTR (Pointer) resource record.

- **Always Update DNS.** Specifies to update forward and reverse DNS lookup zones when a client acquires a lease, regardless of the type of lease request. If this option is selected, the DHCP server updates the A and PTR resource records regardless of the DHCP client's request.

Configuring DNS to Allow Dynamic Updates

To configure a zone for dynamic updates, open the Properties dialog box for the zone in the DNS tool. On the General tab, shown in Figure 10.2, there are three possible selections for the Allow Dynamic Updates option.

- **No.** Disables dynamic updates for the zone.
- **Yes.** Allows all DNS dynamic updates requested for the zone.
- **Only Secure Updates.** Allows only DNS dynamic updates that use secure DNS for the Active Directory–integrated zone.

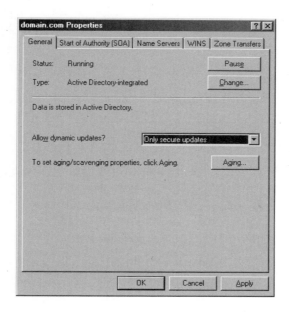

Figure 10.2   Configuring a zone for dynamic updates

By default, communication between DHCP and DNS is not encrypted. However if the zone type is Active Directory Integrated Primary, the Only Secure Updates option appears in the Allow Dynamic Update list. Select this option to enable secure dynamic updates. With secure dynamic updates, the authoritative name server accepts updates only from clients and servers that are authorized to send dynamic updates. Secure dynamic update provides the following benefits:

- It protects zones and resource records from being modified by users without authorization.
- It enables you to specify exactly which users and groups can modify zones and resource records.

Configuring DHCP Scopes in Windows 2000

Windows 2000 extends DHCP functionality to include support for superscopes and multicast scopes. You use these new features to assign IP addresses to a physical network that contains more than one logical subnet. In addition to extended scope support, Windows 2000 includes a set of wizards that make the task of configuring DHCP scopes, superscopes, and multicast scopes easier.

Configuring a Scope

In Windows 2000, you use the Create Scope wizard to configure a new scope. To start the Create Scope wizard, on the Start menu, point to Programs, point to Administrative Tools, and click DHCP. In the console tree, click the name of the DHCP server for which you want to create a scope. Right-click the name of the DHCP server, and then click New Scope.

When you configure a new scope, you specify the information found in Table 10.1.

Table 10.1   Parameters for Creating a New Scope

Parameter	Description
Scope Name	The name of the scope.
Description	An optional description for the scope.
Start IP Address	The starting IP address that can be assigned to a DHCP client from this scope.
End IP Address	The ending IP address that can be assigned to a DHCP client from this scope.
Length	The subnet mask to assign to DHCP clients is automatically filled in based on the IP address range entered, but you can modify it by changing the Length field.

Parameter	Description
Subnet Mask	The subnet mask to assign to DHCP clients. This field is automatically filled in based on the IP address range entered, but you can modify the suggested Subnet Mask.
Exclusion Start IP Address	The starting IP address of the range to exclude from the pool of addresses. The addresses in this exclusion range will not be assigned to DHCP clients. This is important if you have static IP addresses configured on non-DHCP clients. (This is optional.)
Exclusion End IP Address	The ending IP address of the range to exclude from the pool of addresses. The addresses in this exclusion range will not be assigned to DHCP clients. This is important if you have static IP addresses configured on non-DCHP clients. (This is optional.)
Lease Duration Limited To	The number of days, hours, and minutes that a DHCP client lease is available before it must be renewed. The default lease duration is three days.
Lease Duration Unlimited	A parameter that indicates that DHCP leases assigned to clients never expire.

You can also configure some common DHCP options including the following:

- IP addresses of any gateways
- Domain name and the IP address of any DNS servers
- IP addresses of any WINS servers

When you create a new scope, it must be activated before it can start lease distribution. You can choose to activate the new scope during completion of the New Scope wizard, or you can activate it later. To activate a scope later, right-click the scope name, and then click Activate.

Configuring a Superscope

In a Microsoft Windows NT 4.0 network, IP addresses for DHCP clients are limited to a single logical subnet per physical network. The Windows 2000 implementation of DHCP supports superscopes, which provide IP addresses from multiple logical subnets to DHCP clients on a single physical network. In Figure 10.3, SuperscopeA contains Scope1, which contains IP addresses from one logical subnet, and Scope2, which contains IP addresses from a second logical subnet.

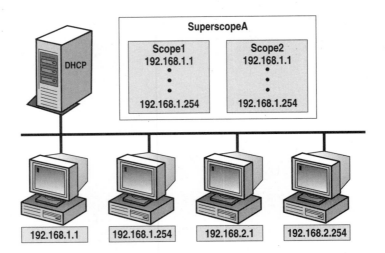

Figure 10.3   Superscope

You use superscopes in a variety of situations, including the following:

- You need to add more hosts on a subnet than originally planned.
- You replace existing address ranges with new address ranges.
- The network uses two DHCP servers to manage separate logical subnets on the same physical subnet.

You use the New Superscope wizard to configure a new superscope. To start the New Superscope wizard, on the Start menu, point to Programs, point to Administrative Tools, and click DHCP. In the console tree, click the name of the DHCP server for which you want to create a superscope. Right-click the name of the DHCP server, and then click New Superscope. In the New Superscope wizard, enter the superscope name, and then specify the scopes to include.

Configuring a Multicast Scope

Multicast DHCP (MDHCP) is an extension to the DHCP protocol standard that you use to support dynamic assignment and configuration of IP multicast addresses on TCP/IP networks. DHCP scopes provide client configuration by allocating ranges of IP addresses from the Class A, B, and C address classes. DHCP in Windows 2000 supports MDHCP in the form of multicast scopes.

Most IP addresses are unique and specific to a single network computer. Multicast addresses are shared by many network computers. When the destination address of an IP datagram is a multicast address, the datagram is forwarded to all members of a multicast group. Multicast address assignment allows selected computers on a network to participate in collaborative application sessions. Typically, conferencing and audio applications use multicasting technology for deploying information to several computers at one time without generating network traffic. Without a multicast scope, users must manually configure multicast addresses. Membership in a multicast group is dynamic, so hosts can leave or join the group at any time. Group membership can be any size and hosts can be members of multiple multicast groups.

Note For more information on multicast addresses, see RFC 1112 and RFC 2236.

You use the New Multicast Scope wizard to configure a new multicast scope. To start the New Multicast Scope wizard, start DHCP, and in the console tree, click the name of the DHCP server for which you want to create a multicast scope. Right-click the name of the DHCP server, and then click New Multicast Scope. In the New Multicast Scope wizard, enter the multicast scope's name and the IP address range. Specify any excluded IP addresses and the lease duration. When prompted, activate the multicast scope.

Examining Option Classes

In a Windows NT 4.0 network, a DHCP server provides the same configuration information to all DHCP clients that receive an IP address. The Windows 2000 implementation of DHCP supports option classes, which you can use to provide unique configurations to client computers. For example, you might configure an option class to provide a group of computers with Internet access. Therefore, you must configure both the DHCP server and DHCP clients to allow option class support.

Windows 2000 supports two types of option classes:

- **Vendor-defined classes.** Configure vendor-defined classes to manage DHCP options that are assigned to clients that are identified by vendor type. For example, you can configure a vendor-defined class to provide a configuration for a specific brand of computer. The vendor-class identifier information is a string of character data interpreted by the DHCP servers. Vendors can choose to define specific vendor class identifiers to convey particular configuration or other identification information about a client. For example, the identifier can encode the client's hardware or software configuration. Most vendor types are derived from the standard reserved-hardware and OS-type abbreviation codes listed in RFC 1700.

- **User-defined classes.** Configure user-defined classes to manage DHCP options that are assigned to clients that require a common configuration that is not based on vendor type; for example, you might want to assign shorter leases to a dial-up client or a laptop portable computer. As of the writing of this training kit, user class options for DHCP is a proposed Internet standard. For more information on DHCP user options, see the Internet Engineering Task Force (IETF) Web site (http://www.ietf.org).

After you define option classes on a DHCP server, you must configure individual scopes with any class-related options that you want to provide to clients.

Using Automatic Private IP Addressing

Windows 2000 supports a new mechanism for automatic IP address assignment for simple local area network (LAN)–based network configurations. This addressing mechanism, called Automatic Private IP Addressing (APIPA), is an extension of dynamic IP address assignment for LAN adapters, enabling the configuration of IP addresses without using static IP address assignment or installing the DHCP Service.

For the APIPA feature to function properly on a computer running Windows 2000, you must configure a network LAN adapter for TCP/IP and click Obtain An IP Address Automatically in the Internet Protocol (TCP/IP) Properties dialog box.

When Windows 2000 starts, TCP/IP attempts to find a DHCP server on the attached network to obtain a dynamically assigned IP address. If there is no DHCP server available, the client cannot obtain an IP address. However, if the Obtain An IP Address Automatically option has been selected, APIPA generates an IP address in the form of 169.254.$x.y$ (where $x.y$ is a unique identifier on the network that the client generates) and a subnet mask of 255.255.0.0.

Note The Internet Assigned Numbers Authority (IANA) has reserved 169.254.0.1 through 169.254.255.254 for APIPA. As a result, APIPA provides an address that is guaranteed not to conflict with routable addresses.

After generating the address, the client computer broadcasts it, and then, if no other computer responds, assigns the address to itself. The computer continues to use this address until it detects and receives configuration information from a DHCP server. This allows the computer to be connected to a LAN hub, to restart without any IP address configuration, and to be able to use TCP/IP for local network access.

Understanding the Limitations of APIPA

APIPA can assign an IP address to DHCP clients automatically. However, APIPA does not generate all of the information that DHCP typically provides, such as the address of a default gateway. Consequently, computers that are enabled with APIPA can communicate only with computers on the same subnet that have also been assigned addresses through APIPA.

Disabling APIPA

By default, the APIPA feature is enabled. However, you can disable this feature. To disable APIPA, add the IPAutoconfigurationEnabled entry to the

HKEY_LOCAL_MACHINE\SYSTEM\CurrentControlSet\Services\Tcpip\
Parameters\Interfaces*GUID_of_the_adapter* subkey in the registry.

The IPAutoconfigurationEnabled entry takes a REG_DWORD data type. To
disable APIPA, specify a value of 0 for the entry.

Practice: Supporting DHCP in Windows 2000

In this practice, you will install and configure the DHCP Service and then add
the DHCP server to the list of authorized servers for the domain.

Exercise 1: Installing the DHCP Service

In this exercise, you will install the DHCP Service on your computer.

▶ **To install the DHCP Service**

1. Log on to your domain as Administrator.
2. Click Start, point to Programs, and then point to Administrative Tools.

   Are there any entries for DHCP?

3. Open Control Panel.
4. Double-click Add/Remove Programs.

   The Add/Remove Programs window appears.
5. Click Add/Remove Windows Components.

   The Windows Components wizard appears.
6. Click Next.
7. Click Networking Services, but do not place a check mark in the box to the
   left of the component.

   Note If the Networking Services check box is already selected, that means
   that some optional networking components have already been installed on this
   computer.
   ---

8. Click Details.

   The Networking Services dialog box appears.
9. Under Subcomponents Of Networking Services, click to place a check mark
   in the box to the left of Dynamic Host Configuration Protocol (DHCP).
10. Click OK.

    You are returned to the Windows Components page.
11. Click Next.

    Windows 2000 Server begins installing the required components.

12. If the Insert Disk dialog box appears, insert the Windows 2000 Advanced Server beta CD-ROM, if necessary, and then click OK. Otherwise, go to step 15.

    The Windows 2000 CD-ROM window appears.

13. Close the Windows 2000 CD-ROM window.

    Windows 2000 Server Setup copies the required files.

14. Remove the CD-ROM.

15. Click Finish to close the Windows Components wizard.

16. Close the Add/Remove Programs window.

17. Minimize Control Panel.

18. Click Start, point to Programs, and then point to Administrative Tools.

    Are there any entries for DHCP?

Exercise 2: Creating and Configuring a DHCP Scope

In this exercise, you create and configure a DHCP scope.

▶   **To create and configure a DHCP scope**

1. On the Administrative Tools menu, click DHCP.

   The DHCP window appears, and a message in the details pane describes how to authorize the DHCP server with Active Directory directory services.

2. On the Action menu, click Authorize.

   Authorization begins and can take several minutes to complete. When authorization is complete, a green upward-pointing arrow appears on the server's icon in the console pane.

3. Right-click Server1 (or the name of your computer), and then click New Scope.

   The New Scope wizard appears.

4. Click Next.

   The Scope Name page appears.

5. Type **Scope1** in the Name box, and then click Next.

   The IP Address Range page appears.

6. Type **192.168.1.70** in the Start IP Address box, and type **192.168.1.140** in the End IP Address box.

Caution If you are on a network, do not assume that you can use this range of addresses. You must check with your network administrator to determine a range of addresses that you can use.

---

7. Ensure that the Mask is 255.255.255.0.

8. Click Next.

    The Add Exclusions page appears.

9. Type **192.168.1.76** in the Start IP Address box.

10. Type **192.168.1.90** in the End IP Address box.

11. Click Add.

12. Notice that 192.168.1.76 to 192.168.1.90 appears in the Excluded Address Range box.

13. Click Next.

    The Lease Duration page appears.

    What is the default lease duration?

14. Click Next to accept the default lease duration.

    The Configure DHCP Options page appears.

15. Click the No option and then click Next.

    The Completing The New Scope Wizard page appears.

16. Click Finish.

    An icon representing the new scope appears in DHCP Manager.

Note The red arrow pointing downward indicates that the scope is not activated.

---

17. Double-click Scope1, right-click Scope1, and then click Activate.

    The red arrow pointing downward disappears indicating that the scope is activated.

▶   **To create a DHCP superscope**

1. Right-click Server 1 (or the name of your computer), and then click New Superscope.

2. In the New Superscope wizard, click Next.

3. On the Superscope Name page, type **superscope** in the Name box, and then click Next.

    The Select Scopes page appears.

4. On the Select Scopes page, click Scope1.

5. Click Next, and then click Finish.

    The superscope appears in the console tree.

▶   **To create a DHCP multicast scope**

1. Right-click Server1 (or the name of your computer), and then click New Multicast Scope.

2. In the New Multicast Scope wizard, click Next.

3. On the Multicast Scope Name page, type **multicast** in the Name box, and then click Next.

   The IP Address Range page appears.

4. On the IP Address Range page, type **224.1.1.1** in the Start IP Address box, type **224.1.1.254** in the End IP Address box, and then click Next.

5. On the Add Exclusions page, click Next.

6. On the Lease Duration page, click Next to accept the default settings.

7. On the Activate Multicast Scope page, ensure the Yes option is selected, and then click Next.

8. Click Finish.

   The multicast scope appears in the console tree.

9. Close the DHCP window.

Lesson Summary

Windows 2000 includes an enhanced implementation of DHCP that simplifies IP address management. In earlier versions of Windows NT, a user could easily create an unauthorized DHCP server on the network. In Windows 2000, DHCP prevents unauthorized DHCP servers from assigning IP addresses—thus reducing this major source of address assignment conflicts. Another enhancement to the Windows 2000 implementation of DHCP is that the DHCP service can now be configured so that when it assigns an IP address to a client, it can also register the IP address with DNS name servers that support the DNS dynamic update protocol. This can help to reduce the administrative effort required to manage DNS name servers.

DHCP in Windows 2000 also has expanded scope support, adding support for superscopes and multicast scopes. A superscope allows you to group scopes so they can provide IP addresses from multiple logical subnets to DHCP clients on a single physical network. Multicast scopes simplify support for Multicast DHCP. Multicast addresses are shared by many network computers. When the destination address of an IP datagram is a multicast address, the datagram is forwarded to all members of a multicast group. Multicast address assignment allows selected computers on a network to participate in collaborative application sessions. Without a multicast scope, users must manually configure multicast addresses.

Other enhancements to the Windows 2000 implementation of DHCP include support for the option classes, which you use to separate and distribute appropriate options for clients with similar or special configuration needs; automatic assignment of IP addresses; and enhanced monitoring and statistical reporting. DHCP clients running Windows 2000 can automatically assign a temporary IP configuration if a DHCP server is unavailable to provide one. Addresses are self-assigned from a network address range that is reserved for private TCP/IP usage and is not used on the Internet. The enhanced monitoring and statistical reporting are found in the DHCP console. The DHCP console provides a graphical display of statistical data to help you monitor system status, such as the number of available addresses versus the number of depleted addresses or the number of leases being processed per second.

Windows 2000 supports a new mechanism for automatic IP address assignment for simple LAN–based network configurations called Automatic Private IP Addressing (APIPA). For APIPA to function properly on a computer running Windows 2000, you must configure a network LAN adapter for TCP/IP and click the Obtain An IP Address Automatically check box in the Internet Protocol (TCP/IP) Properties dialog box. By default, APIPA is enabled; you can disable it by adding the IPAutoconfigurationEnabled entry to the HKEY_ LOCAL_ MACHINE\SYSTEM\CurrentControlSet\Services\Tcpip\Parameters\Interfaces\ *GUID_of_the_adapter* subkey in the registry.

APIPA can assign an IP address to DHCP clients automatically, but it does not generate all of the information that DHCP typically provides, such as the address of a default gateway. Consequently, computers that are enabled with APIPA can communicate only with computers on the same subnet that have also been assigned addresses through APIPA.

Lesson 2: New WINS Functionality

The Windows 2000 implementation of the Windows Internet Name Service (WINS) is an enhanced version of the service provided in Windows NT. WINS registers NetBIOS names and resolves, or translates, them to IP addresses. In Windows 2000, WINS includes a variety of server enhancements, additional client functionality, and an improved management tool. The result is an easier-to-manage and more robust solution for mapping NetBIOS names to IP addresses in TCP/IP networks.

After this lesson, you will be able to

- Describe the new WINS server functionality.
- Describe the new WINS client functionality.

Estimated lesson time: 10 minutes

WINS Server Functionality

You use WINS in Windows 2000 to support clients and applications that rely on NetBIOS names for communication. The Windows 2000 implementation of WINS provides a more powerful and easier-to-manage service for resolving NetBIOS names to IP addresses. These enhancements to WINS server functionality include persistent connections, manual tombstoning, and improved management capabilities.

Persistent Connections

Typically WINS servers disconnect from their replication partners each time replication is completed. When WINS servers are interconnected through high-speed LAN links, it is usually preferable to keep connections open rather than closing them after each replication is completed. Windows 2000 enables you to configure a WINS server to maintain a persistent connection with one or more replication partners. This eliminates the overhead of opening and terminating connections, and it increases the speed of replication.

Manual Tombstoning

In Windows 2000, you can mark a record for deletion and ensure that the tombstone state of the record is replicated to all WINS servers. Tombstoning marks the selected records as tombstoned—that is, they are marked locally as extinct and immediately released from active use by the local WINS server. This allows the tombstoned records to remain present in the server database for purposes of subsequent replication of these records to other servers. When the tombstoned records are replicated, the tombstone status is updated and applied by other WINS servers that store replicated copies of these records. Each replicating WINS server then updates and tombstones these records.

When all WINS servers complete replication of these records and a specified length of time—determined by the Verification Interval—has elapsed, the records are automatically removed from WINS. This prevents the propagation of a copy of an unmarked record to overwrite a record that has been marked for deletion.

Improved Management Capabilities

The administrative tool for configuring WINS is integrated fully with Microsoft Management Console (MMC), providing a more user-friendly environment for configuring the service and for viewing and managing WINS information. In addition, managing the WINS database in Windows 2000 is easier than in earlier versions of Windows. In the Windows 2000 implementation of WINS, you can do the following:

- Filter and search for specific records
- Delete both dynamic and static records
- Select multiple records and perform an action on them all at one time
- Check database consistency
- Export WINS data to a comma-delimited text file

WINS Client Functionality

In addition to improved WINS server functionality, Windows 2000 also includes enhancements to WINS client functionality, including increased fault tolerance and dynamic reregistration.

Increased Fault Tolerance

For a WINS client in a Windows 2000 network, you can specify as many as 12 WINS servers for resolving NetBIOS names to IP addressees. The additional WINS servers provide an extra measure of fault tolerance in the event that the primary and secondary WINS servers fail to respond. If one of the additional WINS servers provides name resolution for a client, the client caches the name resolution to use the next time that the primary and secondary WINS servers fail to resolve the name.

Dynamic Reregistration

In Windows 2000, client functionality is improved to allow a client computer to reregister a NetBIOS name-to-IP-address mapping without the need for the client computer to restart. This is useful for situations in which an incorrect static entry exists or in which a WINS database is restored with an old record, for example. The version ID is updated on the server to cause the record to be replicated to the other WINS servers.

Lesson Summary

The Windows 2000 implementation of WINS is an enhanced version of the service that was provided in Windows NT. The enhancements to WINS server functionality include persistent connections, manual tombstoning, and improved management capabilities.

You can configure a WINS server to maintain a persistent connection with one or more replication partners. This eliminates the overhead of opening and terminating connections, and it increases the speed of replication.

Manual tombstoning allows you to mark a record for deletion and ensure that the tombstone state of the record is replicated to all WINS servers. Each replicating WINS server then updates and tombstones these records. When all WINS servers complete replication of these records and a specified length of time—determined by the Verification Interval—has elapsed, the records are automatically removed from WINS.

Management capabilities are improved in Windows 2000 because the administrative tool for configuring WINS is fully integrated with Microsoft Management Console (MMC). This provides a more user-friendly environment for configuring the service and for viewing and managing WINS information. In addition, managing the WINS database in Windows 2000 is easier than in earlier versions of Windows because you have the ability to filter and search for specific records, delete both dynamic and static records, select multiple records and perform an action on them all at one time, check database consistency, and export WINS data to a comma-delimited text file.

One Windows 2000 enhancement to WINS client functionality is increased fault tolerance. Windows 2000 allows you to specify as many as 12 WINS servers for resolving NetBIOS to IP addresses and dynamic reregistration. The additional WINS servers provide an extra measure of fault tolerance in the event that the primary and secondary WINS servers fail to respond. A second enhancement to WINS client functionality is dynamic reregistration. A client computer can reregister a NetBIOS name-to-IP-address mapping without the need for the client computer to restart.

Review

Here are some questions to help you determine if you have learned enough to move on to the next chapter. If you have difficulty answering these questions, please go back and review the material in this chapter before beginning the next chapter. The answers to these questions are located in Appendix A, "Questions and Answers."

1. What statistical information can you display in the DHCP console?

2. You have installed the DHCP Service on a member server in a domain and have configured a scope, but clients cannot lease an address. You open the DHCP console and notice that the DHCP server icon is marked with a red arrow. What does this mean?

3. How does a DHCP server determine authorization status within a workgroup?

4. You have defined a scope for a subnet and want to add additional IP addresses to the scope. What is the easiest way to complete this task without having to delete the current scope and create a new one?

5. What is the purpose of option classes and what types can you create?

6. If a DHCP client is unable to obtain a lease from a DHCP server, how can the client still gain limited network functionality?

7. How does the Windows 2000 implementation of WINS provide greater fault tolerance for the client?

CHAPTER 11

Managing Disks

About This Chapter

Microsoft Windows 2000 provides two disk storage types: basic disks that use the partitions found in earlier versions of Windows and MS-DOS, and dynamic disks that use volumes which provide more efficient use of space than partitions in computers with multiple hard disks. To simplify the job of managing disks, Windows 2000 includes Disk Management, a graphical tool that consolidates all disk management tasks for both local and remote administration. Disk Management provides shortcut menus to show you which tasks you can perform on the selected object, and includes wizards to guide you through creating partitions and volumes and upgrading disks.

Before You Begin

To complete this chapter

- You must have a computer that meets or exceeds the minimum hardware requirements listed in "Getting Started," on page xxi.

- You must have installed the beta version of Windows 2000 Advanced Server on a computer meeting the specifications listed in the preceding bullet. The computer should be installed as a stand-alone computer in a workgroup and TCP/IP should be the only installed protocol.

- Your computer should be using a static IP address.

- You must have a beta version of Windows 2000 Advanced Server on CD-ROM.

Lesson 1: Introduction to Disk Management

If you have free space on your hard disk, you need to partition and format it so that you can store data on that part of the disk. In addition, if you have more than one hard disk, each disk will also have to be partitioned and formatted so that you can store data on it. Windows 2000 supports two types of disk storage: basic storage and dynamic storage. A physical disk must be either basic or dynamic; you cannot use both storage types on one disk. You can, however, use both types of disk storage in a multidisk system.

After this lesson, you will be able to

- Describe disk management concepts.

Estimated lesson time: 25 minutes

Understanding Basic Storage

Before Windows 2000, the only type of disk storage available was the industry standard that is referred to in Windows 2000 as *basic storage*. It dictates the division of a hard disk into partitions. A *partition* is a portion of the disk that functions as a physically separate unit of storage. Windows 2000 recognizes primary and extended partitions. A disk that is initialized for basic storage is called a *basic disk*. A basic disk can contain primary partitions and extended partitions with logical drives. For Windows 2000, basic storage is the default, so all disks are basic disks until you convert them to dynamic storage. Basic storage in Windows 2000 provides compatibility with disk partitions and sets created with Microsoft Windows NT 4.0.

Partitioning Basic Disks

In Windows 2000, you can create, delete, and format partitions without having to restart your computer to make the changes effective. When you create partitions, you should leave a minimum of 1 megabyte (MB) of unallocated space on the disk in case you decide later to convert the basic disk to a dynamic disk. The conversion process creates a 1 MB region at the end of the dynamic disk in which it stores a database that tracks the configuration of all dynamic disks in the computer.

You can divide a basic disk into *primary* and *extended* partitions. This allows you to separate different types of information, such as user data on one partition and applications on another. A basic disk can contain up to four primary partitions, or up to three primary partitions and one extended partition, for a maximum of four partitions, and only one partition can be an extended partition (see Figure 11.1.)

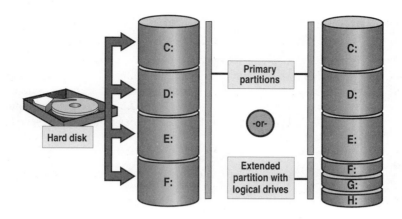

Figure 11.1   Partition types

Primary Partitions

Windows 2000 can use one of the primary partitions to start the computer. The computer looks for the boot files to start the operating system on the primary partition that has been designated as the *active* partition. Only a primary partition can be marked as the active partition and only one partition on a single hard disk can be active at a time. To dual boot Windows 2000 with Microsoft Windows 95 or MS-DOS, the active partition must be formatted as file allocation table (FAT) because Windows 95 cannot read a partition formatted as FAT32 or NT file system (NTFS).

Note Microsoft Windows 98 and Microsoft Windows 95 Operating System Release 2 (OSR2), an enhanced version of Windows 95, can read partitions formatted with FAT32. To dual boot with Windows 98 or Windows 95 OSR2, the active partition must be formatted as FAT or FAT32.

Extended Partitions

There can be only one extended partition on a hard disk, so it is important to include all remaining free space in the extended partition. Unlike primary partitions, you do not format extended partitions or assign drive letters to them. You divide extended partitions into segments. Each segment is a *logical drive*. You assign a drive letter to each logical drive and format it with a file system.

Note The Windows 2000 *system partition* is the active partition that contains the hardware-specific files required to load the operating system. The Windows 2000 *boot partition* is the primary partition or logical drive where the operating system files are installed. The boot partition and the system partition can be the same partition. However, the system partition *must* be on the active partition, typically drive C, while the system partition can be on another primary partition, or on an extended partition.

Introducing Dynamic Storage

A disk that you convert from basic storage to dynamic storage is a *dynamic disk*. Only Windows 2000 supports dynamic disks. Dynamic disks contain dynamic volumes, which can consist of a portion, or portions, of one or more physical disks. A dynamic disk can contain simple volumes, spanned volumes, mirrored volumes, striped volumes, and redundant array of independent disks–5 (RAID-5) volumes. These volume types will be discussed shortly.

Dynamic storage has several advantages:

- Volumes can be extended to include noncontiguous space on the available disks.

- There is no limit on the number of volumes you can create per disk.

- Disk configuration information is stored on the disk, rather than in the registry or in other places where it might not be accurately updated. The disk configuration information is also replicated to all other dynamic disks so that one disk failure will not obstruct access to data on other disks.

Note Removable storage devices contain primary partitions only. You cannot create extended partitions, logical drives, or dynamic volumes on removable storage devices. You cannot mark a primary partition on a removable storage device as active.

Choosing a Volume Type on Dynamic Disks

You can convert basic disks to dynamic storage and then create Windows 2000 volumes. Consider which volume type best suits your needs for efficient use of disk space, performance, and fault tolerance. *Fault tolerance* is the ability of a computer or operating system to respond to a catastrophic event without loss of data. In Windows 2000, mirrored volumes and RAID-5 volumes are fault tolerant.

Simple Volume

A *simple volume* contains disk space from a single disk and provides no fault tolerance. A simple volume can be mirrored to provide fault tolerance.

Spanned Volume

A *spanned volume* includes disk space from two or more disks (up to 32 disks). Windows 2000 writes data to a spanned volume on the first disk, completely filling the space, and continues in this manner through each disk that you include in the spanned volume. A spanned volume provides no fault tolerance. If any disk in a spanned volume fails, the data in the entire volume is lost. Spanned volumes in Windows 2000 are similar to volume sets in Windows NT 4.0.

Mirrored Volume

A *mirrored volume* consists of two identical copies of a simple volume, each on a separate hard disk. Mirrored volumes provide fault tolerance in the event of hard disk failure. Mirrored volumes in Windows 2000 are similar to mirror sets in Windows NT 4.0.

Striped Volume

A s*triped volume* combines areas of free space from multiple hard disks, up to 32, into one logical volume. In a striped volume, Windows 2000 optimizes performance by adding data to all disks at the same rate. If a disk in a striped volume fails, the data in the entire volume is lost. Striped volumes in Windows 2000 are similar to stripe sets in Windows NT 4.0.

RAID-5 Volume

A *RAID-5* volume is a fault-tolerant striped volume. Windows 2000 adds a parity-information stripe to each disk partition in the volume. Windows 2000 uses the parity-information stripe to reconstruct data when a physical disk fails. A minimum of three hard disks is required in a RAID-5 volume. RAID-5 volumes are similar to stripe sets with parity in Windows NT 4.0.

Creating multiple partitions or volumes on a single hard disk allows you to efficiently organize data for tasks such as backing up. For example, partition one-third of a hard disk for the operating system, one-third for applications, and one-third for data. Then, when you back up your data, you can back up the entire partition instead of just a specific folder.

Choosing a File System

Windows 2000 supports the NTFS, FAT, and FAT32 file systems. Use NTFS when you require a partition to have file- and folder-level security, disk compression, disk quotas, or encryption. Windows 2000 and Windows NT are the only operating systems that can access data on a local hard disk that is formatted with NTFS. If you plan to promote a server to a domain controller, format the installation (boot) partition with NTFS.

FAT and FAT32 allow access by, and compatibility with, other operating systems. To dual boot Windows 2000 and another operating system, format the system partition with either FAT or FAT32. FAT and FAT32 do not offer many of the features that are supported by NTFS, for example file-level security. Therefore, in most situations, you should format the hard disk with NTFS. The only reason to use FAT or FAT32 is for dual booting.

Note For a review of file systems, see Chapter 2, "Installing Windows 2000."

Introducing the Disk Management Tool

You can access the Disk Management tool in the Computer Management console. You use the Disk Management tool to configure and manage your storage space and perform all your disk management tasks. Because the Disk Management tool is an MMC snap-in, it uses the interface, menu structure, and shortcut menus you are familiar with from other MMC snap-ins (see Figure 11.2).

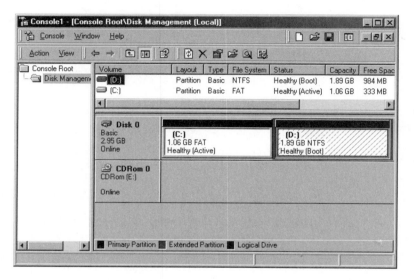

Figure 11.2   The Disk Management tool

You can also create a separate console for the Disk Management tool. When you create a separate console and add the Disk Management snap-in, you have the option of focusing the tool on the local computer or on another computer for remote administration of that computer. As a member of the Administrators or Server Operators group, you can manage disks on a computer running Windows 2000 that is a member of the domain or a trusted domain from any other computer running Windows 2000 in the network.

Disk Management displays the storage system of the computer in either a graphical view or in a list. Important operating information about the disks, partitions, and volumes in your computer is contained in the Properties dialog boxes.

Disk Properties

To view disk properties in Disk Management, select a disk, right-click it, and then click Properties. Table 11.1 describes the information in the Properties dialog box for a disk.

Table 11.1   Disk Properties

Property	Description
Disk	The number for the disk in the system
Type	Type of storage (basic, dynamic, or removable)
Status	Online, offline, *foreign* (disks from another computer), or unknown
Capacity	The total capacity of the disk
Unallocated Space	The amount of available free space
Device Type	Integrated Device Electronics (IDE), Small Computer System Interface (SCSI), or Enhanced IDE (EIDE)
Hardware Vendor	The hardware vendor for the disk and the device type (disk, CD-ROM, DVD-ROM, and so on)
Adapter Name	The type of controller to which the disk is attached
Volumes contained on this disk	The volumes that exist on the disk and their total capacity

Partition and Volume Properties

To view partition or volume properties in Disk Management, select a partition or volume, right-click it, and then click Properties. Table 11.2 describes the information that appears and the tasks that you can perform on the tabs in the Properties dialog box for a partition or volume.

Table 11.2   Partition and Volume Properties

On this tab	You can
General	View the volume label, type, file system, and used or free space.
Tools	Perform the tasks of error-checking, backup, and defragmentation.
Hardware	Lists the storage devices installed. This tab is the same for all volumes.
Sharing	Set shared volume parameters and permissions.
Web Sharing	Share folders through Microsoft Internet Information Services (IIS). This tab only appears if IIS is installed.
Security	Set NTFS access permissions. This tab is only available when the file format is NTFS.
Quota	Set user quotas for NTFS volumes.

Lesson Summary

Windows 2000 supports basic storage and dynamic storage. A disk initialized for basic storage is called a basic disk and can contain primary partitions, extended partitions, and logical drives. All versions of Microsoft Windows, MS-DOS, and Windows 2000 support basic storage. For Windows 2000, basic storage is the default, so all disks are basic disks unless you convert them to dynamic storage.

Dynamic storage creates a single partition that includes the entire disk. You divide dynamic disks into volumes, which can consist of a portion, or portions, of one or more physical disks. A dynamic disk can contain simple volumes, spanned volumes, mirrored volumes, striped volumes, and RAID-5 volumes. Dynamic storage has several advantages over basic storage: volumes can be extended to include noncontiguous space on the available disks; there is no limit on the number of volumes you can create per disk; and disk configuration information is stored on the disk and replicated to all other dynamic disks, so that one disk failure will not obstruct access to data on the other disks.

After you create partitions on a basic disk or create volumes on a dynamic disk, you must format the partition or volume with a specific file system. Windows 2000 supports NTFS, FAT, or FAT32. The file system that you choose affects disk operations. This includes how you control user access to data, how data is stored, hard disk capacity, and which operating systems can gain access to the data on the hard disk. Use the Disk Management tool to configure and manage your network storage space.

Lesson 2: Common Disk Management Tasks

The Disk Management tool provides a central location for disk information and management tasks, such as creating and deleting partitions and volumes. Common disk management tasks include the following:

- Converting storage types
- Creating and extending simple volumes
- Creating and extending spanned volumes
- Creating striped volumes
- Adding disks
- Changing storage type
- Viewing and updating information
- Managing disks on a remote computer

After this lesson, you will be able to

- Identify common disk management tasks.
- Upgrade a basic disk to a dynamic disk.
- Create a new volume.
- Extend a simple volume.
- Mount a simple volume.

Estimated lesson time: 60 minutes

Upgrading Basic Disks to Dynamic Disks

You can convert a disk from basic storage to dynamic storage at any time with no loss of data. To upgrade (convert) a basic disk to a dynamic disk, open the Disk Management tool, right-click the basic disk that you want to upgrade, and then click Upgrade To Dynamic Disk. A wizard provides on-screen instructions. If the disk you are upgrading contains either the boot or system partition, or both, you need to restart the computer to complete the upgrade process.

Important As a precaution, you should always have the data on a disk backed up before you convert the storage type from basic to dynamic.

When you convert a basic disk to a dynamic disk, any existing partitions on the basic disk become volumes. Table 11.3 describes the results of converting a disk from basic storage to dynamic storage.

Table 11.3   Basic Disk and Dynamic Disk Organization

Basic disk organization (before conversion)	Dynamic disk organization (after conversion)
System partition	Simple volume
Boot partition	Simple volume
Primary partition	Simple volume
Extended partition	Simple volume for each logical drive and any free space becomes unallocated space
Logical drive	Simple volume
Volume set Windows NT 4.0 or Windows 2000	Spanned volume
Stripe set Windows NT 4.0 or Windows 2000	Striped volume
Mirror set Windows NT 4.0 or Windows 2000	Mirrored volume
Stripe set with parity Windows NT 4.0 or Windows 2000	RAID-5 volume

Note Any disks that you upgrade must contain at least 1 MB of unallocated space for the upgrade to succeed.

Reverting to a Basic Disk from a Dynamic Disk

You must delete all volumes from the dynamic disk before you can revert the storage type of the disk to basic. After deleting all volumes on the disk, to revert a dynamic disk to a basic disk, open Disk Management, right-click the dynamic disk that you want to change back to a basic disk, and then click Revert To Basic Disk. If you want to revert the dynamic disk on which Windows 2000 is installed, you will have to reinstall Windows 2000.

Creating and Extending Simple Volumes

A simple volume contains disk space on a single disk. A partition and a simple volume may seem like similar uses of disk space; however, a simple volume does not have the size limits that a partition has, nor is there a restriction on the number of volumes you can create on a single disk. You can create a simple volume and format it with NTFS, FAT, or FAT32.

To create a simple volume, open the Disk Management tool, right-click unallocated space on the dynamic disk where you want to create the simple volume, and then click Create Volume. A wizard provides on-screen instructions.

In addition, you can extend a simple volume to include unallocated space on the same disk; however, you can extend a simple volume only if it is formatted with

NTFS. You can extend a simple volume to include either contiguous or noncontiguous unallocated space on the same disk. However, you cannot extend a system or boot volume. (A system or boot volume is created when you convert a system or boot partition to dynamic storage.) To extend an NTFS simple volume, right-click the simple volume that you want to extend, click Extend Volume, and then follow the instructions on your screen. When you extend a simple volume to another disk, it becomes a spanned volume.

Note A simple volume is not fault tolerant, but you can mirror a simple volume.

Creating and Extending Spanned Volumes

A spanned volume consists of disk space from multiple disks (from 2 to 32) combined into one large volume, as shown in Figure 11.3. Spanned volumes enable you to use the total available free space on multiple disks more effectively. You can create spanned volumes only on dynamic disks, but the areas of free space that you combine to create a spanned volume can be different sizes. Spanned volumes cannot be part of a mirror volume or striped volume and are not fault tolerant.

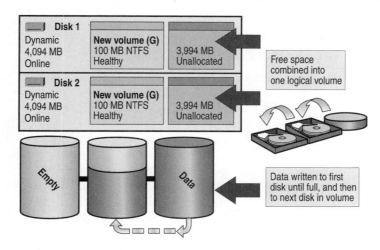

Figure 11.3 Creating and extending spanned volumes

Windows 2000 writes data to the first disk in a spanned volume, completely filling the space, and continues in this manner through each disk that you include in the spanned volume. When any disk in a spanned volume fails, all data in the entire volume is lost. You can create spanned volumes on disks formatted with FAT, FAT32, or NTFS.

By deleting smaller volumes and combining them into one spanned volume, you can free drive letters for other uses and create a large volume for file system use.

Another benefit of spanned volumes is the ability to add space to an existing volume when it is full. For example, when a database on a volume is about to grow beyond the size of the volume, you could add another disk to the system and then add that space to the existing volume.

Creating a Spanned Volume

To create a spanned volume, open the Disk Management tool, right-click unallocated space on one of the dynamic disks where you want to create the spanned volume, and then click Create Volume. In the Create Volume wizard, click Next, click Spanned Volume, and then follow the instructions on your screen.

Extending a Spanned Volume

You can extend an existing spanned volume that is formatted with NTFS by adding free space. The Disk Management tool formats the new area without affecting any existing files on the original volume. You cannot extend volumes formatted with FAT or FAT32. You can extend spanned volumes on dynamic disks onto a maximum of 32 dynamic disks.

Important After a spanned volume is extended, no portion of it can be deleted without deleting the entire spanned volume.

Creating Striped Volumes

You create striped volumes, similar to spanned volumes, by combining areas of free space from 2 to 32 disks into one volume. Among the Windows 2000 Server disk management strategies, striped volumes provide the best performance. In a striped volume, data is written evenly across all physical disks in 64-kilobyte (KB) units (see Figure 11.4). Because the striped volume performs as a single hard disk, Windows 2000 can issue and process concurrent input/output (I/O) commands on all hard disks that are in the striped volume simultaneously. In this way, striped volumes can increase the speed of system I/O.

With a striped volume, Windows 2000 writes data to multiple disks, similar to spanned volumes, except that on a striped volume Windows 2000 writes files across all disks so that data is added to all disks at the same rate. Like spanned volumes, striped volumes do not provide fault tolerance. If a disk in a striped volume fails, the data in the entire volume is lost. You cannot extend or mirror striped volumes.

To create a striped volume, open the Disk Management tool, right-click unallocated space on one of the dynamic disks where you want to create the striped volume, and then click Create Volume. In the Create Volume wizard, click Next, click Striped Volume, and then follow the instructions on your screen.

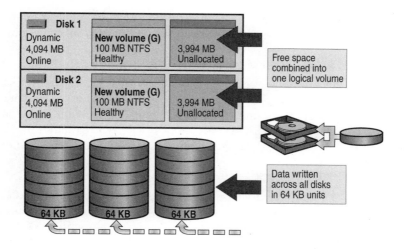

Figure 11.4 Benefits of working with striped volumes

Adding New Hard Disks

To increase your disk storage, you can add new disks to a computer or move a disk or group of disks from one computer to another. If the computer to which you are adding disks does not support *hot swapping* (the ability to add or remove disks without shutting down the computer), shut down the computer, add the disks, and then restart the computer. The new disks will now appear in the Disk Management console.

To add a new disk to a computer that supports hot swapping, install or attach the new hard disk (or disks), and then in the Disk Management tool, click Rescan Disks on the Action menu. You must use the Rescan Disks command every time that you remove or add disks to a computer that supports hot swapping. It should not be necessary to restart the computer when you add a new disk to your computer. However, you might need to restart the computer if Disk Management does not detect the new disk after you run Rescan Disks.

Adding Hard Disks Removed from Another Computer

There may be times you want to uninstall or remove a disk from one computer and then install the hard disk in a different computer. In most cases, disks from another computer are imported automatically. However, if the status of the disk appears as Foreign, you must right-click the new disk, and then click Import Foreign Disk. A wizard provides on-screen instructions.

The disks are grouped according to the computer name they were moved from. To specify the disks from the group that you want to add, click Select Disk. However, if you do not have any dynamic disks installed, all of the disks are added regardless of the disks that you select.

When you move a dynamic disk to your computer from another computer running Windows 2000, you can see and use any existing volumes on that disk.

Failed: Incomplete Volume

If an imported volume's status appears as Failed: Incomplete Volume, you have imported a disk that contains a spanned or a striped volume but have failed to import one or more disks that contain the remaining portions of the spanned or striped volume. This also applies to RAID-5 volumes if two or more disks were not imported. You must import the remaining disks to complete the volume.

Failed Redundancy

If the imported volume's status appears as Failed Redundancy, you have imported a mirror volume or a RAID-5 volume but have failed to import one or more volumes that contain the remaining portions of the mirror or RAID-5 volume. You will still be able to access data on the volume, but redundancy is lost. You must import the remaining disks to complete the volume.

Managing Drive Letters and Paths

Windows 2000 allows the static assignment of drive letters to partitions, volumes, and CD-ROM drives. This means that you permanently assign a drive letter to a specific partition, volume, or CD-ROM drive. It is often convenient to assign drive letters to removable devices that cause the devices to appear after the permanent partitions and volumes on the computer.

You can use the Disk Management tool to mount a local drive to any empty folder on a local NTFS partition or volume. Mounting a drive at an empty folder assigns a drive path rather than a drive letter to the drive. This allows you to use mounted drives to access more than 26 drives on your computer because mounted drives are not subject to the 26-drive limit imposed by drive letters. Mounting at a folder allows you to use an intuitive name for the folder, such as Project Data. Users would then save their documents to the Project Data folder rather than to a drive letter. In Windows 2000, you can add or rearrange storage devices without the drive path failing because drive paths retain their association to the drive.

Assigning, Changing, or Removing Drive Letters

You can use up to 24 drive letters, from C through Z. Drive letters A and B are reserved for floppy disk drives. However, if you only have one floppy disk drive, you can use the letter B for a network drive. When you add a new hard disk to an existing computer system, it will not affect previously assigned drive letters.

To assign, change, or remove a drive letter, open the Disk Management tool, right-click a partition, logical drive, or volume, and then click Change Drive Letter And Path. In the Drive Letter And Paths dialog box, you can do one of the following:

- To assign a drive letter, click Add, click a drive letter, and then click OK.
- To remove a drive letter, click the drive letter and then click Remove.
- To modify a drive letter, click the drive letter that you want to modify and then click Modify. Click the drive letter that you want to use, and then click OK.

Assigning or Removing Drive Paths

Windows 2000 assigns a drive path and not a drive letter to a drive when you mount a local drive at an empty folder on a local partition or volume formatted with NTFS. You can create drive paths for partitions and volumes, and you can format a mounted drive with any Windows 2000–supported file system.

Note You can view all drive paths in Disk Management by clicking View and then clicking All Drive Paths.

To assign or remove a drive path, open Disk Management, right-click the partition or volume, and then click Change Drive Letter And Path. In the Drive Letter And Paths dialog box, do one of the following:

- To create a new drive path, click Add and then type the path to the empty folder or click Browse to locate it. When the correct path is entered, click OK.
- If you are administering a local computer, you can browse folders on that computer to locate the folder to which you want to mount the drive. If you are administering a remote computer, browsing is disabled and you must type the path to an existing folder.
- To remove a drive path, click the drive path and then click Remove.

Note You cannot modify a drive path. If you need to change a drive path, you must remove it and then create a new drive path with the changed information.

Managing Mirror Sets on Basic Disks

Mirror sets that you created with Windows NT 4.0 are retained when you upgrade the computer to Windows 2000. The disks that make up the mirror set are initialized as basic. The Disk Management tool offers limited support for mirror sets on basic disks. You can repair, resynchronize, break, and delete existing mirror sets, but you cannot create new mirror sets on basic disks in Windows 2000.

If a basic disk that contains part of a mirror set is disconnected or fails, the status of the mirror set becomes Failed Redundancy and the status of the disk remains Online. If this happens, you can try to repair the volume.

Repairing a Mirror Set

You must have an additional basic disk with enough space for a new mirror to repair a mirror set on a basic disk. You cannot use a dynamic disk to repair a mirror set. If an additional basic disk is not available, the Repair Volume option is unavailable and you cannot repair the mirror set.

When you repair a mirror set, the Disk Management tool creates a new mirror on a separate basic disk and then resynchronizes the new mirror set. During the repair volume process, the status of the mirror set changes to Regenerating and then Healthy. If the status does not return to Healthy, right-click the mirror set and then click Resynchronize Mirror.

To repair a mirror set on a basic disk, open the Disk Management tool, right-click the mirror set that you want to repair, click Repair Volume, and then follow the instructions on your screen.

Resynchronizing Mirror Sets

Resynchronize a mirror set when data on one of the disks is incomplete or out-dated. If one disk in a mirror set is removed, for example, data will be written to the remaining disk. The mirror set is then no longer fault tolerant. When you replace the missing disk, you must resynchronize the mirror set to update the information on the replaced disk. Resynchronize Mirror is an option on the short-cut (right-click) menu for a mirror set.

Breaking Mirror Sets

Breaking a mirror set creates two independent partitions or logical drives. The data is no longer redundant and no data is deleted. For example, if you determine that the data you store in the mirror set is not vital enough to require fault tolerance and you need more disk storage space, you can break the mirror set to use both partitions for storage. To break a mirror set, open the Disk Management tool, right-click the mirror set that you want to break, and then click Break Mirror.

Deleting Mirror Sets

When you want to recover the use of both partitions that comprise a mirror set and do not want to save the data stored in the mirror set, you can delete the mirror set rather than breaking it. Deleting a mirror set deletes all of the data that the set contains, in addition to the partitions that make up the set. You can delete only the entire mirror set. To delete a mirror set, open the Disk Management tool, right-click the mirror set that you want to delete, and then click Delete Volume.

Managing Volume Sets and Stripe Sets on Basic Disks

When you no longer want a volume set or a stripe set, or you have a problem with a faulty disk drive, you can delete the set. When you have a problem with a faulty disk drive that is part of a stripe set with parity, you can attempt to repair the stripe set with parity or delete it.

Deleting Volume Sets and Stripe Sets

Volume sets and stripe sets that you created with Windows NT 4.0 are retained when you upgrade the computer to Windows 2000. The disks that make up the volume set or stripe set are initialized as basic. Disk Management offers limited support for volume sets and stripe sets on basic disks. You can delete volume sets and stripe sets, but you cannot create new ones on basic disks in Windows 2000.

Deleting a volume set or stripe set deletes all of the data that the set contains, in addition to the partitions that make up the set. You can delete only entire volume sets and stripe sets. To delete a volume set or a stripe set, right-click the volume set or stripe set that you want to delete, and then click Delete Volume.

Repairing and Deleting Stripe Sets with Parity

Stripe sets with parity that you created with Windows NT 4.0 are retained when you upgrade the computer to Windows 2000. The disks that make up the stripe set with parity are initialized as basic. Disk Management provides limited support for stripe sets with parity on basic disks. You can repair, regenerate the parity of, and delete stripe sets with parity, but you cannot create new stripe sets with parity on basic disks in Windows 2000.

If a basic disk that contains part of a stripe set with parity is disconnected or fails, the status of the stripe set with parity becomes Failed Redundancy and the status of the disk remains Online. If this happens, you can try to repair the set. Repairing a stripe set with parity on a basic disk requires an additional basic disk with sufficient free space for part of the stripe set with parity. You cannot use a dynamic disk to repair a stripe set with parity. If an additional basic disk is not available, the Repair Volume option is unavailable and you cannot repair the set.

Disk Management relocates part of the stripe set with parity to a separate basic disk, regenerates the parity, and then returns the status of the set to Healthy when you repair a stripe set with parity on a basic disk.

To repair a stripe set with parity on a basic disk, open the Disk Management tool, right-click the stripe set with parity that you want to repair, and then click Repair Volume.

During the Repair Volume process, the status of the stripe set with parity changes to Regenerating and then Healthy. If the status of the set does not return to Healthy, right-click the stripe set with parity, and then click Regenerate Parity.

Deleting a stripe set with parity deletes all of the data that the set contains, in addition to the partitions that make up the set. You can delete only entire stripe sets with parity. To delete a stripe set with parity on a basic disk, right-click the stripe set with parity that you want to delete, and then click Delete Volume.

Practice: Working with Dynamic Storage

In this practice, you will upgrade a basic disk to a dynamic disk. You will create a folder for mounting a volume and then create and mount a simple volume.

Exercise 1: Upgrading a Disk

In this exercise, you will use the Disk Management tool to upgrade a basic disk to a dynamic disk.

▶ **To upgrade a basic disk**

1. Ensure that you are logged on as Administrator.
2. Right-click My Computer, and then click Manage.

   The Computer Management console window appears.
3. In the console tree, double-click Storage, and then click Disk Management.

   Notice that Disk 0 is a Basic disk.
4. In the lower-right pane of Computer Management, right-click Disk 0, and then click Upgrade To Dynamic Disk.

   The Upgrade To Dynamic Disk dialog box appears.
5. Ensure that Disk 0 is the only disk selected for upgrade, and then click OK.

   The Confirm Upgrade To Dynamic Disk dialog box appears.
6. Click Upgrade.

   The Disk Management message box appears, warning you that you will not be able to boot previous versions of Windows from any volumes on this disk.

   Note If you are dual booting with another operating system, for example Windows 95 or Windows 98 loaded on Drive C, these operating systems will no longer run. Only Windows 2000 can access a dynamic drive.
   ---

7. Click Yes.

   The Upgrade Disks message box appears, indicating that file systems on any of the disks to be upgraded will be force dismounted.
8. Click Yes.

The Confirm dialog box will appear, informing you that a reboot will take place to complete the upgrade process if you are upgrading a disk containing a boot or system partition or if one of the partitions being upgraded is in use.

9. Click OK if the prompt appears, and your computer will restart. Otherwise the upgrade process is complete.

► **To confirm the upgrade**

1. Log on as Administrator.

   The System Settings Change dialog box appears, prompting you to restart your computer. This is not required and is a limitation of this prerelease version of Windows 2000.

2. Click No.

3. Right-click My Computer, and then click Manage.

4. In the Computer Management console tree, double-click Storage, and then click Disk Management.

   Notice that Disk 0 is now a dynamic disk and that drive C is a simple volume.

5. Minimize Computer Management.

Exercise 2: Creating and Mounting a Volume

In this exercise, you will use the Disk Management tool to create a new simple volume and mount the new volume onto an existing folder on another volume.

► **To create a folder for mounting the new volume**

1. Right-click My Computer, click Explore, and then click Local Disk (C:).

   Note If drive C is not formatted with NTFS, click the volume that is formatted with NTFS and contains the Windows 2000 files.

2. On the File menu, click New, and then click Folder.

3. Type **Mount** and then press Enter.

► **To create and mount a new simple volume**

1. Restore Computer Management.

2. Right-click the remaining unallocated space on Disk 0 in the lower-right pane, and then click Create Volume.

   The Create Volume wizard appears.

3. Click Next.

   The Select Volume Type page appears. Notice that Simple Volume is the only available option.

4. Click Next.

   The Select Disks page appears.

5. Type **50** in the For Selected Disk box, and then click Next.

6. Click Next.

   The Assign Drive Letter Or Path page appears.

7. Click Mount This Volume At An Empty Folder That Supports Drive Paths, and then type **c:\mount**

8. Click Next.

   The Format Volume page appears.

9. Type **Mounted Volume** in the Volume Label box.

10. Click Perform A Quick Format, and then click Next.

11. Click Finish.

    The new volume is created, formatted, and mounted on the C:\Mount folder; or, if C is not formatted with NTFS, it is mounted where you created the Mount folder.

12. Leave Computer Management open.

▶   **To examine the new volume**

1. Open Microsoft Windows Explorer.

2. Click Local Disk (C:) to display its contents.

Note If you mounted your volume on a drive other than drive C, click that drive instead.

---

3. Right-click Mount, and then click Properties.

   The Mount Properties dialog box appears.

   What type of folder is C:\Mount or X:\Mount (where X is the drive on which you mounted the volume)?

4. Click OK.

5. Close Windows Explorer.

▶   **To extend a volume**

1. In the lower-right pane of Computer Management right-click Mounted Volume (C:), and then click Extend Volume.

2. In the Extend Volume wizard, click Next.

3. On the For Select Disks page, under Size, type **50** in the For All Selected Disks box, and click Next.

4. Click Finish.

Drive C is extended to include an additional 50 MB of disk space.

5. Close Computer Management.

Lesson Summary

The Disk Management tool provides a central location for disk information and management tasks, such as creating and deleting partitions and volumes. With the proper permissions, you can manage disks locally and on remote computers. In addition to monitoring disk information, some of the other disk management tasks that you might need to perform include adding and removing hard disks and changing the disk storage type.

Common disk management tasks include upgrading from a basic disk to a dynamic disk, creating and extending simple volumes, creating and extending spanned volumes, creating striped volumes, adding disks, changing storage type, viewing and updating information, and managing disks on a remote computer. In the practice portion of this lesson, you used the Disk Management tool to upgrade a basic disk to a dynamic disk, to create a new simple volume and mount the new volume onto an existing folder on another volume, and to extend a volume.

Review

Here are some questions to help you determine if you have learned enough to move on to the next chapter. If you have difficulty answering these questions, please go back and review the material in this chapter before beginning the next chapter. The answers to these questions are located in Appendix A, "Questions and Answers."

1. You install a new 10-gigabyte (GB) disk drive that you want to divide into five equal 2-GB sections. What are your options?

2. How do you configure the Disk Management tool for remote administration of other computers?

3. You are trying to create a striped volume on your Windows 2000 Advanced Server in order to improve performance. You confirm that you have enough unallocated disk space on two disks in your computer, but when you right-click an area of unallocated space on a disk, your only option is to create a partition. What is the problem and how would you resolve it?

4. You add a new disk to your computer and attempt to extend an existing volume to include the unallocated space on the new disk, but the option to extend the volume is not available. What is the problem and how would you resolve it?

5. You dual boot your computer with Windows 98 and Windows 2000. You upgrade a second drive, which you are using to archive files, from basic storage to dynamic storage. The next time you try to access your archived files from Windows 98, you are unable to read the files. Why?

C H A P T E R   1 2

Implementing Disaster Protection

About This Chapter

Disaster protection involves the efforts by support professionals to prevent computer disasters and to minimize the amount of time a computer is nonfunctional in the event of a system failure. A *computer disaster* is any event that renders a computer unable to start. The causes of computer disasters range from hardware failure to a complete system loss, such as in the case of fire.

Microsoft Windows 2000 includes a variety of features that are designed to help you recover from computer disasters. These disaster protection features include support for fault-tolerant volumes, advanced startup options, the Recovery Console, the Backup utility. Understanding these features is essential to developing and implementing effective disaster protection and recovery plans.

Before You Begin

To complete this chapter

- You must have a computer that meets or exceeds the minimum hardware requirements listed in "Getting Started," on page xxi.
- You must have installed the beta version of Windows 2000 Advanced Server on a computer meeting the specifications listed in the preceding bullet. The computer should be installed as a stand-alone computer in a workgroup and TCP/IP should be the only installed protocol.
- Your computer should be using a static IP address.

Lesson 1: Using Fault-Tolerant Volumes

Microsoft Windows 2000 Server includes support for two types of fault-tolerant volumes: mirrored volumes and RAID-5 volumes. Similar to mirror sets and stripe sets with parity in Microsoft Windows NT Server 4.0, Windows 2000 fault-tolerant volumes write data on multiple disks. Understanding how to use fault-tolerant volumes can help to protect data in the event of a disk failure.

Note Fault-tolerant volumes in the Windows 2000 family of server products, which include Windows 2000 Server, Windows 2000 Advanced Server, and Windows 2000 Datacenter, are only available on dynamic disks. Microsoft Windows 2000 Professional does not support fault-tolerant volumes.

After this lesson, you will be able to

- Use Windows 2000 fault-tolerant volumes.

Estimated lesson time: 10 minutes

Implementing Fault-Tolerant Volumes

You can use fault tolerance to help protect data against disk failures. In Windows 2000 Server, you create mirrored and RAID-5 volumes from unallocated space by using the Create Volume wizard in Computer Management.

To create a mirrored or RAID-5 volume from unallocated space, you would do the following:

1. In Computer Management, expand Storage, and then click Disk Management.
2. Right-click an area of unallocated space, and then click Create Volume.
3. Click Next, and then, on the Select Volume Type page, specify the type of volume to create.

   Table 12.1 describes the additional options you can specify in the Create Volume wizard.

Table 12.1   Create Volume Wizard Options

Option	Description
Select Disks	The dynamic disks that will make up the volume. For mirrored volumes, you can select only two disks. For RAID-5 volumes, you must select at least three disks.
Volume Size	The amount of unallocated disk space to use on each selected dynamic disk.
Assign A Drive Letter Or Path	A drive letter or path for the volume that you are creating.
Format Volume	Formatting options for the volume.

4. After you specify the appropriate options, click Finish to create the volume.

To mirror an existing volume, you would do the following:

1. After you specify the appropriate options, click Finish to create the volume.
2. Select the second disk in the mirrored volume, and then click OK.

Recovering a Failed Mirrored Volume

When one member of a mirrored volume fails, the other member continues to operate, though it is no longer fault tolerant. To prevent potential data loss, you must recover the mirrored volume as soon as possible. The status of the failed volume appears in Disk Management as Failed Redundancy, and one of the disks will appear as Offline, Missing, or Online (Errors). The method that you use to recover the mirrored volume depends on the status of the disk.

Recovering a Disk Identified as Offline or Missing

To recover a mirrored volume if the disk status is either Offline or Missing, you would do the following:

1. Ensure that the disk is attached to the computer and has power.
2. In the Disk Management window, right-click the disk that is identified as Missing or Offline, and then click Reactivate Disk.

   The status of the disk should return to Healthy, and the mirrored volume should regenerate automatically.

Recovering a Disk Identified as Online (Errors)

To recover a mirrored volume if the disk status is Online (Errors), in the Disk Management window, right-click the disk, and then click Reactivate Disk. The status of the disk should return to Healthy, and the mirrored volume should regenerate automatically.

Note If a disk continues to appear as Online (Errors), it might be about to fail. You should replace the disk as soon as possible.

Replacing a Disk and Reestablishing a Mirrored Volume

If the preceding procedures fail to reactivate the disk or if the status of the volume does not return to Healthy, you must replace the failed disk and reestablish the mirrored volume:

To create a new mirrored volume, you would do the following:

1. In the Disk Management window, right-click the mirrored volume on the failed disk, and then click Remove Mirror.

2. In the Remove Mirror dialog box, click the failed disk, and then click Remove Mirror.

3. Click Yes when prompted to confirm your choice.

4. Right-click the volume that you want to mirror, and then click Add Mirror.

5. Select the second disk in the mirrored volume, and then click OK.

Recovering a Failed RAID-5 Volume

When one member of a RAID-5 volume fails, the other members continue to operate, though the volume is no longer fault-tolerant. To prevent potential data loss, you must recover the RAID-5 volume as soon as possible.

The status of the failed volume appears in the Disk Management window as Failed Redundancy, and one of the disks will appear as Offline, Missing, or Online (Errors). The method that you use to recover the RAID-5 volume depends on the status of the disk.

Recovering a Disk Identified as Offline or Missing

To recover a RAID-5 volume if the disk status is either Offline or Missing, you would do the following:

1. Ensure that the disk is attached to the computer and has power.

2. In the Disk Management window, right-click the disk that is identified as Missing or Offline, and then click Reactivate Disk.

   The status of the disk should return to Healthy, and the RAID-5 volume should regenerate automatically.

Recovering a Disk Identified as Online (Errors)

To recover a RAID-5 volume if the disk status is Online (Errors), in the Disk Management window, right-click the disk, and then click Reactivate Disk. The status of the disk should return to Healthy, and the RAID-5 volume should regenerate automatically.

Note If a disk continues to appear as Online (Errors), it might be about to fail. You should replace the disk as soon as possible.

Replacing a Disk and Regenerating a RAID-5 Volume

If the preceding procedures fail to reactivate the disk or if the status of the volume does not return to Healthy, you must replace the failed disk and regenerate the RAID-5 volume.

To regenerate a RAID-5 volume using a different disk, you would do the following:

1. In the Disk Management window, right-click the RAID-5 volume on the failed disk, and then click Repair Volume.

2. In the Repair RAID-5 Volume dialog box, select the disk that will replace the failed disk in the RAID-5 volume, and then click OK.

Lesson Summary

The Microsoft Windows 2000 family of server products includes support for two types of fault-tolerant volumes: mirrored volumes and RAID-5 volumes. You can use fault tolerance to help protect data against disk failures. In Windows 2000 Advanced Server, you create mirrored and RAID-5 volumes from unallocated space by using the Create Volume wizard in the Storage node of Computer Management.

If one member of a mirrored volume fails, the other member will continue to operate, but it is no longer fault tolerant. The status of the failed volume appears in the Disk Management window as Failed Redundancy, and one of the disks will appear as Offline, Missing, or Online (Errors). If the disk status is either Offline or Missing, ensure that the disk is attached to the computer and has power.

To recover a mirrored volume, in the Disk Management window, right-click the disk that is identified as Offline, Missing, or Online (Errors), and then click Reactivate Disk. If the disk fails to reactivate or if the status of the volume does not return to Healthy, you must replace the failed disk and reestablish the mirrored volume. To create a new mirrored volume, use the Disk Management tool to remove the existing mirror and then to create a new mirror.

When one member of a RAID-5 volume fails, the other members continue to operate, though the volume is no longer fault-tolerant. The status of the failed volume appears in the Disk Management window as Failed Redundancy, and one of the disks will appear as Offline, Missing, or Online (Errors). If the disk status is either Offline or Missing, ensure that the disk is attached to the computer and has power.

To recover a RAID-5 volume, in the Disk Management window, right-click the disk that is identified as Offline, Missing, or Online (Errors), and then click Reactivate Disk. If the disk fails to reactivate or if the status of the volume does not return to Healthy, you must replace the failed disk and regenerate the RAID-5 volume. To regenerate a RAID-5 volume using a different disk, in the Disk Management console window, right-click the RAID-5 volume on the failed disk, and then click Repair Volume. In the Repair RAID-5 Volume dialog box, select the disk that will replace the failed disk in the RAID-5 volume, and then click OK.

Lesson 2: Using Advanced Startup Options

Windows 2000 includes advanced startup options for use in troubleshooting and repairing startup problems, maintaining and repairing the directory services based on Active Directory technology, and connecting the computer to a debugger. These new startup options enhance the ability to diagnose and resolve driver incompatibility and startup problems in Windows 2000.

After this lesson, you will be able to

- Describe the advanced startup options.

Estimated lesson time: 5 minutes

Displaying the Advanced Startup Options

To display the advanced startup options, press F8 during the operating system selection phase of the Windows 2000 startup process. Table 12.2 describes the Windows 2000 advanced startup options.

Table 12.2   Advanced Startup Options

Option	Description
Safe Mode	Loads only the basic devices and drivers that are required to start the computer, including the mouse, keyboard, mass storage devices, base video, and the standard, default set of system services. This option also creates a log file.
Safe Mode With Networking	Loads only the basic devices and drivers that are required to start the computer and enable networking. This option also creates a log file.
Safe Mode With Command Prompt	Loads safe mode options but starts a command prompt instead of Windows Explorer. This option also creates a log file.
Enable Boot Logging	Creates a log file that references all of the drivers and services that the system loads (or does not load). This log file is called Ntbtlog.txt and is located in the *systemroot* folder (the folder that contains the Windows 2000 system files).
Enable VGA Mode	Loads the basic VGA driver. This mode is useful if a video driver is preventing Windows 2000 from starting properly.
Last Known Good Configuration	Uses the last known good configuration information that is stored in the registry to start the computer.

(continued)

Option	Description
Directory Services Restore Mode (Windows 2000 Domain Controllers Only)	Allows restoration and maintenance of Active Directory directory services and restoration of the Sysvol folder on domain controllers.
Debugging Mode	Sends debugging information to another computer through a serial cable.

Lesson Summary

The advanced startup options available in Windows 2000 include Safe Mode, Enable Boot Logging, Enable VGA Mode, Last Known Good Configuration, Directory Services Restore Mode, and Debugging Mode. These options allow you to attempt to restart your computer when there is a problem with a normal boot.

Lesson 3: Using the Recovery Console

The Windows 2000 Recovery Console is a command-line interface that you can use to perform a variety of troubleshooting and recovery tasks, including the following:

- Starting and stopping services
- Reading and writing data on a local drive (including drives that are formatted with the NTFS file system)
- Formatting hard disks

After this lesson, you will be able to
- Install and use the Recovery Console.

Estimated lesson time: 20 minutes

Installing and Starting the Recovery Console

To install the Recovery Console, start a command prompt in Windows 2000, change to the I386 (or Alpha) folder on the Windows 2000 CD-ROM, and then run the Winnt32 command with the /cmdcons switch. After you install the Recovery Console, you can access it from the startup menu. You can also access the Recovery Console by using the Windows 2000 Setup disks or the Windows 2000 CD-ROM to start your computer and then selecting the Recovery Console option when you are prompted to choose repair options.

After you start the Recovery Console, you must specify which installation of Windows 2000 you want to log on to (if you have a dual boot or multiple boot configuration), and then you must log on as the Administrator user.

Understanding the Recovery Console Commands

There are a number of commands available in the Recovery Console. Table 12.3 describes some of these commands.

Table 12.3   Recovery Console Commands

Command	Description
Chdir (cd)	Displays the name of the current folder or changes the current folder
Chkdsk	Checks a disk and displays a status report
Cls	Clears the screen
Copy	Copies a single file to another location

(continued)

Command	Description
Delete (del)	Deletes one or more files
Dir	Displays a list of files and subfolders in a folder
Disable	Disables a system service or a device driver
Enable	Starts or enables a system service or a device driver
Exit	Exits the Recovery Console and restarts your computer
Fdisk	Manages partitions on your hard disks
Fixboot	Writes a new partition boot sector onto the system partition
Fixmbr	Repairs the master boot record of the partition boot sector
Format	Formats a disk
Help	Lists the commands that you can use in the Recovery Console
Logon	Logs on to a Windows 2000 installation
Map	Displays the drive letter mappings
Mkdir (md)	Creates a folder
More	Displays a text file
Rmdir (rd)	Deletes a folder
Rename (ren)	Renames a single file
Systemroot	Sets the current folder to the systemroot folder of the system that you are currently logged on to
Type	Displays a text file

Practice: Using the Recovery Console

In this practice, you will install and start the Recovery Console. You will look at Help to determine the commands available in the Recovery Console, you will use Listsrv to view the services, and then you will use the Disable command to disable the Alerter service.

Exercise 1: Installing the Windows 2000 Recovery Console

In this exercise, you will install the Recovery Console.

▶ **To install the Recovery Console**

1. Log on as Administrator.

2. Insert the CD-ROM that you used to install Microsoft Windows 2000 Advanced Server into the CD-ROM drive.

3. When the Microsoft Windows 2000 CD window appears, close it.

4. In the Run dialog box, type **<X>:\i386\winnt32 /cmdcons** (where *<X>* represents the letter assigned to your CD-ROM drive), and then click OK.

    The Windows 2000 Setup dialog box appears.

5. Click Yes to install the Windows 2000 Recovery Console.

   Windows 2000 Setup installs the Windows 2000 Recovery Console to your hard disk.

6. Click OK to close the Windows 2000 Advanced Server Setup dialog box.

Exercise 2: Using the Windows 2000 Recovery Console

In this exercise, you will use the Help command to view the available commands. You will then view and scroll through a list of all available services. Finally, you will disable the Alerter service.

1. Restart your computer.
2. Select Microsoft Windows 2000 Command Console from the boot loader menu.

   The Windows 2000 Recovery Console starts up and prompts you to select which Windows 2000 installation you would like to log on to. If you have more than one Windows 2000 installation on this computer, they will be listed here.

3. Type **1** and then press Enter.
4. Type **password** when prompted for the Administrator password, and then press Enter.
5. Type **help** and then press Enter to see the list of available commands.
6. To view all available services, type **listsvc** and press Enter.
7. Press Spacebar to scroll through the page of available services.
8. To disable a service, type **disable /?**, and then press Enter.
9. Type **disable alerter**, and then press Enter.

   You are prompted that the Alerter service has a start type of SERVICE_AUTO_START, but that it is now disabled, with a start type of SERVICE_DISABLED.

10. Type **exit** and then press Enter to restart your computer.
11. Click OK.

Exercise 3: Restarting the Alerter Service

In this exercise, you will confirm that the Alerter service is disabled, and then you will restart it.

1. Log on as Administrator.
2. Open Computer Management, expand Services And Applications, and then click Services.

   Notice that the Start Up value for the Alerter service is Disabled.

3. Double-click Alerter, change the Startup Type to Automatic, and then click OK.

4. Right-click Alerter, and then click Start.

5. Close Computer Management.

6. Restart your computer.

Lesson Summary

The Windows 2000 Recovery Console is a command-line interface that you can use to perform a variety of troubleshooting and recovery tasks, including starting and stopping services, reading and writing data on a local drive, and formatting hard disks. You install the Recovery Console by starting a command prompt, changing to the I386 (or Alpha) folder on the Windows 2000 CD-ROM, and running the Winnt32 command along with the /cmdcons switch. After you install the Recovery Console, you can access it from the startup menu or by using the Windows 2000 Setup disks or the Windows 2000 CD-ROM to start your computer and then selecting the Recovery Console option when you are prompted to choose repair options.

Lesson 4: Using the Backup Utility

Windows 2000 includes an enhanced, graphical backup utility that is designed to help you protect data from accidental loss as a result of hardware or storage media failure. You can use the Backup utility to do the following:

- Back up files and folders
- Back up system state data
- Schedule a backup
- Restore files and folders
- Restore Active Directory directory services

Note You can also use the Backup utility to create an Emergency Repair Disk.

The Backup utility supports a variety of storage devices and media, including tape drives, logical drives, removable disks, and recordable CD-ROM drives. In addition, the Backup utility includes wizards that are designed to make using the utility easier and more efficient. Effective use of the Backup utility can help ensure a quick system recovery in the event of a failure.

After this lesson, you will be able to

- Back up files and folders.
- Back up the system state data.
- Restore files and folders.
- Restore Active Directory directory services.

Estimated lesson time: 40 minutes

Backing Up Files and Folders

You can use the Backup utility to archive files and folders on volumes that are formatted with either file allocation table (FAT) or the NTFS file system. The Backup utility includes a Backup wizard, which steps you through the entire backup process. However, you can also create a backup job without using the wizard. To access the Backup utility, click Start, point to Programs, point to Accessories, point to System Tools, and click Backup. The Backup window appears, as shown in Figure 12.1. To begin the backup process, click the Backup tab (see Figure 12.2) and then select the drives, folders, or files you want to back up. Then click the Start Backup button.

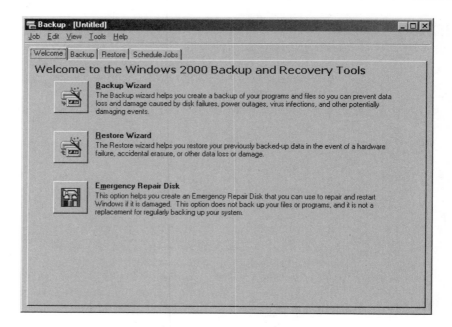

Figure 12.1   The Backup window's Welcome tab

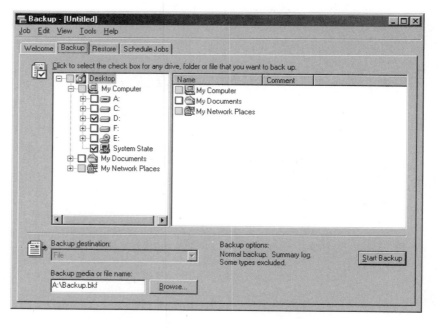

Figure 12.2   Select the data to be backed up on the Backup tab.

Backing Up System State Data

You can use the Backup utility in Windows 2000 to back up the system state data, which includes the following system components:

- **Registry:** A database repository for information about a computer's configuration. It contains information such as user profiles, the programs installed on the computer and the types of documents each can create, property settings for folders and program icons, what hardware exists on the system, and which ports are in use.

- **Component Services Class Registration database:** A database that stores class registrations.

- **System startup files:** Ntldr and Ntdetect.com for Intel-based systems and Osloader.exe for Digital-alpha-based systems.

- **Certificate Services database:** A database that stores the issued certificates. A certificate is a file used for authentication and secure exchange of data on nonsecured networks, such as the Internet.

- **Active Directory directory services:** The directory that stores information about network resources, as well as all the services that make the information available and useful. The resources stored in the directory—such as user data, printers, servers, databases, groups, computers, and security policies—are known as objects.

- **Sysvol folder:** The shared system volume, which is a folder structure that exists on all Windows 2000 domain controllers. It stores scripts and some of the group policy objects for both the current domain as well as the enterprise. The default location for the shared system volume is *systemroot*\Sysvol.

On computers running Windows 2000 Professional, the system state includes the registry, the Component Services Class Registration database, and system startup files.

On computers running Windows 2000 Server operating systems, the system state includes the registry, the Component Services Class Registration database, and system startup files, and if the computer is also a certificate server, the system state also includes the Certificate Services database.

On computers running Windows 2000 Server operating systems that are installed as domain controllers, the system state includes the registry, the Component Services Class Registration database, system startup files, the Certificate Services database, Active Directory directory services, and the Sysvol folder.

Note You cannot back up individual components of the system state data.

You can back up the system state data on a local computer in one of the following three ways:

- In the Backup wizard, on the What To Back Up page, click Only Back Up The System State Data.
- In the Backup wizard, on the Items To Back Up page, expand My Computer, and then select the check box to the left of System State.
- In the Backup utility, on the Backup tab, expand My Computer, and then select the System State check box.

Scheduling a Backup

Windows 2000 integrates the Backup utility with the Task Scheduler service. As a result, you can use the Backup utility to schedule a backup. You can schedule a backup to occur at regular intervals or during periods of relative inactivity on a network (see Figure 12.3).

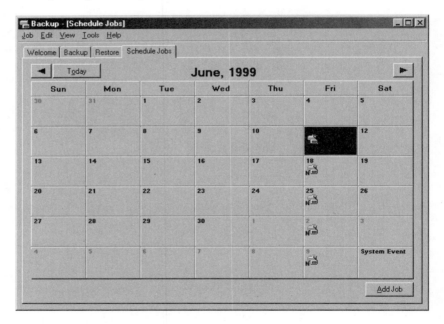

Figure 12.3   A backup scheduled for a weekly interval

To schedule a backup, follow the procedure identified to back up files and folders. When the Backup Job Information dialog box appears, you would click Schedule and then do the following:

Note If the Backup dialog box appears, indicating that you must save the backup selections before you can schedule a backup, click Yes, specify the appropriate information in the Save Selections dialog box, and then click Save.

1. In the Set Account Information dialog box, specify the user name and password of the account under whose security context you want the scheduled backup to run. You must specify an account that has been granted the Back Up Files And Directories privilege.

   Note The Set Account Information dialog box will not appear if Task Scheduler is already running.

2. In the Scheduled Job Options dialog box, specify a job name, and then click Properties.
3. In the Schedule Job dialog box, specify the date, time, and frequency parameters for the scheduled backup. Then close the Scheduled Job Options dialog box.

   Note You can view scheduled jobs on the Schedule Jobs tab in the Backup utility.

Restoring Files and Folders

You can use the Backup utility in Windows 2000 to restore files and folders. The Backup utility includes a Restore wizard that steps you through the entire restore process. However, you can also restore files and folders without using the wizard.

To restore files and folders without using the wizard, open the Backup utility, and then specify the following:

- The folders or files to restore.
- A restore location. You can restore files to the original location, an alternate location, or to a single folder.
- Restore options, such as whether to replace existing files with backup files.

Caution To avoid data loss and to preserve all file and folder features, you should restore data that is archived from a Windows 2000 NTFS volume to another Windows 2000 NTFS volume. Restoring the data to a FAT volume or to a Windows NT 4.0 NTFS volume might result in the loss of access permissions, Encrypting File System (EFS) settings, disk quota information, mounted drive information, or Remote Storage information.

Restoring Active Directory Directory Services

You can use the Backup utility to restore Active Directory directory services during the process of replacing a failed domain controller, to repair a damaged Active Directory database, or to recover one or more objects that are accidentally deleted from Active Directory directory services.

Failed Domain Controllers

If a domain controller fails completely, you must first restart the computer and make sure Windows 2000 is running. Then you can use the Backup utility to restore the latest version of the system state data, which includes Active Directory directory services.

After you have restored Active Directory directory services, Windows 2000 automatically does the following:

- Performs a consistency check on and reindexes the Active Directory database.
- Updates Active Directory directory services and the File Replication Service with data from their replication partners.

Damaged Active Directory Databases

If the operating system on a domain controller is functioning normally, but the Active Directory database is damaged, you must restart the computer, select the Directory Services Restore Mode advanced startup option, and then use the Backup utility to restore the latest system state data.

After you have restored the Active Directory database, restart the computer, and Windows 2000 will reindex the Active Directory database and update Active Directory directory services and the File Replication Service.

Authoritative Restores

Restoring deleted objects in a distributed environment presents a challenge. If you restore the most recent copy of the Active Directory database that contains the deleted objects, those objects will be deleted when replication occurs because the objects are marked for deletion in the replicas of the database.

To prevent this from occurring, you can perform an authoritative restore. When you restore an object authoritatively, it persists after replication even though it is marked for deletion in the replicas of the database.

To perform an authoritative restore, you would do the following:

1. Restart the computer, press F8, and select the Directory Services Restore Mode from the Windows 2000 Advanced Options menu.

Note If your system is set up for dual booting and you are prompted to select an operating system, select it and press Enter.

---

2. Restore the system state data from the most recent backup that contains the objects that you want to recover.

3. When the restore is complete, run Ntdsutil.exe.

4. Type **authoritative restore** at the command prompt.

5. Type **restore subtree distinguished_name_of_object** at the authoritative restore prompt.

   For example, if you are the administrator of a domain called domain.com and you want to restore an organizational unit (OU) called Sales, which existed directly below the domain, you would type

   restore subtree OU=Sales,DC=domain,DC=com

6. Exit Ntdsutil by typing **quit** at the prompt, and then restart the computer.

The restored object is marked as authoritative and will be replicated to all domain controllers in the domain.

Practice: Using the Backup Utility to Restore Active Directory Directory Services

In this practice, you will back up the system state using Windows 2000 Backup. You will delete an OU and then perform an authoritative restore.

Exercise 1: Backing Up the System State Data

In this exercise, you will backup the system state using Windows 2000 Backup. You will then delete an OU.

▶ **To back up the system data**

1. On the Start menu, point to Programs, point to Accessories, point to System Tools, and then click Backup.

2. Click the Backup Wizard button on the Welcome tab.

   The Backup wizard starts.

3. Click Next.

4. On the What To Back Up page, click Only Backup The System State Data, and then click Next.

5. On the Where To Store The Backup page, type **C:\SysState** in the Backup Media Or File Name box, and then click Next.

6. On the Completing The Backup Wizard page, click the Advanced button.

7. On the Type Of Backup page, click Next.

8. On the How To Back Up page, click Next.

9. On the Media Options page, click Next.

10. On the Backup Label page, type **Practice** in both the Backup Label and Media Label boxes, and then click Next.

11. On the When To Back Up page, click Next.

12. On the Completing The Backup Wizard page, click Finish.

    Backup begins backing up the system state data.

13. When the backup is complete, click Close in the Backup Program dialog box, and then close Backup.

Exercise 2: Deleting an OU

In this exercise, you will delete the Production OU.

▶ **To delete an OU**

1. Open Active Directory Users and Computers.

2. Expand domain.com.

3. Delete the Production OU. Click the Yes button to confirm the deletion.

Note If a message box appears to warn you about the presence of objects within the Production container, click Yes to confirm the deletion.

---

4. Close Active Directory Users and Computers.

Exercise 3: Performing an Authoritative Restore of Active Directory Directory Services

In this exercise, you will perform an authoritative restore of the Active Directory directory services and recover the Production OU.

▶ **To restore Active Directory directory services**

1. Restart the computer.

2. When the boot loader menu appears, press F8.

3. Select Directory Services Restore Mode and press Enter.

4. Press Enter to select the Microsoft Windows 2000 Advanced Server operating system.

The Welcome To Windows dialog box appears. This will take a few minutes.

5. Log on as Administrator.

A Desktop dialog box appears informing you that you are in safe mode.

6. Click OK.

7. Open Backup, and then click Restore Wizard on the Welcome tab.

8. Click Next.

9. On the What To Restore page, expand File, expand Practice, and then click the System State check box to select it.

There should be a check mark in the box indicating that System State is selected.

10. Click Next.

11. On the Completing The Restore Wizard page, click Finish.

12. In the Enter Backup File Name dialog box, verify that C:\SysState appears in the Restore From Backup File box, and then click OK.

The Restore Progress dialog box appears. The restore process will take a few minutes.

13. When the restore is complete, click Close.

The Backup dialog box appears, prompting you to restart the computer.

14. Click No, and then close Backup.

Note If you were to click Yes in step 14, you would have done a non-authoritative restore. You clicked No, so that you can perform the next procedure and make it an authoritative restore.

► **To make the restore authoritative**

1. Open a command prompt.

2. Type **ntdsutil** and then press Enter.

3. At the ntdsutil: prompt, type **authoritative restore** and then press Enter.

4. Type **restore subtree OU=Production,DC=domain,DC=com** at the authoritative restore: prompt, and then press Enter.

The Authoritative Restore Confirmation Dialog message box appears asking if you are sure you want to perform this authoritative restore.

5. Click Yes.

The ntdsutil utility begins to restore the OU. When the restore process is complete, the authoritative restore prompt returns.

6. At the authoritative restore: prompt, type **quit** and then press Enter.

7. At the ntdsutil: prompt, type **quit** and then press Enter.

8. Type **exit** and press Enter to close the command prompt, and then restart the computer.

Exercise 4: Verifying the Authoritative Restore

In this exercise, you will verify the authoritative restore by verifying that the Production OU was restored.

▶ **To verify the Production OU was restored**

1. Log on as Administrator.

2. Open Active Directory Users and Computers.

3. Expand domain.com.

4. Verify that the Production OU is listed.

5. Close Active Directory Users and Computers.

Lesson Summary

Windows 2000 includes an enhanced, graphical backup utility that is designed to help you protect data from accidental loss as a result of hardware or storage media failure. You can use the Backup utility to back up files and folders, back up system state data, schedule a backup, restore files and folders, and restore Active Directory directory services.

The system state data that you back up depends on the operating system running on the computer. On computers running Windows 2000 Professional, the system state data includes the registry, the Component Services Class Registration database, and system startup files. On computers running Windows 2000 Server operating systems, the system state data includes the same files as does Windows 2000 Professional. If the computer is also a certificate server, the system state data also includes the Certificate Services database. On computers running Windows 2000 Server operating systems that are installed as domain controllers, the system state includes the registry, the Component Services Class Registration database, system startup files, the Certificate Services database, Active Directory directory services, and the Sysvol folder.

Windows 2000 integrates the Backup utility with the Task Scheduler service. As a result, you can use the Backup utility to schedule a backup. You can schedule a backup to occur at regular intervals or during periods of relative inactivity on a network.

You use the Backup utility in Windows 2000 to restore files and folders. The Backup utility includes a Restore wizard that steps you through the entire restore process. You can also use the Backup utility to restore Active Directory directory services. You can restore Active Directory directory services during the process of replacing a failed domain controller to repair a damaged Active Directory database, or to recover one or more objects that are accidentally deleted from Active Directory directory services.

Lesson 5: Performing an Emergency Repair

If Windows 2000 fails to start, you can use the Windows 2000 emergency repair disk (ERD) you created to perform an emergency repair of your system. After you have installed Windows 2000, you use the Backup utility to create an ERD.

After this lesson, you will be able to

- Explain how to create an ERD.
- Explain how to perform an emergency repair.

Estimated lesson time: 15 minutes

Creating an Emergency Repair Disk

You use the Backup utility to create an emergency repair disk for your system installation. To create the ERD, you would carry out the following steps:

1. Click Start, point to Programs, point to Accessories, point to System Tools, and then click Backup.

   Backup will open and display the Welcome page, as shown in Figure 12.1 on page 354.

2. On the Welcome tab, click the Emergency Repair Disk button.

   The Emergency Repair Diskette dialog box appears, prompting you to insert a blank, formatted disk into drive A.

3. Insert a blank, formatted disk into drive A.

   The dialog box also prompts you to back up the registry to the repair directory (see Figure 12.4).

4. Select the check box labeled Also Backup The Registry To The Repair Directory.

5. Click OK.

   The Backup utility creates an ERD and copies the registry to the repair directory.

   A dialog box appears indicating that the ERD was successfully created and prompting you to label the diskette Emergency Repair Disk and note the date.

6. Remove the diskette, label it, and date it.

7. Click OK to close the dialog box.
8. Close the Backup utility.

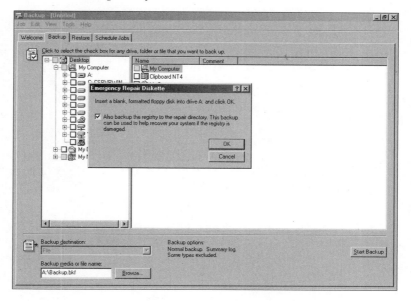

Figure 12.4 Backing up the registry to the repair directory.

Repairing a Damaged Windows 2000 Installation

If your Windows 2000 installation won't start, you can perform an emergency repair to attempt to repair the damaged Windows 2000 installation. You should have previously created an emergency repair disk (ERD) to repair your system.

1. If your computer can boot from the CD-ROM drive, insert your Windows 2000 CD-ROM and allow your system to boot from the CD-ROM.

Note If your Intel-based computer does not boot from the CD-ROM drive, insert Setup disk 1 into drive A, and then restart your computer. When prompted insert disks 2, 3, and 4.

After your computer starts, the Setup program will start. You will be asked if you want to continue installing Windows 2000.

2. Press Enter to continue.

   You will be prompted to choose whether you want to continue installing Windows 2000 or repair your current system.

3. Press R to start repairing your damaged system.

   Now you are prompted to choose whether you want to repair your system using the Recovery console or the emergency repair process.

4. Press R if you want to use the emergency repair process.

   You are prompted to choose the type of repair, Manual or Fast.

Note In most cases you should choose the Fast emergency repair option. It does not require any user intervention and will try to repair problems with the registry. You should only choose Manual if you are very familiar with your system and the files installed on it. Also, the manual emergency repair does not allow you to attempt to repair the registry.

---

5. Press F to choose Fast repair.

   You are prompted to press Enter if you have the ERD and L if you do not.

6. Press Enter.

Note If you do not have the ERD, Setup will still attempt to repair your system. However, if you do not have your ERD, Windows 2000 may not be able to locate and repair your installation.

   You are prompted to insert your ERD.

7. Insert the ERD and press Enter.

   If you chose the fast repair method, Setup will proceed automatically. It will typically examine your disks, attempt to fix errors, and finally prompt you to remove the ERD floppy disk to allow the machine to attempt to reboot the repaired operating system.

Lesson Summary

In this lesson you learned that if Windows 2000 fails to start, you can use an Emergency Repair Disk (ERD) to try to repair the system. You create an ERD by clicking Emergency Repair Disk on the Welcome tab of the Backup utility. You must create an ERD before the problem arises; it is too late to create an ERD once the system won't boot. Using your ERD and your CD-ROM, you can run an emergency repair and attempt to recover your system.

Review

Here are some questions to help you determine if you have learned enough to move on to the next chapter. If you have difficulty answering these questions, please go back and review the material in this chapter before beginning the next chapter. The answers to these questions are located in Appendix A, "Questions and Answers."

1. What requirement applies to disks used to create new fault-tolerant volumes in Windows 2000?

2. After installing a new hardware device, you restart your computer and log on. Immediately after logging on, your computer fails with a stop error that indicates the problem resulted from the new device driver. How would you solve this problem?

3. Describe two methods for accessing the Windows 2000 Recovery Console.

4. An administrator on your network has accidentally deleted an OU containing several thousand user objects. Assuming you have a recent backup of Active Directory directory services, how would you recover the deleted OU?

5. What are the two types of emergency repair and what are the differences between them?

C H A P T E R   1 3

Upgrading a Network to Windows 2000

About This Chapter

As a network administrator or support professional, you will derive many benefits from upgrading a Microsoft Windows NT 4.0 network to Microsoft Windows 2000, including improved security, easier management, and improved administration. The process of upgrading a Windows NT 4.0 network to Windows 2000 varies depending on your existing Windows NT 4.0 network infrastructure and your organization's business requirements. This chapter examines the upgrade process, specifically as it relates to upgrading Windows NT 4.0 domain models.

Before You Begin

To complete this chapter

- You must have a computer that meets or exceeds the minimum hardware requirements listed in "Getting Started," on page xxi.

- You must have installed the beta version of Windows 2000 Advanced Server on a computer meeting the specifications listed in the preceding bullet. The computer should be installed as a domain controller in a domain and TCP/IP should be the only installed protocol.

- Your computer should be using a static IP address.

Lesson 1: Planning a Network Upgrade

Your network is a critical resource, one that's imperative to the business success of your organization. As such, it is extremely important that you thoroughly plan any network changes or modifications before performing a network upgrade. When you plan and prepare for a network upgrade, you help ensure the upgraded network works properly once completed and that the chosen structure satisfies the business requirements of your organization.

After this lesson, you will be able to
- Plan a network upgrade to Windows 2000.

Estimated lesson time: 20 minutes

Understanding the Upgrade Process

To be better able to plan your upgrade, you need to understand the upgrade process. Upgrading your network from Windows NT 4.0 to Windows 2000 occurs in several discrete steps, as follows:

1. Establishing the root domain of the Windows 2000 Network
2. Upgrading member servers and client computers
3. Upgrading the primary domain controllers to Windows 2000
4. Upgrading the backup domain controllers to Windows 2000
5. Switching the domain from mixed to native mode

Note These steps will be explained later in this chapter.

You can upgrade member servers and client computers running Windows 95, Windows 98, or Windows NT Workstation 3.51 or 4.0 at any time before or after you upgrade your domain controllers. Member servers and client computers are not dependent upon directory services based on Active Directory technology to operate on the network. By upgrading your member servers and clients first, you can take advantage of the benefits of the new Windows 2000 features, and then upgrade to Active Directory directory services as organizational resources permit.

Choosing an Upgrade Model

The model you choose for your Windows 2000 upgrade depends on the Windows NT 4.0 domain structure in your existing network.

Upgrading the Single Domain Model

In a single domain model, the Windows NT 4.0 primary domain controller (PDC) maintains the master copy of the Security Account Manager (SAM) database. The SAM database can be replicated to one or more backup domain controllers (BDCs). In Windows NT 4.0, the single domain model is the simplest architecture you can use.

If you have a Windows NT 4.0 single domain, you can upgrade it to a single Windows 2000 Active Directory domain. With Active Directory directory services, you will be able to manage the domain much more easily by using organizational units (OUs) within the domain to reflect the structure of your organization.

Upgrading the Single Master Domain Model

In Windows NT 4.0, a single master domain model consists of multiple domains, with one domain designated as the master domain. The master domain is the domain where user accounts and global groups are created. The resource domains contain computer accounts and built-in accounts, but do not normally contain user or group accounts. The resource domains trust the master domain.

If you have a Windows NT 4.0 single master domain model, you can upgrade it to a Windows 2000 Active Directory domain tree. In this case, the master domain becomes the root domain of the tree. This makes it much easier to manage the domain by using OUs within the domain to reflect the structure of the organization.

Upgrading the Multiple Master Domain Model

In Windows NT 4.0, the multiple master domain model consists of more than one master domain and one or more resource domains that trust every master domain. This model is often used when organizations contain a large number of accounts, or when domain synchronization traffic between geographically separate sites is undesirable.

If you have a Windows NT 4.0 multiple master domain model, you can also upgrade to a Windows 2000 Active Directory domain tree. To do this, create a new empty root domain, and then upgrade the master domains to child domains of the new root domain. Finally, add any resource domains as child domains of the appropriate upgraded master domains.

Upgrading the Complete Trust Domain Model

In Windows NT 4.0, the complete trust domain model consists of multiple domains, but no master domain. All domains maintain their own user accounts and global groups. All domains trust each other, and administration is decentralized.

If you have a Windows NT 4.0 complete trust domain model, you can upgrade it to a Windows 2000 Active Directory domain tree. Each division within the organization will maintain its own domain as a child of a common, empty root domain. Trust relationships are automatic and transitive, so administrators no longer need to manage relationships.

If each of your Windows NT 4.0 domains represent a subsidiary that operates under a different name, you could alternatively upgrade these domains into a forest, with each domain representing the root of its own tree. This approach works best for separate companies or divisions that need to maintain limited communication, rather than for a single company.

Migrating to Active Directory Directory Services

You must carefully consider the following questions before you migrate your network from Windows NT 4.0 to Windows 2000. Careful thought and planning here will help ensure a successful network upgrade.

Consider these questions when planning the Active Directory Migration to Windows 2000:

- Have you identified any domain controllers running critical services, such as Dynamic Host Configuration Protocol (DHCP) and Windows Internet Naming Service (WINS), and created a disaster recovery plan for these domain controllers?
- Can you roll back your system if you encounter problems?
- Can you identify the site structure for replication?
- Can you use your existing Domain Name System (DNS) servers or do you need to add new servers?
- Do you need to establish a root zone on your network?
- What do you plan to call your domains?

If you can answer these questions, you are ready to proceed with the network upgrade.

Developing a Naming Strategy

An effective naming strategy is important to help your organization take advantage of Windows 2000 functionality. An effective naming strategy makes it easier for users to log on to the network and to locate network resources.

Every Active Directory domain must have a corresponding DNS domain. If you have an existing DNS namespace, it shouldn't determine your Active Directory structure. Rather, DNS should accommodate Active Directory directory services. It is possible to keep your existing DNS namespace and create a new one for Active Directory directory services.

As you create a DNS namespace, consider the following domain guidelines and standard naming conventions:

- The number of domain levels is determined by Active Directory directory services. DNS provides a naming service to Active Directory directory services, so the number of DNS domains is determined by your Active Directory domain structure. Any existing DNS naming structure should not determine your Active Directory domain structure.

- Use unique names. Each subdomain must have a unique name within its parent domain to ensure that the name is unique throughout the DNS namespace.

- Avoid lengthy domain names. This is especially important if you have many levels of domains because you might potentially exceed naming limitations. Domain names can be up to 63 characters, including the periods. The total length cannot exceed 255 characters.

Note Windows 2000 does not support case-sensitive domain names.

- Use standard DNS characters and Unicode characters.
  - Windows 2000 supports the following standard DNS characters: A–Z, a–z, 0–9, and the hyphen (-).
  - The DNS Service also supports the Unicode character set. The Unicode character set includes additional characters not found in the ASCII character set, which are required for languages such as French, German, and Spanish.
  - Only use Unicode characters if all servers running the DNS Service in your environment support Unicode.

Note For more information on the Unicode character set, see Request for Comment (RFC) 2044. For more information on DNS characters, see RFC 1123.

Adapting Windows 2000 to an Existing Network Structure

You can often adapt Windows 2000 DNS and Active Directory directory services to an existing network structure. As you plan your upgrade, examine your existing DNS servers to see if you can use them as part of your Windows 2000 network.

Using an Existing DNS Server

To use an existing DNS server for Active Directory directory services, it must support the following:

- **Service location resource records.** For more information see RFC 2052.
- **Dynamic update protocol for DNS.** For more information see RFC 2136.

If your existing DNS servers do not support RFC 2052 and RFC 2136, you must install and configure a DNS server that does. The DNS Service included with Windows 2000 allows you to set up a DNS server that meets these RFC requirements.

Creating a Root Zone

You configure a root zone for your intranet in only two instances:

- **When you are not connecting to the Internet.** The root level domain is for your intranet only.

- **When using a proxy service to gain access to the Internet.** You create the root of your local DNS namespace. The proxy service handles translation and connection necessary to access the Internet.

Lesson Summary

Careful planning will help ensure that your upgraded network will work properly. After you complete your planning, the first step in upgrading your network is to establish the root domain of the Windows 2000 network. The next three steps are to upgrade your PDCs, your BDCs, and your member servers and client computers. The last step in upgrading your network is switching the domain from mixed mode to native mode.

The model you choose for your Windows 2000 upgrade depends upon the Windows NT 4.0 domain structure in your existing network. Upgrade a Windows NT 4.0 single domain to a single Active Directory domain, and use organizational units (OUs) within the domain to reflect the structure of your organization. Upgrade a Windows NT 4.0 single master domain model to an Active Directory domain tree. The master domain becomes the root domain of the tree, and you can use OUs within the domain to reflect the structure of the organization.

Upgrade a Windows NT 4.0 multiple master domain model to an Active Directory domain tree. Create a new empty root domain, and then upgrade the master domains to child domains of the new root domain, and add any resource domains as child domains of the appropriate upgraded master domains. Upgrade a Windows NT 4.0 complete trust domain model to an Active Directory domain tree. Each division within the organization will maintain its own domain as a child of a common, empty root domain. Trust relationships are automatic and transitive, so administrators no longer need to manage relationships.

Every Active Directory domain must have a corresponding DNS domain. If your existing DNS server does not support service location resource records (see RFC 2052) and dynamic update protocol for DNS (see RFC 2136), you must install and configure a DNS server that does. The DNS Service included with Windows 2000 allows you to set up a DNS server that meets these RFC requirements.

Lesson 2: Establishing the Root Domain

The root domain in Active Directory directory services is the top branch of the enterprise namespace. Other domains in the tree are subdomains below the root domain. All other domains refer to the root domain as the root of the enterprise. If you fail to plan and establish the root domain correctly, you can compromise your network structure from the beginning. For example, if you use the incorrect root name, all child domains will inherit this incorrect name as part of their name.

After you have planned your network upgrade, the first step in upgrading your network to Windows 2000 is to establish the root domain. There are two options for establishing the root domain:

- Migrate an existing Windows NT 4.0 domain to a Windows 2000 root domain.
- Create a new Windows 2000 root domain.

The option you use depends on the domain model you use in your existing Windows NT 4.0 network.

After this lesson, you will be able to

- Determine whether to migrate an existing domain to a root domain or to create a new root domain for a Windows 2000 network.

Estimated lesson time: 10 minutes

Migrating an Existing Domain to a New Root Domain

You upgrade an existing domain to serve as the new root domain when your existing Windows NT 4.0 network uses one of these two domain models:

- Single domain model
- Single master domain model

In these two models, user accounts and global groups are created in a single domain, called the master domain. In the single master domain model, only computer accounts and resources are created in the resource domains. The resource domains trust the master domain.

Upgrading the Master Domain

When you upgrade the master domain to Active Directory directory services first, it forms the root of a new domain tree. In the single master domain model, you then upgrade the resource domains to become child domains of the root domain.

Migrating Objects to Active Directory Directory Services

The following objects migrate from Windows NT to Active Directory directory services during an upgrade:

- User accounts migrate to the users container.
- Computer accounts migrate to the computers container.
- Global groups migrate to the users container.
- Local groups migrate to the users container.
- Built-in groups migrate to the built-in container.
- Permissions for the NTFS file system files, printers, and local groups.

Creating Organizational Units

In Windows NT 4.0, administrators used domains to manage users and delegate administrative control. In Windows 2000, administrators use OUs to organize computers and users, delegate authority, and manage group policy.

Your OU structure can model your organizational, geopolitical, or administrative structure. Combine objects into a logical hierarchy of OUs that represent either of the following for your company:

- **Organizational model.** This model is based on departmental or geographical boundaries. For example, company A is organized into departments and has a research department, a development department, and a sales department. In this company, the administrators use different computer settings and deploy different applications for each department. You would create a Research OU, a Development OU, and a Sales OU, and you would place users and computers into these OUs as relevant. You would then use group policy to administer these settings and distribute applications.

- **Administrative model.** This model is based on which administrators are responsible for managing specific users and resources across the network. For example, company B uses separate IS managers for each location in the company. The IS managers in each location manage the users and computers in that location. You would create organizational units for each location and move the users and computers into these OUs. You would then delegate administrative control of those OUs to the appropriate IS managers.

To improve management and administration of users and computers in your company, examine your organizational structure, and then create OUs in the upgraded master domain to meet your business requirements.

Creating a New Root Domain

You create a new root domain for your Windows 2000 network when your existing Windows NT 4.0 network uses one of the following two domain models:

- Multiple master domain model
- Complete trust model

With these models, more than one domain contains user accounts and global groups. Therefore, you must establish a new root domain, and then upgrade the master domains to be children of this new root domain.

You can also upgrade these domain models to a forest with multiple disjointed namespaces. However, this would only be a viable option in an organization with many separate companies that had little need for intercommunication.

Note You must have two or more domain controllers in the root domain of your organization. If you only have one domain controller in the root domain of your organization and that domain controller fails after you migrate other child domains, you cannot run the Active Directory Installation wizard again to create a new domain controller for the root domain. In case of a failure such as this, you would have to restore the domain controller from backup or re-create your entire Active Directory structure.

Lesson Summary

The root domain in Active Directory directory services is the top branch of the enterprise namespace. All other domains in the tree are subdomains below the root domain and refer to the root domain as the root of the enterprise. If you fail to plan and establish the root domain correctly, you can compromise your network structure from the beginning.

After you have planned your network upgrade, the first step in upgrading your network to Windows 2000 is to establish the root domain. You can migrate an existing Windows NT 4.0 domain to a Windows 2000 root domain, or you can create a new Windows 2000 root domain. You upgrade an existing domain to serve as the new root domain when your existing Windows NT 4.0 network uses the single domain model or the single master domain model.

You create a new root domain for your Windows 2000 network when your existing Windows NT 4.0 network uses either the multiple master domain model or the complete trust model. With these models, more than one domain contains user accounts and global groups. Therefore, you must establish a new root domain, and then upgrade the master domains to be children of this new root domain.

Lesson 3: Upgrading Domain Controllers and Member Servers

In Windows NT 4.0, the PDC and the BDCs authenticate domain logons and maintain the directory database for the domain. You upgrade domain controllers and member servers running previous versions of Windows NT to either Windows 2000 Server or Windows 2000 Advanced Server. Once you upgrade all of your domain controllers to Windows 2000, you can take full advantage of the enhanced administrative features offered in Windows 2000 by switching the domain from mixed mode to native mode. This allows the domain to fully use the new features of Active Directory directory services.

After this lesson, you will be able to

- Explain how to upgrade domain controllers to Windows 2000.
- Explain how to upgrade and promote member servers to Windows 2000.

Estimated lesson time: 25 minutes

Identifying Server Upgrade Paths

You upgrade domain controllers and member servers running previous versions of Windows NT to either Windows 2000 Server or Windows 2000 Advanced Server. Table 13.1 lists the upgrade paths for server operating systems.

Table 13.1   Windows 2000 Upgrade Paths for Member Servers

Upgrade from	Upgrade to
PDC or BDC running Windows NT Server 3.51 or 4.0	Domain controller, Windows 2000 Server, or Windows 2000 Advanced Server.
Member server running Windows NT Server 3.51 or 4.0	Windows 2000 Server or Windows 2000 Advanced Server. After the upgrade, you can change it to a domain controller if required.
Windows NT Advanced Server 3.1, Windows NT Server version 3.5	Windows NT Server, version 3.51 or 4.0 first, then upgrade to Windows 2000 Server or Windows 2000 Advanced Server.

Upgrading Domain Controllers

In Windows 2000 networks, all domain controllers running Windows 2000 have equal status in the domain. When you upgrade Windows NT 4.0 or 3.51 PDCs and BDCs to Windows 2000, there is no longer a distinction between PDCs and BDCs. Instead, they become peer domain controllers.

Upgrading Member Servers

You also upgrade member servers running Windows NT Server 3.51 and 4.0 to Windows 2000. This allows them to take advantage of Active Directory directory services. You can promote these member servers to domain controllers as necessary.

Preparing to Upgrade

Before you start the upgrade process, there are a couple of things you need to do to prepare to upgrade your domain controllers and member servers. First of all, make sure that all your computers meet the minimum hardware requirements for Windows 2000 Server and Advanced Server. Then prepare a rollback strategy in case there are any upgrade problems. Finally prepare the domain controllers and member servers for the upgrade.

Note The first thing you should do before your upgrade is to make sure that your computers meet the minimum hardware requirements. See "Hardware Requirements," page 22, for a list of the minimum hardware requirements.

Creating a Rollback Strategy

To create a rollback strategy, preserve one BDC with the current directory database. To do this, synchronize a BDC with the PDC, and then take the fully synchronized BDC offline. Keep this BDC available until you are certain the upgrade is successful. If problems occur during the upgrade, you can reinstate the offline BDC, promote it to a PDC, and recover your system state.

Preparing the Domain Controllers and Member Servers

There are some steps you should do to prepare your domain controllers and member servers to be upgraded. Before you start the Windows 2000 Setup wizard, you should do the following:

1. Remove any virus scanners, third-party network service, or client software. Read the Release Notes file (Relnotes on the Windows 2000 CD-ROM) for information about any known problems with specific applications.

2. Disconnect the serial cable that connects an uninterruptible power supply (UPS) device. During setup, Windows 2000 attempts to detect devices connected to serial ports, which can cause problems with UPS equipment.

3. If your system contains Industry Standard Architecture (ISA) devices that are non–Plug and Play, set your system basic input/output system (BIOS) to reserve all interrupt requests (IRQs) currently in use by non–Plug and Play ISA devices. Failure to do so might result in the error message INACCESSABLE_BOOT_DEVICE. In some cases, the non–Plug and Play ISA devices might not function.

Upgrading a Primary Domain Controller

You upgrade the PDC to Windows 2000 first, and then use the Active Directory Installation wizard to configure the new domain.

Upgrading the Domain Controller

To complete the domain controller upgrade process, you would do the following:

1. If you are upgrading from a CD-ROM, insert the Windows 2000 CD-ROM into the CD-ROM drive. The Windows 2000 Setup wizard starts automatically.

   If you are upgrading from the network, run Winnt32.exe, which is located in the shared folder that contains the Windows 2000 installation files.

2. The setup program upgrades the operating system.

3. The computer reboots and automatically logs on as Administrator.

4. The Active Directory Installation wizard automatically runs.

5. Configure the new domain using the guidelines explained below.

Configuring the Domain

When the setup program finishes, the computer restarts and Windows 2000 automatically logs on as Administrator. The Active Directory Installation wizard (Dcpromo.exe) starts and helps you to configure the new domain environment and to migrate user, group, and computer accounts to Active Directory directory services.

To use the Active Directory Installation wizard to configure the new domain environment, follow the on-screen instructions. When prompted, select the appropriate configuration options.

Table 13.2 describes the configuration options in the Active Directory Installation wizard when configuring a domain environment:

Table 13.2   Windows 2000 Upgrade Paths for Member Servers

Select this option	If you are upgrading
Domain Controller For A New domain	A PDC. This option creates a new Windows 2000 domain.
Create A New Domain Tree *or* Create A New Child Domain In An Existing Domain Tree	A PDC in the first Windows 2000 domain in a tree. A PDC in a new domain in an existing tree
Create A New Forest Of Domain Trees *or* Place This New Domain Tree In An Existing Forest	A PDC in a new domain in an existing tree. A PDC in a new domain tree in an existing forest. This option enables users to access resources in the other trees.

Upgrading Backup Domain Controllers

After you upgrade the PDC for the domain to Windows 2000, you upgrade the BDCs to Windows 2000. You use the same process to upgrade BDCs as you do to upgrade PDCs. Start the Windows 2000 Setup wizard to begin the installation process. Follow the onscreen instructions to complete the upgrade.

After the operating system upgrade is complete, the Active Directory Installation wizard runs to allow you to configure the domain. To complete the upgrade, select the Additional Domain Controller In Existing Domain option in the Active Directory Installation wizard. This adds the upgraded computer to the existing domain as a domain controller.

Note The Windows 2000 Setup wizard will not let you upgrade a BDC until after the PDC has been upgraded. The Setup wizard checks the operating system version of the PDC before starting the upgrade to verify the PDC upgrade has already occurred.

When you upgrade a BDC, you must ensure that the system clock on the BDC is synchronized with the system clock on the domain controllers in your network. The Active Directory Installation wizard prompts you for an administrative username and password that is used to add the additional domain controller to the domain. If the difference in the system clocks is too great, the user account you specify will not be accepted, and you will be unable to join the domain.

Switching from Mixed to Native Mode

After you upgrade all domain controllers on your network, you switch the domain from mixed mode to native mode. This allows the network to take full advantage of Windows 2000 functionality.

Understanding Mixed Mode

When you first create a domain, the domain runs in mixed mode. A mixed mode domain enables Windows 2000 domain controllers to interact with other domain controllers that are running versions of Windows NT Server. Domain controllers running versions of Windows NT are referred to as downlevel domain controllers.

In mixed mode

- The domain still uses the upgraded PDC as the domain master for replication with BDCs running Windows NT Server 3.51 or 4.0.

- Computers upgraded from Windows NT Workstation 4.0 or Windows NT Server 4.0 continue to use Windows NT 4.0 system policy.

- Group functionality new to Windows 2000 Server, such as the ability to nest groups, is not available.

Understanding Native Mode

After you upgrade all the domain controllers, and if you do not plan to add any additional downlevel domain controllers to the domain, you can switch the domain to native mode. A native mode domain contains only Windows 2000 Server domain controllers.

In native mode

- The PDC is no longer the domain master for replication. Instead, all domain controllers replicate with each other as peers.
- Windows NT Server 3.51 or 4.0 domain controllers cannot function in a native Windows 2000 domain.
- Computers upgraded from Windows NT Workstation 4.0 or Windows NT Server 4.0 use Windows 2000 group policy instead of Windows NT 4.0 system policy.
- Group functionality new to Windows 2000 becomes available.

Switching the Domain to Native Mode

To switch domain controllers from mixed to native mode, you would do the following:

1. Click Start, point to Programs, point to Administrative Tools, and then click Active Directory Domains And Trusts.
2. Expand your domain and then open the properties for *your_domain.*
3. On the General page, click Change Mode.

   The Active Directory Service displays a warning stating that once you change the domain mode to native mode, you cannot change back to mixed mode.
4. Click Yes, and then click OK to close the properties page for *your_domain.*

Note After switching to native mode, Windows 2000 might prompt you to restart all domain controllers in your domain. If you get this message, you do not need to restart any domain controllers. This message is the result of an error in the beta release of Windows 2000.

Upgrading and Promoting Member Servers

You can upgrade your member servers to Windows 2000 before, during, or after the domain upgrade process. In addition, you can promote member servers to domain controllers after the operating system upgrade, as necessary.

Upgrading a Member Server to Windows 2000

To upgrade the member server to Windows 2000, insert the CD-ROM and follow the on-screen instructions to complete the upgrade. After the upgrade, the member server will still be a member of its domain or workgroup. During an upgrade, local user and group accounts are stored in the registry of the member server and do not get moved to Active Directory directory services.

Note When you upgrade a member server that is running the DHCP Service, be sure to authorize the DHCP Service in Active Directory directory services, or the service will not start. Servers running the DHCP Service are not automatically authorized when upgraded to Windows 2000.

Promoting a Member Server to a Domain Controller

To promote a member server to a domain controller, run Dcpromo.exe after upgrading to Windows 2000.

When you promote the domain controller, local user and group accounts on the member server are moved to Active Directory directory services. This maintains the permissions previously assigned to resources on that server.

Lesson Summary

You upgrade domain controllers and member servers running previous versions of Windows NT to either Windows 2000 Server or Windows 2000 Advanced Server. All domain controllers running Windows 2000 have equal status in the domain. When you upgrade Windows NT 4.0 or 3.51 PDCs and BDCs to Windows 2000, there is no longer a distinction between PDCs and BDCs. Instead, they become peer domain controllers.

You also upgrade member servers running Windows NT Server 3.51 and 4.0 to Windows 2000. This allows them to take advantage of Active Directory directory services. You can promote these member servers to domain controllers as necessary.

Before you start the upgrade process, make sure that all your computers meet the minimum hardware requirements for Windows 2000 Server and Advanced Server. You should also prepare a rollback strategy in case there are any upgrade problems and prepare the domain controllers and member servers for the upgrade.

After you upgrade all domain controllers on your network, you switch the domain from mixed mode to native mode. This allows the network to take full advantage of Windows 2000 functionality. When you first create a domain, the domain runs in mixed mode. A mixed mode domain enables Windows 2000 domain controllers to interact with other domain controllers that are running versions of Windows NT Server.

Lesson 4: Upgrading Client Operating Systems

You upgrade most Windows client operating systems directly to Windows 2000 in order to take advantage of the new features offered in Windows 2000 Professional operating system. However, before upgrading client operating systems to Windows 2000, you must ensure that the computer hardware meets the minimum Windows 2000 hardware requirements. You must also check the Hardware Compatibility List (HCL) or test the computers for hardware compatibility using the Windows 2000 Compatibility tool. You want to ensure the hardware is compatible with Windows 2000 so that there are no surprises when you start the upgrade on a large number of client computers.

For client systems that use compatible hardware, you upgrade them directly to Windows 2000. If there are Windows 95 and 98 client systems using incompatible or insufficient hardware, you can still take advantage of the Active Directory functionality on these systems by using the Windows 2000 Directory Services Client.

After this lesson, you will be able to

- Explain how to upgrade older Windows client operating systems to Windows 2000.

Estimated lesson time: 20 minutes

Identifying Client Upgrade Paths

You can upgrade most client computers running older versions of Windows directly to Windows 2000. However, computers running Windows NT 3.1 or 3.5 require an additional step. Table 13.3 lists the Windows 2000 Professional upgrade paths for client operating systems.

Note Windows 2000 Professional also upgrades all released service packs for Windows NT Workstation 3.51 and 4.0.

Table 13.3   Windows 2000 Professional Upgrade Paths for Client Operating Systems

Upgrade from	Upgrade to
Windows 95 and Windows 98	Windows 2000 Professional
Windows NT Workstation 3.51 and 4.0	Windows 2000 Professional
Windows NT 3.1 or 3.5	Windows NT 3.51 or 4.0 first, and then Windows 2000 Professional

Note Before you upgrade a client computer to Windows 2000 Professional, make sure that it meets the minimum hardware requirements. See "Hardware Requirements," page 22, for a list of the minimum hardware requirements.

Generating a Hardware Compatibility Report

You generate a hardware and software compatibility report using the Windows 2000 Compatibility tool. This tool runs automatically during system upgrades, but it is recommended that you run this tool before beginning the upgrade to identify any hardware and software problems. This is especially true when upgrading many computers with similar hardware, so compatibility problems can be fixed before the upgrade begins.

Generating the Report

To generate a compatibility report using the Windows 2000 Compatibility tool, select Run on the Start menu and type **Winnt32 /checkupgradeonly**. By using the /checkupgradeonly switch, Winnt32 launches the first part of the Windows 2000 setup program. Instead of running the entire setup process, it only checks for compatible hardware and software. This generates a report that you can analyze to determine what system components are Windows 2000–compatible.

Reviewing the Report

The report generated by running Winnt32 /checkupgradeonly is a text document, named Winnt32.log. It is created in the installation directory; you can view it in the tool or save it as a text file.

The report documents the system hardware and software that is incompatible with Windows 2000. It also identifies whether you need to obtain an upgrade pack for software installed on the system and any additional changes or modifications you must make to the system to maintain functionality in Windows 2000.

Upgrading Compatible Windows 95 and Windows 98 Computers

For client systems that test as compatible with Windows 2000, you run the Windows 2000 setup program (winnt32.exe) to complete the upgrade process.

To upgrade Windows 95 and Windows 98 computers, you would do the following:

1. Run the winnt32.exe command.

2. Accept the license agreement.

3. If the computer you are upgrading is already a member of a domain, you must create a computer account in that domain. Windows 95 and 98 clients do not require a computer account, but Windows 2000 Professional clients do.

4. You are asked to provide upgrade packs for any applications that might need them. Upgrade packs update software so it works with Windows 2000. Upgrade packs are available from the software vendor.

5. You are prompted to upgrade to NTFS. Select the upgrade if you do not plan to set up the client computer to dual boot.

6. The Windows 2000 Compatibility tool runs, generating a report. If the report shows the computer as Windows 2000–compatible, continue with the upgrade. If the report shows the computer to be incompatible with Windows 2000, terminate the upgrade process.

7. The upgrade finishes without further user intervention. After the upgrade is complete, you must enter the password for the local computer Administrator account.

If your computer is Windows 2000–compatible, it is now upgraded and is a member of your domain. If your computer is not Windows 2000–compatible, you must upgrade your hardware, if possible, or you can install the Directory Service Client.

Installing the Directory Service Client

Windows 95 or Windows 98 computers that do not meet the hardware compatibility requirements can still take advantage of Active Directory directory services by using the Directory Service Client. The Directory Service Client upgrades Windows 95 and 98 systems so that they support Active Directory features, including the ability to do the following:

- Use fault-tolerant Dfs
- Search Active Directory directory services
- Change your password on any domain controller

Note Before installing the Directory Service Client on a computer running Windows 95, you must install Internet Explorer 4.01 or greater and enable the Active Desktop component. Otherwise, the Directory Service Client Setup wizard will not run.

To install the Directory Service Client on a non–Windows 2000 compatible computer, you would do the following:

1. In the \Clients\Win9x folder of the Windows 2000 Server or Advanced Server beta CD-ROM, run the dsclient.exe command.

   The Directory Service Client Setup wizard starts.

2. Click Next.

   The License Agreement page appears.

3. Click I Accept This Agreement, and then click Next to continue.

   The Ready To Install page appears, prompting you to confirm that you want to install Directory Service Client.

4. Click Finish to complete the install.

5. When prompted, click Yes to restart the computer.

Upgrading Windows NT 3.51 and 4.0 Clients

The upgrade process for computers running Windows NT 3.51 and 4.0 is similar to the upgrade process for computers running Windows 95 and Windows 98.

Verifying Compatibility

Before you perform the upgrade, you must verify that the systems are compatible with Windows 2000. Use the Windows 2000 Compatibility tool to identify any potential problems before you start the upgrade.

Upgrading Compatible Systems

Windows NT 3.51 and 4.0 computers that meet the hardware compatibility requirements can upgrade directly to Windows 2000. To perform the upgrade process, you would do the following:

1. Insert the Windows 2000 CD-ROM in the CD-ROM drive.

2. Click Start, and then click Run.

3. In the Run box, type X:\i386\winnt32 and then press Enter (where X is the drive letter for your CD-ROM drive).

   The Welcome To The Windows 2000 Setup Wizard page appears.

4. Click Upgrade To Windows 2000 (Recommended) and then click Next.

   The License Agreement page is displayed.

5. Read the license agreement and then click I Accept This Agreement.

6. Click Next.

   The Upgrading to the Windows 2000 NTFS File System page appears.

7. Click Yes, Upgrade My Drive, and then click Next.

The Copying Installation Files page appears.

The Restarting The Computer page appears and the computer will now restart.

The upgrade finishes without further user intervention.

Using Incompatible Systems

Computers running Windows NT 3.51 or Windows NT 4.0 that do not meet the hardware compatibility requirements can still log on to a Windows 2000 network, but they will not be able to take advantage of many of the Windows 2000 features. No Directory Services Client is available for computers running Windows NT 3.51 or Windows NT 4.0.

Lesson Summary

You can upgrade most client computers running older versions of Windows directly to Windows 2000. However, computers running Windows NT 3.1 or Windows NT 3.5 must first be upgraded to Windows NT 3.51 or Windows NT 4.0, and then you can upgrade them to Windows 2000 Professional.

Before you upgrade a client computer to Windows 2000 Professional, make sure that it meets the minimum hardware requirements. You can generate a hardware and software compatibility report using the Windows 2000 Compatibility tool. This tool runs automatically during system upgrades, but it is recommended that you run this tool before beginning the upgrade to identify any hardware and software problems. This is especially true when upgrading many computers with similar hardware, so compatibility problems can be fixed before the upgrade begins.

For client systems that test as compatible with Windows 2000, you run the Windows 2000 setup program (winnt32.exe) to complete the upgrade process. If your computer is not Windows 2000–compatible, you must upgrade your hardware, if possible, or you can install the Directory Service Client. Windows 95 or Windows 98 computers that do not meet the hardware compatibility requirements can still take advantage of Active Directory by using the Directory Service Client. The Directory Service Client upgrades Windows 95 and 98 systems so that they support Active Directory features, including the ability to use fault-tolerant Dfs, search Active Directory directory services, and change your password on any domain controller.

Review

Here are some questions to help you determine if you have learned the material presented in this chapter. If you have difficulty answering these questions, please go back and review the material in this chapter. The answers to these questions are located in Appendix A, "Questions and Answers."

1. You have a server running Windows NT 3.5 and SNA server. You want to upgrade this server to Windows 2000. Can this server be upgraded to Windows 2000? If so, what is the upgrade path?

2. You have a laptop running Windows 95 and you want to upgrade it to Windows 2000. The computer has 16 MB of RAM, and this can be upgraded to 24 MB. Can you upgrade this computer to Windows 2000? If not, how would you make it so this computer is able to access Active Directory directory services?

3. You are about to install Active Directory directory services in your network, and you want to use your existing DNS servers to support Active Directory directory services. What two features must be supported by the DNS server?

4. Your organization currently uses a Windows NT 4.0 single master domain model. Your organization has decided to upgrade to Windows 2000 and Active Directory directory services. How will you establish the root domain for your organization and what system recovery step should you take?

5. Your organization wants to migrate to Active Directory directory services from a multiple master domain model. They created a new empty root domain and now wish to upgrade their existing Windows NT 4.0 domains. Explain the steps you must use to upgrade the master domains, and then the resource domains.

6. Your organization has a Windows NT 4.0 member server in a domain that has been upgraded to Active Directory directory services. The member server is a print server and you have created local groups on that server and applied permissions to those groups. You also put global groups from the domain into the local groups to give print permissions. What happens to the local groups when you upgrade to Windows 2000?

7. You are about to upgrade a Windows NT 4.0 workstation to Windows 2000 Professional. List two things you should check before starting the upgrade process.

A P P E N D I X   A

Questions and Answers

Page 1

Chapter 1
The Microsoft Windows 2000 Platform

Page 20

Review Questions

1. You have been asked to install a file and print server for your department of 50 people. Which operating system would you choose from the Windows 2000 platform?

   Windows 2000 Server.

2. Your department has now grown to support over 500 people, all of whom need access to your server's file services. They also require 24-hour access to these services. Which operating system from the Windows 2000 platform would you now choose?

   Windows 2000 Advanced Server.

3. Users in your organization are complaining that they cannot locate the printers that they need to print to. Identify the component in Windows 2000 that addresses this business problem, and explain how it addresses the problem.

   Active Directory directory services. Active Directory directory services integration with Windows 2000 makes all shared printers in your domain available as objects in Active Directory directory services.

4. Your organization provides users with access to a large number of programs for everyday use. The help desk is receiving many calls from people who are having difficulty finding the applications that they need because of a very large and confusing Start menu structure. How does Windows 2000 solve this problem?

   Personalized Menus can be activated to keep track of the programs you use and to update the Programs menu so that it presents only the programs that you use most often. Applications that you use less frequently are hidden from normal view, making the Start menu easier to use.

5. Identify three of the features that make Windows 2000 Professional the best desktop operating system for a business environment.

Improvements to the user interface, a graphical scheduling utility, improved hardware support, and support for ACPI.

6. List three of the features that help to simplify management of a Windows 2000 network.

Microsoft Management Console (MMC), group policy, DNS dynamic update protocol, Active Directory directory services, Windows Management Instrumentation (WMI), Remote Storage, Windows Script Host, Indexing Service.

Page 21

Chapter 2
Installing Windows 2000

Page 61

Review Questions

1. Your company has decided to install Windows 2000 Professional on all new computers that are purchased for desktop users. What should you do before you purchase new computers to ensure that Windows 2000 can be installed and run without difficulty?

Verify that the hardware components meet the minimum requirements for Windows 2000. Also, verify that all of the hardware components that are installed in the new computers are on the Windows 2000 HCL. If a component is not listed, contact the manufacturer to verify that a Windows 2000 driver is available.

2. You are attempting to install Windows 2000 Professional from a CD-ROM; however, you have discovered that your computer does not support booting from the CD-ROM drive. How can you install Windows 2000?

Start the computer by using the Setup boot disks. When prompted, insert the Windows 2000 Workstation CD-ROM, and then continue Setup.

3. You are installing Windows 2000 Advanced Server on a computer that will be a member server in an existing Windows 2000 domain. You want to add the computer to the domain during installation. What information do you need, and what computers must be available on the network, before you run the Setup program?

You need the DNS domain name of the domain that you are joining. You must also make sure that a computer account for the member server exists in the domain or you must have the user name and password of a user account in the domain with the authority to create computer accounts in the domain. A server running the DNS Service and a domain controller in the domain you are joining must be available on the network.

4. You are using the CD-ROM to install Windows 2000 Advanced Server on a computer that was previously running another operating system. How should you configure the hard disk to simplify the installation process?

Use a disk partitioning tool to remove any existing partitions, and then create and format a new partition for the Windows 2000 installation.

5. You are installing Windows 2000 over the network. Before you install to a client computer, what must you do?

Locate the path to the shared installation files on the distribution server. Create a 500 MB FAT partition on the target computer (1 GB recommended). Create a client disk with a network client so that you can connect from the computer, without an operating system, to the distribution server.

Page 63

Chapter 3
Configuring the DNS Service

Page 91   ▶   **To create a pointer record for your DNS server**

2. Click 192.168.1.*x* Subnet.

What types of records exist in the reverse lookup zone?

Start of Authority (SOA) and Name Server (NS).

Page 92   ▶   **To test your DNS Server using Nslookup**

2. At the command prompt, type **nslookup** and then press Enter.

Record your results in the following table.

Parameter	Value
Default server	**Server1.microsoft.com.** **(Answers will vary if you did not use Server1 as your computer name or domain1 as your DNS domain name.)**
Address	**192.168.1.201.** **(Answers will vary if you did not use 192.168.1.201 as the static IP address for your server.)**

Page 97

Review Questions

1. What is the function of each of the following DNS components?

Domain name space

The domain name space provides the hierarchical structure for the DNS distributed database.

Zones

Zones are used to divide the domain name space into administrative units.

Name servers

Name servers store the zone information and perform name resolution for their authoritative domain name spaces.

2. Why would you want to have multiple name servers?

Installing multiple name servers provides redundancy, reduces the load on the server that stores the primary zone database file, and allows for faster access speed for remote locations.

3. What is difference between a forward lookup query and a reverse lookup query?

A forward lookup query resolves a name to an IP address. A reverse lookup query resolves an IP address to a name.

4. When would you configure a server as a root server?

Configure a name server as a root server only if you will not be connecting to the Internet or if you are using a proxy server to gain access to the Internet.

5. Why do you create forward and reverse lookup zones?

A name server must have at least one forward lookup zone. A forward lookup zone enables name resolution.

A reverse lookup zone is needed for troubleshooting utilities, such as Nslookup, and to record names instead of IP addresses in IIS logs.

6. What is the difference between Dynamic DNS and DNS?

Dynamic DNS allows automatic updates to the primary server's zone file. In DNS, you must manually update the file when new hosts or domains are added.

Dynamic DNS also allows a list of authorized servers to initiate updates. This list can include secondary name servers, domain controllers, and other servers that perform network registration for clients, such as servers running WINS and the DHCP Service.

Page 99

Chapter 4
Exploring Microsoft Active Directory Directory Services

Page 127   ▶   **To install Active Directory directory services on a stand-alone server**

10. Ensure that the Sysvol location is C:\Winnt\Sysvol.

What is the one Sysvol location requirement?

Sysvol must be located on a Windows 2000 partition that is formatted as Windows NT file system (NTFS).

What is the function of Sysvol?

Sysvol is a system volume hosted on all Windows 2000 domain controllers. It stores scripts and part of the Group Policy objects for both the current domain and the enterprise.

Page 129   ▶   **To use Active Directory Users and Computers**

2. In the console tree, expand domain.com.

What selections are listed under domain?

Builtin, Computers, Domain Controllers, and Users.

Page 139   **Review Questions**

1. List three of the items that you should check on a server before running the Active Directory Installation wizard.

That you have a partition or volume formatted with NTFS.

That you have adequate hard disk space to store the directory.

The system time and time zone settings.

That you have a DNS server, if you are not going to let Active Directory directory services configure a DNS server while running the wizard.

2. You have installed Active Directory directory services on your corporate network and have upgraded all domain controllers running Windows NT 4.0 to Windows 2000. You now want to create security-type universal groups. What should you do and what console should you use to make the change?

Change from mixed mode to native mode. To do this, you use Active Directory Domains And Trusts on the Administrative Tools menu.

3. You are the administrator of a network in a remote location, and the network connection from the main office to that location has failed. You find you are still able to create user accounts even though the connection has failed, and users are noticing no difference in logon speed. What would you need at the remote location for this to be possible?

A domain controller and a global catalog server. These two components can be on the same computer.

4. Your company has one remote office connected by a 64 Kbps WAN link. Technical support is receiving calls from users in the remote office who are complaining that it is sometimes taking over five minutes to log on. You have configured a domain controller and a global catalog server in the remote office. What is a potential source of the problem? Describe the steps you would take to improve logon times.

It is likely that you haven't configured sites for your network and that domain controllers that are located across the slow WAN link are occasionally authenticating users.

Create a site for your main office and a site for your remote office. Create a subnet object for each network, and associate the subnet with the appropriate site. Make sure that both sites are in the default site link, DEFAULTIPSITELINK.

5. You have three locations (A, B, C) that are connected to a central site (D) by 128 Kbps WAN links, and another remote location (E) connected to the central site by a 256 Kbps WAN link. You create a site for each location. What site links should you create to enable replication to take place, and given only the bandwidth information about the links, what cost should be associated with each site link?

Site Link AD: Cost 2

Site Link BD: Cost 2

Site Link CD: Cost 2

Site Link ED: Cost 1

The cost value is arbitrary. It is only important that the cost of site links be in the same proportions as above.

Page 141

Chapter 5
Administering Active Directory Directory Services

Page 152   ►   **To modify user account properties**

2. Click the Account tab, and then click Logon Hours.

By default, when can a user log on?

All hours on all days are allowed by default.

Page 152   ►   **To test restrictions on logon hours**

4. Click OK to close the Change Password message box.

Were you able to successfully log on as User1? Why or why not?

Yes, because User One has access to the network 24 hours a day, 7 days a week.

5. Repeat steps 1–3 for User Two; use User2 as the new password.

Were you able to successfully log on as User Two? Why or why not?

It depends on the time set on your system clock. If it is between 6:00 AM and 6:00 PM, you should not be able to log on. If it is between 6:00 PM and 6:00 AM, you should be able to log on.

Page 162   ►   **To add members to a universal group**

6. Click OK to close the Universal1 Properties dialog box.

Were you able to successfully add the Managers global group to the universal group? Why or why not?

Yes. A global group can be a member of a universal group.

7. Attempt to repeat steps 1 through 5 to add the Inventory domain local group to the universal group.

Was the Inventory domain local group available for you to add to the universal group? Why or why not?

No. A domain local group cannot be a member of a universal group.

Page 171 ▶ **To view default Active Directory permissions for an OU**

4. In the following table, list the groups that have permissions for the Security OU. If an account has special permissions, just record Special Permissions in the table. You will need to refer to these permissions in the next exercise.

User account or group	Assigned permissions
Authenticated Users	**Read**
System	**Full Control**
Domain Admins	**Full Control**
Enterprise Admins	**Read, Write, Create All Child Objects**
Account Operators	**Special Permissions**
Print Operators	**Special Permissions**

Why are all permission check boxes for some groups blank?

Additional permissions are present, but you cannot view them in this dialog box. To see the unavailable permissions, click the Advanced button.

Are any of the default permissions inherited from the domain, which is the parent object? How can you tell?

The permissions that are assigned to Enterprise Admins are inherited from the parent object. The check boxes for inherited permissions are shaded.

Page 172 ▶ **To view special permissions for an OU**

2. To view the permissions for Account Operators, in the Permission Entries box, click each entry for Account Operators, and then click View/Edit.

The Permission Entry For Security dialog box appears.

What object permissions are assigned to Account Operators? What can Account Operators do in this OU?

The permissions that are assigned to Account Operators are Create User Objects, Delete User Objects, Create Group Objects, Delete Group Objects, Create Computer Objects, and Delete Computer Objects. Account Operators can only create and delete user accounts groups, accounts, and computer accounts.

Do any objects within this OU inherit the permissions assigned to the Account Operators group? Why or why not?

No. Objects within this OU do not inherit these permissions. The dialog box shows that permissions are applied on this object only.

Page 172   ▶   **To test current permissions**

3. In the console tree, expand your domain, and then click Security.

What user objects are visible in the Security OU?

The Secretary and Assistant user accounts.

Which permissions allow you to see these objects? (Hint: refer to your answers in the preceding exercise.)

The Assistant user account automatically belongs to the Authenticated Users built-in group, which has the Read permission for the OU.

Attempt to change the logon hours for Secretary. Were you successful? Why or why not?

No. The Assistant user account does not have the Write permission for this object.

Attempt to change the logon hours for Assistant. Were you successful? Why or why not?

No. The Assistant user account does not have the Write permission for this object.

Page 174   ▶   **To test delegated permissions**

4. Attempt to change the logon hours for both user accounts in the Security OU.

Were you successful? Why or why not?

Yes. The Assistant user account has been assigned the Full Control permission for all objects in the OU. This includes the permission to change the logon hours.

5. Attempt to change the logon hours for a user account in the Users container.

Were you successful? Why or why not?

No. The Assistant user account has been assigned no permissions for the Users OU.

Page 175   **Review Questions**

1. What strategy should you apply when you use domain local and global groups?

Place user accounts (A) into global groups (G), place global groups into domain local groups (DL), and then assign permissions (P) to the domain local group.

2. What determines whether users can locate an object using the global catalog?

The global catalog contains the access permissions for an object. If users do not have the Read permission for an object, they cannot view or locate the object.

3. What happens to the permissions of an object when you move it from one OU to another OU?

Permissions that are assigned directly to the object remain the same. The object also inherits permissions from the new OU. Any permissions that were inherited from the previous OU no longer affect the object.

4. You want to delegate administrative control of all computer accounts in an OU to a specific user. What is the simplest method for assigning the needed permissions?

Right-click the OU and click Delegate Control to run the Delegation Of Control wizard. Assign control of the OU to the user and limit the user's control to computer accounts within that OU.

5. You have the Read permission for the Sales OU. Can you create other OUs within Sales?

No, you must also have the Create Organizational Unit Objects permission to create an OU. You should also have the List Contents permission to view the objects in the container.

6. What is the difference between the naming requirements for user accounts and for computer accounts?

User accounts must have unique names within the OU or container in which you have created them. Computer accounts must have unique names within the Active Directory forest.

Page 177

Chapter 6
Managing Desktop Environments with Group Policy

Page 196   ▶   **To test Group Policy**

1. Log on as ADAdmin with a password of *password*.

Were the following restrictions enforced? Why or why not?
No Run command on the Start menu.
No access to Control Panel from the Start menu.
No My Network Places icon on the desktop.
No Map Network Drive or Disconnect Network Drive on the Tools menu in Windows Explorer.

Yes. The restrictions should be enforced for the Administration OU.

Page 199   **Review Questions**

1. Where do GPOs store Group Policy information?

   GPOs store Group Policy information in a Group Policy Container and in a Group Policy Template.

2. In what order are GPOs implemented through the structure of Active Directory directory services?

   GPOs are implemented in the following order: site, domain, and then organizational unit.

3. Your company has decided to implement some restrictions on what users can and cannot do on their desktops. These restrictions need to be applied to all users in your single domain, with the exception of members of the Software Development group. If the Software Development group had their own organizational unit, how would you accomplish this? How would you accomplish this if all user accounts in the domain, including members of the Software Development group, were in the Users container?

   If the Software Development group had its own OU, you would create a GPO at the domain level, containing the required restrictions. You would then set the Block Policy Inheritance option at the Software Development OU. If all user accounts, including the Software Development group were in the Users container, you would create a GPO at the domain level, containing the required restrictions. Next you would create a security group and add all of the Software Development group accounts to this group. Then you would deny Apply Group Policy permission on the discretionary access control list of the GPO for the new security group.

Page 201   **Chapter 7**
Managing Software by Using Group Policy

Page 224   **Review Questions**

1. What two new technologies in Windows 2000 provide the ability to manage software?

   The two new technologies are the Windows Installer and Windows 2000 Software Installation And Maintenance.

2. You need to deploy two new applications to users in your organization, Microsoft Excel 2000 and Microsoft Word 2000. All users in your company use Word 2000 on a daily basis. All users in the accounting department also use Excel 2000 on a daily basis. Some users outside of the accounting department need occasional access to Excel 2000. If you have a single domain and each department has their own organizational unit, how would you deploy these two applications?

Microsoft Word 2000 would be assigned in a GPO at the domain level. Microsoft Excel 2000 would be assigned in a GPO at the accounting department's organizational unit and would also be published in a GPO at the domain level.

3. Under what circumstances would you choose to assign an application to computers instead of users?

    If the application were required for all users, regardless of which computer they log on to, you would assign the application to computers.

4. You have deployed an application to all users in your organization and now need to upgrade the application to the latest version. For compatibility reasons, you need to allow some users to continue to use the old version. How would you accomplish this?

    You would deploy the new version as an optional upgrade. This will allow users to continue to use the previous version until they are able to upgrade to the new version.

Page 225

Chapter 8
Managing File Resources

Page 246   ▶   **To determine the permissions for a file**

6. Click the Owner tab.

    Who is the current owner of the Owner.txt file?

    The Administrators group.

Page 247   ▶   **To take ownership of a file**

5. Click Advanced to display the Access Control Settings For Owner dialog box, and then click the Owner tab.

    Who is the current owner of Owner.txt?

    The Administrators group.

6. Under Name, select User Four, and then click Apply.

    Who is the current owner of Owner.txt?

    The User Four user account.

Page 253   ▶   **To configure quota management settings for a user**

5. Click OK.

    Windows 2000 displays the Add New Quota Entry dialog box.

    What are the default settings for the user you just set a quota limit for?

    Limit disk space to 10 MB and set warning level to 6 MB. These are the default settings that are selected for drive C.

Page 260   ▶   **To test encrypt files**

3. Start Windows Explorer and open C:\Secret\File1.txt.

What happens?

The Notepad message box informs you that access is denied.

Page 265   **Review Questions**

1. You are the administrator for your organization's network. Management would like to segregate documents so that marketing documents are available to everybody on the network while research and development documents are hidden in a shared folder. How can this be accomplished?

This can be accomplished by publishing the marketing documents and putting the research and development documents in a hidden shared folder.

2. Users are distraught because information they need is scattered throughout the network on various servers. This forces them to remember the names of all of the servers and shared folders on the entire network, which is difficult at best. As the administrator, what can you do to alleviate this problem?

Install Dfs on one computer and create child nodes out of all of the shared folders.

3. Your company utilizes a data center for centralized storage and control of corporate documents. Each user is allocated a certain amount of storage at the data center and the user's department is charged a monthly fee for usage. In the past, the data center's strategy has been to partition the drives on the servers to configure each user's allocation. This creates problems when the allocations must be changed. The data center is going to be upgrading all of its servers to Windows 2000. Which feature of Windows 2000 will make setting the allocations easier?

Windows 2000 supports disk quotas, which allow administrators to dynamically change the quotas.

4. Users complain that access times to the data center's servers has increased over the past few months. What maintenance must be done and when should this be done?

The disks need to be defragmented. This should be done at night or during the weekend to minimize the impact on productivity.

Page 267   # Chapter 9
Configuring Remote Access

Page 297   **Review Questions**

1. What are the advantages of using L2TP over using PPTP?

L2TP supports more types of internetworks, it supports header compression, and it cooperates with IPSec for encryption.

2. Describe the two new settings that must be configured using the Network Connection wizard in regard to sharing the connection.

   The settings are whether you want to allow others who use the computer to use the connection (access to the connection) and whether you want to allow other computers to access resources through this port (sharing the connection once it is established).

3. Why are remote access policies stored on the remote access server and not in Active Directory directory services? Describe a scenario in which this is beneficial.

   By storing remote access policies on the remote access server, policies can vary according to the capabilities of the server. For example, servers having different sizes of modem pools can have different profile settings for multilinking.

4. Which part of a remote access policy is overridden in a mixed-mode domain? Why? Which parts are still effective?

   The access permission setting on the policy is overridden in a mixed-mode domain because the user dial-in setting, Control Access Through Remote Access Policy, is not available. Policy conditions and profiles are still effective.

5. A user in the Sales Group has their dial-in permission set to Allow Access. The user attempts to connect during business hours using an ISDN connection, an IP address of 123.45.1.2, and CHAP authentication. Assuming the following policy is in effect on the remote access server, will the user's connection attempt be accepted?

   The profile must still match the settings of the connection attempt. For example, the profile may specify that another authentication protocol be used instead of CHAP. If this is the case, this attempt would be denied.

Page 299

Chapter 10
Supporting DHCP and WINS

Page 309   ▶   **To install the DHCP Service**

2. Click Start, point to Programs, and then point to Administrative Tools.

   Are there any entries for DHCP?

   No.

18. Click Start, point to Programs, and then point to Administrative Tools.

    Are there any entries for DHCP?

    Yes, the DHCP tool was added to the Administrative Tools menu when the DHCP Service was installed.

Page 310   ▶   **To create and configure a DHCP scope**

13. Click Next.

The Lease Duration page appears.

What is the default lease duration?

Eight days.

Page 317   **Review Questions**

1. What statistical information can you display in the DHCP console?

   You can use the DHCP console to display the total number of scopes and addresses on the server, the number of available addresses versus the number of depleted addresses, and the number of leases being processed per second.

2. You have installed the DHCP Service on a member server in a domain and have configured a scope, but clients cannot lease an address. You open the DHCP console and notice that the DHCP server icon is marked with a red arrow. What does this mean?

   The DHCP Service is not authorized to operate in the domain. A member of the Enterprise Admins group must authorize the DHCP server before the DHCP Service will start on the member server.

3. How does a DHCP server determine authorization status within a workgroup?

   When a DHCP server that is a member of a workgroup starts, it sends a broadcast message. If the DHCP server receives a response from a DHCP server in a domain, the DHCP server that sent the broadcast message assumes that it is unauthorized on the network. If the DHCP server receives a response only from workgroup DHCP servers, the DHCP server that sent the broadcast message determines that it can operate normally.

4. You have defined a scope for a subnet and want to add additional IP addresses to the scope. What is the easiest way to complete this task without having to delete the current scope and create a new one?

   Create a new scope with the additional addresses, and then combine the two defined scopes into a superscope.

5. What is the purpose of option classes and what types can you create?

   You can use DHCP option classes to manage configuration details for DHCP clients within a scope. Windows 2000 supports two types of option classes: vendor-defined and user-defined classes.

6. If a DHCP client is unable to obtain a lease from a DHCP server, how can the client still gain limited network functionality?

   The client can use Automatic Private IP Addressing to generate a unique IP address in the range 169.254.x.y.

7. How does the Windows 2000 implementation of WINS provide greater fault tolerance for the client?

You can configure a WINS client with as many as 12 WINS servers. The additional WINS servers provide an extra measure of fault tolerance in the event that the primary and secondary WINS servers fail to respond.

Page 319

Chapter 11
Managing Disks

Page 338 ▶ **To examine the new volume**

3. Right-click Mount, and then click Properties.

The Mount Properties dialog box appears.

What type of folder is C:\Mount or X:\Mount (where X is the drive on which you mounted the volume)?

Mounted Volume

Page 340

Review Questions

1. You install a new 10-gigabyte (GB) disk drive that you want to divide into five equal 2-GB sections. What are your options?

You can leave the disk as a basic disk and then create a combination of primary partitions (up to three) and logical drives in an extended partition; or, you can upgrade the disk to a dynamic disk and create five 2-GB simple volumes.

2. How do you configure the Disk Management tool for remote administration of other computers?

Add the Computer Management or Disk Management snap-in to an MMC console. You have the option to focus the snap-in on the local computer or another computer. Type in the name of the computer you want to administer remotely.

3. You are trying to create a striped volume on your Windows 2000 Advanced Server in order to improve performance. You confirm that you have enough unallocated disk space on two disks in your computer, but when you right-click an area of unallocated space on a disk, your only option is to create a partition. What is the problem and how would you resolve it?

You can create striped volumes on dynamic disks only. The option to create a partition rather than a volume indicates that the disk you are trying to use is a basic disk. You will need to upgrade all of the disks that you want to use in your striped volume to dynamic disks before you stripe them.

4. You add a new disk to your computer and attempt to extend an existing volume to include the unallocated space on the new disk, but the option to extend the volume is not available. What is the problem and how would you resolve it?

   The existing volume is not formatted with NTFS. You can extend NTFS volumes only. You should back up any data on the existing volume, convert it to NTFS, and then extend the volume.

5. You dual boot your computer with Windows 98 and Windows 2000. You upgrade a second drive, which you are using to archive files, from basic storage to dynamic storage. The next time you try to access your archived files from Windows 98, you are unable to read the files. Why?

   Only Windows 2000 can read dynamic disks.

Page 341

Chapter 12
Implementing Disaster Prevention

Page 367

Review Questions

1. What requirement applies to disks used to create new fault-tolerant volumes in Windows 2000?

   All disks that will be a part of the fault-tolerant volume must be upgraded to dynamic storage.

2. After installing a new hardware device, you restart your computer and log on. Immediately after logging on, your computer fails with a stop error that indicates the problem resulted from the new device driver. How would you solve this problem?

   You would restart the computer and select Safe Mode from the Advanced Options menu. When the computer starts in safe mode, you would remove the device that was causing the stop error.

3. Describe two methods for accessing the Windows 2000 Recovery Console.

   You can access the Windows 2000 Recovery Console by starting the computer from the Windows 2000 CD-ROM or the Windows 2000 boot disks and then choosing the repair option in setup.

   You can also install the Windows 2000 Recovery Console by running Winnt32.exe /cmdcons, and then you can access the Recovery Console from the Windows 2000 startup menu.

4. An administrator on your network has accidentally deleted an OU containing several thousand user objects. Assuming you have a recent backup of Active Directory directory services, how would you recover the deleted OU?

On a domain controller you have backed up recently, restart the domain controller in Directory Services Restore Mode. Using the Backup utility, restore the system state data. Next, using the Ntdsutil.exe utility, mark the deleted OU as authoritative. Restart the domain controller and replicate the changes to the remaining domain controllers.

5. What are the two types of emergency repair and what are the differences between them?

The two types of emergency repair are Manual and Fast. You should normally choose Fast emergency repair because it is the easiest and does not require any user interaction. The fast repair will attempt to repair registry problems. You should only choose Manual emergency repair if you are an experienced user. Manual repair does not allow you to attempt to repair the registry.

Page 369

Chapter 13
Upgrading a Network to Windows 2000

Page 389

Review Questions

1. You have a server running Windows NT 3.5 and SNA server. You want to upgrade this server to Windows 2000. Can this server be upgraded to Windows 2000? If so, what is the upgrade path?

Yes. You must first upgrade to Windows NT Server 3.51 or 4.0, and then upgrade to Windows 2000.

2. You have a laptop running Windows 95 and you want to upgrade it to Windows 2000. The computer has 16 MB of RAM, and this can be upgraded to 24 MB. Can you upgrade this computer to Windows 2000? If not, how would you make it so this computer is able to access Active Directory directory services?

No. You can install the Directory Service Client for Windows 95 or 98. The laptop would then be able to access Active Directory directory services.

3. You are about to install Active Directory directory services in your network, and you want to use your existing DNS servers to support Active Directory directory services. What two features must be supported by the DNS server?

SRV (Service) location resource records and the dynamic update protocol for DNS.

4. Your organization currently uses a Windows NT 4.0 single master domain model. Your organization has decided to upgrade to Windows 2000 and Active Directory directory services. How will you establish the root domain for your organization and what system recovery step should you take?

Upgrade the master domain to Windows 2000 to create the root domain.

To facilitate system recovery in the event of a problem during the upgrade, you should synchronize a BDC with the PDC and keep this BDC offline until you are sure the network upgrade has completed successfully.

5. Your organization wants to migrate to Active Directory directory services from a multiple master domain model. They created a new empty root domain and now wish to upgrade their existing Windows NT 4.0 domains. Explain the steps you must use to upgrade the master domains, and then the resource domains.

   In all domain upgrade cases, the first step is to take a fully synchronized BDC offline to facilitate system recovery in case of problems during the upgrade.

   Next, upgrade the PDCs in the resource domains, and tell the Active Directory Installation wizard to make a new child domain in an existing domain tree. In this case, make the resource domains child domains of the old master domains. Finally, upgrade the BDCs of the resource domains.

6. Your organization has a Windows NT 4.0 member server in a domain that has been upgraded to Active Directory directory services. The member server is a print server and you have created local groups on that server and applied permissions to those groups. You also put global groups from the domain into the local groups to give print permissions. What happens to the local groups when you upgrade to Windows 2000?

   Nothing. The local groups remain, and group membership remains unchanged.

7. You are about to upgrade a Windows NT 4.0 workstation to Windows 2000 Professional. List two things you should check before starting the upgrade process.

   Check that you have at least 32 MB of RAM and enough hard disk space free to complete the upgrade. You should also run the Windows 2000 Compatibility Tool to check that all hardware and software currently installed is compatible with Windows 2000.

APPENDIX B

Creating Setup Disks

Unless your computer supports booting from a CD-ROM drive, you must have the four Microsoft Windows 2000 Server or Windows 2000 Advanced Server Setup disks to complete the installation of Windows 2000 Server or Advanced Server. To create these Setup disks, complete the following procedure.

Note You must complete this procedure on a computer running Windows 2000 or Windows NT with access to a CD-ROM drive. This procedure requires four blank formatted 1.44 MB disks.

To create Windows 2000 Server or Windows 2000 Advanced Server Setup disks, you would do the following:

1. Label the four blank formatted 1.44 MB disks with the appropriate product name, as follows:

   - Windows 2000 Server Setup Disk 1 or Windows 2000 Advanced Server Setup Disk 1

   - Windows 2000 Server Setup Disk 2 or Windows 2000 Advanced Server Setup Disk 2

   - Windows 2000 Server Setup Disk 3 or Windows 2000 Advanced Server Setup Disk 3

   - Windows 2000 Server Setup Disk 4 or Windows 2000 Advanced Server Setup Disk 4

2. Insert the Microsoft Windows 2000 Server or Windows 2000 Advanced Server CD-ROM into the CD-ROM drive.

3. If the Windows 2000 CD-ROM dialog box appears prompting you to upgrade to Windows NT, click No.

4. Start a command prompt.

5. At the command prompt, change to your CD-ROM drive. For example, if your CD-ROM drive letter is E, type **e:** and press Enter.

6. At the command prompt, change to the Bootdisk folder by typing **cd bootdisk** and pressing Enter.

7. With Bootdisk as the active folder, type **makeboot** *a*: (where *a*: is the floppy disk drive) and then press Enter.

   Windows 2000 displays a message indicating that this script creates the four Windows 2000 Setup disks for installing from a CD-ROM. It also indicates that four blank formatted floppy disks are required.

8. Press any key to continue.

   Windows 2000 displays a message prompting you to insert the disk labeled Disk 1.

9. Insert the blank formatted disk labeled Windows 2000 Server Setup Disk 1, or Windows 2000 Advanced Server Setup Disk 1, in drive A and then press any key to continue.

   After Windows 2000 creates the disk image, it displays a message prompting you to insert the disk labeled Disk 2.

10. Remove Disk 1 and insert the blank formatted disk labeled Windows 2000 Server Setup Disk 2, or Windows 2000 Advanced Server Setup Disk 2, in drive A and then press any key to continue.

    After Windows 2000 creates the disk image, it displays a message prompting you to insert the disk labeled Disk 3.

11. Remove Disk 2 and insert the blank formatted disk labeled Windows 2000 Server Setup Disk 3, or Windows 2000 Advanced Server Setup Disk 3, in drive A and then press any key to continue.

    After Windows 2000 creates the disk image, it displays a message prompting you to insert the disk labeled Disk 4.

12. Remove Disk 3 and insert the blank formatted disk labeled Windows 2000 Server Setup Disk 4, or Windows 2000 Advanced Server Setup Disk 4, in drive A and then press any key to continue.

    After Windows 2000 creates the disk image, it displays a message indicating that the imaging process is done.

13. At the command prompt, type **exit** and then press Enter.

14. Remove the disk from drive A and the CD-ROM from the CD-ROM drive.

Index

Ready solutions
for the
IT administrator

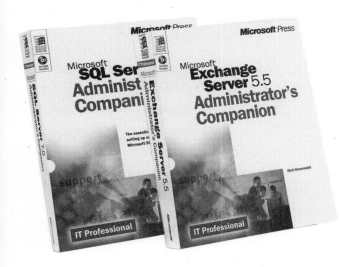

Keep your IT systems up and running with ADMINISTRATOR'S COMPANIONS from Microsoft Press. These expert guides serve as both tutorial and reference for critical deployment and maintenance tasks for Microsoft products and technologies. Packed with real-world expertise, hands-on numbered procedures, and handy workarounds, ADMINISTRATOR'S COMPANIONS deliver ready answers for on-the-job results.

There's no *substitute* for *experience.*

Now you can apply the best practices from real-world implementations of Microsoft technologies with NOTES FROM THE FIELD. Based on the extensive field experiences of Microsoft Consulting Services, these valuable technical references outline tried-and-tested solutions you can use in your own company, right now.

Deploying Microsoft® SQL Server™ 7.0 (Notes from the Field)	Optimizing Network Traffic (Notes from the Field)	Managing a Microsoft Windows NT® Network (Notes from the Field)	**Coming Soon!** Deploying Microsoft Office 2000 (Notes from the Field)
U.S.A. $39.99	**U.S.A.** $39.99	**U.S.A.** $39.99	**U.S.A.** $39.99
U.K. £37.49	U.K. £37.49 [V.A.T. included]	U.K. £37.49 [V.A.T. included]	U.K. £37.49 [V.A.T. included]
Canada $59.99	Canada $59.99	Canada $59.99	Canada $59.99
ISBN 0-7356-0726-5	ISBN 0-7356-0648-X	ISBN 0-7356-0647-1	ISBN 0-7356-0727-3

Microsoft®

mspress.microsoft.com

Microsoft Press Resource Kits— powerhouse resources to minimize costs while maximizing performance

Microsoft® Windows NT® Server 4.0 Resource Kit
ISBN   1-57231-344-7
U.S.A. $149.95
U.K.   £140.99 [V.A.T. included]
Canada $199.95

Microsoft Windows NT Workstation 4.0 Resource Kit
ISBN   1-57231-343-9
U.S.A. $69.95
U.K.   £64.99 [V.A.T. included]
Canada $94.95

Microsoft Internet Information Server Resource Kit
ISBN   1-57231-638-1
U.S.A. $49.99
U.K.   £46.99 [V.A.T. included]
Canada $71.99

Microsoft Office 2000 Resource Kit
ISBN   0-7356-0555-6
U.S.A. $59.99
U.K.   £56.49 [V.A.T. included]
Canada $89.99

Microsoft Internet Explorer Resource Kit
ISBN   1-57231-842-2
U.S.A. $49.99
U.K.   £46.99 [V.A.T. included]
Canada $71.99

Direct from the Microsoft product groups, the resources packed into these best-selling kits meet the demand for hardcore use-now tools and information for the IT professional. Each kit contains precise technical documentation, essential utilities, installation and rollout tactics, planning guides, and upgrade strategies. Use them to save time, reduce cost of ownership, and maximize your organization's technology investment.

Microsoft®

mspress.microsoft.com

Microsoft BackOffice® Resource Kit, Second Edition
ISBN   1-57231-632-2
U.S.A. $199.99
U.K.   £187.99 [V.A.T. included]
Canada $289.99

Microsoft Press® products are available worldwide wherever quality computer books are sold. For more information, contact your book or computer retailer, software reseller, or local Microsoft Sales Office, or visit our Web site at mspress.microsoft.com. To locate your nearest source for Microsoft Press products, or to order directly, call 1-800-MSPRESS in the U.S. (in Canada, call 1-800-268-2222).

Prices and availability dates are subject to change.

The *intelligent* way
to practice for the
MCP exam

If you took the Microsoft Certified Professional (MCP) exam today, would you pass? With the *Readiness Review* MCP exam simulation on CD-ROM, you get a low-risk, low-cost way to find out! Use this electronic assessment tool to take randomly generated, 60-question practice tests, covering actual MCP objectives. Test and retest with different question sets each time, and then consult the companion study guide to review all featured exam items and identify areas for further study. *Readiness Review*—it's the smart way to prep!

Register Today!

Return this
*Upgrading to Microsoft® Windows® 2000
Training Kit, Beta Edition*
registration card today

Microsoft®*Press*
mspress.microsoft.com

OWNER REGISTRATION CARD   1-57231-894-5

Upgrading to Microsoft® Windows® 2000 Training Kit, Beta Edition

_____   _____   _____

FIRST NAME   MIDDLE INITIAL   LAST NAME

_____

INSTITUTION OR COMPANY NAME

_____

ADDRESS

_____

_____   _____   _____

CITY   STATE   ZIP

                                                         (   )
_____   _____

E-MAIL ADDRESS   PHONE NUMBER

U.S. and Canada addresses only. Fill in information above and mail postage-free.
Please mail only the bottom half of this page.

For information about Microsoft Press®
products, visit our Web site at
mspress.microsoft.com

Microsoft®Press